This Book must be returned to
the Library on, or before, the
last date shown below

D1491907

THE
SALERNITAN QUESTIONS

Oxford University Press, Amen House, London E.C.4

GLASGOW   NEW YORK   TORONTO   MELBOURNE   WELLINGTON
BOMBAY   CALCUTTA   MADRAS   KARACHI   LAHORE   DACCA
CAPE TOWN   SALISBURY   NAIROBI   IBADAN   ACCRA
KUALA LUMPUR   HONG KONG

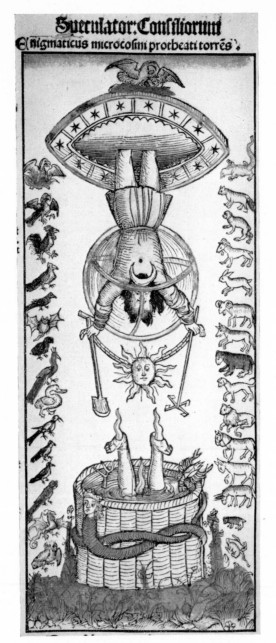

Woodcut from Dietrich Ulsen's *Speculator* Broadside,
Nürnberg, *c.* 1501.
From the unique example in the Bayerische
Staatsbibliothek, Munich.

THE
SALERNITAN QUESTIONS

An Introduction to the
History of Medieval and Renaissance
Problem Literature

BY

BRIAN LAWN

OXFORD
AT THE CLARENDON PRESS
1963

© *Oxford University Press 1963*

PRINTED IN GREAT BRITAIN
AT THE UNIVERSITY PRESS, OXFORD
BY VIVIAN RIDLER
PRINTER TO THE UNIVERSITY

TO THE MEMORY OF
MY FATHER

Felix, qui potuit rerum cognoscere causas,
atque metus omnis et inexorabile fatum
subiecit pedibus strepitumque Acherontis avari.

VIRGIL, Georgics, II

PREFACE

IT has often been stressed that a study of the questions that were asked at any period is of great value for determining the intellectual climate of that period, for tracing the progress of thought in general, and for examining particular problems by means of the case-history method.

Yet there exists no survey of one branch of literature which deals solely with such questions: namely, that which includes the scientific and medical problem books of classical antiquity, of the Middle Ages, of the later Renaissance, and of still more recent times. Perhaps the vast extent of the field and the well-nigh inexplicable tangle in which some parts of it were involved—for example, the various books of problems ascribed to Aristotle —have been a deterrent. Or again, it may have appeared to some that the game was not worth the candle, that the seeming triviality of many of the early questions did not warrant the time it would take to investigate them.

My interest in the subject began with some spare-time research in connexion with a German humanistic manuscript which I acquired some years ago. I found that this contained a contemporary transcript of the remarkable *Speculator* Broadside, composed by the humanist-physician Dietrich Ulsen and printed at Nürnberg *c.* 1501. I then discovered that Ulsen had used a large part of a medieval Latin poem, the *Questiones phisicales*, and next that this belonged to a hitherto unknown collection or family of scientific and medical questions that had been put together at Salerno about the year 1200. By now I was fairly committed; there was no retreat, and in tracing the origin and subsequent influence of these 'questions' I was led to explore the wide, uncharted seas of scientific and medical problem literature in the West. So much for how the book came to be written.

It remains to record my thanks and obligations to those who have helped and encouraged me in my labours: to Professor Leonard Forster of Selwyn College, Cambridge, who kindly read through an early draft of the section on Ulsen and the *Speculator*, and gave me valuable advice and assistance; to Dr. Ashworth Underwood of the Wellcome Historical Medical Museum, for encouragement in the early days of my research; and, above all, to Dr. R. W. Hunt, Keeper of Western Manuscripts in the Bodleian Library, for having had the patience to read through an extended version of my book in manuscript and for much helpful criticism.

Then there are the many librarians and other officials of libraries, too numerous to list in full, who have met my repeated requests for photostats of manuscripts or of books in their keeping, with unfailing courtesy and goodwill. Special thanks, however, are due to the following keepers of manuscripts and archivists who have very kindly replied, sometimes at considerable length, to my queries regarding material not directly accessible to me: Mme D. Bloch, Bibliothèque Nationale, Paris; Dr. H. Boese, Öffentliche Wissenschaftliche Bibliothek, Berlin; Dr. Max Burckhardt, Öffentliche Bibliothek der Universitaat, Basel; Mlle Th. d'Alverny, Bibliothèque Nationale, Paris; Dr. H. D. Emanuel, University College of Wales; Alec T. Gaydin, Records Office, Gloucester; Professor Dr. Antoni Knot, Biblioteka Uniwersytecka, Wrocław (Breslau); R. O. Mackenna, M.A., University Library, Glasgow; E. F. D. Roberts, National Library of Scotland, Edinburgh; Dr. P. Ruf, Bayerische Staatsbibliothek, Munich; Dr. Franz Unterkircher, Österreichische Nationalbibliothek, Vienna; Dr. K. G. Van Acker, Bibliotheek der Rijksuniversiteit, Ghent; F. P. White, M.A., St. John's College Library, Cambridge; Dorothy M. Williamson, Lincolnshire Archives Committee; Dr. Martin Wittek, Bibliothèque Royale, Brussels; Dr. Jerzy Zathey, Biblioteka Jagiellonska, Crakow.

I am also grateful to the authorities of the Bayerische Staatsbibliothek, Munich, for allowing me to use a reproduction of the woodcut from their unique copy of Ulsen's *Speculator* Broadside as a frontispiece.

Finally, it would be hard indeed to express adequate thanks to the Delegates of the Clarendon Press, who have so generously consented to the publication of this book, and to the staff and advisers of the Press, who have so patiently and competently dealt with the many problems that arose, and given much valuable advice, particularly in connexion with the texts and translations of the *Speculator* and *Questiones phisicales*.

B. L.

London, September 1962

CONTENTS

Contents

INTRODUCTION

IT has long been known that Salerno was the birthplace and nursery of what has been called the scientific renaissance; that the masters there were the first, in the Latin West, to make use of the newly translated Aristotelian books, the *libri naturales*, in scientific and medical writings; and that, particularly during the twelfth century, the *civitas Hippocratica* became a centre for the diffusion of philosophical and scientific doctrines, as well as a school renowned far and wide for its medical teaching. Yet little attention has been paid to this other, more scientific, side of the school's activities. It is true that several of the writings of Urso of Calabria, perhaps the most influential master who flourished during the golden age of Salernitan learning, have been edited at one time or another. But his most voluminous and, in some respects, most important work, the *De commixtionibus elementorum*, still remains unedited and there exists no adequate critical study of his work as a whole, or of its subsequent influence on the scientific heritage of the West.

The Salernitan questions constitute a hitherto entirely unknown and unsuspected source for both the scientific and medical teaching at Salerno. Gradually increasing over the years and probably representing the work of several masters, by about 1200 they received additions, either by Urso himself or by a pupil, which distil the very essence of the master's thought; and the group, as a whole, gives the clearest picture that has yet emerged of exactly what was taught in the school at that time. The literary form used was the entirely didactic one of simple question and answer; concise, clear, easily memorized, this was the form used by both masters and pupils, and the one through which these particular doctrines were diffused throughout the length and breadth of Europe, as time went on.

Earlier constituents of the group, which had evidently existed long before the time of Urso, had influenced Adelard of Bath and, to an even greater extent, the Chartrian, William of Conches. About 1200 they were much utilized by Alexander Neckam, and it is probably these questions which supplied him with the greater part of his knowledge of natural philosophy, as displayed in his *De natura rerum* and the later *De laudibus divinae sapientiae*. The influence of the questions in England, in fact, seems to have been particularly strong.

The oldest and most voluminous text of the questions (Bodl. Auct. F. 3. 10) seems to have been copied, in an English hand, *c.* 1200, by a scholar who was in close touch with Hugh de Mapenore, later to become bishop of Hereford, and other members of the Hereford circle: also more than half of the manuscripts of this early group or family of questions, namely five out of nine, are of English provenance.

In the great age of scholasticism, the thirteenth century, many of the questions served as a basis for scholastic disputations in *physica* held in the schools of England, France, Italy, and Germany, and were used by such famous masters as Peter of Spain and Albertus Magnus. Later still they formed part of almost every collection of natural questions or problems, composed during the fourteenth, fifteenth, and sixteenth centuries, until, by the seventeenth century, they had fully entered into the stock of popular scientific, pseudo-scientific, and medical lore, as embodied in the vernacular question books and aids to conversation. Thus their history is continuous and uninterrupted, from the twelfth to the seventeenth century.

Probably at an early period a selection of the questions was arranged in Latin hexameters to make them more attractive and still easier to remember; and it is this metrical version which constitutes the *Questiones phisicales*, extant in two manuscripts of English provenance (Sloane, 1610 and Trinity 580. (R. 3. 1)). About the beginning of the sixteenth century, an early German humanist-physician Dietrich Ulsen, the intimate friend of the poet Conrad Celtis, used a large part of this metrical version in the composition of his curious and little known *Speculator* Broadside, printed at Nürnberg *c.* 1501.

I have thought it worth while to devote a chapter to Ulsen and his Broadside, since the latter is such a good example of the continuity of thought between the Middle Ages and the Renaissance, and has, besides, so many other interesting features; because Ulsen himself was, clearly, a man of unusual talent, a true forerunner, as it appears, of Paracelsus; and, finally, because fresh light is thrown on the part played by Nürnberg, then one of the most cultured cities north of the Alps, in the assimilation and spread of the new learning from Italy.

In addition it has been my intention not only to trace the spread of Salernitan *physica* to other parts of western Europe and, in particular, the influence of the questions, but also to try to show the vast extent of this kind of question literature as a whole and what part it played in the progress of the natural sciences and medicine. In this way it is hoped that the Salernitan questions will be seen in their true perspective.

This has involved giving an account of both pre-Salernitan, traditional Latin questions, and of later collections which swelled the Salernitan stream and added fresh features and characteristics. Thus about 1300 there was a tremendous revival of interest in the problems ascribed to Aristotle in the schools at Paris, under the influence of such masters as Peter of Abano and Jean de Jandun. This provided a new and powerful impetus to the study of this kind of literature, which lasted at least three centuries. From this time onwards, translations of all kinds of Greek problems, some of which had contributed material to the oldest Salernitan questions, continued to play a major part in such collections.

I have included an account of the later, vernacular question books, since not only do they also form a hitherto unexplored field of study, but they are certainly in the direct tradition of the Salernitan and other natural questions, and must have helped in that movement which, beginning in the fourteenth century, resulted in the popularization of science and medicine, and eventually led to the almost universal interest shown in these subjects throughout the civilized world today.

As regards the subject-matter of the Salernitan questions, the bulk of them dealt with anthropology, the various branches of medicine, and zoology; the everyday behaviour of man and beast, ordinary physiological actions and processes, and simple anatomy. In zoology this included a high proportion of the fabled and marvellous attributes of animals, birds, fishes, and reptiles. A lesser number of the questions dealt with meteorology, the effects of lightning, weather lore, the causes of the tides—questions which had been popular since the days of Seneca. Others may be classed as botanical, as distinct from herb lore and pharmacology, and discussed the nutrition, growth, and structure of trees and plants. Another small section dealt with physics, in the modern meaning of the term, and included questions about vacuums, magnetic attraction, vision and colour, and the discussion of simple experiments in connexion with sound, the generation of fire, the testing of wine and vinegar, the softening of egg-shells, and so forth. The smallest number of all dealt with metals, and inquired concerning the floating of iron on quicksilver, the tempering of iron, the purifying of silver, and why gold is unharmed in the fire. But there is a complete absence of alchemy in the sense of questions dealing with the transmutation of metals and chemical processes; and, indeed, the earliest collection to contain questions of this kind is probably the *Questiones Nicolai* attributed to Michael Scot, and associated with the court of Frederick II. To all these questions the Salernitan masters gave qualitative answers, based on physical composition and characteristics. This applied even to those which dealt with zoological fables, and such abstract matters as the various forms of action at a distance. Thus magnetic attraction was explained by the qualities of heat and cold and by *fumositas* derived from the elementary composition and complexion of iron. Fascination, about the only example of magical action, and the fatal glance of the basilisk, were explained by the emission of animal spirits from the eyes, infected with a venomous quality. Little use was made of an indeterminate 'occult virtue', which was to play so large a part in the explanations of similar phenomena given by sixteenth and seventeenth century naturalists. The outlook of the Salernitans, therefore, probably inspired by their long devotion to the doctrines of Greek medicine and by the strictly scientific teaching of Urso, was essentially practical and naturalistic.

In conclusion, apart from the obvious value of the questions in providing a hitherto unknown source-book and encyclopedia of scientific and medical knowledge, fables, folklore, and beliefs for the period about 1200, their long and continuous history makes them exceedingly useful for tracing the continuity and evolution of ideas. Comparison of the answers to the same questions, asked over a number of centuries, is bound to yield important data, and such analyses can be put to a number of uses. I have made several such comparisons throughout this study, with some interesting results.

One such result has been to show that thought in connexion with certain ancient questions relative to human and animal behaviour has not been so static, up to comparatively recent times, as has been supposed. Seemingly simple, these questions proved, in the end, to be among the most difficult to solve in a satisfactory manner. Not capable of an exact mathematical solution they were passed over by the technicians and mathematicians, and having no direct therapeutic value they were neglected by the majority of physicians. Yet some progress was made in answering them. By the seventeenth century psychological motives were beginning to reinforce or replace the physical causes of the earlier inquirers—this leading directly to the modern psychological treatment of human conduct and behaviour.

At the other end of the scale, it will no doubt surprise many readers to know that certain Greek procedures in scientific methodology, such as reasoning by inductive analogy, the processes of definition and resolution, and the confirmation of theory by experiment, were widely taught, in principle, by the didactic *quaestiones et responsiones* found in manuscripts dating from about the ninth century onwards—long before their reintroduction to the Latin West in the Galenic translations of Constantinus. It seems likely, in fact, that a reassessment of the value and importance of this type of question literature will have to be made when more texts are available for study. Here will be found the texts of Ulsen's *Speculator* Broadside and the remainder of the *Questiones phisicales* not used by him, with translations and notes to each question, giving the sources, where possible, and other relevant material. I hope to be able to deal in the same way with the text of the prose Salernitan questions at a later date.

1

Traditional pre-Salernitan, Latin, Scientific and Medical Questions

THE question, in one form or another, played an increasingly important part in the teaching of both theology and secular disciplines, first in the monastic and cathedral schools of the early Middle Ages, and then in the lay schools and universities.

Long before Salerno had achieved fame as the foremost school of medicine in western Europe, traditional questions, dealing with the sciences and medicine, had been available in the Latin West: questions in which were preserved and kept alive many ideas, stemming from the rich heritage of Greek and Roman culture; until, with the advent of what has been called the scientific renaissance in the twelfth century, fresh channels were opened up.

But even with the influx of this new stream of Greek learning, the old questions continued to play their part in the ceaseless quest for knowledge; and it is to them that we must look for some of the oldest ingredients of the Salernitan Questions, one of the main tools of instruction during the early years of this same scientific renaissance, and, subsequently, of great influence during a period of many centuries. Before we study this collection in some detail, therefore, let us see exactly what these traditional questions were, in what works they were to be found, and what were some of the ideas preserved in them.

The compilers of such questions made use, principally, of three literary forms—the essay, the sermon, and the dialogue. To the first belong the *Quaestiones naturales* of Seneca, the *Noctes Atticae* of Aulus Gellius, and a Latin translation of the *Solutiones* of Priscianus Lydus.[1] In all these the questions serve as pegs on which to hang essays or dissertations of various lengths. Seneca's questions, composed during the first century A.D., are confined to meteorology, and their influence may be traced in the meteorological content of nearly every subsequent collection of natural questions composed in the Latin West. Those of Aulus Gellius, belonging to the following century and dispersed in various chapters of his *Noctes Atticae*, are much fewer in number and briefer, though their scope is wider, and they discuss medical as well as physical and meteorological matters.

---

[1] Ed. F. Dubner, together with *Plotini Enneades*, but much more fully by I. Bywater in *Supplementum Aristotelicum*, i, part 2.

But perhaps because many passages are in Greek, they had little influence in the Latin West,[1] except via Macrobius, who used them in his *Saturnalia*. As for Priscianus Lydus, the importance of his *Solutiones* has only recently been realized.[2] Composed in Greek *c.* 529, the work consists of a series of fairly long dissertations in answer to questions put by King Chosroes about such varied matters as the nature of the soul, sleep, dreams, the four seasons, medical remedies, the cause of tides and other meteorological subjects, the action of climate on living things, and the causes of poison in reptiles. There exist four manuscripts of a Latin translation, the oldest being a Corbie codex of the ninth century. From this time onwards, therefore, the *Solutiones* must be numbered among the possible sources of natural philosophy in the West. It may be the source of one question in the Salernitan *Questiones phisicales* (Q. 9. *sompnia*) and Vincent of Beauvais made considerable use of it in his *Speculum naturale*.[3]

The sermon is not the usual place to look for scientific questions; but the nine Homilies of St. Basil of Caesarea on the *Hexaemeron*, composed in the fourth century, contain a fund of interesting questions and answers on cosmology, astronomy, the elements, botany, zoology, and anthropology. The work was very popular and influential throughout the Middle Ages and beyond, mainly through two Latin works, the *Hexaemeron* of St. Ambrose, an adaptation of it, also composed in the fourth century, and the fifth-century translation of Eustathius Afer. St. Basil's sources include the Stoics, Theophrastus, Aelian, Oppian, and, above all, the *Timaeus* of Plato, and the *libri naturales* of Aristotle.[4] Thus, long before the twelfth-century renaissance, a good deal of Peripatetic lore was available through the works of Priscianus Lydus and St. Basil. At the end of the twelfth century Alexander Neckam followed the method of the latter, introducing questions on natural science into his *De natura rerum*, which was nothing more than a series of short, moralizing sermons on all kinds of subjects.

But, on the whole, the sermon was not a popular medium in which to introduce questions of the kind we have been discussing. If natural science was introduced at all it was usually in the form of *exempla* or short anecdotes, often of a marvellous nature, and men preferred, as was only natural, the more scientific dialogue for the discussion of such questions. This form particularly lent itself to the introduction of questions and answers, either between master and pupil, or between a number of friends at a banquet or elsewhere, the so-called *Symposium* or Socratic dialogue,

---

[1] Thus eight questions stem from the pseudo-Aristotelian *Problems* (see Barthélemy-Saint Hilaire, *Les Problèmes d'Aristote*, 1891, I. pp. lxi–vi), but five of its quotations are in Greek.

[2] T. Silverstein, in his paper, 'Adelard, Aristotle and the De Natura Deorum', *C.P.* xlvii (1952), 82–86, drew attention to Macrobius and Priscianus Lydus in connexion with their importance for the general history of Aristotelianism in the West.

[3] See Bywater, op. cit., praefatio, p. xii.

[4] See the excellent introduction to S. Giet's translation of the *Homilies* in the series *Sources Chrétiennes* (Paris, 1949), pp. 47 ff.

immortalized by Plato.[1] In the former case the dialogue was entirely one of exposition, in which the master gradually unfolded to the pupil pre-conceived opinions and dogmatic facts about an art or science; and in this sense it may be called Aristotelian rather than Platonic, resembling those dialogues which Aristotle is supposed to have written, but which are now lost. Again, this dialogue of exposition may be rather diffuse and con-versational in character, as in the dialogues of Cicero, in which the ques-tions play a subsidiary role, or more abrupt and concise, consisting entirely of questions and short answers, *quaestiones et responsiones*, with a minimum of discussion, as in the pseudo-Aristotelian *Problems*, a form which was adopted by the compilers of the Salernitan prose questions.

The Ciceronian dialogue became one of the most important of the established forms of instruction in the *trivium* and *quadrivium*, being used by, amongst others, such famous teachers as Donatus, Victorinus, Augus-tine, and Alcuin; while, early in the twelfth century, it was this form which was adopted by Adelard for his *Quaestiones naturales*. But other writers on medicine and natural philosophy, subjects apart from the *quadrivium*, seemed to prefer the drier, more scientific form of the *quaestiones et re-sponsiones*.[2] Whether this form originated, as Hirzel thought,[3] from the *responsiones* of the Roman jurists, or initially came from Greece, it seems likely that Aristotle was the first to systematize the method and use it for demonstrating all kinds of scientific and medical problems, many of which have survived in the pseudo-Aristotelian *Problems*.[4]

The Stagyrite was imitated at the beginning of the second century by the Greek physician, Soranus, about a century later by Cassius the Iatrosophist, and still later by pseudo-Alexander Aphrodisias. Among Latin writers, however, little interest seems to have been taken in these kinds of problems until about the sixth century. In the definitions of

---

[1] On the contrast between these two types of dialogue, see A. S. Wilkins in his introduction to the *De oratore* of Cicero, 2nd ed., pp. 3 ff.

[2] An outline of the early history of this form of dialogue, as used in both religious and secular literature, is given in Part I of the edition of the *Altercatio Hadriani Augusti et Epicteti Philosophi*, by L. W. Daly and W. Suchier, 1939. But in the case of medicine, the discussion is confined to the pseudo-Galenic *Definitions*, or Ὅροι ἰατρικοί, and the works of Soranus and pseudo-Soranus, whilst the pseudo-Aristotelian *Problems* and other similar works of the Peri-patetic School are entirely left out of the picture. The *Altercatio* itself belongs rather to the domain of the literary riddle than to that of the more serious and technical kind of question we are discussing.

[3] R. Hirzel, *Der Dialog*, ii. 364.

[4] According to E. S. Forster, this seems to have been a gradual compilation formed, 'not much earlier than the first century B.C., and probably a good deal later', from genuine Aristo-telian material and other sources such as the Hippocratic writings and those of Theophrastus. See his 'The pseudo-Aristotelian Problems, their nature and composition', *C.Q.* xxii (1928), 165. E. Richter, *De Aristotelis Problematis*, 1885, would put the date as late as the fifth or sixth century A.D. One of the best general accounts of the *Problems* is the paper by C. Prantl, *A.B.A.W.* vi (1851), 339–77. See also J. Barthélemy-Saint Hilaire's introduction to his translation of the *Problems*, 1891. For detailed bibliography see the preface to the standard Greek text, ed. by Ruelle–Knoellinger–Klek, 1922.

Seneca, Macrobius, and Martianus Capella, *physica* was chiefly concerned with astronomy and meteorology, the grander phenomena of nature, and its ultimate aim and purpose was ethical, as Seneca says, 'to turn us aside from base matters, and lead the soul itself, which needs to be healed and uplifted, away from the body'.[1] Medicine and that part of *physica* which dealt with terrestrial bodies was little esteemed, being classed by Macrobius as the very lowest part or dregs of *physica*,[2] and being altogether excluded from the company of the seven liberal arts by Martianus Capella.[3] Thus probably not until the time of Cassiodorus (*c.* 490–583), who recommended the reading of classical medical texts in Latin translation,[4] was there much interest shown in such works.

The history of the Latin translations of the works of the three Greek writers mentioned above is still obscure. The Numidian physician Caelius Aurelianus was probably the first to translate certain works of Soranus, including his medical questions, in the fifth and sixth centuries. Certainly, by Carolingian times there existed a fairly large number of Latin medical *quaestiones et responsiones*, including substantial fragments of the Soranus–Aurelianus questions and of the problems of pseudo-Alexander and Cassius, which were by no means all medical.

These questions and problems formed part of that corpus of Latin medical texts belonging to the Carolingian period, to whose extent and importance Beccaria has only recently drawn attention. This scholar has succeeded in tracing no fewer than 59 codices belonging to the eighth and ninth centuries, of which 47 definitely belong to the latter century.[5] These figures refer to manuscripts which exclusively contain medical material, but if we take into account miscellaneous manuscripts in which the medical tracts are accompanied by other treatises of a non-medical nature, the total would be 82, and the figure for the ninth century, 68. Again, the number of separate treatises in these manuscripts would amount to several hundred, thus pointing to a considerable body of medical literature existing in the ninth century, both in Italy and the north. Further evidence of this is provided by ninth-century inventories and catalogues, which we have for such monasteries as Corbie, Reichenau, St. Gall, Lorsch, and Murbach.[6]

What these texts were, it is now necessary to examine in some detail,

---

[1] 'Ad hoc proderit nobis inspicere rerum naturam. Primo discedemus a sordidis. Deinde animum ipsum, quo sano magnoque opus est, seducemus a corpore', *Quaest. nat.*, ed. P. Oltramare, i. 118.

[2] 'Medicina autem physicae partis extrema faex est.' *Saturnalia*, vii. 15.

[3] 'Sed quoniam his [medicine and architecture] mortalium rerum cura terrenorumque sollertia est nec cum aethere quicquam habent superisque confine, non incongrue, si fastidio respuuntur.' *De nuptiis phil.*, ed. Eyssenhardt, p. 333.

[4] *Institutiones*, i. 31.

[5] *I codici di medicina del periodo presalernitano*, p. 21.

[6] For a list of such catalogues, &c., see Beccaria, op. cit., pp. 79–86, where the relevant entries regarding medical codices are also given.

since in several cases they represent the earliest impact of certain Greek scientific ideas on Western thought, long before their reintroduction by the translations of Constantinus from the Arabic. As long ago as 1901 Giacosa, in speaking of these early texts in his *Magistri Salernitani nondum editi*, pointed out that they were quite clearly divided into theoretical (*patologica*) and practical (*terapeutica*).[1] By the latter he meant, especially, the numerous *antidotaria*, herbals, and *materiae medicae*, but we can add to these the treatises on phlebotomy, urinoscopy, pulse, dietetics, mid-wifery, bathing, and weights and measures. Some of these are translations from the Greek and, rightly or wrongly, are ascribed to such famous physicians as Hippocrates, Galen, Oribasius (the *Euporista*), Dioscorides, Soranus, and Alexander of Tralles. Others are works, also often spurious, of late Roman physicians, such as Theodorus Priscianus, pseudo-Pliny Secundus, Gargilius Martial, Quintus Serenus, Cassius Felix, Apuleius, and Marcellus Empiricus.

Probably because this practical section constitutes the bulk of the early texts, it has been much more fully dealt with than the theoretical portion, and had greater emphasis laid upon it by historians of medieval medicine. I will only note here that at least three of these practical texts are in the form of *quaestiones et responsiones*, namely the pseudo-Hippocratic *De phlebotomia*, the translation of the *Gynaecia* of Soranos, and the *Disputatio Platonis et Aristotelis*.[2] Of the second or theoretical portion, only such classical texts as those of Caelius Aurelianus (*De morb. acut. et chron.*), Oribasius (*Synopsis*), and Celsus are at all widely known—while quite a numerous class of minor writings is still comparatively little known, and therefore deserves much fuller investigation.

Even with regard to the classical texts, however, it is not, perhaps, fully realized that they were available to the Latin West as early as the ninth and tenth centuries, and, in the case of Oribasius, a good deal earlier. The book on chronic diseases (*Tardarum passionum Lib. V*) of Caelius Aurelianus existed at Lorsch in the ninth to tenth century, as we know from two catalogues of that date. This very manuscript was used by Johann Sichard for his edition of the work printed at Basel in 1529,[3] but it has since com-pletely disappeared, except for two leaves which were discovered in 1921, by J. Ilberg, in a codex at Zwickau.[4] The book on acute diseases (*Acutarum passionum Lib. III*) by the same author, was edited four years later, in 1533

[1] Giacosa, *Mag. Sal.*, p. xxiv.

[2] See Caelius Aurelianus, *Gynaecia*, ed. M. F. and I. E. Drabkin. It appears that there are extant parts of two translations of the *Gynaecia* of Soranus, one by Caelius the other by Mustio, and that the Greek physician also incorporated sections on gynaecology into his *Medicinales responsiones*, which embraced the whole of medicine, and parts of which, translated by Caelius, are also extant. We shall discuss this latter work below. The *Disputatio Platonis et Aristotelis* was edited by Normann, *Sudhoffs Archiv* xxiii (1930), 68–73.

[3] On the fate of the manuscripts at Lorsch, and the vicissitudes which befell this codex, see Rose, *Anecdota Graeca et Graecolatina*, ii. 163 ff.

[4] Beccaria, op. cit., pp. 82 and 235.

at Paris, by Johann Gunther, again from an early codex,[1] but this time there are no entries in early catalogues which could help us, and no portions of the manuscript have so far turned up. Parts of the *Synopsis* (*conspectus ad Eustathium filium*) of Oribasius were known in a pre-Carolingian Latin translation, still existing in four early manuscripts, ranging from the sixth to the ninth century; whilst a later translation also exists, in fragmentary form, in a further seven codices, dating from the ninth to the twelfth century.[2] Celsus, *De medicina* also exists in three early codices, two of which belong to the ninth and tenth centuries, and was quoted by Gerbert at the end of the tenth century.[3] But much more often found in manuscripts of the ninth and tenth centuries are the treatises recommended by Cassiodorus in the sixth century, pseudo-Galen, *ad Glauconem de medendi methodo*, the *Aphorisms* of Hippocrates with an anonymous commentary, and the so-called Aurelius–Esculapius text.[4] These are found associated with certain other theoretical texts, such as pseudo-Hippocratic and other anonymous *Epistolae*, *Epist. Vindiciani*, Isidore, *Etymologiae Lib. IV* (*De medicina*), the *Sapientia artis medicinae*, pseudo-Aristotelian *Problemata*, the translation by Caelius Aurelianus of the *Medicinales responsiones* of Soranus, and the pseudo-Soranic *Isagoge* or *Introductio ad medicinam*, also known as *Quaestiones medicinales*.

Giacosa had noted this association of tracts, and thought that it formed the theoretical portion of a complete *summa* of medicine which existed in south Italy at that early date, and was still to be found, in various stages of completeness, in a number of Italian manuscripts. In some manuscripts only the practical part of the *summa* is found, as in Casin. 69 (ixth cent.) and Lucca 296 (ix–x cent.), to mention only the earliest noticed by Giacosa; in others both the theoretical and the practical, as in Casin. 97 (ix[1] cent.) and 225 (xi[2] cent.), the former being more complete and more representative of the whole *summa*, the latter having the practical part represented only by *antidotaria*.[5]

In order to show the correspondence between them I have compared the theoretical contents of the last two Casinensian manuscripts mentioned by Giacosa with those of six other codices of the same period (ix–xi cent.). See Table 1. The regularity with which these texts turn up in association with each other tends to confirm Giacosa's theory of a *summa* of medicine, which, if not always exactly the same, was at least constructed along similar lines, and which exactly corresponded to the *collectanea* and chrestomathies

---

[1] Rose, op. cit., p. 166.

[2] All these codices will be found listed in *Oribasius Latinus*, hrsg. H. Mørland, i. 3 ff. See also Loren C. MacKinney, *Early Medieval Medicine*, pp. 111 ff.

[3] Vat. Lat. 5951 (ix[1] cent.), Florent. Laurent. Plut. 73. 1 (ix–x cent.), Bibl. Nat. Lat. 7028 (x–xi cent.). The last manuscript was in the library of Otto III, where it was probably seen by Gerbert when he was in the service of the emperor. See the Prolegomena to Celsus, *Opera*, rec. F. Marx (*C.M.L.* i), p. xxxviii, and MacKinney, op. cit., p. 117 ff.

[4] See above, p. 4.

[5] Giacosa, *Mag. Sal.*, pp. xxi ff. (Lucca 296 is called 236 in error).

TABLE I

A Comparison of the Theoretical Contents of Medical Codices of the ninth, tenth, and eleventh centuries

The number following B refers to the number of the codex in Professor Beccaria's *I codici di medicina del periodo presalernitano*, Rome, 1956.

	Casin. V. 97 x^1. B 95	Casin. V. 225 xii^2. B 96	Montp. 185 xi. B 16	Hunterian V. 3·2, x^1. B 73	Brit. Mus. Addit. 8928, x. B 84	Reichenau 120 ix. B 56	Bibl. Nat. Lat. 11219 ix. B 35	Chartres 62 x^2. B 10
Hip. *Aphor.* and *Com.*	199^v–282	..	1^v–98	34–147^v	..	120–181^v, 200–204^v	1^r–11^v	..
Epist. 'frustra'	24	..	116^v	24^v–25	6^v	..	..	..
,, 'non satis'	24	..	116^v	25	..	..	..	..
,, 'ne ignorans'	24–26	30–33	117^v–119^v	25–27^v	13–14	..	15–17	..
,, Hip. ad Antiochum	20^v–23^v	..	113–115^v	..	11^v–13	..	41^{r-v}	..
,, 'interea'	..	..	..	27^v	14	..	12	..
,, 'in primo'	23^v–24	..	115^v–116^v	..	..	..	..	..
,, *De disciplina artis med.*	..	..	..	..	..	..	12^v–14	16–36^v, 40^v–53^v
Galen, *Epist. ad Glauconem*	33–89	34–35	119^v–129^v	30^v–31^v	..	..	..	..
,, *De sectis*	4^v–6	..	136^v–154^v	27^v–28^v	8–9	185^v–187^v	..	..
Vindicianus, *Epist. ad Pentadium*	13^v–20^v	17–20	101–102^v	15–17	1^v–5^v	..	..	..
Isidore, *Etym.* iv.	12^v–13^v	3–17	105–113	3–11^v	1^{r-v}, 11^v	..	..	..
Sapientia artis med.	109–199^v	1–3	..	1–3	11^{r-v}	18–95^v	24^v–26, 39^v–41	74–109
Aurelius–Esculapius text	10^v–12^v	..	..	..	..	..	20^r–24^v	..
pseudo-Arist., *Prob.* (*Vetust. trans.*)	..	26–30	..	..	..	..	..	..
Caelius Aurelianus *Med. responsiones*	..	..	..	..	..	102–15	26–32^v	..
pseudo-Soranus, *Quaestiones med.*	..	..	..	..	..	..	20^{r-v}	1–16

dealing with the subjects of the *trivium* and *quadrivium* dating from the same period.

The idea of a combination of theory and practice was a continuation of the tradition of Cassiodorus, who recommended to the monks of Vivarium, besides the above-mentioned theoretical works, the practical *Herbarium* of Dioscorides and the *De herbis* attributed to Hippocrates. Now, as regards these various theoretical texts, we need only discuss here, following the particular line of our investigation, the corpus of medical *quaestiones*, for the most part based on Greek originals, to which I have already referred, and which, as it happens, is probably one of the least widely known parts of the *summa*.

Let us take the *Medicinales responsiones* of Caelius Aurelianus first. Like the books on acute and chronic diseases, this work was derived from the Greek of Soranus, existed in at least three books, and embraced the whole of medicine in the easily digestible, introductory form of question and answer.[1] It also formerly existed at Lorsch in the tenth century, like the larger work on chronic diseases, according to the above-mentioned two catalogues, but, like the other codex, this manuscript has since disappeared.[2] We possess portions of the text, however, in the *De salutaribus praeceptis* and *De significatione diaeticarum passionum* of Caelius Aurelianus, both edited by V. Rose in 1870,[3] the former from Reichenau 120 (IX cent.) ff. 102–7, and Brit. Mus. Sloane, 1122 (XI cent.) ff. 1–7ᵛ, the latter from Reichenau 120 ff. 107–15. Another fragment of the *De salutaribus praeceptis* has since been found in Vendôme 109 (XI cent.) ff. 87ᵛ–88,[4] and it seems to me that Bibl. Nat. Lat. 11219 (IX cent.) ff. 26–32ᵛ, *Liber interrogationis Yppocratis medici*, is an abbreviated form of this text, consisting of the questions with short summaries of the answers.[5]

It appears that this introductory work was used later on by Soranus–Caelius Aurelianus in the compilation of the longer and more elaborate work on acute and chronic diseases, where, sometimes, the question form and the very wording of the *responsiones* is retained.[6] Traces of it are also

---

[1] As we learn from the beginning of the Soranus–Caelius *Lib. de acut. pass.* 'Nam interrogationum ac responsionum libros, quibus omnem medicinam breviter dixi, iamdudum ad Lucretium nostrum perscriptos aptissime destinavi.' *Caelii Aureliani, De morbis acutis et chronicis*, rec. J. C. Amman, Lib. I, p. 1.   [2] Rose, *Anecdota*, ii. 166.

[3] Ibid., 183–240.   [4] Beccaria, *Cod. di med.*, p. 186.

[5] Ibid., p. 168. Sometimes the answers correspond exactly: cf. 'Quid est sanitas? integra viarum aut officiorum naturalium temperies' (Rose, p. 196), 'integra virium atque officiorum naturalium temperies' (11219, f. 26ᵛ, a), where note that *virium* is more likely to be correct than *viarum*. 'Quot vel quibus constat salutare praeceptum? quattuor: qualitate, quantitate, tempore atque ordine' (Rose, p. 198). 'Quod vel quantis constat salutarium praeceptorum? quattuor, id est qualitatem, quantitatem, temperiem et ordinem' (11219, f. 26ᵛ, a). Compare, however, the short answer of 11219 to the question 'Quid magis post lavacrum utile est, potum aut cibum accipere?' 'Et hoc et illud, sitienti tamen post laborem potus potius optimum est. Similiter autem et esurientibus utilis est' (f. 29ᵛ a) with the much longer answer in Rose, p. 199.

[6] e.g. Caelius, *Lib. de acut. pass.* ii, cap. 36 corresponds to question 40 of the *De sig. diaet. pass.*

found in Isidore, *Etym. Lib. IV* (*De medicina*), pseudo-Pliny, and the Aurelius–Esculapius text, which, again, often contains the actual wording.[1]

The *responsiones*, then, had the extremely practical end in view of teaching medicine in an easily assimilated form, and in accordance with the tenets of the methodist sect, of which Soranus was one of the chief exponents. This sect paid little attention to the causes of diseases, but concentrated mainly on their classification, symptoms, differential diagnosis, and therapeutics.

Rather similar to the *responsiones* is the pseudo-Soranic *Isagoge* or *Quaestiones medicinales*, also edited by Rose in 1870[2] from Cotton, Galba E. IV (XIII cent.), ff. 238ᵛ–244ᵛ. Since then, in 1906, H. Stadler[3] has furnished some additions from a more complete text, found in Chartres 62 (X cent.), ff. 1–16, and more recently Beccaria has noted the presence of part of the prologue only, in Bibl. Nat. Lat. 11219, f. 20ʳ⁻ᵛ. Another portion of the prologue is found in Nat. Lib. of Scotland, Adv. Ms. 18. 5. 16 (XII cent.), f. 92ᵛ (mentioned by H. Diels, *Die Handschriften der antiken Aerzte*, ii (1906), p. 94, under the old press-mark of Adv. Lib. A. 5. 42). Finally, I have now discovered a text in Lincoln Cath. Lib. 220 (XII cent.), ff. 22–44 which completes still further the text edited by Rose,[4] and there

---

(Rose, p. 213), and see the numerous references in Rose's critical apparatus and p. 174. Apart from this the *De salutaribus praeceptis* is frequently named in the *De morb. acut. et chron.* (places noted by Rose, p. 172). Fragments of the gynaecological portions of the *Medicinales responsiones* are probably incorporated in the Latin translations of the *Gynaecia* of Soranus, as we now have them. See above p. 5, n. 2.

[1] See Rose, op. cit., pp. 175 ff. A good many of the questions of the *Medicinales responsiones* are incorporated in the Aurelius–Esculapius text, so much so that Rose thinks some lost questions of the former may be recovered from the latter. The Aurelius–Esculapius text, not to be confused with the *De morbis acut. et chron.* of Soranus–Caelius Aurelianus, was composed by a Christian physician from both dogmatic and methodist sources and, in its turn, was to become one of the main sources of the Salernitan *Passionarius*, which we shall discuss below. The text is divided into two portions, often occurring separately, the *Aurelius, de acutis passionibus*, ed. Daremberg, in *Janus* (Breslau), ii (1847), 478–99, 690–731, and the *Esculapius de chronicis passionibus*, printed at the end of *Experimentarius medicinae*, Strassb. 1544. Exactly what text Cassiodorus meant to signify by the words *Caeli Aureli de medicina* will, I suppose, always be a debatable point. Rose thought they referred to the Aurelius text (op. cit., p. 119), Courcelle, that they indicated a compilation from the works of Caelius Aurelianus, and included the Aurelius–Esculapius text and the *Medicinales responsiones* (*Les Lettres grecques en Occident*, pp. 384–6).

[2] *Anecdota*, ii. 243–74.

[3] 'Neu Bruchstücke der *Quaestiones medicinales* des Pseudo-Soranus' in *A.L.L.G.* xiv (1906), 361–8. Stadler only supplies, from the Chartres MS., the first missing portion in the Cottonian text (Rose, p. 254); he refrained from trying to fill in the second gap (Rose, p. 269) and the missing end portion, because he found the order of the questions quite different, and thought the Greek text of pseudo-Galen ὅροι or *Definitiones medicae* (ed. Kuhn, xix. 348 ff.), one of the main sources, should be used to obtain a more correct reading.

[4] This discovery is all the more fortunate, since the Chartres codex, along with many others, suffered very heavy damage during the bombardments of the last war, being 'reduced to a few corroded and burnt fragments' (Beccaria, op. cit., p. 127). Lincoln 220 lacks the prologue and the first part of the questions, but after that seems very complete, offering a different reading for part of the first gap (Rose, p. 254), supplied by Stadler, completely filling the second gap (Rose, p. 269), and supplying the missing terminal portion, which occupies ff. 40–44.

is yet another twelfth-century text in the Metropolitan Chapter Library at Prague, which I have not seen.[1] This work, which is not originally by Soranus, was translated from the Greek by someone who was a much worse translator than Caelius Aurelianus, and seems to be a compilation from methodist sources, the pseudo-Galenic ὅροι or *Definitiones medicae*, and other Galenic material.[2] The prologue had, apparently, an importance of its own, since not only do we find parts of it in two ancient manuscripts, but it was also published by Albanus Torinus in his 1528 (Basel) edition of *De re medica*,[3] with the title *Sorani Ephesii in artem medendi isagoge*.

In this short prologue, which is not in the form of question and answer, we find mentioned the attributes of a good physician, *qualem oporteat esse medicum*, and what he should know, *doctrina artis*. With regard to the latter, the anonymous author, like Isidore, mentions the necessity of the *trivium* and *quadrivium*, and stresses the value of natural philosophy.[4] Here, too, we meet, I believe for the first time in Latin translation, with the well-known Galenic principle which unites reason with experience, expressed in no uncertain terms.[5]

After the prologue come the questions and answers, a method which the author thinks 'more useful to those who are being introduced to medicine, since, in a way, it fashions the minds of the young.'[6] The questions deal with both the practice and the theory of medicine; in the former case discussing anatomy, physiology, pulse lore, the signs and symptoms of diseases, and surgery; in the latter, the classification of diseases, the meaning of certain technical terms, the *principia* and parts of medicine, and the doctrines of the three principal sects.

[1] Cod. Capituli Metropolitani 1358 (XII cent.), ff. 49ᵛ–92ᵛ: 'Incipit liber Sorani loyci de horis ysagogicis—Medicinam quidem invenit Apollo.'

[2] Rose, op. cit., pp. 169 ff.

[3] It also appeared in the collection *Medici antiqui omnes*, Venice, 1547.

[4] 'Nec non et naturae rerum scientiam habeat, ut omnino huius rei non expers esse videatur. his quidem ornatus esse debet qui sumpturus est medicinalem artem . . . grammaticam autem artem ad tantum sciat ut possit intelligere vel exponere quae apud veteres dicta sunt praeteriens artificiosam loquacitatem. rhetoricam quoque sciat ut possit suo patrocinari sermone tractantibus medicinales disciplinas. geometriam item ut aegrorum mensuras et numeros agnoscat ad comprehensionem et complexionem accessionum quae typi appellantur, vel crisin quam periodici faciunt. astrorum quoque ratio scienda est ut cognoscat eorum et occasus et ortus et motus et tempora anni, quia cum ipsis et nostra corpora commutantur, et eorum moderatione et perturbatione aegritudines in hominibus commoventur.' Rose, pp. 244–5.

[5] 'Qui autem vult nostram artem discere optime, is debet unius cuiusque rei doctrinam et corporum naturam et singularium partium operationem cognoscere. qui autem non ita doctus est sed experientiam tantum sine aliqua ratione exercuerit et inhoneste artis professionem risui dederit et sine doctrina rationabili egerit, alienum medicinae opus adhibere videtur quantum ad ipsam artem spectat. ubi enim ratio non diiudicat, necesse est eum ad incommoda pergere qui sola experientia sine aliqua ratione utitur. ratio enim breviter ad utilitatem perducit et tanquam caecam empiricam id est experientiam ducit.' Rose, pp. 246–7.

[6] 'Quem ad modum autem doctrinam percepimus dicendum existimo. et quoniam utilior videtur eis qui ad medicinam introducuntur interrogationum et responsionum modus, quoniam format quodammodo sensus iuvenum, brevi in controversia isagoga tradenda est illis.' Rose, p. 247.

Again, perhaps for the first time in the Latin West, we find exactly and succinctly described the Galenic principles of reasoning by 'inductive analogy',[1] that is of proceeding by way of the more obvious causes and effects to the discovery of the hidden causes of diseases, from which, in turn, a method of cure could be worked out, of the processes of definition and resolution,[2] and of the confirmation of theory by experiment or experience.[3] These matters had been discussed in Galen's *De Sectis* and *Ars medica* (*microtegni, ars parva*), both of which were translated into Latin and commented upon in that language at Ravenna, perhaps as early as the sixth century.[4]

From the present state of our knowledge it is difficult to know whether these translations and commentaries preceded the Latin pseudo-Soranic *Quaestiones*, or vice versa. In any case the former seem to have disappeared to an even greater extent than the latter, having survived in only two manuscripts of the ninth century, one of which contains only a fragment of the *Com. de sectis* (Reichenau 120, ff. 185ᵛ–187ᵛ).[5] It is perhaps significant that, in the latter case, this fragment, like the pseudo-Soranic *Quaestiones*, is associated with other short tracts belonging to what we may call the theoretical part of the medical *summa*; see Table 1. But some of these theoretical tracts seem to have survived much better than others.

---

[1] 'Quid est analogismus? analogismus est ratio ab his quae videntur initium sumens et ad ea pergens quae dubia sunt et minime sensibus comprehenduntur. . . . quid est logica medicina? logica medicina est quae et dogmatica condicio dicitur, ut definitio responsionis utilis efficiatur, ut anatomica ratio consentiat medicinae ut ad utilitatem suam perveniat, et ut ante omnia natura hominis sciatur, causae etiam vitiorum inquirantur et de ipsis ratio curae inveniatur, nec non et analogismo utatur et rationabilem considerationem curae sciat et quae sunt naturales et quae spontaneae operationes, naturales quoque calores, gubernationes causarum manifestarum et non manifestarum, comprehensiones temporum locorum aetatum et vitiorum singulorum inspectiones et actuum singulorum considerationes. haec enim omnia et his similia id est aetas temperantia virtus corporis habitudo calor qualitas consuetudo incessus et ut dictum est actuum singulorum considerationes et tempora anni et eorum qualitates et locorum positiones utilia medicinae ad praesciendas aegritudines esse cognoscuntur, ut ex hoc paratam habeat curae consequentiam. inspicienda etiam sunt vitiosa loca, ut comprehendamus quae vitalia sunt. causarum autem quaedam sunt manifestae, quaedam vero non manifestae. manifestae autem sunt quaedam quae sensibus comprehenduntur . . . non manifestae autem dicuntur causae quae fiunt per sensibilia intrinsecus et quae effugiunt quidem sensus sed per quaedam signa mentis conspiciuntur.' Rose, pp. 253–4.

[2] 'Quid est definitio? definitio est ratio reddita, quae de singulis rebus quales sint ratione definita significat, aut ratio ipsa earum. quarum definitio constat ex genere et specie differentia accidentique, quae per resolutionem ad determinationem proferuntur.' Rose, p. 247.

[3] 'Inventionis autem principium iuxta empiricos quidem est pira id est experientia, iuxta dogmaticos vero experientia cum ratione. quod enim lectio invenit in aphorismis, experimentum confirmavit.' Rose, p. 248.

[4] See O. Temkin, 'Alexandrian Studies on Galen's De Sectis', *B.I.H.M.* iii (1935), 405–30; and, for Ravenna as a centre of medical studies, MacKinney, *Medieval Med.*, pp. 52, 222; Beccaria, 'Il Ritorno della Scienza Classica', *R.S.I.* ii. 1 (1937), 24 ff.; and the same author's *Cod. di med.*, p. 60. It should not be forgotten, also, that the prefatory matter to the *De medicina* of Celsus contains a good deal of valuable information regarding the three main sects, but this work was probably as scarce in Carolingian times as the Galenic commentaries. See above, p. 6.

[5] The other manuscript is Milan (Ambros.) G. 108 Inf., which contains, also, commentaries on the Galenic *De pulsibus* and *Ad Glauconem*.

Thus, the more concise pseudo-Soranic *Quaestiones*, specially adapted for teaching, would probably be more popular, and so stand a better chance of survival, than the longer commentaries and translations. Perhaps one would not be far wrong in thinking that it was through the former, rather than the latter, that the particular doctrines of Galen that we have been discussing first became more widely known in the early Middle Ages. Certainly it seems to me that the almost universal opinion of scholars, up till now, that the ideas of Galen on these subjects were first made known to the Latin West through the translations and writings of Constantinus, will have to be revised. It is instructive to consider that in a tenth-century Chartrian manuscript we find described, in principle, that double inductive-deductive process of reasoning combined with experiment which, as A. C. Crombie has taken pains to show, formed the basis of Grosseteste's experimental method over two centuries later.

To return to the pseudo-Soranic *Quaestiones*, in recommending the study of natural philosophy, and in postulating that the student should begin the study of medicine with the 'physical method', *oportere nos incipere a physica ratione*,[1] which he identifies with the nature and natural operations of the body (physiology), the author is preparing the ground for the later emphasis on *physica* as a whole, and the inclusion of medicine within its sphere. Finally, in stressing the value of the method of *quaestiones et responsiones* in teaching medicine he is carrying on the Peripatetic tradition of Soranus, and helping to establish this as one of the main methods of instruction in scientific, and non-scientific, disciplines.

In Bibl. Nat. Lat. 11219 (f. 39ʳ⁻ᵛ) there is a short *De interrogatione medicinali*, which, as far as I know, is not to be found anywhere else. Perhaps part of a larger work, it consists of a few short questions and answers dealing, in rather an elementary way, with such subjects as the causes of speech and walking, the number and names of the veins in the heart and eye, the nature of the four humours, the kinds of hydropsy, and the meaning of certain technical terms. Another series of questions, beginning *De passionibus unde eveniunt*, is quite often found associated with the *Sapientia artis medicinae*, which was edited by M. Wlaschky in 1928,[2] and of which Beccaria has traced twelve manuscripts dating from the ninth to the eleventh century.[3] These questions deal entirely with the causes of diseases in relation to the humoral theory.

Much more interesting is a collection of Latin *problemata* sometimes ascribed to Aristotle, which exists in a fragmentary form in eight manuscripts dating from the ninth century onwards.[4] Called by Lacombe and

---

[1] Rose, p. 251.   [2] In *Kyklos*, i. 103–13.   [3] *Cod. di med.*, p. 484.

[4] Bamberg, Cod. med. 1 (L. III. 8) (ix¹ cent.), ff. 6ᵛ–7ᵛ. This codex was probably in the library of Otto III, cf. the manuscript of Celsus mentioned above, p. 6, n. 3; Casinen. 97 (x¹ cent.), ff. 10ᵛ–12ᵛ; Casinen. 225 (xi² cent.), ff. 26–30; Brit. Mus. Addit. 8928 (x cent.), ff. 11ʳ⁻ᵛ, the problems we are discussing end 11ᵛ, l. 21; ll. 22–30 contain four questions and

his collaborators the *Vetustissima translatio*,[1] this collection represents the first appearance in the Latin West of *quaestiones et responsiones* which, if not actually by the Stagyrite, contain Aristotelian material, and are directly in the Peripatetic tradition. The problem of their exact origin has not yet been solved. V. Rose, who edited these *problemata* in 1863 from three ancient manuscripts,[2] noted that twenty-four of the questions corresponded to those which go under the name of Alexander Aphrodiseas, another eight to those of Cassius the Iatrosophist, whilst the remaining eleven were untraced. Twenty-three of the pseudo-Alexandrian questions belonged to a late collection of miscellaneous Greek *problemata*, compiled from various sources, including pseudo-Alexander, Cassius, and, possibly, Aristotle himself, and edited in 1857 by Bussemaker, with the title *Problemata inedita*.[3] Whether the remaining twenty problems were originally translated from a more complete version of these Greek *Problemata inedita* is a question which still awaits investigation.

As regards the period of the translation, there is a strong probability that since only fragments remained by Carolingian times the translation had been made much earlier, and had subsequently been neglected. Between the ninth and the mid-thirteenth century, when the much bulkier pseudo-Aristotelian *Problems* in thirty-eight books was translated by Bartholomew of Messina, the *Vetustissima translatio* formed the main source, in the Latin West, for this particular kind of Aristotelian problem, which dealt, in a strictly scientific way, with the causes of phenomena, not always anthropological and medical. It was undoubtedly a source for some of the medical questions discussed in the monastic schools at the end of the eleventh century, the sort of question which has been described by Baudry, abbot of Bourgueil,[4] and, as we shall see, it probably

answers from the *De passionibus unde eveniunt* (not mentioned in Beccaria's analysis of this codex); Brit. Mus., Sloane 634 (xv cent.), f. 9ᵛ; Bruxelles 2419–31 (xii cent.), f. 86ʳ⁻ᵛ; Berlin, lat. qu. 198 (xii cent.), ff. 14–15. An eighth manuscript of the work turned up recently at a sale at Sotheby & Co., 11 July 1960, lot 130, a folio codex of the mid-thirteenth century, which had at one time been in the Benedictine abbey of Cluny. This interesting manuscript contains large portions of the early *summa* of medicine which we have been discussing, both theoretical and practical, as well as some of the later Arabic–Latin translations of Gerard of Cremona, such as works by Rhazes and Avicenna. The *problemata* occupy f. 19ʳ⁻ᵛ. The manuscript was bought by the Bodleian Library, and has been allotted the press mark lat. misc. c. 73. Berlin 165 (Phillipps 1790) (ixᴵ cent.), ff. 34–35ᵛ, lists several components of the early *summa*. Among the titles are 'De interrogatione medicinale', 'proclima (problemata) Arestotilis pylosophi', and 'Proplema aristotili que sunt que mutant corpora'.

[1] *Aristot. Lat. cod. descrip.* i. 40, 86; ii, index; iii, pp. 225–6. Sloane 634 is not listed.

[2] In *Aristoteles Pseudepigraphus*, pp. 666–76, using the three manuscripts mentioned in *Aristot. Lat.* i and ii.

[3] In *Aristotelis Opera omnia*, gr. et lat. iv. 291–334.

[4] In a poem dedicated to the Countess Adèle, daughter of William of Normandy, Baudry gives a long, 88-line, description of both theoretical and practical medicine, extremely valuable for the light it throws on the methods of instruction in France at that early period. See *Les Œuvres poétiques de Baudri de Bourgueil*, ed. Phyllis Abrahams, pp. 196 ff. The description of medicine occupies ll. 1254–1341. This portion of the poem is also found in Dubreuil-

inspired some of the questions of Adelard, William of Conches, and the Salernitan masters.

Finally we come to the other type of dialogue, the Socratic. This form differed very much both in construction, spirit, and aim from those which we have just been discussing. According to Aristotle, 'Two things may be fairly ascribed to Socrates—inductive arguments and universal definitions, both of which are concerned with the starting-point of science.'[1] Plato used these methods in his dialogues, where, by means of rapid and dramatic dialectical arguments, he sought to arrive at the truth in relation to abstract questions, not always attaining it with any dogmatic certainty. So that this kind of dialogue is one of investigation, of search after truth, rather than one of exposition of known truths.

The external form of the Socratic dialogue, particularly that of the *Symposium*, was very popular amongst Greek writers, being adopted by, amongst others, Xenophon, Plutarch, Lucian, and Athenaeus. But none of these Symposia were translated into Latin before the Italian renaissance, so that their influence was very limited in the West before that time. The Platonic dialogues scarcely had a better fate. Cicero's translation of the *Protagoras* disappeared before the sixth century, as did Apuleius' of the *Phaedo*, and both seem to have been known to very few scholars even during the time they were extant. Cicero and Chalcidius (*c.* 350) both translated parts only of the *Timaeus*, and these versions formed the only direct sources for Platonic doctrines during the early Middle Ages. In fact, not until *c.* 1156, when Aristippus translated the *Meno* and *Phaedo*, did Latin scholars have direct access to any more of Plato's dialogues.[2] If we except the lost *Quaestiones conviviales* of Apuleius, Macrobius would appear to be the first to write an original, Latin Symposium which dealt with questions of a medical and scientific nature—the *Saturnalia*. In this work, like the Greek writers mentioned above, he adopts only the external form of this kind of dialogue, and, like Plutarch and Athenaeus, used it for compiling a species of encyclopedia, and for discussing, in as pleasant and easy a way as possible, questions which he thought would interest his son and be of use to him in his future studies. The seventh book of the *Saturnalia* consists largely of a series of questions and answers about natural philosophy; and having already, perhaps, in his *Commentary on the Dream of Scipio*, dealt with what was for him the most important part of *physica*, namely astronomy,[3] he is here more concerned with the lowest portion, the bulk of the questions dealing with anthropology and medicine,

Chambardel, *Les Médecins dans l'ouest de la France au XIe et XIIe siècles*, pp. 54–56. The questions, about thirteen in number, are described in ll. 1286–95.

[1] *Metaphysics*, M. 4 (1078ᵇ).

[2] See R. Klibansky, *The Continuity of the Platonic Tradition*, 2nd ed., pp. 22 ff.

[3] W. H. Stahl in the introduction to his recent translation of the *Commentary*, p. 5, agrees with Wissowa in dating this work before the *Saturnalia*. On the superiority of astronomy to medicine see above, p. 4.

food and drink, the actions of the senses, the differences between the sexes, and *materia medica*. A few, however, are physical in the modern sense, such as those dealing with the temperature of wells, movements in hot water, fanning, honey, oil and wine, and washing clothes.[1]

Macrobius was thus the first in the Latin West to grant to medicine a place, however humble, in the exalted realm of *physica*, and the first to afford a series of natural questions which dealt mainly with the lesser world of man, and inferior bodies. This series was of great influence during the succeeding centuries. Adelard used it, and questions from it are found in the *Questiones phisicales* and other Salernitan collections, as well as in many other collections of natural questions and *problemata*, until as late as the seventeenth century.[2] In spite of its great popularity, however, no other medieval Latin author, as far as I know, adopted this form for the discussion of purely scientific and medical questions, although it was used with great effect in the service of philosophy by such writers as Boethius and John Scotus Erigena.

[1] On the sources for these questions consult P. Courcelle, *Les Lettres grecques en Occident*, 1948, 9–20, and the literature there cited. They will be found to be chiefly the *Banquet (Symposium)* of Plutarch, the *Problems* ascribed to Alexander Aphrodiseas, and the *Noctes Atticae* of Aulus Gellius. Three of the eight questions in the latter work, which stem from the pseudo-Aristotelian *Problems*, are discussed by Macrobius. See above, p. 2, n. 1.

[2] At least twice it has appeared separately, with the titles *Questiones phisice*, Bibl. Nat. Lat. 7412 (XII cent.), ff. 80–89ᵛ, and *Tractatus de naturalibus quorumdam philosophorum questionibus*, Gloucester Cath. 25 (XIII cent.), ff. 34–39, while Vienna, Nationalbibl. 11240 (XVI cent.), contains excerpts from it.

2

The Beginnings of the Scientific Renaissance in South Italy. The Quaestiones naturales of Adelard, and the Prose Salernitan Questions

AT the end of the tenth century the historian Richer, having learnt the rudiments of medicine at Rheims under Gerbert, had to go to Chartres in order to proceed further in his medical studies.[1] He tells us an interesting story, which, whether true or not, reflects the state of medical studies in north France and Salerno at that time.

Two physicians, a Frenchman, Deroldus, and a Salernitan, disputed before the king and queen. Deroldus is represented as being skilled in theory, *litterarum artibus eruditus*, and the Salernitan as being possessed of a certain inborn cleverness and practical ability. Needless to say, the former won the contest to the great discomfiture of the latter.[2] As Kristeller pointed out, the value of the story lies in the fact that it shows that Salerno existed as a separate centre of medicine as early as the end of the tenth century, and that its doctrines were practical rather than theoretical, while in north France theory held the field.[3]

Owing to the restoration of law and order about this time, which once more created conditions favourable to civilization and culture, profane studies, including theoretical medicine, began to rival those of theology not only at Chartres but at several other monastic and cathedral schools north of the Alps.[4] But in Italy the conditions for the development of an independent spirit in culture and learning were even more favourable than they were in the north. In the land of Virgil, Horace, and Ovid teachers and pupils alike had always felt they were the direct heirs of the classical tradition. The lay schools, too, had never entirely ceased after the barbaric invasions, as they had in France, and under Lombard rule they sprang up anew in Pavia, Milan, Benevento, Ravenna, and many other places. Then, as times became more settled, and trade and commerce flourished, the old Roman ideal of a free and vigorous municipal life revived, and more and more of the citizens, including the sons of the

[1] Richer, *Hist.* iv. 50. For an account of the incident see Loren C. MacKinney, *Medieval Med.*, pp. 121 ff.   [2] Richer, *Hist.* ii. 59.
[3] P. O. Kristeller, 'The School of Salerno', *B.H.M.* xvii (1945), 144.
[4] See Clerval, *Les Écoles de Chartres au moyen âge*, p. 27.

nobility, took up the study of the liberal arts in a true, humanistic spirit, and, often with the practical end in view of following the professions of law and medicine, for which the arts were the necessary preliminaries. Thus the secular, rather than the ecclesiastical, element came to predominate in Italian civic life, and its echoes even penetrated to the cloisters of the monasteries, and helped to produce there a more liberal and humanistic outlook, subservient still to theology, it is true, but not entirely entrammelled by it.

In south Italy, during the eleventh century, the heart and centre of humane studies was the great Benedictine abbey of Montecassino, the parent house of the order, where so many important manuscripts originated. After its destruction in 883 by the Saracens, the monks had fled to Teano in Campania, and it was not until 949 that they returned, under the leadership of Aligernus. After a rather unsettled period, during which the work of copying was recommenced, under Abbot Atenolf (1011–22), what Lowe calls 'the golden age of copying' set in. In his book on the Beneventan script, for which Montecassino was the most important centre, he mentions fourteen medical manuscripts in that script dating from the ninth to the eleventh century,[1] four of which we have discussed above.[2] Some of these were actually written in Montecassino, and the others in regions not far distant, the whole forming 'a collection of medical texts exceptional both for quantity and quality'.[3] The subjects of the *trivium* and *quadrivium* received no less attention, and surviving Beneventan manuscripts of a great many classical and profane authors show the overwhelming interest in secular learning of all kinds, especially in the eleventh century.

Montecassino reached the height of its fame under Abbot Desiderius (1058–87), later Pope Victor III, whose greatest friend, Alfanus, was archbishop of Salerno from 1058 until his death in 1085. These two men became the centre of what has been called the south Italian intellectual renaissance of the eleventh century.[4]

Not much of the earliest Salernitan literature has survived. One work, however, belonging to the first half of the eleventh century, is of the greatest interest, namely the so-called *Passionarius* ascribed to a tangible Salernitan personality, Garioponto or Guarimpoto, in at least one eleventh-century manuscript.[5] Now this work is not original, but is entirely a compilation from the Aurelius–Esculapius text, pseudo-Galen *Epistola*

---

[1] E. A. Loew (Lowe), *The Beneventan Script*, p. 18.
[2] pp. 6 ff.
[3] Beccaria, *Cod. di med.*, p. 58.
[4] See H. M. Willard, *Casinensia*, i (1929), 304.
[5] See Kristeller, art. cit., p. 147. Recently Messrs. Dawson & Sons Ltd. possessed a manuscript of the *Passionarius* ascribed to the early eleventh century, with the explicit 'Liber a Guaripotu compositus'. It was catalogued as the earliest known manuscript of this work (Cat. 97, Sept. 1957, item 1). The codex came from the library of Baron Horace de Landau.

ad Glauconem, Paulus Aegineta, Alexander of Tralles, Theodorus Priscianus, and other Graeco-Latin sources[1]—in other words from parts of that *summa* of medicine which we have so often mentioned, and which had been present in south Italy, and in regions north of the Alps, since the ninth century. The author has taken these various tracts, often found haphazardly scattered in different manuscripts, and even when found, to a certain extent, united in one manuscript, always jumbled together, without any order or method—arranged them, epitomized them, and reduced their contents to some sort of logical order, perhaps, as Giacosa suggests,[2] with the object of producing a textbook of medicine which would be useful for teaching purposes. This represents a definite advance, and marks the beginning of a more theoretical tendency in the outlook of Salernitan physicians.

In the second half of the century the writings of Alfanus[3] must have exercised considerable influence in the *civitas Hippocratica*, as Salerno came to be called. Today he is chiefly remembered as a writer of elegant odes and hymns, which were, for Renan, 'a last breath of antiquity'. These, though entirely modelled on the classical tradition, have yet that freshness and living spirit which betray the true humanist, and the scholar of wide and varied tastes.[4]

Of his scientific and philosophical writings, only one seems to have survived—the *Premnon physicon*, a work translated from the Greek of Nemesius, bishop of Emesa in Syria, who had composed it probably during the last decade of the fourth century, with the different title, *On the Nature of Man*.[5] This work contained a good deal of Neoplatonic philosophy, and an even greater amount of theoretical medicine, which stemmed directly from Galen, an author of whom Nemesius was very fond, as may be gathered from the fact that he makes use of no fewer than fifteen treatises of 'the Father of Greek medicine'.

Although Alfanus achieved contemporary fame as a physician, only traces remain of his purely medical writings, such as the two tracts, *De quatuor humoribus* and *De pulsibus*, both edited by Capparoni, and shown by him to be based on lost originals. These, like the poems, carry on the classical tradition, and, as far as we can tell, add nothing new to the stores of Graeco-Latin medicine handed down since Carolingian times. There is no evidence, as far as I am aware, that the *Antidotary* or *Experimenta* attributed to the archbishop of Salerno, in Trinity (Camb.), 1365 (XII

---

[1] See Rose, *Anecdota*, ii (1870), 177–80, and Giacosa, *Mag. Sal.*, p. xxvi.

[2] Op. cit., p. xxxiv.

[3] On Alfanus see M. Schipa, 'Una triade illustre', *Casinensia* i (1929), 157 ff.; Kristeller, 'School of Salerno', pp. 149 ff.; and Raby, *Christian Lat. Poetry*, pp. 242 ff.

[4] Raby, op. cit., p. 245.

[5] A translation of this work, with excellent introduction, commentary, and notes, has recently been published in the *Lib. of Christian Classics*, iv (London, 1955). Alfanus's translation appeared in a critical edition by K. Burkhard at Leipzig in 1917.

cent.), iii, ff. 155 ff. is really by Alfanus, though it must be included in a list of 'possibles'. The same applies to other works which bear his name, and which are mentioned in early catalogues, such as the *Alfani Archiepiscopi liber de medicina*, formerly in the Chapter library at Westminster,[1] and the *Alfani Salernitanensis de quibusdam questionibus medicinalibus*, which was in the library of Christchurch, Canterbury[2] at the time of Henry of Eastry (1284–1331), and possibly considerably earlier. This latter title is particularly interesting, as, if late, it shows the continuing popularity of the archbishop, whilst if contemporary, and really by him or based on a work by him, it is evidence of the direct influence of the corpus of Graeco-Latin medical questions, discussed above, in Salerno at that time.

It is rather dangerous to draw any conclusions from the juxtaposition of texts in medieval manuscripts, but it might be mentioned that the medical questions of Alfanus are associated with *Dinamedus Galieni*, and *Alexander Sophista de curis humani corporis*, both frequently found in early Beneventan manuscripts.

Alfanus thus forms a direct and living link between Montecassino and Salerno, and his humanism, his knowledge of Greek, and theorizing tendencies must have helped a good deal to sow the seed of the Greek scientific tradition, and especially of that of Galen, on Salernitan soil, probably some time before the coming of the African, Constantinus. The process would be greatly helped, too, by the survival of the Greek language in this part of Italy, a heritage of its Byzantine conquerors, and by the close contact which the city still maintained with Byzantium. In fact, Alfanus himself had paid quite a long visit to the Greek capital and the East in 1063, during which he would have had ample opportunities of acquiring Greek codices, and coming into contact with Greek learning.

Constantinus is supposed to have come to Salerno from North Africa about the year 1077.[3] Alfanus appears to have taught him Latin, and to have been so pleased with his first work in that language, a translation of Galen's *Microtegni* or *Ars parva*, that he sent his pupil with it to Abbot Desiderius at Montecassino, with a letter of introduction. Soon afterwards Constantinus adopted the Christian faith, became a monk, and entered the abbey, where he remained until his death in 1087. There, in that active and stimulating centre of the new humanism, he lived and worked, translating from the Arabic, teaching medicine, and infusing a new life into scientific studies. His most important works were translations of Galen and Hippocrates, and of certain Arab and Jewish medical

---

[1] J. A. Robinson and M. R. James, *The Manuscripts of Westminster Abbey*, p. 33.

[2] M. R. James, *The Ancient Libraries of Canterbury and Dover*, p. 59.

[3] On him, see Kristeller, 'School of Salerno', pp. 151 ff. and the literature there cited, and the more recent article by Boubaker ben Yahia, 'Constantin l'Africain et l'école de Salerne', *C.T.* iii (1955), 49–59.

texts, such as the *Pantegni* (*Liber regalis*) of Hali ibn Abbas, the *Viaticum* of Ibn al Dschazzar, and the books on universal and particular diets of Isaac Israeli. Some of the Galenic and Hippocratic theories which the African here presented, this time through Arab media, were not new in the West, as I have tried to show. But he gave a fresh impulse to these theories, and a fuller elaboration of them.[1] If he was not the first to introduce Arab mathematical sciences to the West, certainly we owe to his industry the earliest considerable body of Arab medicine to appear in Latin translation.

This medicine, as well as that contained in the Galenic and Hippocratic texts, was largely practical, and thus tended to carry on the practical tradition which had prevailed at Salerno since the previous century. In spite of this, however, the penetration of these Constantinian translations to Salerno seems, for some reason, to have been very slow.[2] Few Salernitan works belonging with any certainty to the early part of the twelfth century show much influence by them. One explanation may be that the *civitas Hippocratica*, nourished on Greek thought and on Greek and Roman traditions of medicine, was at first hostile to Arab influence in any shape or form—that is, to the reception of all translations from Arabic, even if some of them were based on Greek originals. The writings ascribed to Copho, usually assigned to this early period, have little that derives from this Constantinian material; on the other hand, the so-called second *Demonstratio anatomica* composed c. 1100, the *Anatomia Mauri*,[3] and the anonymous *De curis*[4] are rather more influenced by it.

Two works of Adelard of Bath, the *De eodem et diverso*, and the *Quaestiones naturales*, have hitherto been thought to reflect conditions in the medical schools in south Italy, and particularly in Salerno, and to have been influenced by the writings of the African. In the former work, written c. 1105–10, Adelard records a meeting between himself, after he had just come from Salerno, and a certain Greek philosopher, when they discussed 'both the art of medicine and the nature of things'.[5] This passage clearly shows that the linking together of the studies of medicine and natural science, due to the inclusion of medicine within the more comprehensive sphere of *physica*, was prevalent in south Italy at that time. On the other hand, the work contained no trace of essentially Arab learning.[6] The

---

[1] Notably in Galen's *Ars Parva*, ch. 1, and *De methodo medendi* (*Megategni*), i. 3–4; ii. 7; iii. 1, 2, 7.   [2] Kristeller, art. cit., p. 154.

[3] See G. W. Corner, *Anatomical Texts of the Earlier Medieval Ages*, for these two texts.

[4] Ed. Giacosa, *Mag. Sal.*, pp. 175–279.

[5] Ed. H. Willner, *B.G.P.M.* iv. 1, 1903, p. 33.

[6] The truth of morning dreams (*De eodem*, ed. Willner, p. 13, ll. 29–33) is an idea found in Avicenna's *De Anima*; but it is, originally, a Greek conception which was available in the Latin translation of the *Solutiones* of Priscianus Lydus, long before the appearance of the Latin *De anima* (after 1150). See further on this subject my note on Q. 9 *sompnia*, below, p. 194.

The concept about the localization of the faculties in the brain (*De eodem*, p. 32, l. 33 to p. 33, l. 1) also occurs in the later *Quaestiones naturales*, and will be dealt with below, p. 22.

Quaestiones naturales, written a little later, gave a much better idea of the extent of *physica*, as it existed at that time. Thirty-two out of seventy-six questions deal with anthropology and medicine. The remainder embrace astronomy and cosmology, meteorology, zoology, botany, and physics (*experimenta*), in the modern sense of the word.[1] In other words, the questions, as a whole, covered the same ground which had been gone over before by Seneca and Macrobius, with the important addition of zoology and botany, which neither had included in his collection.

But again the work contained no trace of influence by the Constantinian translations, and no specifically Arab learning.

This may seem rather a dogmatic statement, in the face of many opinions to the contrary. Thus, according to Dr. Singer, 'He wrote a popular dialogue, *Natural Questions*, which is a sort of Compendium of Arab Science.'[2] M. Müller, the editor of the *Quaestiones*, says,

He experienced the strongest influence, right at the beginning of his travels, in Salerno. Perhaps he was the first among the Northerns to be able to enter the school of Constantinus. Of the texts of the African, the translations of Isaac Judeus appear to have afforded him most material, though there is no proof of this. At any rate, what he got from him was Galenical in nature. . . . The first, anthropological, part contains more opinions of the Arabs than the second,[3]

and so forth. Finally, Bliemetzrieder, the author of the most recent book on the English scientist, although admitting that Adelard quotes no Arab authors and gives no detailed accounts of Arab theories, yet tries to show that what he had in mind was to offer a general view of Arab science, a comprehensive summary, in order to show the difference between scholasticism and arabism—particularly from the point of view of the causes of phenomena, theological in the case of scholasticism, natural in the case of arabism;[4] as if this line of thought were the prerogative of the Arabs alone.[5] But as long ago as 1924 Haskins, after giving a résumé of the questions, said, 'In all this there is not much that comes from the Arabic, nor is any Arabic authority or phrase specifically quoted.'[6] He still thought, however, that Adelard had obtained some of his information via Constantinus,

---

[1] To avoid confusion, the Latin *physica* will be used throughout this study to denote the whole field of medieval 'natural philosophy', and the English 'physics' only in the narrower modern sense.   [2] *A Short History of Science*, p. 148.

[3] *Die Quaestiones Naturales*, B.G.P.M. xxxi. 2, 1934, pp. 87, 88.

[4] *Adelhard von Bath*, pp. 94 ff.

[5] Cf. also the statements of H. Gollancz in his translation of the *Questions* and of a later, Hebrew version, *Dodi Ve-Nechdi*, p. xi, 'Adelard was the first to make accessible to the West, by means of translations, the knowledge of the writings of Galen, as of the Arabic and Jewish physicians'; of H. Willner, *Des Adelard von Bath Traktat De Eodem et Diverso*, B.G.P.M. iv. 1, 1903, p. 82, 'Adelard, William (of Conches), and the medical school of Salerno rely upon Constantinus Africanus'; and, more recently, of H. Schipperges, 'Die frühen Übersetzer der arabischen Medizin in chronologischer Sicht', *Sudhoffs Archiv*, 39. 1, 1955, p. 70, 'Here also is the motif of Arabism . . ., although no Arabic author is mentioned, and the influence of Constantinus was of some weight.'   [6] *Med. Science*, 1st ed. (1924), p. 38.

namely, certain theories about the localization of the faculties in the brain, and about the four elements.[1]

As regards the first theory, concerning the seats of imagination, reason, and memory (*Quaest. nat.*, ch. 18), which, before Haskins, both Baumgartner[2] and Willner[3] thought Adelard had obtained from Constantinus, this same theory is found in the so-called *Practica Petroncelli*, a Salernitan text attributed by Sudhoff,[4] in the form in which we now have it, to the middle or second half of the eleventh century, and by Beccaria[5] to about 1035. But even if this work, of somewhat obscure origin, should prove to be a later, post-Constantinian compilation, the theory is also found in Alfanus's translation of the *Premnon physicon* of Nemesius—a source which is much more likely, since it contains the same proof for the localization, depending on injury to the various parts of the brain, that we find in the *Quaestiones naturales*;[6] a proof, by the way, which does not occur in the translations of Constantinus.[7] It is rather difficult to know exactly to which theories Haskins is referring, when he says, 'and certain theories of the elements apparently reached Adelard and the later twelfth century, via Constantine the African'.[8]

The theory of the indissoluble union and commingling of the four elements, not one of which exists in an entirely pure state, found in *Quaestiones Naturales*, chs. 1–5, was frequently found in pre-Constantinian Latin literature, from the translation of the *Hexaemeron* of St. Basil to that of the *Premnon phisicon* of Nemesius.[9]

---

[1] Op. cit., p. 39.   [2] *Die Philosophie des Alanus de Insulis*, B.G.P.M. ii. 4, 1896, p. 94.
[3] Op. cit., p. 81.   [4] Meyer-Steinig und Sudhoff, *Gesch. der Med.*, Jena, 1921, p. 183.
[5] 'Il ritorno della scienza classica', *R.S.I.* ii. 1 (1937), p. 46.
[6] Adelard, *Quaest. nat.*, ch. 18: 'Quicunque igitur primus de cellis illis discretive egit, id ipsum sensuali experimento didicisse auguror. Erat quippe aliquis, qui cum phantastica formarum recollectione bene uteretur, parte illa capitis anteriore laesus est, adeo ut inde virtutem phantasticam amiserit, ratione tamen et memoria non privatus. . . . Non dissimiliter etiam si laesione aliarum partium aliae animae actiones impeditae fuerunt, constare potuit pro certo ut in singulis cellis singulae exerceantur.'
Nemesius, *Premnon physicon* (trans. Alfanus, ed. Burkhard), ch. 13: 'Satis vero est sufficiens demonstratio ab ipso actu membrorum assumpta. Anterioribus etenim ventribus quomodolibet laesis sensus praepediuntur et dinoscibile manet illaesum. Medio vero ventre patiente solo ratio interturbatur et sensus manent integri. Si vero et anteriores et medius venter perpessi fuerint, ratio simul cum sensibus aufertur, posteriori vero patiente memoria corrumpitur sensibus atque mente manentibus illaesis.'
Bliemetzrieder has shown that Adelard almost certainly used Nemesius (trans. Alfanus) in his *De eodem*, see his *Adelhard*, Appendix 2, and thought, moreover, that it is likely that he came across this author in Tours and not in Salerno, ibid., p. 48.
[7] In the *De humana natura* and *Pantegni*, *Theor.* iv. 9 and 19, the faculties are associated with the three cells of the brain, but this association is not made in *Pantegni*, *Theor.* iii. 11, which contains, however, a fuller description of these cells.
[8] Op. cit. (1927), p. 39.
[9] St. Basil, *Hexaemeron*, iv. 5; Chalcidius, *Com. in Timaeus* (ed. Mullach, *Frag. Phil. Graecorum*, Paris, ii (1881)), cccxv–xvi; Macrobius, *Com. in Somn. Scip.* i. 6, and *Sat.* vii. 5; Isidore, *Etym.* xiii, 3; Nemesius, *Prem. phis.*, ch. 5. See also Duhem, *Système*, ii. 481 ff. and T. Gregory, *Anima Mundi*, p. 204.

The theory, found in *Quaestiones Naturales*, ch. 3, that every separate thing is nourished by its like, and that the predominating elementary quality of a thing, i.e. whether it is hot, cold, moist, or dry, determines the attraction of nourishment with a similar quality, occurs in Macrobius, *Saturnalia* vii. 5, and Nemesius, *Premnon phisicon*, i. 6. These two authors apply the principle to man who, combining in himself all four qualities, requires different foods, corresponding to these qualities. Adelard, on the other hand, applies it to plants, which, being separately of different natures, require, each one, a different nourishment.[1] It is noticeable that Adelard does not anywhere discuss the Galenic transformative power (*virtus immutans*) by which the nourishment is changed into the substance of the plant, or animal, and which is mentioned by the Salernitan masters in their answer to a similar question,[2] and in the Constantinian translations.[3]

Again, the theory of the indestructibility of matter, and of the reversion of the elementary particles in bodies to their respective elements, which Thorndike thought Adelard and Hugh of Saint-Victor were the first to enunciate, though he admits the possibility of a common source,[4] and which Müller[5] thought Adelard obtained from the *Pantegni* of Constantinus, had been expressed in a general way by Ovid, and more exactly by Macrobius and Nemesius[6]—either of whom could have been an earlier 'common source' than the *Pantegni*.

---

[1] The theory was known in late Roman medicine also, cf. *Epist. Vindiciani ad Valentinianum imp.*, 'Nam nimirum aestimas, o bone imperator, calidam et frigidam mortalibus inclusam esse corporibus, cum singulae res propriam habeant naturam. Ignis ignem, aqua aquam desiderat', *Marcelli, De Medicamentis*, ed. G. Helmreich, p. 23 (edited from a ninth-century manuscript). Aristotle was perhaps an original source, see Schedler, *Die Philosophie des Macrobius, B.G.P.M.* xiii. 1, 1916, p. 70, where he quotes Arist. *De anima*, iv. 4.

[2] 'Licet ille arbores eundem humorem attrahant, tamen quibusdam propriis virtutibus eisdem naturaliter insitis unum et eundem humorem permutant in propriis naturis, et diversos generant fructus ut in membris est videri. Quamvis omnia membra de sanguine nutriantur, tamen ossa sanguinem in os commutant, nervus in nervum, caro in carnem, et sic de aliis. Et notandum est quod in arboribus quedam sensualitas est que sentit sibi utilia et attrahit, nociva expellit, unde crescit multum et grossum.' Bodl. Auct. F. 3. 10, f. 156ᵛ.

[3] Particularly in *Pantegni, Theor.* iv. 2 and 3, where a detailed account of both animal and plant nourishment is given.

[4] *H.M.E.S.* ii. 36 ff.   [5] *Die Questiones Nat.* in a note to ch. 4.

[6] Adelard, *Quaest.*, ch. 4: 'Et meo certe iudicio in hoc sensibili mundo nihil omnino moritur, nec minor est hodie quam cum creatus est. Si qua enim pars ab una coniunctione solvitur, non perit, sed ad aliam societatem transit.' Ovid, *Met.* xv. 254 ff.:

> 'nec perit in toto quicquam, mihi credite, mundo,
> sed variat faciemque novat, nascique vocatur
> incipere esse aliud, quam quod fuit ante, morique
> desinere illud idem. cum sint huc forsitan illa,
> haec translata illuc, summa tamen omnia constant.'

Macrobius, *Com. in Somn. Scip.* ii. 12: 'Constat, inquam, nihil intra vivum mundum perire; sed eorum quae interire videntur solam mutari speciem: et illud in originem suam atque in ipsa elementa remeare, quod tale quale fuit esse desierit.' Nemesius, *Premnon* (Eng. trans., Telfer, p. 310): 'For the Creator in his wisdom devised that, lest the elements, or the bodies made up of elements, should ever by any means fail, the elements should be convertible both into one another, and into composite bodies, and that composite bodies should be resolvable

Yet another question in which Adelard uses the older source and not the Constantinian is ch. 20, concerning anterior baldness, a pseudo-Alexandrian problem dealt with by Macrobius (*Sat.* vii. 10). Adelard varies slightly the theory of the latter, agreeing with him that the pores in the fore part of the head are larger and more numerous, in order to allow superfluous fumes from the stomach to escape, but then stressing as the final cause, not the dryness caused by evaporation of humours, as Macrobius does, but the loss of continuity of the surface, which does not permit the hairs to take root. Dryness he mentions as a secondary cause. The Galenic theory, on the other hand, as found in Const. *Viaticum*, i, and Galen, *Megategni*, xiv. 18, besides not discussing anterior baldness at all, makes no mention of the pores, and takes into account only the loss or corruption of the humours nourishing the hair.

TABLE 2

Adelard, Quaest. nat.	Possible Latin source	Greek problemata	Salernitan prose questions
Ch. 32	*Vet. trans.* 2	pseudo-Alex. *Prob.* (trans. Gaza), ii. 96; *Prob. ined.* (Bussemaker), ii. 2.	Auct., f. 158ᵛ
„ 38	*Vet. trans.* 18	pseudo-Alex. *Prob.* ii. 106; *Prob. ined.* ii. 13.	Auct., f. 143ᵛ; Pet. f. 13
„ 42	*Vet. trans.* 26	..	Auct., f. 118ᵛ; Pet., f. 9
„ 10	pseudo-Hip. *De cibis*	pseudo-Alex. *Prob.* i. 106	Auct., f. 148; Pet., f. 12
„ 12	..	pseudo-Alex. *Prob.* i. 66	Auct., f. 149ᵛ; Pet. 1ᵛ
„ 47	..	pseudo-Alex. *Prob.* ii. 72	Auct., f. 147ᵛ; Pet., f. 7ᵛ
„ 33	..	pseudo-Arist. *Prob.* xxxiv. 7 (964ª)	..

Without discussing in detail any more of Adelard's questions, it may be said that the closest examination has failed to reveal any exclusively Constantinian influence,[1] thus not only confirming Haskins's suspicions that there was 'not much that comes from the Arabic', but also doing away with the little Arabic content that this scholar allowed.

In addition to the old-established Latin sources mentioned by Thorndike, Haskins, and Müller, among which two of the most prolific are Chalcidius and Macrobius, at least seven of the questions, not including those which could have been transmitted through the latter author, belong to the corpus of pseudo-Alexandrian and pseudo-Aristotelian *problemata*. Three of these, which are also found in the Salernitan questions, are present in the *Vetustissima translatio*, which thus could have been the Graeco-Latin source both for Adelard and for the Salernitan compiler.[2] One of the

into elements again. And so, by process of perpetual transformations, they are kept continually in being.' See also, p. 311 of the same work.

[1] That is, either literal quotations, similar wording or phraseology, or ideas which he could only have got from the Constantinian texts. On the positive side is the fact that his views frequently differ from those expressed in these texts, as the examples mentioned have shown.

[2] That is, the source for the questions, but not for the answers. In only one instance is Adelard's answer the same as the Greek; see below, p. 25.

remaining four questions is discussed in the pseudo-Hippocratic *De cibis*,[1] found in an early-ninth-century St. Gall manuscript (Cod. 762), and may easily have found its way into other Latin treatises on diet. I have not succeeded in finding the other three Greek questions in any early, pre-Constantinian, Latin source. But in Adelard's time there may have been extant a fuller version of the *Vetustissima translatio* than we have today; and it is also likely that these and similar questions[2] were at that time common property in the Greek-speaking districts of south Italy.[3] In one of them, that about the night vision of animals (ch. 12), Adelard's answer, the Salernitan, and the Greek (pseudo-Alexandrian) are all the same, which is extremely unusual. Curiously enough, another rare instance of almost exact agreement between the Salernitan compiler and the English scientist is in their answers to yet another question about vision, which though not extant, as far as I have been able to discover, in any Greek or Graeco-Latin source, yet is distinctly Greek in character.[4]

Adelard's *Quaestiones naturales* then, must, I think, be considered as embodying either his own views or pre-Constantinian medical and scientific material, the latest source being, perhaps, the *Premnon physicon* of Nemesius in the translation of Alfanus. This material was available in Salerno and south Italy; but also, it must be remembered, much, if not all of it, could have been obtained north of the Alps, particularly in north France, where, as we have seen, there had been a considerable interest in disputations (in the non-scholastic sense) and theoretical medicine since at least the end of the tenth century.

But how can we reconcile this state of affairs with Adelard's statements in the dedication and prologue to the *Quaestiones*, which maintained that he had spent seven years in travel with the express purpose of studying Arabic, that his friends urged him to publish something fresh in the way of Arab learning on his return to England, and that, consequently, whenever he adduced anything new, people were not to think that it was his own view but that of the Arabs that he was presenting?—statements which have undoubtedly biased all who have read the *Quaestiones*, causing them to look for Arab learning, and in most cases to imagine that they had found it, when, all the time, it was not really there.

In the first place, although it may have been his intention to study Arabic, he had probably not got very far with it when he composed the

---

[1] Ed. Rose, *Anecdota*, ii. 151–6. For further discussion concerning this particular question, see below, p. 74.

[2] Such as the one about *elephantiasis* (ch. 41) discussed below, p. 205.

[3] In ch. 38 Adelard says 'solet enim vulgariter communis esse quaestio'. Similar remarks could apply to some of the questions emanating from Aristotle and Aelian in the *Questiones phisicales*, for which no early, intermediate Latin source could be found (Q. 21; Q. 76; Q. 98; S. 100). It is very difficult to say just to what extent oral tradition played a part in the transmission of ideas from the Aristotelian and other Greek writings.

[4] *Quaest. nat.*, ch. 30: 'Why it is not as easy to see from light into darkness, as it is to see from darkness into light.' Found also in Pet. 27ᵛ.

Quaestiones, since he quotes no Arab authority, and uses no Arabic words or phrases, as he does later on in his astronomical works.[1] We must, therefore, I think, take Adelard's works at their face value, and assume that, in some of the cases where his answers differ from the earlier Latin, Graeco-Latin, and Salernitan ones, he is, in fact, giving his own opinion; and, in order to make these unfamiliar views (*ignota sententia*) more acceptable, and, at the same time, as he says, preserve his popularity with the ordinary, less educated reader (*apud vulgus*), who might complain of their novelty,[2] attributing them to the Arabs. Thorndike thought that this might have been the case, though he considered that Adelard was slightly satirical, and 'only in part serious', when he made the above statements.[3] At the same time, as this scholar goes on to say, the practice was not at all an uncommon one in the Middle Ages; there are several Latin works ascribed to Arab authors, for which no Arabic original is known, and other cases where obviously Western opinions have appeared under high-sounding Eastern names.[4]

If Adelard obtained nothing in detail from the Arabs and, in particular, from Constantinus, it is scarcely likely that the rather vague generalities and attitudes of mind, which some say he also got from that source, came from there either. Thus the 'rationalistic habit of mind and secular philosophy' mentioned by Haskins,[5] the 'teleological views', stemming from Galen, ascribed to him by Müller,[6] and the naturalism, which Bliemetzrieder thought he got from the Arabs,[7] could all very easily have been obtained in north France or south Italy *c.* 1100, via pre-Constantinian Latin and Graeco-Latin sources.[8]

One other point remains to be mentioned. In speaking of the date of composition of the *Quaestiones* Haskins felt that, on the internal evidence of its contents, this work should be placed early in Adelard's career, 'much earlier than a dedication to Richard of Kent, bishop of Bayeux (1132–42), would imply'.[9] From the reference to Henry I,[10] he thought that Adelard

---

[1] Haskins, *Med. Science*, p. 39.

[2] 'Habet enim haec generatio ingenitum vitium ut nihil quod a modernis reperiatur putet esse recipiendum.' Dedication of the *Quaestiones naturales*.   [3] *H.M.E.S.* ii. 26 ff.

[4] Thus in the twelfth-century treatise *Liber Hermetis Mercurii Triplicis de VI rerum principiis*, we find opinions attributed to Ezich and Almanach, which emanate from a much more ordinary source, namely Macrobius. See the edition of this text by Th. Silverstein in *A.H.D.L.* xxii (1956), 233.   [5] *Med. Science*, loc. cit.

[6] *Quaest. nat.*, p. 82.   [7] *Adelhard v. Bath*, pp. 94 ff.

[8] Rationalism had been gaining ground in north France since the days of Gerbert, and, especially, of Berengar, who lectured at Tours, where Adelard had been a pupil. We have already said something about the secular outlook in France and Italy. The teleological view was, of course, very prevalent with St. Basil and the early Fathers of the Church. Naturalism was especially cultivated at Chartres during the first half of the twelfth century, see T. Gregory, *Anima Mundi*, ch. 4, 'L'Idea di Natura', and the articles quoted by him on p. 177, and J. M. Parent, *La Doctrine de la création dans l'École de Chartres*.   [9] Op. cit., p. 27.

[10] 'Cum in Angliam nuper redierim Henrico Wilhelmi Anglis imperante, quoniam a patria causa studii diu me exceperam, occursus amicorum et iocundus mihi fuit et commodus', beginning of dedication.

must have left England on his travels, either before the king's accession (1100), or after his death (1135), as otherwise 'the king would naturally be taken for granted'. In the former case the seven years' absence mentioned by Adelard would place the treatise not later than 1107, and on account of the dates of the other possible dedicatee, Richard Fitz-Samson, bishop of Bayeux (1107–33), it could not be earlier. Haskins then says, 'The first alternative would tend to place the *Quaestiones* as early as the *De eodem*, whereas they show Arabic influences quite foreign to the *De eodem*, and imply a longer period and wider range of travel.' But I think that we can safely assume now that the last two statements are not applicable, and that, therefore, the date 1107 need not be ruled out on their account. It seems to be generally agreed that the composition of the *De eodem* falls between the dates 1105 and 1110, and that this treatise preceded the *Quaestiones*.[1] If we agree with Haskins's pin-pointing of the year 1107 for the completion of the latter, then the *De eodem*, to be earlier, must have been written *c.* 1105–6.

On the other hand, once we start examining the dedication and prologue for evidence, several difficulties in the way of this theory present themselves. One is that Adelard refers to a time when he was lecturing at Laon seven years before, at the beginning of his travels, and in the *De eodem* does not mention Laon at all, but only refers to the previous year, when he was himself attending lectures at Tours. This would make him a master at the outset of his travels, and a pupil later on. This is, it is true, not an impossible state of affairs, but the 'nephew' was supposed to be present on both occasions, and on the first it was agreed that while Adelard was devoting himself to Arab studies, during his absence, his 'nephew' should continue his usual studies in Gaul.[2] In the *De eodem*, however, he does not refer to this agreement at all, but speaks as if the 'nephew' were entirely ignorant of the reason for his travels.[3]

Now Müller, attaching no importance to the mention of Henry I, and ignoring the inconsistency inherent in the reference to Laon, thought that Adelard began his travels in the year we find him at Tours, that is, in the

---

[1] Haskins, pp. 21 ff.; Müller, p. 77.

[2] *Quaest. nat.* prologue: 'Meministi nepos septennio iam transacto, cum te in gallicis studiis pene puerum iuxta Laudisdunum una cum ceteris auditoribus meis dimiserim, id inter nos convenisse ut Arabum studia ego pro posse meo scrutarer, tu vero gallicarum sententiarum inconstantiam non minus acquireres?'

De eodem (ed. Willner, 1903), p. 4: 'Erat praeterito in anno vir quidam apud Turonium, tum sapientia tum moribus gravis, adeo ut eo tam vulgares quam philosophi uterentur. Sed quid plura de laude eius, cum praesentis aetatis auditores plerumque invidiosi sint, et te eius probitas non lateat, qui una ibi mecum adesses? Hunc ego admodum colebam, studens eius prudentia doctior fieri.'

[3] p. 4, 'Saepenumero admirari soles, nepos, laboriosi itineris mei causam et aliquanto acrius sub nomine levitatis et inconstantiae propositum accusare. . . . Ego rem, quam per biennium celavi, ut tibi morem geram, aperiam; tu vero orationem in fine, ut diem in vespere, diiudica.' From which it appears that Adelard had actually kept the reason for his travels hidden from his 'nephew' for two years. Thorndike, op. cit., pp. 46 ff., mentions these inconsistencies.

year before he completed the *De eodem*, therefore, at the earliest in 1104, at the latest in 1109. Since the *Quaestiones* were said to be written seven years later, he dated this work between 1111 and 1116.[1] In this case, therefore, six years would intervene between the writing of the two treatises.

To escape the inconsistency of the reference to Laon, first Thorndike, and then Bliemetzrieder, thought there were two journeys, the first ending with the writing of the *De eodem* in Sicily, and his return to Laon soon after, *c.* 1111–12, where he taught the *artes* for a time, his 'nephew' being one of his pupils, before setting out on a second journey in quest of Arab learning, which lasted seven years.[2] In this case he would have returned to England about 1120, and written the *Quaestiones* almost immediately; and more than seven years would have elapsed between the two works. In addition, Bliemetzrieder thought that Adelard put aside the work and dedicated it later to Richard of Kent, bishop of Bayeux (1135–42), who, he imagined, was more likely to be a member of Adelard's circle of friends than Richard Fitz-Samson, besides being a greater encourager of learning. This, he believed, would also explain the reference to Henry I, since, when the work was presented to Richard of Kent, sometime after 1135, Henry would be dead, and Stephen on the throne.[3]

What are we to make of all these conflicting theories? In the first place, it is very hard to believe that six or seven years' study separated the writing of the treatises. Their sources are too similar, and neither shows any evidence of Adelard's later Arabic studies, which, by 1126, had enabled him to translate the astronomical tables of al-Khwarizmi. Haskins's initial belief that the *Quaestiones* belonged to the early part of Adelard's career is, I am sure, fully justified by the internal evidence of the text.

Even more incredible is Bliemetzrieder's theory that Adelard put aside the work for over fifteen years, and finally dedicated it to Richard of Kent, long after Adelard himself had obtained a considerable knowledge of Arabic, and after Arab medicine and anthropology had penetrated to Chartres (see Chapter 4), and probably farther afield. If he had indeed put aside the work for so long, it is inconceivable that, under the circumstances, he would not have revised it, brought it up to date, and included at least some Arab learning.

Taking into consideration, then, the more certain dates of the *De eodem*, the dates of the earliest of the two possible dedicatees of the *Quaestiones*, Richard Fitz-Samson, and the fact that the latter treatise was probably written not long after the former, we arrive at the period *c.* 1107–12 for the writing of the *Quaestiones*. The seven years' travel does not seem to make sense, whichever way you look at it. As regards Laon, Adelard could have returned there as a master, for a short period, soon after writing the

---

[1] Op. cit., pp. 76 ff.
[2] Thorndike, op. cit., p. 47; Bliemetzrieder, op. cit., pp. 52 ff.
[3] Op. cit., pp. 82 ff.

De eodem, but, as seems more likely, on his way back to England, and not just before setting out on a fabulous journey to the East. In that case this journey, and the dialogue with the 'nephew', would be fictions introduced to lend greater probability to the 'Arab learning', to enhance the 'story' effect, and so to capture still further the imagination and interest of his would-be readers. This would be nothing unusual. The Ciceronian dialogue form, as I have shown above, was extremely popular for teaching purposes, and Adelard had a long tradition behind him; also the combination of fiction and pseudo-scientific learning was common at that period.[1] Once we admit this explanation, the difficulties and inconsistencies disappear. The reference to Henry I could then be merely a device to lend colour to his story of a long absence for purposes of study, the implication being, as Haskins saw, that he left England long ago, before that monarch came to the throne. The claim to Arab learning and the story of travel in the East, introduced in the dedication and prologue, are continued in the questions themselves. Thus in ch. 6 Adelard makes the Arabs responsible for his rationalism,[2] in ch. 16 he fathers upon an old man, whom he met in Tarsus in Cilicia, a method of studying the anatomy of corpses which is probably Salernitan,[3] and which he would be much more likely to hear about when he was in south Italy.[4] In ch. 32, by another palpable 'device', he makes the 'nephew' weep tears of joy at his arrival home from the East, 'where he had stayed studying so long', in order to illustrate the Greek question about joy causing tears. Finally, in ch. 50, he employs a similar technique, the reference to his crossing a bridge in Antioch during an earthquake, both lending local colour to the travel story, and illustrating the question about the cause of this phenomenon. If this really was the earthquake of 1114 mentioned by Fulcher of Chartres, as Bliemetzrieder thought,[5] it looks, at first sight, as if the *Quaestiones* must have been written after this date. But this, again, would make rather too long an

---

[1] Cf. *Kiranides*, Letter of Prester John, the Alexander legend, and other similar works described by Thorndike. The later French *Roman de Sidrach* and *Livre des secrets aux philosophes*, which contain large numbers of pseudo-scientific questions and answers, are exactly in this tradition. See below, p. 111.

[2] 'Ego enim aliud a magistris arabicis didici ratione duce . . . .'

[3] This method, characterized by allowing fast-running streams to wash the flesh from the bones of corpses, is described in detail in the *Anatomia Richardi Anglici*, which was said by Sudhoff, *Gesch. d. Med. im Überblick* (1921), p. 196, to be definitely Salernitan. Wickersheimer, *Dict. Biog.* ii. 696, although thinking that Richard worked at Montpellier, yet saw many affinities between his writings and the Salernitan treatises, and especially was this so in the case of this anatomical work. In any case there is no doubt that this branch of medicine had been studied from at least the beginning of the century in Salerno, which thus rapidly became the main centre in the West for the study of anatomy. See also Sudhoff, 'Die vierte Salernit. Anatomie', *Archiv* xx (1928), 33–50, and Corner, *Anatomical Texts*.

[4] Apart from anything else, the dedication of the *De eodem* to William, bishop of Syracuse (1105–16), would seem to indicate that Adelard had actually been in south Italy. There is thus no reason to doubt his statement in this treatise about meeting a Greek philosopher on his way south from Salerno, see above, p. 20; it is more consistent with the facts than the statements in the *Quaestiones* which we are discussing.   [5] Op. cit., p. 60.

interval between the two works, ten years, at least, if the *De eodem* was written in 1105, five years, if this tract was written in 1110. It seems more likely that it was a later interpolation, though another possibility is that it was an earlier earthquake, of which Adelard had heard, since these events are by no means rare in those regions.

It must be said, in conclusion, that if Adelard did resort to fiction in order to popularize his ideas, and if it can no longer be said that he was the first to make known to the West the writings of Constantinus and Arabic speculative philosophy, this derogates very little from his unique position in the history of English science. There can be little doubt that he was a true pioneer in introducing Arabic mathematics and astronomy into England, and he was certainly one of the first to state original views on scientific matters, and to speak, in no uncertain terms, against that adherence to authority which was to have such a deadening effect on scientific progress for many years to come. At the same time, as already pointed out, his *Quaestiones* defined the extent of *physica* more fully than any previous Latin work, and, as we shall see, had great influence during the succeeding centuries, particularly in England.

To return to Salerno, evidence of both an increasing theoretical tendency in the studies there, and of the further influence of Constantinus, in the first half of the twelfth century, is afforded by the writings of Mathaeus Platearius, who flourished, according to De Renzi, *c.* 1130–60. He wrote a commentary on the older, Salernitan *Antidotarium Nicolai*, which is, perhaps, the oldest example of a Salernitan commentary, of any kind, known,[1] and a *Liber de simplici medicina*, the so-called *Circa instans*, which was based on the Constantinian *De gradibus simplicium*.[2]

The next step was the writing of much more scientific and logical commentaries on the Constantinian translations themselves, and up to quite recently it had been thought that the physician Maurus (d. 1214), so much praised by his pupil, Gilles of Corbeil, was the first to do this. But P. O. Kristeller has now discovered a still earlier group of commentaries on these texts, which exhibit similar features to those of Maurus, and are almost certainly by Bartholomaeus of Salerno, a well-known physician who flourished *c.* 1150, and was the author of a popular *Practica*.[3] Thus it seems that we will have to put back to about this date the earliest use, in medicine, of a technique which had hitherto been chiefly employed in connexion with the teaching and exposition of grammar, and the entry into its sphere of logical distinctions, and of a more strictly scientific and philosophical outlook.

---

[1] Kristeller, 'School of Salerno', p. 156.
[2] Edited by P. Dorveaux from a thirteenth-century French translation.
[3] See P. O. Kristeller, 'Beiträge der Schule von Salerno zur Entwicklung der Scholastischen Wissenschaft im 12 Jahrhundert', *Artes Liberales*, S.T.G.M. (1959), 84–90. On Bartholomaeus see F. Hartmann, *Die Lit. von Früh- und Hochsalerno*, pp. 18 ff.

A similar revision of judgement is necessary with regard to the use of the newly translated Aristotelian *libri naturales* in scientific and medical writings. Adelard in the *Quaestiones* had attributed opinions to Aristotle, once or twice incorrectly, and seemed familiar with a few Peripatetic theories, two of which ultimately derived from the *Physica*. But there is no evidence that he had before him any known Latin translation of Aristotle's works, and the assumption is that he obtained these scraps of Aristotelian lore at second hand, from indirect sources.[1] On the other hand, Birkenmajer has long ago shown that Maurus had made direct use of certain Greek–Latin translations of the *libri naturales*, in his commentary on the *Isagoge* of Ioannitius, and since then it has been generally accepted that the physicians of Salerno were the first, in the Latin West, to use these books in scientific and medical, as opposed to purely philosophical and theological, writings.[2] In view of the findings of Kristeller, we shall now have to examine the earlier commentaries of Bartholomaeus for evidence of this Aristotelian influence. It seems likely, in fact, that the true beginning, in the West, of what has been called the scientific renaissance, which most modern authorities associate with the recovery of the works of Aristotle, either wholly or in part,[3] dates from about the mid-twelfth century, instead of from *c.* 1180, as was formerly supposed.

From about 1150 onwards, then, Aristotelian doctrines began to play an ever increasing role in Salernitan literature, and other subjects of *physica* began to be studied in Salerno, along with medicine. One witness of this is the fact that the earliest Latin version of Ptolemy's *Almagest* is due to a Salernitan student.[4] A Salernitan physician was also a teacher of logic as early as 1170,[5] and, indeed, the logical developments and excessive argumentation displayed in such a treatise as the *Curae Magistri Ferrarii*, edited by Giacosa,[6] and ascribed by him to the last quarter of the century, show that by this time the physicians of Salerno were well on the road to 'scholastic' medicine.

Perhaps the greatest name in this golden age of Salernitan learning is

---

[1] Haskins, op. cit., pp. 38 ff.

[2] In *Le Rôle joué par les médecins et les naturalistes dans la réception d'Aristote aux XIIe et XIIIe siècles*, pp. 4 ff. L. Minio-Paluello has shown that the *libri naturales* were used, perhaps as early as *c.* 1160 in Normandy, in theological writings, by such men as Robert of Torigny, abbot of Mont-Saint Michel, and Richard Bishop, archdeacon of Coutances; see his 'Jacobus Veneticus Grecus', *Traditio*, viii (1952), 265–304, and, in particular, pp. 292–4.

[3] For Haskins it was 'the entire body of Aristotle's writings . . . supplemented by what the Arabs had gained from the Orient and from their own observation'. *Med. Science*, p. 3. Birkenmajer stresses the importance of the *libri naturales*. *Le Rôle, passim*. Paré and his colleagues stress the Aristotelian influence on the classification of the sciences, and the effects of the *logica nova*, both in revolutionizing teaching, and in inaugurating 'a scientific order of knowledge' (G. Paré, A. Brunet, P. Tremblay, *La Renaissance du XIIe siècle*, pp. 167 ff.). A. C. Crombie connects these same logical factors with the rise of experimental science. *Robert Grosseteste, passim*.

[4] Kristeller, art. cit., p. 160; Haskins, op. cit., pp. 157 ff.

[5] Kristeller, loc. cit.   [6] *Mag. Sal.*, pp. 1–68.

Urso of Calabria. Little seems to be known about the life of this remarkable man. The reference of E. Rota to a document of the year 1163, in which it is stated that Urso was a high-ranking church dignitary in Salerno at that time, is hard to reconcile with the generally accepted date of his death, 1225, as given by Garufi.[1] Urso seems to have been a fairly common name, and the probability is that the ecclesiastic who flourished *c.* 1163 and the physician who died in 1225 were different people, though, as Creutz suggests, the latter may have also been a theologian.[2] Yet another *magister Urso philosophus* is recorded as dying in the late twelfth or early thirteenth century.[3] But the evidence seems to point to a period late in the former century for the *floruit* of Urso the physician. With the possible exception of some fragments contained in the famous Breslau codex of Salernitan writings, assigned to the period *c.* 1170, I know of no manuscripts of any of his works which can be dated, with certainty, to before 1200.[4] He clearly taught Gilles of Corbeil (*c.* 1140–1224), who was formerly thought to have left Salerno to visit Montpellier and Paris *c.* 1180 at the latest. But, as I shall show in chapter four, it is much more likely that Gilles did not come to Paris until *c.* 1194, and that, since his stay at Montpellier was very short, he therefore left Salerno later than 1180. Another poet-physician, Peter of Eboli (*c.* 1160–1219), was also a contemporary of Urso, and mentioned him, in connexion with the solving of a medical question, in his poem *De rebus Siculis*, written after 1194.[5] Finally, the earliest quotations from Urso's works are not found until between 1197 and 1204, the period during which Alexander Neckam wrote his *De natura rerum*, containing passages from Urso's commentary on his own *Aphorisms*,[6] and also, roughly, the period during which the earliest collection of Salernitan prose questions (Auc. F. 3. 10) was copied. The next philosopher to show a knowledge of Urso's writings was the Frenchman, Raoul de Longchamp, who quoted him in his commentary on the

---

[1] *Petri Ansolini de Ebulo, De rebus Siculis carmen*, a cura di Ettore Rota, p. 35. C. A. Garufi, *Necrologio del Liber Confratrum di S. Matteo di Salerno*, p. 183. See also Kristeller, art. cit., p. 161.

[2] R. Creutz, *Urso der letzte des Hochsalerno Arzt, Philosoph, Theologe*, p. 7.

[3] Garufi, op. cit., p. 181.

[4] The best description of the Breslau codex is that given by Sudhoff, 'Die Salernitaner Handschrift in Breslau', *Sudhoffs Archiv* xii (1920), 101–48. The Ursonian fragments are item (26) *De gradibus*, ff. 179^{r-v}, (32) *De saporibus*, f. 188, based on Urso's teaching, (39) *De effectibus qualitatum*, ff. 200^v–201^v, part only, (40) *De effectibus qualitatum accidentalibus*, ff. 201^v–202, based on the *De effect. qualitat.* By far the largest number of Urso manuscripts seems to be in England, but out of a total of nineteen of these the earliest is *c.* 1200, five others are thirteenth-century, the rest later. For a list of these manuscripts, see below, p. 66.

[5]   'Haec ego dum dubia meditarer mente profundum,
          Quae res naturae dimidiasset opus,
          Egregius doctor et vir pietatis amicus
          Explicuit causas talibus Urso michi.'
Ed. cit., p. 35.

[6] See my notes on S. 74 (luscus), S. 81 (vulnus), and S. 83 (lincis radio). Other correspondences occur in the prose Salernitan questions.

Anticlaudianus of Alain de Lille, composed at Montpellier between 1212 and 1225.[1]

Eight works are known to be definitely by Urso, namely, *De effectibus medicinarum, De diebus criticis, De pulsibus, De urinis, Aphorisms,* with his own commentary, *De effectibus qualitatum, De gradibus,* and *De commixtionibus elementorum,* and Sudhoff thought that one of the Salernitan Anatomies should also be attributed to him.[2] Less certain works are: a commentary on the *Canon* of Avicenna, another metrical one, on the *Ars parva (Microtegni)* of Galen, and a *Repressiones.*[3] The tracts *De coloribus* and *De saporibus et odoribus*[4] seem to be later compilations from his works; whilst the *De anima,* also sometimes ascribed to Urso, is to be identified with the *De motu cordis* of the Englishman, Alfred of Sareshel.[5] All of the genuine works seem to be extant except two, the *De diebus criticis* and *De pulsibus,* and of these extant works all have been edited except the *De commixtionibus elementorum,* the most voluminous, and, in some respects, the most important of his writings.

There is no space here to give a detailed account of Urso's doctrines, a task which still awaits completion, although Birkenmajer, Creutz, his principal editor, and more recently, P. O. Kristeller,[6] have all drawn attention to his extreme importance for the history not only of medicine, but of science and philosophy as well. In his two principal scientific works, the *Aphorisms,* with his own commentary, and the *De commixtionibus elementorum,* he covers the whole field of natural philosophy as then known, has a great deal to say about the laws of attraction, alteration, and motion, describes many experiments, including processes used in dyeing and painting, and also discusses such esoteric subjects as dreams, prophecies, fascination, and the ascent of the soul towards God. Because of this combination of mysticism and practical science and philosophy Paul Diepgen saw in Urso the true forerunner of Arnald of Villanova and Paracelsus.[7]

---

[1] This interesting commentary is still unedited; see R. Bossuat's edition of the *Anticlaudianus,* p. 43, where he lists eight manuscripts of Raoul's commentary. See also M. Grabmann, *Handschriftliche Forschungen zum Schrifttum des Wilhelm von Conches, S.B.A.W.,* (1935), x, pp. 31–32, and Birkenmajer, *Le Rôle,* pp. 8 ff. The quotations are listed by C. Matthaes, *Der Salernitaner Arzt Urso,* pp. 6 ff.

[2] 'Die vierte Salernitaner Anatomie', *Sudhoffs Archiv,* xx (1932), 33–50.

[3] See Thorndike and Kibre, *Incipits* (1937), cols. 232, 780. The commentary on the *Ars parva* is by Urso of Lodi, and was expounded at Avignon in 1198. See L. Thorndike, 'Unde versus', *Traditio,* xi (1955), 163. Perhaps the remaining two treatises are by this other Urso.

[4] The tract *De saporibus* was edited by F. Hartmann, from the Breslau codex. See his *Die Literatur von Fruh- und Hochsalerno,* pp. 55–57.

[5] See R. Creutz, op. cit., p. 6. Seven of the eight works mentioned are listed in this treatise of Creutz, the eighth, *De gradibus,* was edited by Sudhoff, *Archiv* xii (1920), 135–8.

[6] Birkenmajer, *Le Rôle,* pp. 4 ff.; Creutz, in the above work, and in 'Die medizinisch-naturphilosophischen Aphorismen und Kommentare des Mag. Urso', *Q.S.G.N.M.* v. 1 (Berlin, 1936), pp. 1–192; Kristeller, art. cit., pp. 161 ff.

[7] In the Introduction to Creutz's edition of the *Aphorisms.*

His sources have not yet been fully investigated, but he certainly used Plato, whom he calls *summus philosophorum*, a good deal, Aristotle to a much greater extent than Maurus,[1] and the Constantinian texts.[2]

Much of the material found in Urso's works is contained in the prose collection of Salernitan questions, to which I have so often referred, the answers sometimes containing long literal quotations; so that, if some of the questions are not actually by Urso, they are almost certainly the work of a pupil, and belong to this most flourishing period of Salernitan learning.[3]

The oldest and most complete text of these questions is found in the Bodleian manuscript, Auct. F. 3. 10 (S.C. 2582), a composite volume, containing five different works, of which the questions form the second, occupying ff. 118–161v. The bulk of the work is written in what may be described as a semi-cursive English court hand of the latter part of the twelfth, or early thirteenth, century.[4] The codex at one time belonged to the Augustinian Priory of St. Thomas the Martyr at Stafford. It consists of nearly five hundred questions and answers. There are references to Salerno in two questions,[5] and in the second of these the solution of King William is given. Of the two kings of Sicily of this name, who reigned during the second half of the twelfth century, the father, William I (1154–66), is perhaps the one most likely to be quoted. He showed a great interest in scientific studies, and encouraged men of learning at his court, like Henricus Aristippus, the translator of Plato and Aristotle from the Greek, and Eugene of Palermo, who was a master of both Greek and Arabic. Most significant is a description of the king, given by Aristippus in the dedication of his translation of the *Phaedo*, 'whose court school he attended, whose every word was a philosophical apophthegm,

---

[1] Birkenmajer, op. cit., p. 4. He used the Greek–Latin, *De gen. et cor.*, *Meteora*, iv, *Physica*, and *De anima*.

[2] Diepgen, loc. cit., characterized Urso's philosophy and medical theory as markedly 'physical'. The vital activities, for instance, and the temperaments, depend on the physical characteristics and movements of the spirits, and on the physical structure of the passages and channels in which they move. He bases theories of language on the physics of speech function.

[3] That Urso had a special talent for solving the most intricate questions in natural philosophy, we learn from Gilles of Corbeil:

> 'Strenuus ambiguos causarum solvere nodos,
> Cuius ab ingenio nulla indecisa recedit
> Quaestio'

(*De laudibus*, i, l. 122, printed in *Aegidii Corboliensis*, *Carmina medica*, ed. Choulant), and from the closing words of Urso's *De com. elem.*: 'Hoc speculo via intelligentiae operatur et nature laberintus aperitur dum ymago nature latentis in eo cernitur et insolubilis questionum nodus explicatur' (Trinity 1154, f. 148v).

[4] ff. 148–149v, 153r–v, 154–161v are written in different hands, perhaps later than that in which the bulk is writtten.

[5] f. 160: 'Queritur unde fit hoc, quod in lombordia et in similibus frigidis et siccis regionibus, cucurbite sunt parve et rotunde; et salerni, et in aliis et in similibus regionibus calidis et humidis inveniuntur subtiles et longa.' f. 161: 'Quidam locus est in partibus salernitanis iuxta castrum iosuni qui in hieme invenitur aridissimus, et nichil aque ibi invenitur. In estate vero inter currit aqua. Rex villelmus sic solvit hanc questionem dicens . . . .'

whose insoluble questions and whose answers left nothing undiscussed, and whose studies embraced everything'.[1] On the other hand, if we may believe Peter of Blois, who was for a time tutor to William II, this monarch was not such a lover of learning as his father was. He began well, but as soon as Peter left the court, 'he threw aside his books, and betook himself to the leisure-hour amusements of the palace'.[2] But William was only a youth then, and later on he may have shown himself more favourable to scientific studies.

In a question dealing with poisonous fungi, mention is made of the famous grammarian and classical scholar, Arnoul d'Orléans (*fl.* 1175), which rather looks as if the writer of this particular question had attended a lecture on Juvenal by this master.[3]

But perhaps the most interesting references are those to five *magistri* in a question about coitus.[4] Three of these seem to be Hereford men, namely Magister Hugh de Mapenore,[5] who later became Bishop of Hereford (1216–19), Mag. Johannes Burgensis, who occurs as a witness in a Hereford document assigned to the period 1185–1205,[6] and Mag. Phillipus Rufus Cornubiensis, who is, perhaps, to be identified with a Mag. Phillip who was a witness in Hereford documents assigned to the years 1200–8,[7] and with a Mag. Phillipus Rufus whose obit year is given as *c.* 1220.[8] The other two names, Mag. Willelmus Chers, and Mag. Reginaldus de Omine, do not seem to occur in surviving Herefordshire documents. There is a Mag. Willelmus medicus, who was a witness in a document assigned to the years 1180–6,[9] but it is impossible to say whether he can be identified with William Chers. The most likely explanation of the mention of Hereford men in connexion with this question, which occurs near the beginning of the collection, and is in that early English hand in which the bulk of the work is written, is that it was an addition by the

---

[1] 'Cuius curia schola comitatus, cuius singula verba philosophica apofthegmata, cuius questiones inextricabiles, cuius solutiones nihil indiscussum, cuius studium nil relinquit intemptatum', quoted Haskins, op. cit., p. 166, and Paré, Brunet, Tremblay, *La Renaissance*, p. 51.

[2] 'Ipse libris abiectis ad otium se contulit palatinum', Paré, Brunet, Tremblay, loc. cit. William II reigned from 1166 to 1189. Peter wrote the above words in a letter to the archbishop of Palermo written *c.* 1173 from the court of Henry II, whose secretary Peter had meanwhile become.

[3] f. 125: 'Mors enim nichil aliud est quam exstincio naturalis caloris in corde; huius rei testimonium accepimus a magistro hernulfo aurerilianus qui cum lectionem in iuvenali pertransiret mentionem facit de boleta, dicens . . . .'

[4] f. 119: 'Est autem notandum quod quidam sunt qui multum apetunt et parum possunt ut colerici. Quidam parum appetunt et multum possunt, ut magister hugo de mapenofre, quidam qui parum possunt et parum apetunt ut magister reginaldus de omine, multum appetunt et parum possunt ut magister philippus rufus cornubiensis, multum appetunt et multum possunt ut magister iohannes burgensis, et precipue magister villelmus chers, cum cassia fistula.'

[5] He became dean *c.* 1201, see Z. N. Brooke, *C.H.J.* viii. 3, p. 182. I am indebted to Dr. H. D. Emanuel, formerly Assistant Keeper of the Dept. of MSS. and Records, Nat. Lib. of Wales, for this and the following references to Herefordshire documents.

[6] Doc. no. 1091.

[7] Docs. nos. 159 and 1358.

[8] Doc. no. 2071.

[9] Doc. no. 1381.

English scholar who copied the questions. This person must have been in close relationship with the members of the circle at Hereford, which has long been known as a centre for the study of Arabic mathematical science in England at that period, and was probably a physician who had studied at Salerno, or elsewhere in France where Salernitan learning had penetrated. He therefore represents the study of the natural sciences and of medicine (*physica* as a whole), in contrast to that of the mathematical sciences, hitherto thought to be the main preoccupation of these Hereford men. We shall return to this aspect of the subject in Chapter 4, when we discuss the spread of this Salernitan *physica* into England.

Another manuscript of these and similar questions, which this time are definitely called Salernitan, is Peterhouse (Camb.) 178, a late-thirteenth-century codex, perhaps of Italian origin, written in a beautifully clear, rounded, Gothic script. This volume was present in the old, 1418, catalogue of the library, and was then classed as a chained book. It is divided into two parts, of which the first consists entirely of medical works, namely, a large part of the *Micrologus* of Richardus Anglicus,[1] and other works possibly by him, the *Tabule Salernitane*, with commentary by Bernardus Provincialis, a *De modo medendi* ascribed to the Salernitan, Copho, and other anonymous works. The second part contains (1) *Questiones sollempnes Salernitane*, ff. 1–39; (2) the tracts on colours, tastes, and odours, compiled from Urso's works ff. 39–43; (3) *Questiones mag. lor(entii)*, ff. 43–51^v; (4) *Tractatus de naturali philosophia*, ff. 51^v–86^v. The *Questiones sollempnes*[2] consist of about 230 questions, of which over 100 are found in the Bodleian manuscript, whilst the *Questiones mag. lor(entii)* contain 70 questions, almost all medical, 66 of which are found in the latter codex.

These questions ascribed to *mag. lor(entius)* are almost certainly the same as those found in MS. 1236, formerly belonging to St. Augustine's Abbey, Canterbury,[3] which have the title *Questiones Salernitane a magro loz composite*, the 'z' probably being a misreading for 'r'. In this case also, the questions are associated with tracts by Richardus Anglicus and a treatise on colours. I have been able to find no other trace of this Mag. Lorentius in Salernitan literature, although Garufi records the death of an unidentified *magister* Laurentius Ramarius in the twelfth century.[4]

---

[1] See E. Wickersheimer, *Dict. Biog.* ii. 694–8.

[2] The denomination *sollempnes* probably means that, at the period when the manuscript was copied, the questions were used in a *disputatio ordinaria, publica,* or *solemnis,* as it was variously called, held in a medical faculty. But in no sense are they *reportationes* of such a disputation; the answers, often identical with those in the earlier Bodleian manuscript, being entirely in the didactic traditional form of the *quaestiones et responsiones.* Such collections could serve, therefore, either as helps for the student in his preparation for such a disputation or as the basis for the 'determinations' of the master in connexion with such questions. In the late thirteenth and fourteenth centuries Salernitan questions were used in disputations of all kinds, and were transmuted into the various forms of the scholastic *quaestio.* See below, Chapter 6.

[3] M. R. James, *Ancient Libraries of Canterbury and Dover,* p. 342.   [4] *Necrologio,* p. 58.

Other smaller collections of prose 'natural questions' clearly belonging to this same early Salernitan group or family, are contained in five other manuscripts, and still others are found added to later collections of problems.[1] The sources for this group are exactly the same as those mentioned in the next chapter for the *Questiones phisicales*, and, for the reasons there mentioned, it is unlikely that any of the questions are later than about the first quarter of the thirteenth century.[2] If this is the *terminus ante quem*, it is much more difficult to say when such questions began to be composed in Salerno. Like other similar collections, they were probably added to as the years progressed, only assuming their present proportions after a considerable period. Some may have come from elsewhere. As we shall see, a number were known in Chartres, probably well before 1135, either originating in that place, or having come thither from Salerno. A very few, which are not influenced by the Constantinian texts, and whose answers are similar to those given by Adelard, probably belong to a still earlier period.[3]

As regards the group as a whole, however, we may note the presence of a proportion, as yet very small, of questions dealing with mineralogy, and in particular, metallurgy—subjects not found at all in Adelard's collection. Otherwise, the extent of *physica* represented is the same as that furnished by the English scientist, and it corresponds, pretty accurately, to that found in contemporary classifications of the sciences.[4] But the

[1] The largest of such collections is that found in Bibl. Nat. Lat. 18081 (XIII cent.), ff. 210^v–227, and attributed to a certain Alanus, briefly described by Thorndike, 'Questiones alani', *Isis*, li (1960), 181–5, where there is also a brief mention of the questions of Magister Lor(entius) found in Pet. 178. The attribution of the former questions to Alain de Lisle is extremely doubtful. Other groups of early questions are found in Corpus Christi, Oxf. 233 (XIII cent.), ff. 21–31^v, from St. Albans; Brit. Mus. Royal 12, G. IV (*c.* 1300), ff. 127–129^v, from the Benedictine Priory, Coventry; Vienna, Nationalbibl. 5207 (XV cent.), ff. 116^v–134^v; Klosterneuburg 274 (XIV cent.), ff. 83^v–85^v. Later collections of natural questions, which contain groups of the earlier, Salernitan, ones, are the *Quedam questiunculae bone naturales* contained in Erfurt, Ampl. octav. 78 (1346), ff. 135–50, and, less completely, in Vienna Nationalbibl. 5371* (XV cent.), ff. 36–39^v; and the *Questiones phisicales* in Cod. Vat. Burghesiani 86 (*c.* 1300), ff. 1–19^v. Still other groups are found added to the *Problemata* of Peter of Spain and the *Quaest. super De animal.* of Albertus Magnus; see below, pp. 78 and 86.

[2] Until these questions have been edited it is difficult to say what proportion, if any, of later questions is to be found in the various manuscripts.

[3] It is very tempting to think that the first series of Salernitan questions was indeed that attributed to Alfanus and at one time in the library of Christchurch; see above, p. 19. We should expect it to consist almost exclusively of Greek questions, and its recovery would perhaps reveal another source for some of Adelard's questions.

[4] Cf. the classifications given by Clarenbald of Arras in his commentary on the *De trinitate* of Boethius, *c.* 1160–70 (ed. W. Jansen, Breslau, 1926, pp. 26 ff.); by the anonymous author of a twelfth-century *summa* of natural philosophy contained in C l m 331 (described by Grabmann in *Wilhelm von Conches*, S.B.A.W. (1935), x, pp. 47–54, and, less fully, in *G.S.M.* ii (1956), 42); by the Salernitan master, Maurus (d. 1214), in his commentary on the *Isagoge* of Ioannitius (Bibl. Nat. Lat. 18499, f. 1^v); by the earlier (*c.* 1150) commentary of the Salernitan, Bartholomaeus, on the same work, recently described by P. O. Kristeller, *Nuove fonti per la medicina Salernitana del secolo XII* (*Rassegna Storica Salernitana*, Anno xviii, 1–4), Salerno, 1958; and by Raoul de Longchamp in his commentary on the *Anticlaudianus* of Alain de Lille, (Bibl. Nat. Lat. 8083, ff. 7^v–9^v), see above, p. 33, and Grabmann, *G.S.M.* ii (1956), 48–54.

proportion of questions dealing with zoology is much higher, and that concerned with cosmology and meteorology, correspondingly much less.[1]

Again, most of the questions are influenced by the Constantinian texts, and by later, Salernitan masters, such as Platearius, Maurus, and, especially, Urso; and thus they represent a later viewpoint than that of Adelard, and one very much coloured, this time, by Arab thought. Apart from this, however, in cases where Adelard and the Salernitans deal with the same problem, the Salernitan answer is not only fuller, often giving combinations of older, and later Galenic theories,[2] but is also much more sensible and practical—a trait which is not always due to Arab influence.

Let us consider some examples which illustrate this more practical tendency. In *Quaestiones naturales*, ch. 9, 'Why do ruminants get up fore-part last?', Adelard compares the beast with men, who, when fresh, begin by lifting heavy weights, coming afterwards to the lighter ones, when they are tired; the inference being that, after resting, and when it has regained its strength, the animal then lifts the heavier hindquarters first. This assumes, of course, that the animal is never still tired when it rises. The Salernitan master tries to give a more natural explanation, saying that the weight of the hindquarters makes it difficult for the animal to rise fore-part first; the inference being that it naturally rises in the way that it finds easiest, and that will cause it least effort.[3] Although still far from being a satisfactory solution, it is a better and more practical one than Adelard's.[4]

Adelard's answer to the question which discusses why a woman does not catch leprosy by intercourse, but a man does, ch. 41, depends entirely on the attractive and repellent properties of the four elementary qualities. The Salernitan attributes the immunity of the woman to her coldness and compactness, which cause a constriction of the pores, and so stop the entrance of the disease, whereas, in the case of the man, the disease enters, *in modum veneni*, both the open pores of the *virga* and the *meatus*, from thence gradually infecting the whole body.[5]

Again, in the answer to the Greek question, ch. 47, 'Why does a live body sink, but a dead one come to the surface?', Adelard once more uses the time-worn elementary qualities. The warm and dry, which cause lightness, appertain to red bile, which is enclosed in the gall-bladder. As long as this organ remains intact, as in the living, the body sinks, but when

---

[1] The first question only of Auct. F. 3. 10 is theological: 'Quare deus factus fuerit homo?'

[2] The Salernitan answer, for instance, to the question about anterior baldness, discussed by Adelard, combines the theories of Macrobius and Galen (Peterhouse 178, ii, f. 9ᵛ).

[3] Pet., f. 11ᵛ: 'Bos posteriora habet anterioribus graviora et ideo prius elevat ea anterioribus ut anteriora ad surgendum gravitate posteriorum non impediantur. Si enim prius anteriora levaret ex nimia posteriorum gravitate debilitaretur, unde cito posset cadere et ideo natura sagax sic dedit ea prius surgere.'

[4] A better account of what actually happens is given in a later answer to this question, made in the faculty of arts at Paris, *c.* 1300; see below, p. 89.

[5] See Note A, p. 205.

the bladder bursts open, as happens in the dead body, the qualities of warmth and dryness escape with the red bile, and spreading through the body, tend, through their lightness, to raise the limbs. Compared with this the Salernitan answer is far nearer the truth in saying that the humours are resolved into a vapour, which, not being able to escape, inflates the body, and so compels it to rise to the surface.[1]

In other cases the Salernitan answer is not so much more practical as physical, compared with the philosophical answer of Adelard, a characteristic due, perhaps, to the influence of Urso. Two questions will suffice to show this; in the first, ch. 15, 'Why does mankind not have horns?', Adelard points out the superiority of human reason, which far transcends the natural weapons of the lower animals. The Salernitans, on the other hand, give purely physical causes, depending on the porosity of the cranium, and so forth.[2] Adelard solves ch. 38, 'Why are human beings unable to walk as soon as they are born, in contrast to the young of the lower animals, who can?', another pseudo-Alexandrian question found this time in the *Vetustissima translatio*, by saying that the weaker and more tender limbs of infants are consonant with reason, and adapted for its activities; but the stronger limbs of beasts are 'out of keeping with the practice of rational virtue'. This answer is in complete contrast to the physical reasons found in the Graeco-Latin[3] and Salernitan collections,[4] the former being based on the distribution of innate heat, and the latter on the presence or absence of menstrual blood in the nourishment.

It is not necessary, for our purpose, to follow the fortunes of the school of Salerno any farther. The researches of Sudhoff and others have established that the earliest form of perhaps the most popular Salernitan work, the *Regimen Sanitatis, Schola Salernitana*, or *Flos medicinae*, as it is variously called, was composed not earlier than the second half of the thirteenth century. Indeed, a good deal of Salernitan medical literature belongs to this century, but the impression, so far, is that it has not the importance of that of the previous century.[5]

---

[1] Auct. 147ᵛ; Pet. 7ᵛ. This resembles the Greek answer found in pseudo-Alexander, *Prob.* (trans. Gaza), ii. 72.   [2] Auct. 130ᵛ; Pet. 5ᵛ.

[3] pseudo-Alex. *Prob.* (trans. Gaza), ii. 26; *Vet. trans.* 18.

[4] Auct. 143ᵛ, 156; Pet. 13.   [5] Kristeller, art. cit., p. 169.

3

The 'Questiones phisicales'

THE *Questiones phisicales* forms the metrical part of the early family of Salernitan questions that we have been discussing.[1] It is found in two manuscripts and less completely in a printed Broadside,[2] and contains 185 questions in 263 hexameters. The style, subject-matter, and above all a detailed analysis of the sources of each question, all point to the end of the twelfth or the very beginning of the thirteenth century as the period of composition. A *terminus ante quem* is afforded by the generally accepted dates between which Michael Scot translated Aristotle's *De animalibus*, i.e. 1217–20,[3] since, with two possible exceptions,[4] the zoological questions, which comprise about a third of the total, are not influenced by this work. It is also noteworthy that the medical questions are not influenced by the translations of Gerard of Cremona, such as those of the *Canon* of Avicenna, and of the works of Rhazes and Albucasis—none of which were available in Salerno before the end of the twelfth century.[5]

A glance at Table 3 will show that the main sources for the questions

[to p. 44

---

[1] The poem seems to have been overlooked by historians of medieval science and medicine; it is not in Thorndike and Kibre, *Incipits* (1937), or in any of the supplements thereto.

[2] Brit. Mus. Sloane 1610, Trinity 580 (R. 3. 1), and Ulsen's *Speculator* (*c.* 1501).

[3] See A. C. Crombie, *Robert Grosseteste*, p. 46.

[4] The question about the bell-wether (Q. 76) may have come from the *Hist. animal.* vi. 19 (573ᵇ), although a characteristic so well known would hardly require a literary source. Another question about the colour of animals (Q. 21) would also appear to stem from the *De gen. animal.* v. 6 (785ᵇ), without any early intermediate Latin source. This problem occurs among those attributed to pseudo-Alexander, and in the Greek *Problemata inedita* listed by Bussemaker, so that it is quite possible that it did exist in Latin translation during pre-Salernitan times, perhaps in a fuller version of the *Vetustissima translatio* than we have at present. The source for a third question about the she-wolf (S. 142) seems to be the *Abbreviatio de animal.* of Avicenna, translated by Michael Scot *c.* 1232. But these three instances are hardly sufficient in themselves to upset the general dating of the work. As in the case of some of Adelard's Greek questions, see above, p. 25, oral tradition may have played a part in the transmission of these ideas; the possibility of later interpolation cannot be ruled out, and parts of Avicenna's Arabic text may have been known in south Italy well before 1232.

[5] The evidence so far collected seems to suggest that none of Gerard's translations reached Salerno before *c.* 1200. The *Chirurgia* of Roger of Salerno (1170) is influenced by the Constantinian translations, but not by the *Canon* of Avicenna and other medical texts translated by Gerard, and the same may be said concerning the *Anatomia Richardi*, or *Nicolai*, which belongs to about the last decade of the century. See Sudhoff, *Gesch. d. Med. in Überblick*, p. 195, the same author's 'Die vierte Salern. Anatom.', *Sudhoffs Archiv*, xx (1928), 33–50, and Corner, *Anatomical Texts, passim*. As we have seen, the Salernitan masters Maurus and Urso used the Greek–Latin translations of the Aristotelian *libri naturales*, not the Arabic–Latin ones of Gerard.

TABLE 3

An Analysis of the Sources

I have only taken account, where possible, of Latin sources. The ultimate Greek sources for many of the questions will be found mentioned in the notes but, as Whittaker pointed out long ago, 'in any case, there is no prospect of an end to the search for sources'[1]—one must set a limit somewhere. To indicate possible steps in the transmission of ideas, I have given alternative sources in brackets, shown by the following symbols.

A = Adelard	Ph. = Physiologus (Dicta Chrysostomi, *c.* 1000, and Phys. Theo-
B = St. Basil (trans.	baldi, *c.* 1100)
Eustathius)	Plat. = Platearius
C = Constantinus	S = Seneca
I = Isidore	U = Urso
M = Macrobius	Vet. = Vetustissima translatio (of the Greek problems)
P = Pliny	

Questions in the *Speculator* are indicated by S., followed by the line number, those in the portion of the *Questiones phisicales* not used by Ulsen, by Q., followed by the line number—a procedure which will be followed throughout this study, and which will enable any question to be quickly traced in the texts and notes.

1. TRADITIONAL LATIN SOURCES

(a) THE CLASSICAL POETS

Virgil

S. 40 rerum nat.
42 signosum
52 cerastes
63 luce lupina (P.I)
95 ventus equam (P.U)
Q. 16 marini fluctus (P.M)
60 imbres, ventos, nubes
    fulmina, tonitrus (S.P.I)
67 marmor lacrimis

Ovid

S. 34 chaos (M.I)
38 nexus elem.
40 motus in igne
43 discord. rer. sem.
45 terram medio (P.A.U)
77 ursus (P.I)
91 pavo
152 serpens (I.Ph.)
Q. 58 sideris casus (S.P.A)

Lucretius

S. 48 ether (P. Maurus)
56 magnes (P.I.U)
85 canis (P)
Q. 35 ecco (P)
44 putei latices (S.M)
49 oleum (P)

Horace

S. 83 lincis radio (P.U)
Q. 9 sompnia (Ovid. Priscianus Lydus. A)

Lucan

Q. 52 piscis brevis (P.I)

Claudian

Q. 5 nare sagaces

(b) THE ENCYCLOPEDISTS

Pliny

S. 50 lacticis imago
52 cerastes (I)
54 adamante (I)
59 emathites (Plat.)
68 hyrundo
69 fenix (I.Ph.)
70 vipera (B.I.Ph.)

76 catulis (U)
84 lux aquile (I.U)
88 castor (I.Ph.)
93 mula
104 galli cantus
112 fructus, flos (U)
114 cerasa, persica
    nux (C.U)

---

[1] *Macrobius*, p. 18.

S. 119 oliva, lauro (C)
  121 rogus auro
  125 canis
      psittacus (I)
  128 holor
      basiliscus (I)
  129 mulier
  131 cornua (A.U)
  138 leo (I)
  140 lepus
  145 ydroforbitico (C)
  149 solsequio (I.U)
  153 muliebre caput
  157 ruta (C.U)
  158 philomena
Q. 6 cancer
  10 lactuca (C)
  12 agnus heris (C)
  13 columba
  17 circulus imbres
  18 cornix
  38 compassio porcis
  41 coitus
  54 porcam
  63 mane rubor (U)
  66 commotus piscis

  72 testibus
  75 arbor
  81 mors (C)
  86 ungula
  89 senior (M)
92-93 semel et sepe pariant.
  94 cauda
  100 ciminum (C.U)
  103 menstrua
  104 mulier submersa
  127 dentes
  131 aloe (C)

Solinus

S. 57 gagates

Isidore

S. 76 leonis fetum (Ph.U)
  89 bubo (U)
  90 vespertilio
  159 pulmo, cor etc.
Q. 38 murilegus (A.U)
  41 rinoceros (Ph.)
  47 leporis
  69 cervus (Ph.)
  70 nani
  132 subacellis

(c) THE PHILOSOPHERS

Seneca

Q. 27 hauster, boreas etc. (P)
  56 potus (P)
  109 solis calor (U)
  111 bruma, grandinis (P.U)

Macrobius

S. 129 puer

Q. 36 in sompnos?
  45 vellus ovium (C)
  103 eunuchus (Vet.)
  107 barba, mulier, vox
  119 vini frig. (Vet.)
  121 piper, sinapis
  125 in gyrum motus
  126 cibaria cruda

(d) CLASSICAL ROMAN MEDICINE

Theodorus Priscianus

S. 59 peonia (C)

2. EARLY GREEK–LATIN TRANSLATIONS

Physiologus

S. 73 struthio
  80 talpam (U)
  80 salamandram (U)
  126 pica?
Q. 7 leo?
  22 arbor aves (Giraldus Cambrensis; U)
  91 leo?

St. Basil

S. 64 turtur (Ph.)
  108 coturnix

Physionomia (Loxus, Arist. Polemon)
Q. 32 parvum tumidum (U)

Vetustissima translatio
S. 155 pregnantes (Soranus. C.U)

3. ARABIC–LATIN TRANSLATIONS

Constantinus

S. 49 humores
61 epar spodium
61 stomacho galangam (Plat.)
62 cerebro muscum (Plat.)
136 singultum
Q. 11 faba
19 mel?
53 decoctio carnes?
57 convertibilis cibis
71 leprosus
79 sternutare
101 pauca vorans

Belenus-Apollonius

S. 71 apis (U)
95 sambuci

Jorach

S. 71 cornicula
109 passeris

Aristotle

Q. 21 varium . . . colorem?
76 aries?

Avicenna

S. 142 lupa

4. THE WRITINGS OF SALERNITAN MASTERS

Afflacius

Q. 31 cellula frigescat?

Platearius

S. 146 mirrha
147 muscus
Q. 1 acetum

Maurus

Q. 123 allia

Urso

S. 73 piscis
74 luscus?

81 vulnus
94 nepita cattam
Q. 15 viror in flore
25 medulla
27 urine radius
33 campana (1)
123 allia
130 lunare iubar

Gilles of Corbeil

Q. 24 circulus urine

5. OTHER SOURCES

Biblical

S. 133 Samsonis
Q. 82 Jacob vergas. (I.U)

Aelian (no intermediate Latin source)

S. 100 vervex

Aristotle (no intermediate Latin source)

Q. 98 volucres

6. UNCERTAIN ORIGIN

S. 96 membra bovina (A)
121 algeat aurum
122 asellum
136 sternutatio (John of Salisbury)
143 simia
Q. 50 caseum
73 aves rapaces
77 artheticis piper
80 cadaver

85 ovum
87 frigore magno
96 leprosi sperma (A)
97 natare (Hildegarde)
105 lumina
114 officium vocis
115 balbutiente
116 de vulnere Iesus
118 nocte magis morituri

} Probably Salernitan

may be grouped under four headings, namely (1) traditional Latin sources, such as the classical poets, Virgil, Ovid, Lucretius, Horace, Lucan, Claudian; the encyclopedists, Pliny, Solinus, and Isidore, and the writings of Seneca and Macrobius. (2) Early Greek–Latin translations, such as *Physiologus*, St. Basil's *Hexaemeron*, a *Physionomia*, the *Solutiones* of Priscianus Lydus, and the *Vetustissima translatio*. (3) Translations of Arabic and Jewish medical and scientific writings, such as the corpus translated by Constantinus, and other less known Arabic–Latin translations, ascribed to such hypothetical authors as Jorach and Belenus (Apollonius). Finally, (4) the writings of the Salernitan masters, Afflacius, Matthaeus Platearius, Maurus, Urso, and Gilles of Corbeil. Many of the questions are found in the *De natura rerum* (1197–1204) of Alexander Neckam, and in the later metrical summary of this work, the *De laudibus divinae sapientiae* (*c.* 1213).[1] That this author knew of these, or similar, collections of questions, there can be no doubt. The *De natura rerum* teems with references to them, and much of the material is in the form of question and answer.[2] He also makes frequent references to 'the diligent investigators of natural things', who are presumably the same as 'the well informed in physical matters'[3]—the masters who lectured and compiled lists of such questions and answers for their pupils. One such master, who influenced Neckam considerably, was, in fact, Urso of Calabria, as Birkenmajer and Dr. R. W. Hunt pointed out long ago.[4]

In the case of the *Questiones phisicales*, very few of the questions are in Neckam only, and are not in the Salernitan prose collections or explained by any anterior source. Probably there are not more than five such questions, namely S.121 *aurum*, where Neckam has *madet* instead of *algeat*, and so the reference is not exact. Both Thomas of Cantimpré and Vincent of Beauvais agree with the *Questiones phisicales*, which makes it probable that the latter is correct, and that there is some earlier source, as yet untraced.

Two of the questions refer to stories, one about a magpie, S. 126 *pica*, the other about a lion, Q. 7 *leo*. The former is repeated by Vincent, who attributes it to *Physiologus*, and doubtless it was in some early version of this elusive work, now lost; the latter may easily have had a similar origin in some collection of beast stories well known to the early Salernitan masters.

Another question about honey (Q. 19) is, it is true, exactly represented in Neckam's *De natura rerum*, but I have no doubt that it is inspired by

---

[1] 80 out of 185 of the subjects are found in these two works of Neckam. The references will be found in the notes to the *Speculator* and *Questiones*.

[2] Ed. Thos. Wright (Rolls Series), London, 1863, pp. 66, 93, 121, 123, 124, 163, 164, 174, 228, 267, 268.

[3] Ed. cit., pp. 177 and 93.

[4] A. Birkenmajer, *Le Rôle*, p. 4; R. W. Hunt, 'English Learning in the Late Twelfth Century', *T.R.H.S.* 4th ser., vol. xix, London (1936), p. 25.

the corpus of Galenic and Arabic—Jewish medical writings translated by Constantinus, where I have found a relevant passage, although not the exact reference. In the question about the bell sounding near water, Q. 33 *campana*, Neckam has *clarior sonus*, the *Questiones*, *plus iuvet auditum*. In both cases the question is associated with the one about the bell breaking if it is struck when tightly bound with a fine thread, a question which is definitely Salernitan, being found both in Urso and in the prose collection. The latter has rather a similar question, *quare propter foramina superius clarius sonat tintinabulum*, and the probability is that all three questions are Salernitan in origin.

On the whole, then, there is nothing in these five questions to suggest that they derived specifically from Neckam; on the contrary, all the evidence seems to point to the fact that these, in common with many others, were common property among the Salernitan masters from whom Neckam directly, or indirectly, derived the bulk of his knowledge about natural things.[1] Similar considerations point to Neckam's not being the author of the *Questiones phisicales*, as a whole, since, although there are one or two correspondences, such as Neckam's use of the opening line, from Claudian, 'Sepe mihi dubiam traxit sententia mentem' in a poem about wine,[2] and the resemblance of his description of the laurel in *De laud.*, p. 485, to that in l. 120 of the *Speculator*,[3] the discrepancies are far more numerous. Thus if we compare Neckam's metrical treatment, in the *De laud.* and its supplement, contained in Bibl. Nat. Lat. 11867, of ideas common to that poem and the *Questiones*, we shall find in nearly every case a difference in vocabulary and methods of expression.[4] These reasons are perhaps not conclusive by themselves, but there remains the fact that, as far as is known, Neckam never taught *physica* or medicine,

[1] About 89 of the questions in the *Questiones phisicales* are represented, more or less exactly, in the Salernitan prose collection. The correspondence between the latter, which contains the answers as well, and Neckam's prose *De natura rerum* is very close, consisting at times of a literal transcription. See my notes.

[2]   'Qualiter Anglorum possem describere gentem
              Sepe michi dubiam traxit sententia mentem',
M. Esposito, 'On some unpublished poems attributed to Alexander Neckam', *E.H.R.* xxx (1915), 456. This line from Claudian also forms the incipit of a metrical *Ars dictaminis* attributed to a magister Gaufridus Bononiensis; see H. Walther, *Initia Carminum ac Versuum medii aevi*, i.

[3] S. 120   Perpetuam lauro que confert causa virorem? }
   De laud. }
   p. 485 } Perpetuo laurus stat nobilitata virore. }

[4] A few examples must suffice.

   S. 126   Cur pica loquax latitare volentes
                    Accuset? }

   De laud. } Exploratores deprendit cauta latentes. }
   p. 388 }

   S. 63   Cur raucescat homo subito quem luce lupina }
                    Perstringit facies? }

   De laud. } At lupus aspectu subito tibi praeripit usum }
   p. 488 }   Vocis, naturae consona causa subest. }

and that, therefore, it is extremely unlikely that he would write a purely didactic poem on this subject. Finally, the author of the *Questiones* includes several gynaecological questions, a type which is hardly dealt with at all by the English theologian.[1]

Didactic poems were very much in fashion round about the turn of the twelfth century, particularly in Salerno, the medical writings of Gilles of Corbeil being entirely in verse, and the huge *Flos medicinae*, increased by the assiduous editorship of De Renzi to 3,526 verses, attests the continuing popularity of this form of instruction.[2] It was adopted as an aid to memory to help the student who could not afford the costly parchment for taking down lecture notes, let alone manuscripts of any kind, and so had to rely on a capacious memory in his search for knowledge; because it was thought more pleasing to the ear than prose; and finally because it was more compact and concise. Gilles of Corbeil refers more than once to the advantages of these metrical compositions,[3] and there is no doubt that he is a much more likely candidate for the authorship of the *Questiones* than Neckam. Unfortunately the subject matter of his extant poems differs so much from that of the *Questiones* that comparison is difficult. There are, it is true, striking correspondences in style and vocabulary,[4] but one would

S. 73	Cur visu solo duris stans incubat ovis Strutio?
De laud. p. 384	Adde quod ipsius radiorum mira potestas Pulvere quae sterili liquerat ova fovet.
B.N. lat. 11867, f. 219	Strutio fulgentis radii virtute tenellam Inclusam prolem rumpere claustra iubet.
ibid. f. 221	Tunc vi nature radii virtute potentis Rumpuntur prime testea s(c)epta domus.
Q.38	Cur nocte magis discernere visu Possit murilegus?
De laud. p. 490	Muricipes melius atrae caligine noctis Quam de luce vident, cognita causa subest.

It may be noted that Neckam does not seem to use the word *hieronoxa* S. 60 (*yeranoxia*, Sl. 1610) for epilepsy, preferring 'epilempsis' *De laud.*, p. 478, 'epilemticus' *De nat. rer.* i. 60, or 'epilenticus' *De nat. rer.* ii. 155.

[1] About the only two places where he mentions such subjects are *De nat. rer.* ii. 156, where he discusses the evil effects of the menstrual profluvia in women, his object being to humble the pride of man with the thought that he is born from the only animal that menstruates, and *De laud.*, p. 496, where he briefly mentions one of the causes why a woman is not infected with leprosy on coition but a man is. Cf. above, p. 38, for Adelard's treatment of this Salernitan question.

[2] See above, p. 39. For an account of the wide scope of this sort of mnemonic verse see L. Thorndike, 'Unde versus', *Traditio*, xi (1955), 163–93.

[3] In the Prologues to the *De urinis* and the *De pulsibus*, both edited by Choulant in the *Carmina medica*.

[4] These similarities are particularly noticeable in the *Viaticus* (ed. V. Rose, 1907). Here we find the use of *yeronoxa* (l. 320) and cf. the following:

Q. 12	Cur minuat dans *incentiva caloris* Agnus heris?
Viat. 1496	Cibus hoc dampnum potusque ministrat grossitie laedens, aut *incentiva caloris* exacuens renem.

hesitate to ascribe the work to Gilles on these grounds alone and without further evidence. Perhaps this evidence will, in time, be forthcoming.

The field covered by the questions is exactly the same as that which we have already noted in connexion with the prose collection. Just over one-third deals with anthropology and medicine, including *materia medica*, another third with zoology, and the remainder with cosmology and meteorology, botany, mineralogy, and a small ill-defined class which we may call *experimenta* or physics; the proportions of all these subjects corresponding, roughly, to those in the prose Salernitan questions.[1] A more detailed discussion of the sources and other particulars regarding each question will be found in the notes to the *Speculator* and *Questiones phisicales*, so that it only remains to mention here some of the main points of interest in connexion with each group.

The first group contains little that is not found either in the old-established Latin sources, or in the corpus of medical writings current at Salerno during the second half of the twelfth century and later. A few of the questions I have been unable to trace to this latter source, although they may quite possibly emanate from it. On the other hand, it is equally possible that they represent material which, in Salernitan literature, has only survived in this question form. These questions are, S. 136 *sternutatio*, Q. 50 *caseum*, Q. 87 *frigore magno*, Q. 96 *leprosi sperma*, Q. 97 *natare*, Q. 114 *officium vocis*, Q. 115 *balbutiente*, Q. 116 *de vulnere lesus*, Q. 118 *nocte morituri*, all of which are also contained in the prose collection. Questions S. 136, Q. 96, Q. 97, Q. 118 point to a Salernitan source for material hitherto found for the first time, I believe, in John of Salisbury, Adelard, Hildegarde, and Peter of Abano. Q. 104 *mulier submersa* is interesting, since it affords a very rare example of a case in which the Salernitan masters held an opinion exactly opposite to that of Pliny. S. 95 *sambuci*

S. 105	Cur luciferi quasi iura
	vendicet?
Viat. 114	Cum colerae rabies motus sibi *vendicat* horam

S. 52.	Cerastes
	Accusent lachrymis presens *latitare* venenum.
Viat. 362	Stomachum cum noxia morbi
	causa replet, dolor *accusat* qui virus ibidem
	allegat *latitare* mali.

This unusual use of *accuso* in the sense of 'allege' or 'tell' occurs in three other places in the *Speculator*, viz. ll. 81, 122, 127, and frequently in the *Viaticus*, where it is used in describing the symptoms of diseases, e.g.

1113.	Lumbricos haec *accusant*, os discolor, oris
	fetor, pruritus naris. . . .
2196.	*Accusat* coleram facies citrina rubore
	commixto, dolor in dextra plus parte flagellat.

and cf. also ll. 464 and 1661.

[1] The figures are, anthropology and medicine, including materia medica, 66; zoology 66; cosmology and meteorology 29; botany 11; experimenta 11; mineralogy 2.

seems to indicate that the *De sensibus* of the mysterious Belenus or Apollonius was known and utilized at Salerno, before ideas from it became more widespread through the popular, encyclopedic, *De finibus rerum naturalium* of Arnold of Saxony, composed *c.* 1225.

The zoological questions are equal in number to those in the group we have just been discussing, and thus account for another third of the total. By far the most prolific source for these is Pliny, but a few come from Isidore, Physiologus, and the classical Latin poets, while two or three may originate from Arabo-Latin sources such as the *De sensibus* of Belenus–Apollonius, S. 71 *apis*, and the *De animalibus* of Jorach, S. 71 *cornicula* and S. 109 *passeris*, a work which, like the *De sensibus*, was later popularized in the *De finibus* of Arnold of Saxony. S. 100 *vervex* is a case of an ancient belief, first mentioned by the Greek author, Aelian (III cent.), which is discussed for the first time in the Latin West, in these Salernitan questions—at considerable length, in fact, in the prose collection. S. 73 *piscis* and, probably, 74 *luscus* contain what must be among the earliest references to colour blindness in the West. S. 94 *Nepita cattam* points to a Salernitan origin for a superstition about cats and catmint. Q. 38 *compassio porcis* is an interesting example of a belief which may have arisen through the misunderstanding of a corrupt passage in Pliny.

About one-sixth of the questions is devoted to cosmology, meteorology, and kindred subjects, and these questions all stem from classical Latin authors such as Virgil, Ovid, Lucretius, Pliny, and Seneca.

Eleven questions deal with botany, all probably inspired by Pliny, and an equal number discuss *experimenta* or physics, in the modern sense. Of these latter, S. 54 and 57, concerning magnetic power, and Q. 49, about the floating of oil on water, stem from classical sources, whilst Q. 82, about Jacob's rods, is biblical, and was first discussed in the West by St. Augustine. The remaining seven are definitely Salernitan in origin, or were first introduced to the West through Salernitan masters. These are S. 147 *muscus*, Q. 1, *acetum*, 31 *cellula*, 33 *campana* (two questions), 85 *ovum*, 130 *lunare iubar*.[1]

Finally, as regards mineralogy, only two questions, regarding the properties of gold, belong to this subject, S. 121 *aurum*, the first probably Salernitan, the second stemming from Pliny. This small proportion of mineralogy, already mentioned in connexion with the prose questions, is characteristic of the whole group. It is also evident in Neckam's *De natura rerum*, where only four short chapters are devoted to metals (ii. 52–55). This would seem to indicate that in the West there was little interest in alchemy and metallurgy round about 1200, although it is certainly an improvement on the attitude of Adelard and the earlier compilers, who gave no space at all to these subjects. By 1236 at the latest

---

[1] These are, on the whole, more practical than the corresponding physical questions of Adelard, a characteristic we have already discussed, see above, p. 38.

the picture had entirely changed, and the *Questiones Nicolai Peripatetici*, attributed to Michael Scot, shows a very strong interest in alchemy and allied subjects, at the court of Frederick II.[1]

We may note, in conclusion, the relatively small number of questions devoted to magic and superstition in the spheres of anthropology, medicine, and *experimenta*, probably not more than five,[2] but the rather high proportion in zoology, twenty-four out of sixty-six questions.[3] At the same time, such answers to these questions as are found in the prose collection all attempt a naturalistic solution, based on physical properties; not one resorts to a supernatural or occult cause, the favourite explanation of many sixteenth- and seventeenth-century naturalists.

[1] These questions will be discussed in Chapter 5.

[2] S. 81 vulnus; 133 Samson; 136 sternutatio. Q. 82 Jacob, varias vergas; 130 lunare iubar.

[3] S. 63 luce lupina; 64 turtur; 69 fenix; 70 vipera; 71 apis; 71 cornicula; 73 strutio; 76 catulus leonis; 77 ursus; 80 talpa; 80 salamandra; 83 lynx; 88 castor; 91 pavo; 94 cattam; 95 equam; 100 vervex; 128 holor; 128 basilisc; 140 lepus. Q. 22 arbor aves; 41 rinoceros; 52 remora; 69 cervus.

4

The Spread of Salernitan 'Physica' to Chartres, England, and Paris

1. CHARTRES

WE saw in Chapter 2 that, even if conditions were not quite so favourable for independent inquiry in north France as they were in Italy, yet in the former region profane studies had secured a sure foothold in the monastic and cathedral schools by the end of the tenth century. Chartres, in particular, had by then obtained a reputation for the study of theoretical medicine long before such studies had reached Salerno. A considerable time in fact was to elapse before the latter city was able to equal its northern rival in the comprehensive study of *physica*, and eventually surpass it, by virtue of its closer contact with Greek and Arab learning, the stimulus of the south Italian intellectual renaissance, and the greater facilities which it enjoyed as a secular school of medicine which was particularly easy of access.

At the threshold of the twelfth century the school at Chartres became renowned for a species of Neoplatonic natural philosophy, influenced considerably by the *Timaeus* (through the translation and commentary of Chalcidius), Boethius, Macrobius, Nemesius, and the Hermetic Asclepius[1]. The wide variety of reading in the school is shown by the works listed in the *Eptateuchon* of Thierry of Chartres (before 1155)[2] and by the manuscripts which have survived until recent times. We find that the library was rich, not only in classical texts belonging to the *trivium*, but also in those dealing with the mathematical sciences, especially in Arabo-Latin astronomical and astrological works, and that it possessed the corpus of Constantinian translations. Typical of the humanistic philosophy professed at Chartres is the *De mundi universitate* of Bernard Silvestris (*c.* 1147),[3] dedicated to Thierry and resembling in many ways the *De sex dierum operibus* of that master.

But the best account of the natural sciences and medicine cultivated at Chartres during this period is to be found in the *De Philosophia mundi*

---

[1] Clerval characterized the school as 'Aristotelian in its method, and Platonic in its spirit and ideas', and modern research has only confirmed this opinion.

[2] Listed by Clerval, *Les Écoles de Chartres*, pp. 222 ff.

[3] The best recent account of this work is T. Silverstein's 'The Fabulous Cosmogony of Bernardus Silvestris', *M.P.* xlvi (2) (1948), 92–116.

and its later revision, the *Dragmaticon* or *Summa super naturalibus quae-stionibus et responsionibus*, as it is sometimes called, of William of Conches. Several of the questions in these works are identical with those found in the *Quaestiones naturales* of Adelard and in the Salernitan collection, and a comparison of the answers found in these various texts has revealed some interesting facts.

The earlier *De philosophia*, written, according to recent scholarship, during the first ten years of William's mastership at Chartres, i.e. 1120–30, (or 1125–35),[1] contains at least 24 of Adelard's questions, of which the greater number (16) are meteorological.[2] In this latter type of question some of the answers contain passages which are so similar in thought and construction to those in Adelard's answers that there can, I think, be little doubt that William had the *Quaestiones* before him, rather than any common source, such as Seneca.[3] In other cases he has elaborated Adelard's answer, and improved upon it by the addition of more technical material.

Thus in the chapter on tides (iii. 14) William only mentions the theories of Macrobius and the one depending on submarine mountains, both discussed by Adelard (ch. 52). But a little later (iii. 21) he gives the lunar theory. In discussing the causes of winds (iii. 15) he devotes most of the chapter to describing and classifying the winds caused by the ocean tides, and only mentions very briefly the two causes given by Adelard (chs. 59, 63). The chapter on the phases of the moon (ii. 32), taken largely from Macrobius, is also much fuller and more technical, and he again only mentions Adelard's explanation (ch. 70), based on the elementary qualities, at the very end.[4] In the question which asks whether stars really do fall, when they seem to do so (iii. 12), William gives the same explanation of the cause of flashes of light appearing in the night sky as Adelard does (ch. 73), and then goes on to explain why an existing star should appear to an observer to fall and vanish from its position in the heavens. Adelard gives no such explanation, but only tells us why it is that such

---

[1] See Tullio Gregory, *Anima Mundi*, pp. 5 ff. Editions used: *P.L.* clxxii, cols. 39–102; *P.L.* xc, cols. 1127–78.

[2]

De philosophia		*Quaest. nat.*	*De philosophia*		*Quaest. nat.*
iii. 16	=	51	iii. 15	=	63
„ 14		52	„ 10		64
„ 17		54	„ 10		65 and 66
„ 16		55	ii. 31		69
„ 18		56	„ 32		70
„ 18		57	„ 27		71
„ 15		59	„ 25		72
			iii. 12		73

[3] See Note B, p. 205–6.

[4] *De philos.* ii. 32: 'Cum luna frigida et humida sit, quamvis a sole illuminetur, aliquam partem sui retinet, quae aliquid obscuritatis naturaliter inibi semper apparet.' *Quaest. nat.* 70: 'Magis igitur terrestre, aquaticum, aereum quam igneum esse arbitrandum est. Sed et terrestris et aquatica et aerea essentia umbrae generativa est. Lunare igitur corpus umbratile esse necesse est.'

flashes are thought to issue from the body of a star, which was not part of the question at all.

Finally, in some cases William seems definitely to disagree with the English philosopher. Thus, in discussing the causes of thunder and lightning (iii. 10), William adheres to the Senecan theory of the movement and collision of air and winds, which is only incidentally mentioned by Adelard (chs. 66, 73), and does not mention at all the latter's main explanation, which is based on the breaking up of vast masses of ice which float about in the upper regions of the air (ch. 64).[1] He also disagrees with Adelard's belief that lightning can by itself produce a stony substance (thunderbolt) (ch. 66).[2] Except for the questions about the tides and thunder and lightning, these meteorological matters do not seem to be discussed in any extant prose collection of Salernitan questions, although one or two more occur in the metrical *Questiones phisicales*, and there is no evidence that in this class of question either William or Adelard followed the Salernitan compilers.

The case is far otherwise with the remaining eight Adelardian questions discussed by William. Of these, one is botanical, another zoological, and the remaining six deal with anthropology and medicine. Some of these questions we have already discussed in Chapter 2, when we were comparing Adelard's answers with the Salernitan ones.

In the botanical question which discusses how a graft is able to grow, since it has a different nature from the stock, yet has to live on the nourishment drawn from the ground by the latter for itself (iv. 7), William seems to follow Adelard, implying that different kinds of nourishment are drawn from the earth by the stock, and that this keeps what agrees with its own nature, and passes on to the graft that which is suitable for the latter.[3] At the same time his mention of the transmutation of the nourishment into the substance of the tree, that is, of the process of digestion, affords a correspondence with the Salernitan answer to a similar question, based on the Constantinian translations.[4]

The zoological question, also Salernitan,[5] 'Why do some animals ruminate, others not?' (Adelard ch. 7), is only mentioned by William (iv. 7), and not answered either in the *De philosophia* or the later revision.

William (iv. 24) gives the same theory of the location of the faculties in

---

[1] Perhaps Adelard got this idea from Lucretius, *De rer. nat.* vi. 157–8: 'denique saepe geli multus fragor atque ruina / grandinis in magnis sonitum dat nubibus alte.'

[2] A belief transmitted by Nemesius, *Premnon physicon*, ch. 5, which could have been Adelard's source, in this case.

[3] 'Hoc per truncum ascendit, truncusque *quod suae naturae est conveniens, continet*, naturalique calore illud digerens, in medullam et truncum et corticem transmutat. Quod vero ad surculum ascendit, surculus similiter, *quod sibi convenit, in sui naturam digerit*', *De philos.* iv. 7. 'Trahit truncus et sibi et alii, quod sibi trahit, retinet, quod alii, eidem transfert', *Quaest. nat.*, ch. 6. William's answer in the later *Dragmaticon* (p. 232) is even closer to Adelard's.

[4] See above, p. 23.

[5] Pet. 1; Auct. 156ᵛ.

the brain as Adelard (ch. 18), and the same proof from injury. But this time he quotes Constantinus, and there is no doubt that in this case the African is the source for that part of the answer which deals with the threefold location. In the question about sight (iv. 26), William mentions three out of the four theories discussed by Adelard (ch. 23), and agrees with him that the 'extramission theory' is the best. In this case his discussion of the subject is not so full as Adelard's. He is also very brief about hearing, only mentioning the Boethian theory (iv. 28) put by Adelard into the mouth of the 'nephew' asking the question (ch. 21).

William's answer to the question about the new-born infant's inability to walk is based on the Salernitan physiological reason, rather than on Adelard's purely rational one.[1]

The last two questions about catching leprosy by coition (*De. philos.* iv. 14; *Quaest. nat.*, ch. 41), and why women, though colder, are more wanton than men (*De philos.* iv. 14; *Quaest. nat.*, ch. 42), he postpones answering, 'lest, in discussing, for any length of time, such matters as these, I should offend the ears of the monks, in case this my work should ever come into their hands'.[2]

Now these last three questions form part of a group of fourteen which deal with gynaecology and midwifery, all of which occur both in the *De philosophia* and the Salernitan prose questions, almost in the same order.[3] Two of the remaining eleven questions of this group are, again, not answered in the *De philosophia*,[4] but all the others are, and the answers are literal transcriptions of the Salernitan ones, though often greatly abbreviated and with the omission of whole sentences.[5] In the light of the

---

[1] 'Quare homo cum natus est non graditur. Inde est quod caetera animalia, ex quo nata sunt, gradiuntur; homo non graditur, quia ex sanguine menstruato homo in utero nutritur', *De philos.* iv. 14. See above, p. 39.

[2] 'Unde cum mulieres frigidiores sint viris, luxuriosae magis sunt illis. Unde post coitum leprosi mulier non laedatur, accedens vero vir, leprosus efficiatur dicere postponamus, ne corda religiosorum, si forte hoc opus nostrum in manibus acceperint, diu loquendo de tali re offendamus.'

[3]

		De philosophia		Auct. F. 3. 10	
iv.	8	sperma	=	f. 118	question	4
,,	9	pueritia et coitus		119	,,	9
,,	9	tempus coitus		118ᵛ	,,	8
,,	9	complexio et coitus		118ᵛ	,,	6
,,	11	causa sterilitatis		119ᵛ	,,	13
,,	12	nolens potest concipere		119	,,	11
,,	13	menstrua		120ᵛ	,,	21
,,	14	natus est non graditur		143ᵛ	,,	226
,,	14	mulieres post concept.		120ᵛ	,,	23
,,	14	mulieres frigidiores		118ᵛ	,,	7
,,	14	coitum leprosi		119ᵛ	,,	14
,,	15	de formatione hominis		120ᵛ	,,	24
,,	16	puer in utero		120ᵛ	,,	25
,,	17	nati in septimo mense		120ᵛ	,,	26

[4] iv. 9 'complexio et coitus'; iv. 14 'mulieres post concept.'.

[5] The following example will illustrate this. *De philos.* iv. 8: 'Quid sit sperma. Cum igitur ex spermate conceptio hominis fiat, de ipso aliquid dicamus. Sperma ergo est virile semen,

above-quoted remark of William, there is little doubt, I think, that this abbreviation was intentional.

In this case, therefore, the Salernitan questions form another, hitherto unknown, source for the writings of one of the most important masters of the Chartrian school, and at the same time, because of the close literal agreement, they will be of the greatest use to any future editor of the *De philosophia*, and, as we shall see, of the *Dragmaticon*—both of which, as it happens, are in urgent need of re-edition.

From another point of view William's use of the Constantinian translations and of these Salernitan questions shows quite definitely that these writings, in one form or another, had reached northern France, and Chartres in particular, well before 1135.

The *De philosophia* is called by William an imperfect work of his youth,[1] and it is preceded by only two other short works, the commentary on *De consolatione philosophiae* of Boethius and the first gloss on the *Timaeus*. It seems best, therefore, to place the *De philosophia* near the beginning of his teaching period,[2] rather than at the middle or end, that is, *c.* 1122–7, when William would be about thirty-two years old.

Whether the answers to the gynaecological questions used by William were originally composed in Chartres, and only later incorporated into the Salernitan collection, is a matter which cannot be decided from the evidence so far available. At the moment I am assuming the more obvious explanation that they came north with the Constantinian material. There is no doubt that the questions themselves were very old, probably stemming from a lost Greek collection. As mentioned earlier, Adelard could have come across them on either side of the Alps, but since he definitely mentions a visit to Salerno in his more reliable *De eodem*, it is again perhaps more reasonable to suppose that he heard of them in that place, or elsewhere in south Italy.

---

ex pura substantia omnium membrorum compositum. Quod vero ex substantia omnium membrorum illud sit compositum, ex hoc apparet, quod omnia membra inde creantur, naturaque est, ut similia ex consimilibus nascantur. Aliud item ad hoc est argumentum quod si pater in aliquo membro aliquam incurabilem infirmitatem obtineat, ut chiragram vel podagram, filius in eodem membro eamdem obtinebit infirmitatem.' Auct. f. 118, qu. 4: '*Sperma est semen hominis ex sinceriore et puriore substancia omnium membrorum* et humorum et praecipue sanguinis qui est totius corporis nutrimentum *compositum*, sine quo nec corpus nec corporis membra regi nec nutriri possunt. Sed nisi aliquid verisimile argumentum incredibile est, indiximus aliquid de omnibus membris in spermate continetur. Natura exigit quod *similia ex similibus nascantur*, ut caro ex carne, os ex osse, et sic de similibus. Videmus enim quod ipsa elementata a quibus originem sumunt contrahunt similitudinem. Ut igitur humano corpore bina membra possint praeparari ratio est aliquid de spermate in omnibus membris contineri, quemadmodum ex parentis materia fetus. *Ad hoc quidem aliud habeamus argumentum, videmus enim quod si pater aliquem infirmitatem incurabilem in aliquo suo membro obtineat, ut ciragram vel podagram, filius in eodem membro similem incurrit infirmitatem,* et hoc nonnisi quia in germine contraxit infirmitatis illius causam et originem.'

[1] 'Libellus noster, qui philosophia inscribitur, quem in iuventute nostra imperfectum, utpote imperfecti, composuimus', *Dragmaticon* (ed. Gratarolo, Strassburg, 1567), p. 6.

[2] See above, p. 51.

In any case, it is clear that quite early in the twelfth century men were becoming dissatisfied with the traditional answers to many of these questions, and that they were beginning to formulate new ones, based on other pre-Constantinian material, or on their own private opinions, as in the case of Adelard, or on the new, Arabic–Latin translations made by Constantinus, as in the case of the Salernitan masters and William of Conches. Let us now glance at the later *Dragmaticon*.

After his long term of teaching at Chartres, William retired from active life, and accepted a post as tutor to the young Henry Plantagenet, son to Duke Geoffrey the Fair. Here, in the duke's household in Normandy, between the years 1146 and 1149, as Gregory thinks,[1] he wrote the *Dragmaticon*, his most mature work and the one giving the completest exposition of his system of philosophy. This work, written in the form of a dialogue between himself and his noble patron, is modelled on the earlier *De philosophia*, but he omits some theological material which had given offence in influential quarters, and adds a good deal of new information respecting *physica* in its most comprehensive sense, in an attempt to bring his account as up to date as possible.

It is true that he does not include zoology, as he hinted that he might do in the earlier *De philosophia*,[2] but the meteorology is greatly increased by the addition of copious extracts from Seneca's *Quaestiones naturales*,[3] the astronomy is augmented by fresh material obtained from recent Arabic–Latin translations, there are eight botanical questions, as compared with only one in the earlier treatise, and there is much more anthropology and medicine.

Five of the botanical questions correspond to the first six chapters in Adelard's *Quaestiones naturales*, and, as in the case of the meteorological questions in the *De philosophia*, he follows the English philosopher very closely in his answers.[4]

In the question about the inability of infants to walk (p. 249), he now gives, in addition to the Salernitan physiological answer of the *De philosophia*, Adelard's argument based on *ratio hominis*, and his discussion

---

[1] *Anima Mundi*, p. 8.

[2] *P.L.* clxxii, col. 88.

[3] See note B, p. 205.

[4] Cf. *Dragmaticon*, p. 233: 'Non solum de herbis et arboribus sed de omni corpore hoc affirmo, quod ex quatuor constat elementis, quod per actiones et resolutiones probari potest. Quod enim adhaerent, terra est, quod in altum crescant, ignis est, quod dilatantur et spissantur, aqua et aeris.' Adelard, *Quaest. nat.* 1: 'Itaque cum in terreo isto, licet subtiliter pulverizato, quatuor causae sint, necessario inde quoddam compositum surgit, terreum maxime, aquaticum parum, aereum minus, igneum minime, per terram cohaerens, per aquam diffundens, per aerem et ignem surgens. Nisi enim in eo ignis inesset, motum ad superiora non haberet. Nisi item aqua vel aer inesset, in latum diffundi non posset. Postremo nisi terra id praestaret, cohaerentiam non haberet.' Here note that the latter part of Adelard's answer, coupling the actions of water and air, exactly corresponds to the sense of the passage in the *Dragmaticon*, and is not consistent with the first part of his answer, where he joins air with fire, and gives it the totally different action of raising the plant.

of anterior baldness (p. 273) is again an exact paraphrase of Adelard's answer (ch. 20).

On the other hand, the answers to a group of twelve questions dealing with generation and gynaecology are much abbreviated, literal transcriptions of the Salernitan ones, as they were in the *De philosophia*. Here we find the answers to the four questions in this field[1] which William postponed answering in his earlier work, for fear of offending the monks, as well as three other similar questions not mentioned before.

These two writings of William, judging by the very large number of surviving manuscripts, extracts, and summaries,[2] were even more popular and influential than Adelard's *Quaestiones*. The *Dragmaticon* became, in fact, 'the most up-to-date scientific encyclopedia which it was possible to write in the mid-twelfth century',[3] since in addition to the traditional Latin and Graeco-Latin, pre-Constantinian material used by Adelard it contained information taken from scientific and medical works translated from the Arabic, including the Constantinian corpus, and later Salernitan writings.

As for the *De philosophia*, this work, rather than the *Quaestiones* of Adelard, deserves the epithets bestowed upon the latter work by so many scholars in the past, and must have been one of the very earliest writings to disseminate a knowledge of Arabic medicine and Salernitan *physica* north of the Alps—even though its author had probably never wandered far afield from his beloved Chartres during his 'twenty years and more' mastership there.

2. ENGLAND

During the late eleventh and twelfth centuries there were several channels through which the latest scientific and medical knowledge flowed into England. Arabic science either came directly from Spain through such men as Petrus Alphonsi, Adelard, Robert of Chester, and Daniel of Morley, or indirectly from Lorraine through Robert de Losinga, bishop of Hereford, Walcher, prior of Malvern, and other Lotharingians.[4] At the cathedral school of Chartres there had been, according to Clerval, quite a colony of English students from the time of the great

---

[1] These include the two answered by Adelard, see above, p. 53, and it is noteworthy that William prefers the more advanced Salernitan solutions to those of the Englishman, in questions of this kind.

[2] See T. Gregory, *Anima Mundi*, p. 9, n. 6. At least 68 manuscripts of the *De philosophia* are known, and 67 of the *Dragmaticon*.

[3] 'Opera ancora scarsamente studiata e pure essenziale nello sviluppo del pensiero di Guglielmo e della cultura del XII secolo: essa infatti rappresenta l'enciclopedia scientifica piú "aggiornata" che si potesse scrivere alla metà del secolo, e questa è anche la causa della sua larghissima diffusione', T. Gregory, op. cit., p. 226.

[4] See Haskins, *Med. Science*, *passim* and particularly ch. vi, and J. W. Thompson, 'The Introduction of Arabic Science into Lorraine in the Tenth Century', *Isis*, xii (1929), 184–93.

Ivo.[1] John of Salisbury had studied for three years under William of Conches, and, as we have seen, Henry II had received instruction during his youth from the same master. Chartrian philosophy could also come indirectly from Spain, through such treatises as the *De essentiis* of the Dalmatian, Hermann of Carinthia. But perhaps the closest and most numerous ties of all were established with south Italy and Sicily, and it is with these that we are most concerned at the moment.

It will be remembered that Adelard of Bath dedicated his earliest treatise, the *De eodem* (*c.* 1105–10), to William, bishop of Syracuse, whom he addresses as *omnium mathematicarum artium eruditissime.*[2] So that, long before the establishment of the Royal Court at Palermo, the mathematical sciences at least were cultivated in Sicily, and Adelard appears to be the first English scholar to have had scientific and literary relations with that island and south Italy.

In the time of Roger II, the chancellor, Robert of Selby, was an Englishman who entertained visiting noblemen and diplomats from his homeland such as St. William of York and John of Salisbury, who made several visits to that region.[3]

In the reign of William I, Aristippus dedicated his translation of the *Phaedo*, finished 1156, to a certain 'Roboratus', who is about to return from Sicily to his home in England. Haskins, with some probability, has identified this person with Robert of Cricklade,[4] prior of St. Frideswide's at Oxford from *c.* 1140 to 1180 and author of a *Compendium*, in nine books, of Pliny's *Natural history*, which he dedicated to Henry II. The scholar, Gervase of Tilbury, came from England to serve under William II, and Peter of Blois, after tutoring this king, returned from Sicily to become secretary to Henry II.

Several learned Englishmen held high ecclesiastical offices in Sicily during the reign of William II,[5] and the marriage of this monarch in 1177 to Joanna, daughter of Henry II, still further cemented the relations between the two countries. All this intercommunication, one would have thought, must have helped to introduce the new learning from south Italy and Sicily into England from the return of Adelard onwards. A certain amount of Salernitan *physica* could also have come, indirectly, through Chartres and the writings of William of Conches. But the main contribution of Adelard in this particular field was, as we have seen, the exact expression of a more comprehensive content of *physica* as a whole; in detail this philosopher did not express the views of Salernitan masters as found in the prose questions, but rather those belonging to the spheres

---

[1] *Les Écoles de Chartres*, p. 180.   [2] Ed. H. Willner, *B.G.P.M.* iv. 1 (1903), p. 3.
[3] Haskins, op. cit., p. 156.
[4] Ibid., p. 169.
[5] See W. Stubbs, *Seventeen Lectures*, ch. 6, 'Learning and Literature at the Court of Henry II', and Haskins, op. cit., p. 187.

of pre-Salernitan science and medicine, with, possibly, an addition of some of his own. In any case either through the complete loss of many manuscripts, or for other reasons, during the twelfth-century there is a very real scarcity of the sort of work that might utilize Salernitan *physica*, in any shape or form, so that we have to wait until the threshold of the thirteenth century for direct evidence of the penetration of the Salernitan questions into England.

Thus Daniel of Morley,[1] in his *De naturis*[2] dedicated to Bishop John of Norwich (1175–89), quotes the *Quaestiones* of Adelard,[3] but shows no knowledge of the Constantinian translations or Salernitan *physica*. He does, however, use the *De philosophia* of William of Conches a good deal,[4] and therefore must have had indirect knowledge of these two subjects. The fact that his interests lay mainly in the direction of cosmology, astronomy, meteorology, and element lore need not have precluded his reading the Constantinian translations, since they contain much useful information on the elements, and in fact are quoted in that connexion by the Chartrian philosopher.[5] But we should hardly expect Daniel to make use of the Salernitan medical material in the *De philosophia*, since medicine and the allied biological sciences seem to lie entirely outside the range of his studies. In the one place where it might be expected that he would be influenced by the Salernitan questions, if he knew them, that is, in a botanical question about evergreens, he gives an answer different from that in this collection, and, incidentally, from that given by Isaac, *De dietis*, translated by Constantinus.[6] William of Conches does not discuss this question in the *De philosophia*, but it does occur in the later *Dragmaticon* (1146–9). Again, however, Daniel's answer, although slightly similar, cannot be said to be derived from that of William.[7]

Now this negative evidence, though by no means conclusive, does tend to point to the fact that at the time when the *De naturis* was written the Constantinian translations and the Salernitan questions were not widely known in England. It becomes a matter of some importance, then, especially in view of the scarcity of similar English works belonging to that early period, to know as accurately as we can when this event took place. Up to now it has been assumed by everyone without exception that Daniel wrote the *De naturis* after his return from Spain and after he had

---

[1] On Daniel of Morley see V. Rose, 'Ptolomeus und die Schule von Toledo', *Hermes*, viii (1874), 327–49; C. Singer, 'Daniel of Morley', *Isis*, iii (1920–1), 263–9; Haskins, op. cit., pp. 126–7; M. Müller, 'Die Stellung des Daniel von Morley in der Wissenschaft des Mittelalters', *P.J.* xli. 3 (1928), 301–37; Thorndike, *H.M.E.S.* ii. 171–81; T. Silverstein, 'Daniel of Morley', *M.S.* x (1948), 179–96.

[2] Ed. Sudhoff, *A.G.N.T.* viii. 1 (Leipzig, 1917), 1–40, with corrections by Birkenmajer, ibid. ix. 1 (1920), 45–51.   [3] See below, p. 61, n. 1.

[4] See Silverstein, art. cit., pp. 193 ff.

[5] *De philos.* i, ch. 2.   [6] See Note C, p. 207.

[7] 'Virentia quae spissum et crassum habent humorem, neque sole neque alio accidente possunt facile desiccari, unde continue virent.' *Dragmaticon* (1567), p. 231.

attended lectures there by Gerard of Cremona, during the period 1175–89. Let us examine the internal evidence of the treatise a little closer.

In the first place the book is not in the least such as we should expect a pupil of Gerard of Cremona to write. It exactly resembles such treatises as the *De essentiis* (1143) of Hermann of Carinthia, and the anonymous *Lib. de VI rerum principiis* (*c.* 1140), with their mixture of Chartrian philosophy, Arabic–Latin translations of John of Spain, traditional Latin sources, and pseudo-Hermetic writings;[1] in other words, it is typical of that transitional period, before the translations of Gerard had become known. T. Silverstein, one of the latest scholars to discuss the work, has pointed out that three of its main sources were: John of Spain's translation of Alfragani's *Rudimenta astronomica*, made about 1135, not that of Gerard; Hermann of Carinthia's version of Albumazar's *Maius Introductorium*, made before 1143, not John of Spain's translation; and an anonymous translation of Alfarabi's *De ortu scientiarum*, not the *De divisione philosophiae* of Gundissalinus.[2] He still thought, however, that Daniel had used Gerard's translations of three Aristotelian works, the *Physica*, *De celo et mundo*, and the *De gen. et corr.*[3] But Birkenmajer had conclusively shown in 1930 that Daniel in these cases too had not used Gerard's versions, but, for the first two, had relied on an anonymous *De celo et mundo*, ascribed in various manuscripts to Avicenna, and printed in the Venetian 1508 edition of his philosophical works, and, for the *De gen. et corr.*, on the earlier Greek–Latin version made by an anonymous translator.[4] Daniel, it is true, actually mentions Gerard's translation of Ptolemy's *Almagest*, finished in 1175,[5] but he shows no knowledge of its contents, as Silverstein has shown.[6]

[1] The *De essentiis* was edited by P. Manuel Alonso, Univ. Pontificia, Comillas (Santander), 1946, and see T. Silverstein, 'Hermann of Carinthia and Greek', *Medioevo e Rinascimento, Studi in onore di Bruno Nardi* (Florence, 1955), ii. 681–99. The *Lib. de VI rerum principiis* was edited by T. Silverstein, *A.H.D.L.* xxii (1956), 217–301.

[2] See his 'Daniel of Morley', *M.S.* x (1948), 182 ff.

[3] Ibid., p. 180. The identity of a fourth work, the *Liber luminum*, is, as Silverstein says, still doubtful, and he did not succeed in finding the quotation, 'Licet enim philosophus in libro luminum aquam albidam nominaverit' (ed. Sudhoff, p. 11). It is possible that the reference is to the pseudo-Aristotelian Περὶ χρωμάτων, *De coloribus*, in which this particular idea of the individual colours of the elements is found and of which two Greek–Latin translations are known, one by Bartholomew of Messina (*fl.* 1258–66), the other by William of Moerbeke (*fl. c.* 1260–86). See E. Franceschini, 'Sulle versioni latini medievali del Περὶ χρωμάτων', *Autour d'Aristote*, pp. 451–69. Was there an earlier version? Certainly the doctrine of elementary colours was known in western Europe long before the time of these two translators. Not only is it found in Daniel's *De naturis*, but it also occurs in the *Lib. Apollonii de secretis naturae* (*c.* 1143), Bibl. Nat. Lat. 13951, f. 28, discussed in the next chapter, and *c.* 1200 was well known to Urso and the Salernitan masters; cf. his *De effect. qual.*, ed. C. Matthaes, p. 27; *De commixt. elem.*, Trinity 1154, f. 138; *Aphor. Gloss.* 80, 81; and the *De coloribus*, Pet. 178, ii. 40 ff.   [4] *Le Rôle*, pp. 3–4.

[5] 'Cum vero predicta et cetera talium in hunc modum necessario evenire, in isagogis zaphiris auditoribus suis affirmaret, Girardus Tholetanus, qui Galippo mixtarabe interpretante Almagesti latinavit, obstupui . . .', ed. cit., pp. 39–40.

[6] Art. cit., p. 181.

But, still clinging to his belief that Daniel must have been influenced in some way by this work of Gerard, he prints a passage from the *De naturis*, dealing with the sphericity of the heavens, side by side with a corresponding passage from the *Almagest*, to show, as he says, 'the one place where the *Almagest* itself may seem most likely to lie behind Daniel's text', although he admits that the passage, 'shows little trace of the language of Gerard's surviving version'.[1]

In fact, the passage is again taken, almost literally, from the anonymous *De celo* ascribed to Avicenna.[2] We must conclude, then, that Daniel either had no knowledge of the translations of Gerard, made in the second half of the twelfth century, or, if he had, made no use of them. Did he know any of the translations of Gundissalinus and his helpers, which are now attributed to that same period after 1150?[3] There is no certain evidence that he did. The name of the translator of Alfarabi's *De ortu scientiarum* is not given in any of the numerous manuscripts, and it is only tentatively ascribed to Gundissalinus by Baur, Baeumker, its editor, and others, on the insufficient grounds that it is used by the Spaniard in his *De divisione philosophiae*, and found, in several manuscripts, placed near this work.[4]

H. Bédoret, assuming that Daniel had been a pupil of Gerard, thought it more likely that the latter was the translator[5]—but this is rather putting the cart before the horse; if, as seems most likely, Daniel had not been a pupil of Gerard, or, at any rate, had not used any other translations of his, the ground for this belief vanishes. Similar remarks apply to the pseudo-Avicennian *De celo*. Again, the name of the translator is not given in any of the manuscripts, and though later copyists and compilers of catalogues have sometimes attributed the work to Gundissalinus, in the words of M.-Th. d'Alverny, one of the latest to give an opinion, 'only a close study of the vocabulary and the methods of translation can definitely decide the answer',[6] a remark which also applies, of course, to the *De ortu scientiarum*. If these two translations are not the work of either Gundissalinus or Gerard, perhaps the most likely candidate would be John of Spain,

---

[1] pp. 181–2.

[2] 'Ex partibus sibi consimilibus etiam necessaria erat ei figura talis quia erat corpus finitum, tunc ex omnibus figuris sperica fuit ei convenientior. Ideo quod ex omnibus corporibus figura sperica est magis consimilium partium, sicut ex figuriis aliis habentibus superficiem circulus est partium magis consimilium. Ceterarum autem figurarum corporearum aut superficialium nulla congruit celo. Ideo quod omnes diversarum sunt partium et non consimilium, ergo ex hiis que diximus patet quod ex omnibus figuris sperica est convenientior celo.' Avicenna, *Opera*, Venice, 1508, i, f. 40 (*De celo*, cap. 8).

[3] See M.-Th. d'Alverney, 'Notes sur les traductions médiévales d'Avicenne', *A.H.D.L.* xix (1953), 343 ff., and P. Manuel Alonso Alonso, *Temas filosoficos medievales*, Comillas (Santander), 1959, *passim*.

[4] Gundissalinus, *De div. philos.*, ed. Baur, *B.G.P.M.* iv. 2–3 (1903), 159–60, Alfarabi, *De ortu scient.*, ed. C. Baeumker, *B.G.P.M.* xix. 3 (1916), 9–10.

[5] 'Les Premières Traductions tolédanes de philosophie, œuvres d'Alfarabi', *R.N.P.* xli (1938), 91.   [6] Art. cit., p. 352.

whose translations Daniel certainly used, and who has been often confused with Gundissalinus's collaborator, 'magister Johannes'.

Besides quoting from the above translations, Daniel used Adelard's *Quaestiones naturales*[1] and his treatise on the astrolabe. Now Adelard's *De opere astrolapsus* was dedicated to the young Henry Plantagenet sometime between 1142 and 1149,[2] which gives us the former date as a *terminus post quem* for the composition of the *De naturis*. In addition we have no positive information, at the moment, that Daniel used any work written after 1149; whereas, on the contrary, all the known dates of works which he certainly used fall before this date, and ideologically the treatise belongs to the first half of the century rather than to the second, as Silverstein realized.[3]

These facts raise some interesting problems. Did Daniel, for instance, visit Toledo much earlier than *c.* 1175, perhaps as early as *c.* 1150, before Gerard had made the bulk of his many translations, but not before he and his collaborator, the Mozarab Gallibus, had commenced to lecture?

According to the notice prefixed to the list of his works drawn up by his pupils,[4] Gerard first visited Spain in search of a copy of Ptolemy's *Almagest* in Latin translation, which he was unable to find in Italy. Such a translation from the Greek existed, however, *c.* 1160, in Sicily;[5] therefore he probably came to Toledo before this date, even if not as early as the mid-century, a supposition made more probable by the fact that it must have taken him many years to complete all his very numerous translations.

Daniel mentions, at the end of his treatise, Gerard's translation of the

---

[1] Silverstein, 'Daniel of Morley', p. 190, where note that Daniel's quotation of Adelard is prefixed by the words *ut ait philosophus*, so that the latter term did not always apply to Aristotle. It therefore follows that no special significance can be attached to Daniel's similar use of this word in connexion with the *Liber luminum*; see above, p. 59, n. 3. F. Bliemetzrieder, 'Lit. Vorlagen des Lib. de naturis', *A.G.M.N.T.* x (1927), 338–44, and M. Müller, 'Die Stellung des Daniel v. Morley', *P.J.* xli. 3 (1928), 301–37, have both drawn attention to Daniel's great indebtedness to Adelard.

[2] See Haskins, *Med. Science*, p. 29; T. Gregory, *Anima Mundi*, p. 8; F. Bliemetzrieder, *Adelhard von Bath*, p. 137. The latter thought that the year 1149, just after Henry had returned to England, was the most likely date of the dedication. Gregory, the latest scholar to give an opinion, adhered to the period 1146–9, when the future king was in Normandy. Haskins, on the other hand, believed that the treatise was written between 1142 and 1146, 'whilst Henry, between the ages of nine and thirteen, was living in his Uncle's household at Bristol under the tutorship of Master Matthew'.   [3] Art. cit., pp. 179 and 189.

[4] Printed by Boncompagni, *Gherardo Cremonese*, pp. 3–7.

[5] See above, p. 31. Another Greek–Latin translation, belonging to about the same period, was that of the fourth book of the *Meteora*, made by Henricus Aristippus, who also worked in Sicily. This version was known to Gerard, who for that reason did not translate this book when he came to make his version of the *Meteora* from the Arabic, as he says, 'Liber Aristotelis Methaurorum tractatus iii. Quartum autem non transtulit, eo quod sane invenit eum translatum' (Boncompagni, op. cit.). It does not follow, of course, that because Gerard knew this translation he should also know that of the *Almagest*. On the other hand it does make it extremely probable that he would have found the latter, had it been written, when he was particularly searching for it.

Almagest, usually assigned to the year 1175. But first Steinschneider[1] and then Miss Wingate[2] have cast doubts on even this, the only date mentioned in connexion with any of Gerard's translations. The latter scholar pointed out that it was likely that this translation was Gerard's 'first considerable task', since this was the very book that had brought him to Spain, and since he was assisted in it by Gallibus, who, apparently, did not help him later on, and that 'it is hardly credible that Gerard can have completed the eighty-odd versions that stand to his credit between the years 1175 and 1187' (the date of his death). The same scholar also thought it 'not impossible' that the date 1175 at the end of the Laurentian manuscript, itself a thirteenth-century copy, referred to the year in which the work was previously copied by the scribe Thaddeus of Hungary.[3] It seems to me that these suggestions are not unreasonable, and they would certainly receive added support if it could be shown, beyond reasonable doubt, that Daniel's visit to Toledo was much earlier than it is now thought to be.

But even if all the internal evidence of the text itself does seem to indicate that Daniel both visited Spain and wrote the *De naturis* a good deal earlier than 1175, there still remains the dedication to his 'lord and spiritual Father', Bishop John of Norwich, and the prologue to the first book in which a meeting with this prelate is mentioned. The problem is similar to the one that faced us in the case of Adelard, and, indeed, the resemblance of this prologue to the preliminary matter of the *Quaestiones* is very striking.[4] In both there is mention of a return to England, after a period spent abroad in search of Arab learning, a meeting with friends, and a request that the author should give an account of what he had learnt on his travels—Bishop John taking the place of the 'nephew' of Adelard— almost as if this had become a sort of stereotyped formula for introducing popular scientific texts. We have shown that little reliance can be placed on Adelard's inconsistent tales, either for dating the *Quaestiones* or for establishing biographical details, and the question naturally presents itself, to what extent is Daniel's account reliable?

Apart from this, however, the dates of the dedicatee must, in both cases, be a decisive factor. Sometime between 1175 and 1200 Daniel certainly dedicated to Bishop John a work which, to all appearances, he had written much earlier. Unlike Adelard's *Quaestiones* the treatise, this time, did contain quite a lot of Arab learning, and Daniel may not have thought that any revision was necessary, and may have considered that the older translations which he had used were quite as good as the new ones. Or

---

[1] *E.U.*, p. 19.

[2] S. D. Wingate, *The Medieval Latin Versions of the Aristotelian Scientific Corpus*, p. 35.

[3] Ibid., p. 36, n. 26. The whole colophon is printed by Haskins, *Med. Science*, p. 104, n. 139.

[4] Bliemetzrieder was the first to draw attention to this, printing parallel passages in his above-quoted article, pp. 340 ff.

he may have completely lost touch with scientific matters, owing to pressure of another kind of work. Records have been found of him as late in the century as 1184–7, 1198, and 1199, when he became parson of Flitcham, and he was, apparently, still alive in 1205.[1] But no other scientific works or, indeed, works of any kind by him have so far been discovered.

After 1150 it might be thought that Salernitan doctrines would find their way into English writings, either directly or indirectly. But again, no such evidence exists at the moment. During the greater part of the second half of the century we cannot point even to one treatise from which to elicit information of any kind regarding the use of the prose questions, and even the existence of such questions in England at a period *c.* 1170 rests on the extremely slender evidence of a reference in a catalogue to a single manuscript which is not now extant.[2]

So we come to the very threshold of the thirteenth century, and to the consideration of the works of the two friends, Alfred of Sareshel and Alexander Neckam. Exactly when the former wrote the *De motu cordis* is not known, but, from the use in it of other works of his, the mature knowledge displayed, and the obit year of the dedicatee, Neckam, it has usually been assigned to the period 1210–15.[3] The interesting thing from our point of view is that, although dealing with theoretical medicine, it shows only a slight acquaintance with the Constantinian translations, and none at all with the Salernitan questions. On the other hand, the *De natura rerum* of his friend, probably written earlier (1197–1204),[4] makes much greater use of the African's translations, and, as we have seen, is thoroughly imbued with the Salernitan doctrines, as contained in the prose questions and the works of Urso. It seems that there were two distinct, concomitant currents of thought—the one laying greater emphasis on metaphysics and Aristotelian psychology and physiology, the other following the more down-to-earth and practical Salernitan *physica*; and these two trends may be traced, in varying degrees, throughout the entire course of the thirteenth century.[5]

---

[1] See J. C. Russell, 'Hereford and Arabic Science in England', *Isis*, xviii (1932), 23.

[2] See below, p. 67.

[3] The period established by Baeumker, the editor of *De motu cordis*, *B.G.P.M.* xiii (1923), 1–2, and confirmed by S. D. Wingate, op. cit., pp. 55–59, where she discusses, in some detail, the order of Alfred's works. J. C. Russell, however, thought that the date of composition should be much earlier, basing his conclusion on the wording of the dedication to Neckam, *ad magistrum magnum Alexandrum Nequam,* and that it was written while Neckam was still a master in the schools, but late enough for him to have achieved fame in that sphere, giving the period as 1185–95. But there is no real reason why Neckam should not have been called *magistrum* even after he had become a monk. See J. C. Russell, art. cit., pp. 18 ff.

[4] The latest and best printed summary of Neckam's life is in A. B. Emden, *A Biographical Register of the University of Oxford to A.D. 1500*, ii. 1342. See also D. A. Callus, 'Introduction of Aristotelian Learning to Oxford', *P.B.A.* xxix (1943), 9.

[5] They are visible in Neckam himself, who displays a more metaphysical and psychological trend in his *Speculum Speculationum* written later, between 1204 and 1213. See D. A. Callus, art. cit., p. 10, and the same scholar's 'John Blund on the Soul', *Autour d'Aristote*, pp. 491 ff.

Now where did Neckam acquire his evidently extremely detailed knowledge of Salernitan natural science and medicine? Born at St. Albans in 1157, he studied the liberal arts, theology, medicine, and civil and canon law at Paris (*c.* 1175–1182), returned to teach at Dunstable (1183–4), and St. Albans (1185–*c.* 1190), and lectured on theology at Oxford in the last decade of the century, later becoming a canon (1197–1201), and, finally, abbot of Cirencester (1213), where he remained until his death in 1217. He appears to have visited Rome, but there is no evidence that he went farther south, or that he ever visited Chartres or Spain. It is conceivable, of course, that Neckam may have obtained his knowledge of Salernitan *physica* at Paris while he was studying medicine there. But I do not think he did. For reasons which I shall give below, I think Salernitan medicine came later to that city, that is, after Neckam had left, and that it is much more likely that he acquired his knowledge of it in England, after his return from the Continent.

As it happens, Matthew, the brother of Warin, abbot of St. Albans (1183–95), had studied medicine at Salerno, and these two were friendly with two Salernitans, Fabianus and Robertus de Salerno, all four entering the monastery together.[1] Thus it is not hard to imagine that Neckam continued his medical studies when he became master of the school at St. Albans *c.* 1185. A knowledge of what books there were in the library there in the time of Warin would be of tremendous help. But, unfortunately, no such catalogue has survived, and the bulk of the library, which must have been very large and important, has disappeared. A few volumes, it is true, are still to be found in existing libraries, but there are not many scientific and medical texts among them, and what there are are all later than the twelfth century.

Again, it is possible that Neckam renewed his study of *physica* much later on, after he had joined the Austin canons at Cirencester. Most of his numerous works were written after his retirement from the schools, and consequently when he had much more leisure for study and composition.[2] At Cirencester Neckam would be within reach of Hereford, which, since the previous century, had been known as a centre for the study of the mathematical sciences, especially astronomy and astrology.[3] But was medicine taught there? The most that we can say is that men who studied this subject were friendly with scholars who lived at Hereford. Thus Alfred of Sareshel dedicated his version of the *De plantis* to Roger, a canon at Hereford who wrote several astronomical works.[4] J. C. Russell

---

[1] *Chronica Monast. S. Albani*, ed. H. T. Riley (1863), i. 195.

[2] This was probably one of the reasons why he had embraced the monastic life: 'Est etenim in confesso Nechamum, accrescente matura aetate, sectae canonicorum Augustinianorum se addixisse; ea tamen lege atque omine, ut sanctius viveret, et quietius studeret', J. Leland, *Comm. de script. Brit.*, ed. A. Hall, i. 241.

[3] See Haskins, *Med. Science*, ch. 6, and J. C. Russell, art. cit.

[4] Haskins, op. cit., pp. 124 ff.

sought to identify a certain 'magister Aldredus,' found in Hereford documents of *c.* 1175, with Alfred of Sareshel.[1] But his arguments seem rather unconvincing, and there is no proof at all that the latter ever dwelt at Hereford. At about the turn of the century the writer of Auct F. 3. 10 was certainly in close touch with Hereford men, as we have seen. But that is about all. It is a curious thing, too, that when Roger's fellow canon, Simon du Fresne, wrote a poem to Giraldus Cambrensis, *c.* 1195–7, inviting him to come to Hereford, although he mentions amongst the scholastic attractions the usual seven liberal arts, including geomancy, the study of both the old and the new law, and that part of *physica* which deals with the elements, the first matter, and the origin of the world, he entirely leaves out medicine and the allied biological sciences.[2] Again, the library catalogue can give us no help; for, although of some 220 surviving manuscripts 114 were reckoned by M. R. James to be old possessions of the cathedral, some 50 of these being of the twelfth century or earlier, the secular portion of the library, with the exception of a single volume of Cicero's *Rhetoric*, seems to have entirely disappeared.[3]

Thus, although Neckam was friendly with Alfred of Sareshel, and it is very tempting to think that he may have known the writer of Auct. F. 3. 10, the links connecting him with Hereford are extremely fragile.

From the beginning of the thirteenth century onwards, the picture is quite different. As we shall see in Chapter 6, Salernitan questions then began to be used as the basis for scholastic disputations in medicine, both in England and Paris; and they were also discussed in medical treatises, such as the *Compendium medicinae* of Gilbert Anglicus, written during the early years of the century.[4] Henceforth, too, there is no dearth of manuscript evidence for at least the existence in England of books dealing with Salernitan *physica*. The five English manuscripts of the questions include the oldest and most voluminous text (Auct. F. 3. 10), and the only two known texts of the *Questiones phisicales*.[5] Of the four manuscripts of the questions not of English origin, the important Peterhouse 178 has certainly been in England since 1418. Now C.C. Oxf. 233 had previously found its way, at some time or another, into John Dee's library at Mortlake,[6] which contained one of the richest collections of

---

[1] Art. cit., p. 19.

[2] See R. W. Hunt, 'English Learning', pp. 36 ff.

[3] See the introduction, by M. R. James, to A. T. Bannister's *Catalogue of the Manuscripts in the Hereford Cathedral Library*, Hereford, 1927.

[4] Ed. Lyons 1510, f. 337, contains the Adelardian question about coitus and leprosy discussed above, p. 38. Fols. 47 ff. discuss Salernitan questions about vinegar, and f. 128 has a question about night vision, the answer to which corresponds to that of the Salernitan masters. On Gilbert see J. F. Payne, *B.M.J.* ii (1904), 1282–4; H. E. Handerson, *Gilbert Anglicus*; E. Wickersheimer, *Dict. Biog.* i. 191 ff.; J. C. Russell, *Dict. of Writers*, pp. 38 ff.

[5] For the other manuscripts see above, p. 37.

[6] See M. R. James, *Lists of Manuscripts formerly owned by Dr. John Dee*, List C, no. 153. It was originally a St. Albans manuscript and it contains a reference to Salerno on f. 22ᵛ.

scientific and medical codices that had been formed, up to that period, in England—many of the volumes being of English provenance. Other manuscripts in this library which contained Salernitan material, or other problems in natural philosophy, were: the remarkable Galba E. IV (*c.* 1200), a Bury St. Edmunds book, which contains, besides the pseudo-Soranic *Quaestiones medicinales*, edited by V. Rose,[1] Adelard's *Quaestiones naturales*, the *Premnon physicon* of Nemesius, in the translation of Alfanus, the pseudo-Galenic *De spermate*, translated by Constantinus, and a collection of short fragments and treatises on the elements, which Haskins thought originated in south Italy;[2] Cotton, Vesp. A ii (13) (XIV cent.), the *Solutiones* of Priscianus Lydus; Ashmole 1471 (31) (XIV cent.), the *Problemata* of Peter of Spain, described below;[3] St. John's Camb. 171 (G. 3), (XIII cent.), from St. Augustine's, Canterbury (no. 1485), William of Conches, *De philosophia mundi*, and another manuscript containing this work was James's List, T. 13. In addition, there were no less than four codices containing works by Urso of Calabria, all rather late in date;[4] and, indeed, the number of manuscripts of this author in English libraries is very remarkable.[5]

Dee's Library contained a surprisingly large number of volumes from St. Augustine's Abbey, Canterbury, which had probably come to him via John Twyne, who had procured them at the Dissolution. The cathedral priory of Christchurch also contained many scientific and medical codices, so that from the evidence of the manuscripts alone Canterbury might well have been another possible centre during the twelfth and early thirteenth centuries for the study of *physica*. For Christchurchth ere exists a list of the secular portion of the library, composed *c.* 1170,[6] but unfortunately the scribe has omitted the medical books.

Some idea of what there may have been, however, is afforded by the later catalogue, compiled in the time of Henry of Eastry (1284–1331).[7] This contains many of the volumes in the older list, and, indeed, the first part of the catalogue, which is arranged by subjects,[8] was thought by its

---

[1] See above, p. 9.   [2] Op. cit., pp. 93–95.   [3] p. 77.

[4] List C, 3 = Trinity 1154 (*c.* 1400), perhaps written in Flanders, but belonged to the Dominicans of London in 1421; C. 84 = Digby 71, transcribed by Dee himself in 1557; *Lists . . .*, p. 36 mentions Digby 192 (XIV cent.), which at one time contained works by Urso, and C.C. Oxf. 223 (XV cent.).

[5] I have noted the following, not counting the four Dee MSS.: Bodley 680 (2597) (XIII cent.), from Thorney; Digby 37 (XIV cent.), from Oriel Coll.; Digby 153 (XIV cent.), from the Franciscan convent at Canterbury; Digby 161 (XIV cent.), English provenance; Digby 206 (XIV cent.); Balliol 285 (XIII cent.), given by William Rede, bishop of Chichester; New Coll., Oxf. 171 (*c.* 1300); Oriel 28 (XV cent.); Trinity, Camb. 912 (R. 14. 40), iii. 4 (*c.* 1200); St. John's, Camb. 99 (D. 24), 17 (XIII cent.), from St. Augustine's, Canterbury; Peterhouse, 178. ii (XIII cent.) (*De Coloribus*, based on works by Urso); Brit. Mus. Royal 5. C. iii (XV cent.), formerly owned by Archbishop Cranmer and John, Lord Lumley; Sloane 75 (XV cent.); Arundel 295 (XIV cent.), German provenance; Gloucester Cath. 25 (XIII cent.), originally a Worcester book.

[6] Ed. M. R. James, *The Ancient Libraries of Canterbury and Dover*, pp. 1–12.

[7] Ibid., pp. 13–142.   [8] Nos. 1–502.

editor to refer almost entirely to the older portion of the library, as it existed up to about 1170. Under *physica* we get a list of fifty-nine codices, containing many more separate treatises. These consist of Graeco-Latin medical classics, the Constantinian corpus, herbals, lapidaries, and bestiaries, with a good proportion of Salernitan texts.[1]

The late catalogues, of the fifteenth and fourteenth centuries respectively, of St. Augustine's and Dover Priory, are also very rich in scientific and medical books.[2] It is impossible to say, of course, what proportion of these were early possessions, but they probably reflect a continuing tradition of studies in these subjects.

Quite large groups of medical manuscripts are also to be found in the libraries at Durham and Worcester, several dating from an early period, and including Salernitan texts.[3]

All this points to a considerable interest in *physica* centred in religious houses throughout England during the late twelfth and early thirteenth centuries. But at the moment we are lamentably short of information about the precise nature of such studies and about the men who took part in them at that time.

3. PARIS

In Paris the full development in scientific activity came late. Even before the time of Abelard (1079–1142) the Isle de France had become the chief centre in Europe for the study of theology and logic (the *artes sermocinales*), and although other subjects were included in the curriculum, such as those of the *quadrivium*, law, and medicine, they played but a minor part in the intellectual life of the city during the greater part of the twelfth century.

---

[1] These include the medical questions of Alfanus discussed above (488), the works of Gilles of Corbeil (446), the *Liber aureus* of Afflacius (453, 459), the *Passionarius* of Garioponto (5 copies, 462–6), *De regimine sanitatis* (475), *Practica Bartholomei* (464, 475), Trotula (475), Platearius (470, 476, 477), *Experimenta Salernitana* (476), Mag. Ferrarius, *De febribus* (477), *Antidotarium Nicholai* (477), Rogerinus (501), and *Questiones magistri Rogeri* (771). *Questiones de arte phisice* (513) may or may not be Salernitan. Two of these texts are almost certainly later than 1170, viz. the works of Gilles (466) and the *De reg. sanit.* (475).

[2] See M. R. James, op. cit., pp. 173–406 and pp. 407–95. Among these codices we note, in St. Augustine's, the questions of Mag. Lor(entius) (1236) noticed above and, again, other natural questions of doubtful origin (1423); and, in Dover Priory, Urso's *De effect. qualit.* (352), a *Quest. de phisica* (344), which from the identifying words appears to be Salernitan, and a *Questiones de naturis rerum*, in a volume of theology (211), which appears to be Adelard's *Quaestiones*.

[3] Three of the Worcester MSS. may have belonged to Bishop Mauger (1200–12), who had been personal physician to Richard I. See Floyer and Hamilton, *Cat. of Worcester Manuscripts* (1906), p. xii. No evidence exists pointing to friendly relations between this bishop and Neckam, although the latter was buried in Worcester Cathedral and was on good terms with Silvester de Evesham, bishop of Worcester at the time of his death. To the medical manuscripts in Floyer and Hamilton should be added Gloucester 25 (XIII cent.), which came from Worcester and contains works by Urso, see above, Brit. Mus. Addit. 25031 (XIII cent.), also a Worcester codex (see *Catalogus Lib. Manuscriptorum Bibl. Wigorniensis*, ed. P. Young and N. R. Ker, pp. 79–80), and Harley 5228 (XII–XIII cents.).

In Hugh of Saint-Victor's classification of the sciences,[1] theology was placed at the summit, *logica*, which included the whole of the *trivium*, was given a separate division, and the method or *ratio* of practical medicine was relegated to one of the mechanical arts; there was no explicit reference to theoretical medicine at all, although it was doubtless studied along traditional Hippocratic, Galenic, and Neoplatonic lines.[2] It is scarcely surprising, therefore, that the Victorine's approach to this subject was not made in that spirit of 'scientific humanism'[3] which was such a characteristic of the masters of Chartres. One tendency in Paris was for the more serious minded to use the material of *physica* for biblical exegesis and for teleological and mystical purposes, as we should expect, indeed, in the case of those who were primarily mystics and theologians.[4]

But there was another factor which retarded the advance of scientific progress. By the time of John of Salisbury, if not before, the passion for disputing had begun to get out of hand, and a wrong use of dialectic was beginning to invade all fields of study, both theological and secular.[5] In *physica* this led to the opposing camps of the theorizing *physici* and the practitioners, so scathingly denounced by John in the *Polycraticus*.[6] The other tendency, then, in this field, was for the younger and more irresponsible men to indulge in vain and empty speculations which led nowhere and were often, indeed, in opposition to the Faith.[7] By Godfrey of Saint-Victor's time things had not improved, and they may even have got worse, judging by the bitter lines[8] in his metrical *Fons philosophiae*, written in 1178, where he echoes the sentiments of John about the abuse of

---

[1] Given in *Didascalicon, Lib. II (P.L.* clxxvi, cols. 751 ff.).

[2] In *Didasc.* ii. 27, Hugh gives a brief description of medicine, which is sixth in order, in the *divisio mechanicae*. This description is based on traditional, entirely practical, medicine. But earlier on he had made it quite clear that only the *ratio* of the mechanical arts was included in philosophy, not the performance itself. 'Potest namque idem actus et ad philosophiam pertinere secundum rationem suam, et ab ea excludi secundum administrationem, verbi gratia . . . agriculturae ratio philosophi est, administratio rustici', col. 745. This theory or method of practical medicine is quite distinct from the theoretical medicine, anthropology, and physiology which had formed a part of *physica* since the time of Macrobius, in many classifications, and which was not directly concerned with medical practice.

[3] See Paré, Brunet, Tremblay, *La Renaissance du XIIe siècle*, pp. 194–7.

[4] For these uses of the *quadrivium* and *physica* see Hugh of Saint-Victor, *De sacramentis*, Prologue, ch. 6 (*P.L.* clxxvi, col. 185), quoted in *La Renaissance du XIIe siècle*, p. 234.

[5] See the excellent résumé in *La Renaissance*, pp. 197–206, 'Les Dialecticiens'.

[6] ii. 29. *P.L.* cxcix, cols. 475 ff.

[7] On the other hand all the disputations were not vain, and some useful work was probably accomplished. John had said 'Non enim omnes erroris arguo . . .', *Polycrat.*, loc. cit.

[8]　　　　　　　　　　'Hinc inflantur animi, surgunt acres ire:
　　　　　　　　　　　　Stultum dialectica facit insanire.'
Fons philosophiae, ed. P. Michaud-Quantin, p. 40, cf. John's
　　　　　　　　　　'Si quis credatur logicus, hoc satis est.
　　　　　　Insanire putes potius quam philosophari,
　　　　　　　　Seria sunt etenim cuncta molesta nimis,
　　　　　　Dulcescunt nugae, vultum sapientis abhorrent,
　　　　　　　Tormenti genus est saepe videre librum'.
Entheticus, ll. 116–20, *P.L.* cxcix, col. 967.

dialectic, and speaks very harshly about the followers of the mechanical arts.[1]

Towards the end of the century, however, an event took place which was, eventually, to lead to an improvement in the study of medicine in the French capital. This was the coming of the poet-physician, Gilles of Corbeil (*c.* 1140–*c.* 1224), from Salerno, after a short stay *en route* at Montpellier. Invoked by Gabriel Naudé as 'The first Genius and Tutelary God of the Faculty of Medicine',[2] he has long been considered as the founder and originator of medical studies in Paris; and one gains the impression, in reading histories of medicine, that before he came there was no study of that subject at all in that city.[3] This is, I think, to take his own verses much too literally.[4] It seems, however, that he found much the same state of affairs as John of Salisbury and Godfrey of Saint-Victor had found before him. In almost the very words of the former, he condemns the inexperienced tiro, returning from his studies too soon, to boast, wrangle, and dispute about *quosdam physicae nodos.*[5] So that, in bringing advanced Salernitan medicine to Paris, he must have given a new impulse to such studies, and helped to lay the foundation for the revival of science and medicine that took place there much later, in the next century.

Exactly when he came to Paris is a question that needs clarifying. Since the days of C. Vieillard, author of the principal book on Gilles, and V. Rose, his second editor, it has been customary to say that he arrived probably before 1175, certainly before 1181. Some facts have recently come to light,

[1]   'Cum venissem propius invenitur primo
            Locis in campestribus, pede montis imo,
            Quem dicunt mechanicum fons obductus limo,
            Ranarum palustrium sordidatus fimo.

            Dulces rudi populo quamvis sint lutosi,
            Quamvis sint insipidi, quamvis venenosi.'

Fons philosophiae, p. 36. He is, it is true, less severe against the followers of the mechanical arts in his later *Microcosmus* (ed. Ph. Delhaye, Lille, 1951), chs. 55, 56, 57.

[2] 'Primum vestrae Facultatis genium et tutelarem Deum, Aegidium Corboliensem.' Gabriel Naudé, *De antiquitate et dignitate Scholae Medicae Parisiensis*, quoted by C. Vieillard, *Gilles de Corbeil*, p. 37.

[3] e.g. 'Medical teaching went on there at least from 1210, when Gilles de Corbeil left Salerno to become physician to Philip Augustus', Castiglioni, *Hist. of Med.*, 1947, p. 328.

[4] See below, p. 70, n. 5.

[5]   'Medicum vitare decebit
            Qui novus et medicae rudis est tirunculus artis,
            Qui crudus de doctoris fornace recedens,
            Verborum lites sed nullos attulit actus:
            Gutture qui tumidus dum ventos garrit inanes,
            Assuetus quosdam physicae dissolvere nodos,
            Tactus avaritia, multum metuenda peritis,
            Curandi morbos excelsa negotia curat:'

De laudibus et virtutibus compositorum medicaminum, iii, ll. 549–56, ed. by L. Choulant in *Aegidius Corboliensis, Carmina medica*. Cf. John of Salisbury, *Metalogicon*, i. 4. *P.L.* cxcix, col. 830.

however, which make it appear that these dates are much too early. The evidence for the first date depends on lines 2347–8 of Gilles's *Viaticus*,[1] written after he came to Paris,

> Cessent manare fluenta
> fontis Adamatici, Parvipontana columna
> submissim deponat onus.

These lines were thought by Rose and Vieillard[2] to mean that Gilles had been a pupil of the famous English logician, Adam of the Petit Pont, or Adam of Balsham, the friend and counsellor of John of Salisbury, whom they further identified with that Adam who left Paris in 1175 to become bishop of St. Asaph. L. Minio-Paluello, however, in his recent paper on the *Ars disserendi* of Adam of Balsham,[3] shows clearly that the two Adams are not the same; the first dying perhaps before 1159, the second being not an Englishman but a Welshman, with no connexion with the Petit Pont, who died in 1181.[4] The other date, 1181, depends on the very intangible evidence of a passage in the first prologue to the *De laudibus*, where Gilles begs a certain 'Romoaldus' to look with favour upon this new work of his, and upon the inauguration of the study of *physica* in Paris.[5] Now De Renzi and, after him, Vieillard identify this person as Romualdus Guarna, archbishop of Salerno, who died in 1181.[6] On the other hand, as Vieillard has pointed out, a much more definite *terminus post quem* is afforded by Gilles's reference in Book iii to the sack of Salerno by Henry VI of Germany, an event which took place in 1194.[7] De Renzi and Vieillard got over this discrepancy between the two dates by supposing that the first book was written before 1181, and the third after 1194, more than twelve years later. But it would surely be much simpler to accept the fact that 'Romoaldus' does not refer to the archbishop, or that, if it does, Gilles was addressing his departed spirit—since in the same prologue he apostrophizes two Salernitan masters who were certainly dead at the time of writing, Platearius and Musandinus. Apart from this, however, an earlier passage, also in this first prologue, would seem to indicate that the whole work was finished when the latter was written. Addressing his book, he tells it to go forth into the world with a light heart and a firm step, since it is now grown-up and fully fledged, and it is no

---

[1] Ed. V. Rose.   [2] See Vieillard, op. cit., p. 441.

[3] In *M.R.S.* iii (1954), 116–69.

[4] See pp. 165–6.

[5]
> 'Ipse [Romoaldus] novo faveat operi, nec Parisianas
> Aestimet indignum physicam resonare camoenas,
> Nam logices ubi fons scaturit, ubi plenius artis
> Excolitur ratio, sibi physica figere sedem
> Gaudet, et ancillis non dedignatur adesse.'

De laud. . . . comp. med. i, ll. 140–4.

[6] See De Renzi, *Col. Salern.* iv. 569 ff., and Vieillard, op. cit., pp. 35 and 43 ff.

[7] Not 1193, as mentioned by Vieillard, op. cit., p. 43.

longer fitting that it should lie in a cradle fit only for stammering infants.[1]
By this far-fetched metaphor he must surely mean that the whole work
has passed beyond the stage of composition, and is now complete and
ready to be given to the world.[2] He would scarcely use these words in
relation to the first book only of the work, even if he published it separately,
and there is no evidence that he did do this.

The most reasonable hypothesis seems to be, then, that Gilles began his
De laudibus, at the earliest, a year or so before 1194, and finished it not
long after that date.[3] It follows from this that the commencement of his
medical lectures, implied in this poem, took place roughly during the same
period. He could not have been a pupil of Adam of Balsham, so that the
Adamatici of the poem, which, in any case, is only a conjecture of Rose for
the *adamantis* of one manuscript and the *adaratici* of another,[4] is either
wrong or, if correct, must refer to the school on the Petit Pont, perhaps
founded by Adam of Balsham many years before, of which Gilles calls
himself 'a column' (*Parvipontana columna*). It is not clear whether this
means that he was a master there or a pupil. The school was famous for
dialectic in the time of Godfrey of Saint-Victor, who greatly praises its
masters,[5] and it is possible that Gilles attended a course of lectures in the
artes there, before he started his own lectures in *physica*. On the other
hand, a medical school is known to have had its seat near or on the Petit
Pont at least by the middle of the thirteenth century,[6] and thus it is equally
possible that Gilles founded this particular school, and started his lectures
c. 1194, perhaps in or near the same building used by the masters in arts.

[1]
   'Vade liber felix. Nam cum provectior aetas
   Jam tua sit, densisque habeas pubescere plumis
   Dedecus esse potest puerili incumbere nido,
   Et cunas colere balbis infantibus aptas:
   I, cave ne titubes, firmo vestigia gressu
   Dirige, cum rectis habeas procedere talis.'
De laud. . . . . *comp. med.* i, ll. 58–63.

[2] Vieillard, for some extraordinary reason, thought that the *provectior aetas* referred to the
author as well as the poem, see op. cit., p. 43.

[3] De Renzi, while recognizing that the above-quoted lines could very well apply to the dead
Romualdus, op. cit., p. 572, based his main argument against the poem's having been commenced
after 1181 on its length, and on the fact that the reference to the sack of Salerno comes 2,167
lines after the reference to Romualdus. 'It is almost impossible', he says, 'that so many lines
could have been written contemporaneously', p. 574. But to put more than twelve years
between the two passages is, surely, to underrate the abilities of the poet. De Renzi was also
obsessed with the idea of putting the commencement of the *De laudibus* exactly in the middle
of Gilles's working life, which he supposed lasted from *c.* 1160 to his death *c.* 1224. Thus he
thought that the *De urinis*, *De pulsibus*, and the first two books of the *De laudibus* were composed
before 1181, and the last two books of the *De laudibus*, the *Viaticus*, and the *Hierapigra*, after
1193, op. cit., p. 574. It is true that the first two are early works and the last two late ones,
the *Viaticus* coming after the *De laudibus* and the *Hierapigra* being assigned to the period
1219–23, but I can see no valid reason why the *De laudibus* should be made to fill the whole
of the intervening period.

[4] See L. Minio-Paluello's above-mentioned paper, p. 165.

[5] *Fons philosophiae*, ll. 277–96.

[6] Minio-Paluello, art. cit., p. 165.

Another 'column' of the Petit Pont was Alexander Neckam (*Modici Pontis parva columna fui*),[1] but in his case we know that he studied the *artes* in Paris, besides civil and canon law, theology, and medicine, and he refers elsewhere to the dialectical subtleties of the Petit Pont.[2] Thus there can be little doubt that it was the arts school of the Petit Pont that he attended during his stay in Paris. The duration of this stay is not so easy to determine. But, according to Dr. R. W. Hunt, the latest scholar to examine the question, he began his studies there about 1175, when he would be eighteen years old, and left for England, to become master at Dunstable school, about 1182. Thus it now seems certain that he left Paris a long time before Gilles of Corbeil had started to lecture on Salernitan medicine. He says that he heard lectures on Hippocrates and Galen, *Audivi canones Hippocratem cum Galieno*;[3] perhaps, that is, on parts of that early *summa* of classical texts which had been available since the ninth and tenth centuries, and used as the basis of medical instruction in many ecclesiastical schools. The penetration of the prose Salernitan questions to Paris in the first half of the thirteenth century is well attested by the text of 141 of them, contained in Bibl. Nat. Lat. 18081, mentioned above (p. 37). This codex formerly belonged to the Cathedral of Notre-Dame and, as M. d'Alverney tells me, was written in Paris about 1230–40. With the rise of the university system, and owing to the greater emphasis laid on the study of theoretical medicine in the writings of such men as Gilles of Corbeil, Constantinus, and Gundissalinus, a separate 'faculty' was created for this subject *c*. 1213;[4] though, for some time, the natural sciences, which included medicine, continued to be taught in the faculty of arts, so that separation was by no means complete. In the medical faculty the components of the *ars medicinae*[5] probably formed the main basis for lectures and scholastic disputations. But there is evidence that the *physica* taught there and in the faculty of arts, in spite of an increasing Aristotelian bias, continued to draw inspiration from the Salernitan questions throughout the whole of the thirteenth century. We shall discuss this evidence in Chapter 6.

[1] *De laudibus divinae sapientiae*, ed. Thomas Wright, p. 503.

[2] 'Subtilitati Parvipontane veritatis aequiparetur', *De nominibus utensilium* in *A Volume of Vocabularies*, ed. Thos. Wright, 1857, p. 103.

[3] *De laudibus*, p. 503.

[4] It is not known exactly when this 'separation' took place. The earliest mention of a separate faculty for the study of medicine occurs in an agreement of 1213 which recognizes the right of each faculty to testify to the qualifications of candidates to the licence in its own department (Rashdall, *Univ.* i. 324). For a long time the medical faculty had no fixed domicile, the regent masters met in the churches, at first in Sainte-Geneviève-la-Petite or in the capitulary hall of the Convent des Mathurins, which remained an habitual place of assembly until as late as 1500. Instruction was given in the houses of masters and bachelors, and disputes took place in the dwellings of the disputants. Not until 1470 did the faculty acquire a house of its own in the Rue de la Bucherie (E. Wickersheimer, *Commentaires de la Faculté de Médecine*, pp. lix–lx).

[5] A name sometimes given to the Constantinian corpus, with the addition of Philaretus, *De pulsibus*, and Theophilus, *De urinis*, often found together in manuscripts.

5

Scientific Question Literature in Spain and at the Court of Frederick II

DURING the twelfth century the chief role played by Spain in the scientific renaissance seems to have been the diffusion, mainly to France and England, of Arab science and medicine in Latin translation, whereby arose in these disciplines a tradition which for some time remained entirely separate from that which came from south Italy.

Among these Spanish Arabic–Latin translations were no books of problems, in the strict, Aristotelian sense, but one very interesting work does make considerable use of the form of the *quaestiones et responsiones*, and proves yet another little-known, indirect source for the influx of Greek medicine and science into western Europe. This is the so-called *Liber Apollonii de secretis naturae*, translated from Arabic or Hebrew by Hugo of Santalla, perhaps before 1143.[1] J. Ruska has pointed out the affinities of the original work with the Hermetic *Emerald Table*, and suggested that this prototype was composed in Arabic, not before the sixth century A.D. and not later than about 750, when it was in the hands of the alchemist, Geber.[2] The interesting thing is, that, mingled with the oriental mysticism, astrology and alchemy, there is a high proportion of Greek science, which embraces the whole field of *physica*, as it was known in the twelfth century. The incipit of the translation shows the wide extent of the work, *Incipit liber Apollonii de principalibus rerum causis et primo de celestibus corporibus et stellis et plantis, et etiam de mineriis et animantibus, tandem de homine.*

---

[1] On this work see J. G. Wenrich, *De auctorum graecorum versionibus et commentariis Syriacis, Arabicis, Armeniacis, Persicisque Commentatio*, pp. 237 ff.; F. Nau, 'Une ancienne traduction latine du Bélinous arabe', *R.O.C.*, xii (1907), 99–106; Haskins, *Med. Science*, pp. 79 ff.; J. Ruska, *Tabula Smaragdina*, pp. 177–80; T. Silverstein, 'Hermann of Carinthia and Greek', *Studi in onore di Bruno Nardi*, ii. 697. Only one manuscript is known, Bibl. Nat. Lat. 13951 (XII cent.), ff. 1–31.

[2] Extensive extracts from the Arab version are given, in French translation, by de Sacy, *N.E.* iv (1799), 107–58, and this version is analysed by J. Ruska, op. cit., pp. 124–63. See also P. Festugière, *La Révélation d'Hermès Trismégiste*, i. 395 ff., who notes that the final Arabic form was composed *c.* 825 by a heterodox Mussulman, who published it under the name of Apollonius of Tyana. This name in Arabic, Bâlînûs Tûwânî, gave rise to numerous latinized versions such as Belinus, Bolinus, Balbinus, Belbetus, Belletus, &c. Several magical and alchemical works are ascribed to this author, see L. Thorndike, *H.M.E.S.* i. 267; ii. 234 and 282 f.; Steinschneider, *E.U.*, § 144; ibid., 'Apollonius von Thyana (oder Balinus) bei den Arabern', *Z.D.M.G.* xlv (1891), 439–46; and ibid., *A.U.* (1896), § 140.

A large part of the book is in the form of the *quaestiones et responsiones*, namely those sections dealing with plants, animals, and man, but, although several of the questions are the same as or similar to those dealt with by the Salernitan masters, Adelard, and William of Conches,[1] it does not appear that any of these were influenced by the *De secretis*, any similarity in doctrines and ideas being solely due to the fact that both drew upon Greek sources.[2] The question about the non-micturition of birds, one of the Greek questions dealt with by Adelard,[3] shows very well how this type of question was differently handled by the various compilers. Aristotle had said that birds lack bladders because they are dry in nature, drink little, and whatever moisture is present, when they do drink, is absorbed inwardly.[4] Pseudo-Alexander, said that they both lacked bladders and did not urinate because much moisture was needed for the formation and growth of the feathers, and absorbed through the continual vibration of the wings. But he added that their dung contained much moisture, thereby implying that, after drinking, they did get rid of some excess fluid by excretion.[5] The pseudo-Hippocratic *De cibis*, extant in Latin translation since the ninth century, gave the cause of these two characteristics, again, as absorption of the moisture, but this time induced by the excessive heat of their stomachs.[6] Adelard maintained that birds required no fluid for their nourishment, but that the little fluid that they did drink was solely for the lubrication of the dry substances which they consumed, and which would otherwise cause them pain and difficulty in swallowing. Therefore there was not enough fluid left to be excreted.[7] The Salernitan compiler, after pointing out that the lack of a bladder need not necessarily be a cause of non-micturition, since urine could be generated elsewhere, attributed the lack of excess moisture both to the dryness of birds and of their food, and to the fact that any moisture that is present helps to form the feathers— in this respect following pseudo-Alexander.[8] Finally, the *De secretis* states simply that both the urine and the faeces have the same exit, implying, as pseudo-Alexander had done, that the two products are mixed, and thus that birds only appear not to urinate.[9]

The extent of the influence of the Latin *Liber Apollonii* has not yet been

---

[1] Cf. 'unde viror in arboribus, quare decidant folia' (Bibl. Nat. Lat. 13951, f. 19ᵛ), 'unde fructus, unde folia, unde fiat cortex, unde fiat testa' (20ᵛ), 'de fructuum diversitate' (21), 'quare aves non mingant' (23ᵛ), 'unde mors in homine' (25), 'unde fiant cornua' (26), 'quare homo quod dulce est appetat, et amarum devitet, quare visus remotiora quam auris percipiat' (27), 'de fluxu capillorum' (29), 'de diverso parturiendi tempore' (30ᵛ).

[2] Another work attributed to Belinus-Apollonius, however, the *De sensibus*, extracts from which are found in the *De finibus rerum naturalium* of Arnold of Saxony, was perhaps known to the writer of the Salernitan metrical *Questiones phisicales*. See my notes to questions S. 71 and 95.

[3] See above, p. 25.

[4] *Prob.* x. 7. 891ᵇ. 18; *Hist. animal.* ii. 16. 506ᵇ25; *Part. animal.* iii. 8. 671ᵃ.

[5] *Prob.* (trans. Gaza), i. 106.   [6] Rose, *Anecdota*, ii. 151–2.

[7] *Quaest. nat.*, ch. 10.   [8] Auct. f. 148.   [9] f. 23ᵛ.

fully investigated. It was perhaps used by Hermann of Carinthia in his *De essentiis*, written in 1143 and dedicated to the Englishman, Robert of Chester.[1] On the other hand, it is curious that no trace of it appears in two, nearly contemporary, similar works, namely, Daniel of Morley's *De naturis*,[2] and the *Liber de VI rerum principiis*—although T. Silverstein has noted interesting parallels in subject-matter in the case of the latter.[3]

One of the translators from Arabic Michael Scot, after translating the *De animalibus* of Aristotle (1217–20), left Toledo *c.* 1224, and, after a few years spent in the service of the Popes, came to Palermo in or soon after 1227. There he remained, in the service of the emperor Frederick II (1215–50), until his death in 1236.

In the *magna curia* a very different atmosphere prevailed. Here was not merely the translation and interpretation of the works of others, but an extremely active, practical research and inquiry in the various branches of the natural sciences, stimulated by the continual curiosity and genuine interest of the emperor in these subjects.[4]

Perhaps here originated the custom of sending abroad lists of difficult questions for solution. One such collection, dealing with rather abstract, philosophical matters, the so-called *Sicilian Questions*, was sent by the emperor, *c.* 1237–42, to several eastern philosophers, before being finally answered by the Spaniard, ibn Sab'in.[5] Other sets of questions dealing this time with the mathematical sciences, geometry, astronomy, and optics, were sent to places as far afield as Mosul, Toledo, and Egypt.[6] Yet other questions were addressed by Frederick to Michael Scot, and these have survived as part of a comprehensive work by the latter on the natural sciences, and have been in part edited by Haskins.[7] They deal chiefly with theology, cosmology, and meteorology, with long digressions

[1] As T. Silverstein has pointed out, it is difficult to be certain that Hermann used the Latin text; but he certainly knew the work, either in the version of Hugo or in the original Arabic; 'Hermann of Carinthia and Greek', pp. 696 ff.

[2] The question about evergreens in the *De naturis*, which we discussed above, p. 58, occurs also in the *Lib. Apollonii*, where the answer is very close to that given by Isaac, *De diet. univ.*, and quite different from the solutions of Daniel and the Salernitan masters: 'Frigus enim in aere precellens, calorem ut qui contrarium vitabat in terram depulit. Arborum vero radices quia igneus ardor convalescebat calefacte, humorem in superioribus commorantem, ad depellendum contrarium et igneos vitandum calores, inferius attraxerunt. Aqua igitur in ramis ipsis decrescente, et folia perierunt. Quare alia perpetuo maneant. Quedam rursum arbores humoris redundancia iuvante, perpetuo frondibus ornantur propriis. Nam dum calor ignis in ipsis radicibus humoris multiplicem inveniret copiam, ut de supernis adminicula ducerentur nulla fuit necessitas. Sicque humor per universas arboris venas affluenter discurrens, quemlibet noxium depellens vaporem, ex sue equalitatis moderancia, ne arbor viduaretur foliis effecit.' Bibl. Nat. Lat. 13951, f. 20. Cf. Note C below, p. 207.

[3] In his edition of the work, *A.H.D.L.* xxii (1956), 219.

[4] See Haskins, *Med. Science*, chs. 12–14.

[5] Published by M. Amari, *J.A.* 5e ser. i (1853), 240–74, and, more fully, by A. F. Mehren, ibid. 7e ser. xiv (1879), 341–454. See Haskins, op. cit., pp. 264 ff., and Grabmann, *M.G.* ii, ch. 5, pp. 128 ff., where the reader will find an analysis of the questions and an appreciation.

[6] See Haskins, op. cit., p. 265, and the literature there cited.

[7] Op. cit., pp. 292–8.

about the earth, different kinds of waters, and metals. But much more interesting are the still unedited *Questiones Nicolai Peripatetici* ascribed to Michael by Albertus Magnus (*Meteora*, iii. 4. 26), and tentatively accepted as his by such scholars as Renan, Duhem, Haskins, and Birkenmajer.[1]

These questions, which, later on, were to be used a good deal by the great Paduan physician Peter of Abano,[2] deal with meteorology, botany, mineralogy, and alchemy, as well as medicine, anthropology, and dietetics, and they are chiefly remarkable for their extremely practical nature, and the description of several physical experiments.[3] We recognize a few of the questions as Salernitan,[4] but on the whole, they represent a later tradition which was more concerned with practical mineralogy and alchemy,[5] and exactly reflect the experimental nature of Frederick's inquiries.

On the death of Michael Scot, Theodore of Antioch succeeded him as court physician and astrologer, and a self-styled pupil of his was Petrus Hispanus, Peter of Spain, the future Pope John XXI (d. 1277), placed by Dante amongst the *sommi dottori* in the Heaven of the Sun, famous logician, and praised by Ptolemy of Lucca for his skill in medicine.[6] He

---

[1] Renan, *Averroes*, Paris, 1869, pp. 209 ff.; Duhem, *Système*, iii. 244 ff.; Haskins, op. cit., p. 279; Birkenmajer, *Le Rôle*, pp. 9 ff. The latter traced five manuscripts of the work, listed in *Aristoteles Latinus*, *codices descripsit*. See *Pars posterior*, index, p. 1334. To these should be added Bodl. Digby 153 (XIV cent.), ff. 168–74, Lincoln Cath. 113 (XIV cent.), ff. 146–56, Bibl. Nat. Lat. 7156 (XIV cent.), ff. 42ᵛ–48ᵛ, and Bibl. Nat. Lat. 16089 (*c.* 1300), f. 153ᵛ (fragment only).

[2] In his *Conciliator* finished at Padua in 1310.

[3] Cf. 'quomodo generatur sulphur et auripigmentum' (Bibl. Nat. Lat. 7156, f. 43), 'quomodo possint haberi rose in die nativitatis Domini' (43ᵛ), 'quare ventosa attrahit sanguinem' (43ᵛ, cf. the Salernitan Auct. 133ᵛ), 'quomodo sophisticatur aqua que videtur esse vinum' (43ᵛ), 'quomodo probatur si argentum habet cuprum admixtum' (44), 'quomodo caro decoquitur citius' (46), 'propter quod dulcia scito saturant' (46), 'quare turres cadunt propter sonum campanarum' (47), 'ad sciendum utrum in musto sit aqua' (47, a Salernitan question, see Pet. 178, ii, f. 14ᵛ and my note on *Questiones phisicales*, Q. 84), 'quomodo ex vino fit aqua ardens' (47ᵛ), 'quare differunt ligna decisa et pleniluno et in novissimo' (47ᵛ), 'quare minimum frigus in estate magis ledit corpus quam maximum in yeme' (48).

[4] Three meteorological questions are Salernitan, viz. those on the rainbow (42ᵛ), on the appearance of a circle round the moon (42ᵛ), and on the earthquake (43). Besides the two physical questions mentioned in the last note, the following is also Salernitan, 'quomodo de vino fit acetum' (f. 48, cf. Pet. f. 35 and Auct. f. 159).

[5] Other questions of this sort are: 'quomodo dealbatur auripigmentum vel sulfur ad facienda alia metalla' (f. 44), 'quomodo plumbum potest pulverizari' (45ᵛ), 'quomodo ex auro fit pulvis mutato colore. et hoc est etiam artificium quo utuntur saraceni in deferendo suum aurum de terra in terram . . .' (46), 'quare plumbum consolidatur stagno' (46ᵛ), 'quare alkimisti utuntur borace' (46ᵛ). These questions betray the Arabic origin of alchemy and are, perhaps, the earliest dealing with this subject to appear in Latin.

[6] The fundamental works for an account of his life and writings are: R. Stapper, *Papst Johannes xxi*, Thorndike, *H.M.E.S.* ii (1929), ch. 58; Sarton, *Introd.* ii (1932), 889–92; M. Grabmann, *M.G.* ii (1936), 124 ff.; ibid., *Schriften des Petrus Hispanus*, *S.B.A.W.* (1936), ix; E. Wickersheimer, *Dict. Biog.* ii. 638 ff.; P. M. Alonso, *Scientia Libri De Anima*, Madrid, 1941 (introduction and full bibliography); *Bibliografia geral portuguesa*, ii (1944), 167–394; *Revista portuguesa de filosofia*, viii (3), 1952, a special number devoted entirely to Peter to commemorate the 675th anniversary of his death; Diaz y Diaz, *Index script. lat. medii aevi hispanorum* (1959), 290–5.

was a voluminous writer, thirty-six works being listed by M. Alonso,[1] not including those mentioned by earlier writers, but not yet found. He wrote on logic, medicine, natural philosophy, and metaphysics, and his writings include many commentaries, 'scholastic' in form, on the Aristotelian *libri naturales*, the Constantinian corpus, and the *opera* of pseudo-Dionysius the Aeropagite—a remarkable achievement which places him in the very front rank of mid-thirteenth-century scholars. Unfortunately, very little is known about the details of his early life.[2] After studying logic at the Arts faculty in Paris under William of Shyreswood, he became a professor in the same faculty at Siena *c.* 1246–50, and possibly taught medicine there as well. Probably it was while he was at this place that he had literary relations with the emperor and his court, dedicating a letter on *regimen sanitatis* to Frederick, and composing a *Liber de oculo* at the request of his pupil, Gherardo di Sabionetta, who was a translator from the Arabic, employed by the emperor.

Now there is a series of non-scholastic questions, fairly common in medieval manuscripts, with the explicit, *128 Questiones secundum Magistrum de Yspania* in one manuscript, and actually ascribed to Peter in another.[3] There is no doubt, I think, that these are the hitherto unidentified *Problemata* listed among Peter's writings by Nicolas Antonio and Ptolemy of Lucca,[4] since literal transcriptions of most of the questions and answers are found incorporated in Peter's commentary on Aristotle's *De animalibus*.[5] This commentary, as far as is known, was the first to be written on this text, which had been translated by Michael Scot several years before, and to a certain extent it was

---

[1] In the bibliography prefixed to his edition of Peter's Commentary on the *De anima*, Madrid, pp. 13–25. This is six more than he had given in his earlier edition of the *Scientia libri de anima*, pp. 7–18.

[2] There is a completely unfounded tradition that Peter studied medicine at Montpellier, first mentioned by J. Astruc, *Mémoires pour servir à l'histoire de la Faculté de médecine de Montpellier*, pp. 303–5.

[3] Incipit, 'Queritur quare omne animal volatile sit' (Thorndike and Kibre, *Incipits* (1937), col. 557). I have traced the following nine manuscripts: Bibl. Nat. Lat. 7798 (XIV cent.), ff. 83–89, 'expl. 128 Questiones secundum Magistrum de Yspania'; Toulouse 220 (XIV cent.), ff. 237–45, with the titles of the questions in Catalan; Bodl. Ashmole 1471 (XIV cent.), ff. 169–73, 60 questions only; Milan, Ambros. N. 9. sup. (XIV cent.), ff. 115–28; Florence, Bibl. Nazionale Centrale, convent. soppr. J. IX. 26 (*c.* 1500), ff. 1–12, 'expl. problemata magistri Petri Yspani que sunt numero centum vigintiseptem'; Venice, Bibl. Marciana lat. f. a. 534 (Val. xiv. 59), (XIV cent.), ff. 26–31, 91 questions; Metz 296 (no. 9) (1458), destroyed in the last war; Würzburg Univ. M. p. med. f. 2. (XIII cent.) a fragment of two leaves only, described in I. Schwarz, *Die medizinischen Handschriften der kgl. Universitätsbibl. in Würzburg*, no. 49, p. 44; Breslau (Wrocław) Univ. Bibl. IV. Q. 158 (1414), ff. 254–85 (126 questions).

[4] Nicolas Antonio, *Bibl. hisp. vet.*, ii. 75–77, 'item 10, *Problemata*'. The list is reprinted by M. Alonso in his edition of Peter's *Scient. lib. de anima*, pp. 23–24. Ptolemy of Lucca, *Hist. eccles.*, xxiii. 21 (p. 1176), 'Fecit et librum de problematibus iuxta modum et formam libri Aristotelis'.

[5] The commentary, still unedited, is found in only one manuscript, Madrid, Bibl. Nacional 1877 (late XIII cent.), ff. 256–290ᵛ. It is described by Grabmann in two of his works, *Schriften des Petrus Hispanus*, S.B.A.W. (1936) ix, 100–2, and *Handschriften spanischer Bibliotheken*, S.B.A.W. (1928), v. 101–13.

scholastic in character, like Peter's other commentaries. The rigid, dialectical pattern, with statement of the question, discussion of the opposing arguments, and final solution, is not followed throughout, however, as it is, for example, in Peter's *Quaestiones de anima*.[1] In the majority of cases a passage from the Aristotelian text suggests to Peter, or perhaps to one of his pupils, a series of questions, which are then answered, one after the other, simply and without argument—the whole work obviously being based on lectures, perhaps those given by the master whilst he was at Siena.[2] It is a selection of these comparatively short *quaestiones et responsiones* which forms the *128 Questiones secundum Magistrum de Yspania*. Whether this text is a summary prepared by a pupil or the work of Peter himself are questions which will have to be decided later.[3] Perhaps the former alternative is the more likely one, since the answers are sometimes abbreviated, and the terminology not always quite so exact.

The collection continues exactly the tradition of the didactic Salernitan questions, several of which are found in these *problemata*.[4] But the answers show, again, a later development, and are influenced by the *De animalibus* of Aristotle and Avicenna, and of other Spanish translations. Thus the collection represents the next stage in the development of this kind of zoological and anthropological question, which took place after about 1232, the *terminus ante quem* for Michael Scot's translation of the *Abbreviatio de animalibus* of Avicenna.[5]

The presence of the Salernitan questions in Peter's commentaries[6] shows that, probably about 1250, they were being used in lectures on the *libri naturales* of Aristotle, and so were continuing to play an important part in the scientific education of the period—in spite of the tremendous spate of new material which had by then flooded the schools.

Finally, to mention yet another series of scientific questions connected with the *magna curia*, there are the *problemata* which, according to Albertus Magnus, were translated from the Greek for the Emperor Frederick by a certain 'magister David', 'cuius ratio est in quodam libro de problematibus

[1] Ed. by M. Alonso.

[2] See Grabmann's remarks to this effect, *S.B.A.W.* (1936), ix. 102.

[3] The collection never exceeds 128 in number, and the questions are always in the same order, so we have to do with a definite *opus* put together by someone in the thirteenth century, the date of the earliest manuscript, and frequently copied in the next century—not with a series of differing extracts, made at various later dates.

[4] Two of the manuscripts which I have examined contain a number of the old Salernitan questions and answers in addition to Peter's series, viz. Bibl. Nat. Lat. 7798, which has seven Salernitan questions at the end, after the explicit of the *128 Questiones*, and the Venetian Marciana lat. f.a. 534, which is preceded by a series of 34 Salernitan questions.

[5] See Note D, p. 207, for two Greek questions discussed previously by Adelard and the Salernitans which both show this development and illustrate Peter's way of dealing with this kind of question in the commentary.

[6] Still other Salernitan questions are found in Peter's voluminous commentary on Isaac Israeli's books on *Universal and Particular Diets*, printed in the Lyons 1515 edition of Isaac's *Opera* and discussed by Thorndike, *H.M.E.S.* ii. 502–10, where he lists several of the questions.

quibusdam quem transtulit quidam David imperatori Friderico de greco in latinum et incipit, "Cum essem in Grecia".[1] Now there are two texts known with this incipit, one fragment contained in Bodl. Digby 67 (XIV cent.), ff. 96v–97v, edited by Rose in 1886 among the *Fragmenta* of Aristotle,[2] and the other, a much fuller text, contained in Ghent 5 (1479), ff. 158v–183.

In 1932 Birkenmajer, who had earlier drawn attention to the works of 'Magister David' without naming any manuscripts,[3] pointed out that the fragment edited by Rose was by this master.[4] In the following year he announced the discovery of two more related fragments, clearly by the same author, one contained in Bibl. Nat. Lat. 15453 (1243), f. 215r–v, the other in Vienna, Nationalbibl. 4753 (XIV cent.), ff. 141r–143v, and showed that this author, the mysterious 'magister David', was none other than the well-known philosopher David of Dinant, whose writings had been included in the general condemnations of Aristotle's *libri naturales* made at Paris in 1210 and 1215.[5]

These manuscripts appear to represent four distinct works, namely, (1) Ghent, 5, ff. 158v–182v, which has the title *Liber de effectibus colere nigre in homine et de multis aliis dubiis determinatis per Aristotelem;* (2) ibid., ff. 182v–183, a sort of Prologue, incipit, *Aptideni commilitoni meo in gimnasio greco magister David salutem*, which corresponds to Bibl. Nat. Lat. 15453, ff. 215r–v; (3) the Digby fragment entitled *Quedam questiones naturales edite siue facte ab Aristotele;* (4) the Vienna fragment with the title, *Tractatus Adverrois de generatione animalium*.[6] The only two of these which contain questions are (1) and (3), which have the same incipits but different texts. Both are compendiums of Aristotelian learning, the Digby fragment containing ten problems based on the *Meteora*, and dealing mainly with winds, and Ghent 5 containing several taken again from the *Meteora*, and also from the *De animalibus*, *Physica*, *Parva naturalia*, and *Problemata*, the style being based on that of the latter work, and showing no trace of disputations or lectures.

A few of the questions are old favourites, particularly those dealing with sight, generation, and meteorology; but they are not influenced by the Salernitan masters, who also discussed them, and we look in vain for any of the typically Salernitan zoological and anthropological questions, such as we found were used by Peter of Spain. On the other hand,

---

[1] *Commentary on the Politics*, quoted by Birkenmajer, 'Découverte de fragments manuscrits de David de Dinant', *R.N.P.* (1933), 220–9.

[2] *Arist. Fragmenta*, pp. 183–8.

[3] In *Le Rôle*, p. 10.

[4] In *Classement des ouvrages attribués à Aristote par le moyen âge latin*, p. 11.

[5] In the article quoted in n. 1 above.

[6] M. Kurdziałek is at present preparing a complete edition of these fragments, of which he has already edited the anatomical and embryological sections found in the Ghent, Paris, and Vienna manuscripts. See his 'Anatomische und embryologische Ausserungen Davids von Dinant', *Sudhoffs Archiv*, xlv. 1 (1961), 1–22.

here and there we find echoes of Peripatetic lore which had been popularized by Adelard of Bath nearly one and a half centuries before, such as
the theories of the indestructibility of matter,[1] and of the nourishment of
like by like, particularly as it effects plants. In this latter case David compares plant nourishment with that of the body by the blood, in a manner
reminiscent of the Salernitan answer to this type of question, rather than
of Adelard's. But the common source is, almost certainly, the *Pantegni*
of Constantinus, since, like the latter, David mentions the example of
farmers who, in order to sweeten salt ground, plant therein salt-natured
herbs, which were supposed to extract all the salt from the ground for
their own nourishment.[2]

Another botanical question seems inspired by some work of Hippocrates,[3] but with these exceptions, both works are typical of that increasing interest in the Aristotelian *libri naturales*, which was taking place at
that time, and are particularly interesting, since, according to Birkenmajer, David used Greek texts of these books and not intermediate Latin
translations.[4] Certainly this must have been the case with the pseudo-
Aristotelian *Problems*, which were not translated into Latin until the
time of Frederick's son, King Manfred of Sicily (1258–66).[5] Two medical
works of his own are cited by David, neither of which has so far been
traced, the *De spermate*, and the *De anatomia venarum et arteriorum et ner-
vorum totius corporis*.

[1] Ghent 5, f. 162: 'Nam et antiquissimis philosophis visum fuit nullum corpus perire aut
alterari, sed elementales corporis particulas tantummodo congregari et disgregari.' Cf. above,
p. 23.

[2] Ibid.: 'Motus naturalis tamen videtur fieri similitudinis causa. Nam unumquodque vadit
ad simile sibi et ei coheret, huius autem indicium quod cum omnes humores cuiusque saporis
sint in terra seminaliter, et per minutias omnes quidem plante attrahunt a terra humores sibi
consimiles. Similiter autem et in sanguine animalis sunt particule cuiusque saporis, fumusque
sunt a sanguine resolutus, constat quod ex hiis omnibus particulis omnes partes corporis ad se
trahunt particulas sibi consimiles ab hoc fumo in totum corpus disperso, unde et coherentia
partium corporis videtur fieri similitudinis causa.' See also f. 164ᵛ: 'Queritur de omnibus
plantis qualiter nutriantur a terra. Dico quodlibet eorum attrahere partes similes a terra, quod
probatur quia si terra sit propter salsedinem sui infecunda, et inserantur salse herbe, fiet dulcis
et fecunda, salsis eius partibus habentibus nutrimentum salsarum herbarum, unde manifestum
est terram habere particulas cuiuslibet saporis, saporesque diversos inesse in fontibus et stagnis
a terra.' The questions resemble Adelard's chs. 1 and 4, but the answers are quite different,
being based on *Pantegni, Theor.* iv. 2.

[3] Ghent 5, f. 164: 'Querit ypocras quare in herbis prius crescat stipes et postmodum producitur
radix, in arboribus autem prius inter terram producatur radix quam subtollatur stipes a terra.
Dicit autem ypocras . . . .' It would be interesting to know David's source for this question,
which may have afforded him material for his other remarks about plant nourishment. The attribution to Hippocrates probably has reference to a spurious work.

[4] *Le Rôle*, p. 10.   [5] See below, p. 93.

6

Salernitan Questions in Scholastic Disputations of the Thirteenth and Fourteenth Centuries

DURING the thirteenth and fourteenth centuries the scholastic *quaestio* or disputation supplanted the older, traditional forms of question technique in the schools, and came to be, as F. Pelster put it, 'the very kernel and apex of the whole scientific instruction'.[1] But the older questions continued to form the basis for such disputations, both as regards the question itself and the summing up by the master, which was often, apparently, couched in the very words of the older answers. One witness for this we have already seen in the Peterhouse manuscript of the Salernitan prose questions, where the title, *Sollempnes*, probably means that the questions were used in a *disputatio ordinaria* held in a medical faculty.[2] In other cases the answers show a later development, both as regards subject-matter, such as the use of the Spanish Arabic–Latin translations, and technique, when the full *reportatio*, with all the arguments for and against, as well as the summing up, is given. Now these Salernitan questions are not only found in disputations held in medical faculties, but also, and to an even greater extent, in those connected with the faculties of arts and theology. Further, they occur not only in lectures and disputations on definite books, whether Aristotelian or belonging to the *ars medicinae*, but also, again to an even greater extent, in independent disputations *de quolibet*, about anything, not confined to the elucidation of particular books in the curriculum. As an example of the former variety, we have already discussed the questions of Peter of Spain, which resulted from his lectures on the Aristotelian *De animalibus*, but which are not strictly scholastic in the form in which we now have them. There are not many other examples of either variety which can definitely be attributed to the first half of the thirteenth century. The first indication that such questions were being used in the faculty of arts at Paris is to be found in an interesting list of questions contained in the still anonymous *De disciplina scholarium*, composed *c.* 1230.[3] In this treatise the author tells us about his

---

[1] A. G. Little and F. Pelster, *Oxford Theology and Theologians*, p. 29.
[2] See above, p. 36.
[3] There are many early printed editions, but the most convenient edition is that in *P.L.* lxiv,

experiences as a student in Paris, where he evidently attended the faculty of arts. Wishing to satirize the jargon of the students of his day, in much the same way as Rabelais was to do three centuries later, when he parodied the speech of the Limosin scholar, and also to show their inconstancy and waywardness, he gives a list of thirty-seven difficult questions—the sort of question with which such students were wont to occupy themselves, before quickly going on to something else.[1] These questions embrace theology, astronomy, astrology, element lore, meteorology, optics, mineralogy, anthropology, and zoology. The bulk stem from old-established Latin sources, or from astrological works translated from Arabic before the thirteenth century, and many had been discussed before by Seneca, Macrobius, Adelard, William of Conches, the Salernitans, and Alexander Neckam.

Typically Salernitan are three questions about the transferance of hereditary qualities in the foetus, and one about the migration of birds;[2] while other meteorological ones, such as those about earthquakes, thunder and lightning, and the temperature of wells in summer and winter, could equally well have come from Seneca or the Salernitans. Two things may be noted about the questions as a whole. In the first place, few are directly influenced by the new Aristotle. Three questions about the number of the heavens, the manner of their juxtaposition, and their movements contrast the opinions of Aristotle and those of the theologians—but that is about all.

It will be recalled that, at about the time the *De disciplina* was written, the ban on the reading of the Aristotelian *libri naturales* in the Faculty of Arts at Paris was still in force, and external evidence seems to confirm

cols. 1223-38. Discussions of the work will be found in F. G. Freytag, *Adparatus Litterarius* i. 250-4; Jean Porcher, 'Le *De disciplina scholarium*: traité du XIII⁰ siècle faussement attribué à Boèce', in *Positions des thèses de l'école nationale des chartes*; P. Lehmann, *Pseudo-Antike Literatur des Mittelalters*, pp. 27-28; Haskins, *Medieval Culture*, pp. 73-74; Grabmann, *Schriften des Petrus Hispanus, S.B.A.W.* (1936) ix. 5-6; A. Steiner, 'The Authorship of the *De disciplina scholarium*, *Speculum*, xii (1937), 81-84; E. P. Goldschmidt, *Medieval Texts and their First Appearance in Print*, pp. 24-27; F. van Steenberghen, *Aristotle in the West*, Louvain, 1955, p. 76. A critical edition is still very much to be desired.

[1] The author pictures the questions as being written in three zones on the *capacitas semicirculi Cratonis*, a curious phrase thus explained by the gloss in the Cologne (Quentell) 1493 edition, sig. D4, 'voluit studere questiones difficiles scriptas in sede Cratonis rotunda ad modum semicirculi multis depicta questionibus'. But who was Crato, and what exactly was meant by 'sedes', and why should the questions be written there? Has it any connexion with where questions for disputation were posted up before they were disputed in the appropriate faculty? The first zone was said to have seven questions and the second nine, but in these two zones there are seven subordinate questions; in the last zone the number of questions is fourteen, thus bringing the total up to thirty-seven. The passage containing the questions is found in ch. 3 (*P.L.* lxiv, col. 1229).

[2] 'Cum unum generantium sit album et aliud nigrum, quare generatum ex his album et nigrum non est, et quare generatum quandoque in extremitatibus assimilatur patri, in caeteris parturienti, quandoque neutri generantium.' Cf. the Salernitan question, 'Quare fetus aliquando formam accipiat patris, aliquando matris, aliquando utriusque.' (Auct. f. 137.) 'Quae sit natura pennatorum estivalium, in hyeme deficientium, et conversim.' Cf. ll. 67-68 of the *Speculator*.

that these books were neither commented upon nor lectured on during the period *c.* 1210–*c.* 1240. These questions suggest that the gap in the curriculum may have been filled, not only by an increased study in logic and ethics,[1] but also, to some extent, by independent lectures or disputations in *physica*, which were less exclusively Aristotelian, less controversial in character, and more eclectic and universal. In the second place, a special importance seems to have been attached to the questions themselves, judging by the number of elucidations and commentaries which exist in connexion with the questions only[2]—apart from the mass of larger commentaries on the entire work.

In another early collection of independent scholastic questions in *physica* we are more fortunate in having the determinations as well. This series, contained in two manuscripts of English provenance,[3] has every appearance of having been composed in the first half of the century, rather than in the second, and is almost certainly of English origin. It has the title, *Questiones naturales arti phisice competentes*,[4] and contains 48 questions, not including 5 repeats, of which 31 deal with medicine and anthropology, 6 with zoology, 3 with element lore, 3 with *experimenta*, 2 with meteorology, 2 with botany, and 1 with astronomy. Both the wording of the title and the preponderance of medical questions, as well as its association with other purely medical tracts in both manuscripts, indicate that the disputations were held in connexion with the study of medicine in particular, rather than with that of a more general, Aristotelian *physica*, as taught *in artibus*. It will be noted that the questions cover exactly the same field as do those of the *Quaestiones naturales* of Adelard, composed early in the twelfth century. In fact seven of them correspond to those asked by the English philosopher, and three of the answers to these resemble, more or less exactly, the solutions of Adelard. Sixteen questions are Salernitan, and here, too, a few of the answers resemble those provided by the Salernitan masters, although a completely different wording is used.

Now not all the questions are disputed at length, with arguments for and against; some have only the brief determination of the master, and amongst this latter variety are nine which are literal transcriptions from

---

[1] See F. van Steenberghen, op. cit., ch. 5, and particularly pp. 100–8.

[2] The earliest of such commentaries on the questions that I have found is contained in Basel O. IV. 35, a codex which in 1282 had belonged to the south German monastery of Rottweil on the Neckar, and was written about the mid-thirteenth century. The commentary occupies ff. 76ᵛ–77 and has the incipit 'Nota quod chrato habuit quamdam sedem' (Th. and K. 1942, 357, with the reading *thraco*). It is unfortunately incomplete, dealing with the first eighteen questions only. Other commentaries are found in Arundel 52 (*c.* 1300), ff. 58–62, by William of Wheatley, in Budapest Mus. Nat., cod. lat. 247 (1431), ff. 1–4, and Klagenfurt, Studienbibl. cod. pap. 21 (1464), ff. 201ᵛ–213. Also the determinations on the questions by Raymundus Palasinus were published in the Lyon 1510 edition of the *De consolatione* of Boethius, which also contained the *De disciplina* with the commentary of Badius Ascensius.

[3] Bodleian, e Mus. 219 (XIII cent. late), ff. 141–145b and Merton 324 (XV cent.), ff.144–150ᵛ.

[4] Incipit, 'Omnia corpora ex quatuor elementis' (Th. and K. 1937, 462).

the *Vetustissima translatio* of ancient Greek problems, as regards both the question and the answer. Thus again we notice that mixture of two techniques which we found in the commentary of Peter of Spain on the *De animalibus*, and which was, in fact, to continue until the end of the scholastic period. In the medical questions use is made of the *Tegni* of Galen, of the *De pulsibus* ascribed to Philaretus, and of other components of the *ars medicinae*. Two questions dealing with the action of heat in digesting food and in dispersing the products of disease almost certainly stem from Urso's *Aphorisms* and glosses, and two more which discuss the intension and remission of qualities are probably from the same source, and foreshadow the overwhelming interest in this particular subject which was to be a feature of the school associated with Merton College in the following century.

The Adelard–Salernitan tradition had been strong in England, as we have seen, while the absence of such subjects as mineralogy and alchemy, and, in particular, of any direct influence by the 'new Aristotle', points to an early date. The use of the *Vetustissima translatio*, instead of Bartholomew's translation of the pseudo-Aristotelian *Problems*, made between 1258 and 1266, is not conclusive, since, as we shall see, the latter does not appear to have been much used in the north before the end of the century, and it was certainly not widespread until after 1300.

Sometime in the second quarter of the thirteenth century all opposition to the study of the Aristotelian scientific books collapsed in Paris, and lectures and disputations on them began to be held in the faculty of arts once more. Roger Bacon, who may have been preceded by Robert Kilwardby, began to lecture there about 1245, and his questions on these books are the earliest, belonging to this period, that have so far come to light. Unfortunately his questions on the *De animalibus* have not been found, and so no comparison is possible with the zoological Salernitan questions, or with those in the commentary of Peter of Spain on this book, written at about the same time that Bacon was lecturing. In the case of the *Quaestiones de plantis*,[1] however, it is possible to see Bacon's contribution to questions which had interested Adelard, William of Conches, and the Salernitans. A series of nineteen questions in this work dispute about the nutrition of plants in true scholastic fashion, and another eleven deal with the problem of grafting. As one would expect, Bacon adopts the peripatetic viewpoint of Adelard, depending on the theory of nourishment of like by like, and the actions of the elementary qualities, which for him, as for the latter, are the principal factors in the two processes. But it is interesting to see how Bacon's much wider knowledge of the *libri naturales* and stricter use of Aristotelian dialectic make him reach conclusions quite different from those expressed by the earlier philosopher. Thus, although he agrees with the latter that plants of different complexions require

[1] Ed. R. Steele and F. Delorme, *Opera hactenus inedita*, fasc. xi.

different kinds of nourishment, suitable to the predominating elementary qualities, he differs from Adelard, and, incidentally from the Salernitans, in maintaining that a graft will not grow on a stock of completely different complexion—basing his argument on the Aristotelian definitions of 'contrariety' and 'diversity'.[1] Again, and for the same reasons, Bacon was moved to ask questions about these subjects which had not occurred to the earlier writer, such as whether the stock and the graft obtain new souls after grafting, whether the nature of the stock is changed into that of the graft, or vice versa, and whether the two make one according to essence and number. Both the different answer and the new questions show a logical and ontological treatment which had not been attempted before, though it is questionable whether, in this case, such treatment was an improvement on the more practical approach of the Salernitans to what were, after all, essentially practical problems.[2]

In the second half of the century the use of Salernitan questions became much more widespread. Several, for instance, are found in the *Quaestiones super De animalibus* of Albertus Magnus, the reports of his lectures on the *De animalibus* given at Cologne in 1258.[3] Less metaphysical and dialectical than the questions of Bacon, these questions are closely modelled on Peter of Spain's commentary on the same book, many of the questions are the same, and the technique, with its mixture of disputations and simple *quaestiones et responsiones*, exactly similar. The determinations of the Salernitan questions used by Albert as a rule closely resemble the answers given by the Salernitan masters. Sometimes he amplifies these, and discusses opposite points of view, and in a few cases he supplies a different answer, not always an improvement on the earlier, Salernitan one.[4]

[1] 'Diversitas in specie quedam facit quandam diversitatem, quia contrarietas est inter album et nigrum, diversitas est inter album et dulce, et magis conveniunt album et nigrum quam album et dulce; et contrarietas facit ad transmutationem sicut patet in elementis, diversitas non; et quia diversitas est inter plantas, ideo non potest aliquando una in aliam transmutari', *De plantis*, p. 250. Cf. Adelard, *Quaest. nat.*, ch. 6; William of Conches, *De philosophia*, iv. 7; Pet. 16ᵛ, Auct. f. 156ᵛ. See above, pp. 23, 52.

[2] For a discussion of Bacon's methods, illustrated by examples taken from the *De plantis*, see S. C. Easton, *Roger Bacon and his Search for a Universal Science*, pp. 62–66.

[3] Ed. E. Filthaut, *Opera omnia Alberti Magni*, xii. This work must not be confused with Albert's *De animalibus Lib. XXVI*, which is not in question form, and which was written later, between 1262 and 1268.

[4] Thus, in seeking to explain the supposed poisonous properties of human saliva, Albert put forward the extraordinary idea that anything which is in its proper place (*in ordine*) is friendly (*amicabile*), but out of its place (*extra ordinem*) harmful (*inimicabile*). Thus blood inside the body is friendly (innocuous) but outside it harmful, which is proved by the fact that if an ox looks at his own blood outside his body, he becomes mad (*incidit in rabiem*), 'quod probavi Coloniae semel coram fratribus'. The same thing applies to human saliva, which is very harmful to the human body when outside it. Lib. VII, qu. 39 (ed. cit., p. 187).

The Salernitans maintained that not everyone's saliva was poisonous, but only that of a person who had either been conceived during a menstrual period or been nourished during infancy with corrupt milk, or had been fed during his youth on bad food. Also the saliva had to be that of a fasting person, a good meal dulled the action of the poison: Auct. f. 122ᵛ, Pet. f. 15ᵛ. Both Albert and the Salernitans mentioned, in this connexion, the custom of archers who anointed their arrows with their own saliva in order to make the wounds more deadly.

Also, as in some manuscripts of the *Problemata* of Peter of Spain, we find a series of Salernitan questions added to three of the manuscripts of Albert's *Quaestiones*.[1] These, twenty-four in number, have been annexed to Lib. IV by the editor.[2] Twenty-one of them are literal transcriptions from the Salernitan collection, six of these stemming from the *Questiones mag. lorentii*. In two questions the answers are similar, but the wording is different, and in one other, part of the answer is different. But I think there is little doubt that the whole group belongs to that early family of Salernitan questions whose history we are tracing, and that these questions must now be added to the list of those not by Albert, given in the *Prolegomena*.[3]

A similar state of affairs existed in the medical faculties, where the Salernitan questions continued to inspire lectures and disputations on the components of the *ars medicinae*. A good example, belonging to this period, is the commentary of Taddeo di Alderotto (1223–95) on the *Isagoge of Ioannitius*,[4] the result of disputations probably held at Bologna *c.* 1277, which contains many such questions.

Two other independent, quodlibetical disputations, which are probably medical, are particularly interesting, as they show the continuation of the Adelard–Salernitan tradition, which we have so often noticed, in England. The first is contained in Brit. Mus. Royal 12. B. XII, a composite medical manuscript from the Arundel–Lumley collection, part of which came from Newark Priory in Surrey.

The questions with which we are concerned occupy ff. 102ᵛ–104ᵛ, and are written in a small, neat English court hand of the second half of the thirteenth century.[5] There are twenty-nine of them, and of these, eighteen deal with medicine and anthropology, four with zoology, three with element lore, two with botany, one with astronomy, and one, which discusses a method for making meat tender, could be put under the heading of *experimenta*. Again it will be noted that the field covered is the same as that which we found in the earlier, Bodleian collection (e Mus. 219), which had been determined by the *Quaestiones* of Adelard of Bath. But in this case only two questions remind us of those discussed by the Englishman, namely those which deal with the nourishment of like by like, and the process of grafting, and only four questions are Salernitan.

The chief differences are the more elaborate pattern of argumentation developed in some of the questions, and the greater quotation of authorities. Among these we find Aristotle, and indeed the whole tone of the collection is much more Aristotelian than that of the earlier one, and there is direct

---

[1] Listed on p. xxxviii of Filthaut's *Prolegomena*. The manuscripts are the three best ones.
[2] Ed. cit., pp. 148–53.
[3] p. xlv.
[4] I have used the edition of Venice, 1527.
[5] The incipit is 'Queritur utrum fleobotomia precedat farmaciam' (Th. and K. 1937, 755).

influence by the *libri naturales* (*De animalibus*). In the medical questions much use is made of the Constantinian corpus of translations, with quotations of Galen, Isaac, and Constantinus. But the name that occurs most frequently is a certain 'magister Egidius', who furnishes most of the determinations. Warner and Gilson tentatively suggest Gilles (Egidius) of Corbeil,[1] but I think that this would be dating the collection much too early, the probability being that the disputations took place, roughly, at about the time the manuscript was written.

A shorter late-thirteenth-century collection is contained in Bodley 679, a manuscript which formerly belonged to St. Augustine's, Canterbury, and which was given to the library by Thomas Twyne in 1612. The contents are miscellaneous and include the *De divisione philosophiae* of Gundissalinus, the *De sphera* of Sacrobosco, a *compotus* by Grosseteste, the *De philosophia mundi* of William of Conches, the *Quaestiones* of Adelard, the *Imago mundi* of Honorius of Autun, and tracts on medicine, the five senses, alchemy, and canon law. The questions occupy ff. 101–103ᵛ, and have the incipit *Quaestionis titulus fuit de motu humorum*. The first deals with the humours of the body, then come three questions about the stomach, followed by four about drunkenness. All these are argued at considerable length, and Galen and Avicenna seem to be the chief authorities. Right at the end there is a group of four Salernitan questions with extremely abbreviated answers, presumably consisting of the determinations only, one of which had been discussed by Adelard.[2] This interesting manuscript shows once more, then, the continuation of the Salernitan tradition in England, that combination of two techniques which we have noticed several times already, and the lasting influence of Adelard, here shown, not so much by the extent of the field of inquiry and the inclusion of one of his questions, as by the juxtaposition, in the manuscript, of his complete work.

The extent to which Salernitan questions were being used in the second half of the century is also shown by the frequency of their occurrence in *Quodlibeta* belonging to the theological faculties—a kind of scholastic exercise which probably indicated, better than any other, the general intellectual temper of the day, and what questions agitated the minds of those who moved in university circles, as Glorieux has pointed out.[3] Thus we find in the *Quodlibeta* of such famous masters as Richard of Middleton, Roger Marston, Gilles of Rome, Godefroid de Fontaines, and James of Viterbo such Salernitan questions as, whether birth in the eighth month is

---

[1] *Catalogue of Western Manuscripts in the Old Royal and King's Collections in the British Museum*, 1921, ii. 14.

[2] The question is the one about ruminants rising hindquarters first, see above, p. 38. The answer combines ideas obtained from Adelard and the Salernitans.

[3] In the introductions to his two volumes of *La Littérature quodlibétique de 1260 à 1320*. The excellent subject indexes show how wide is the field covered by the *quodlibeta*.

as good as that in the ninth or seventh, whether a wise father generally begets a foolish son, why the tall are dull, the short quick-witted, why one laughs about trifles but not about serious matters, why wounds bleed in the presence of the murderer, why men go bald, and have beards, but women are without these characteristics, whether whole or finely divided foods are better for eating, and questions about vision, optics (the formation of images in mirrors), the actions of lightning, fascination, and sleep-walking. All these are disputed with the full and elaborate technique of the *Quodlibeta*, which about this time had reached the very apogee of their development—a far cry, indeed, from the simple *quaestiones et responsiones* of the earlier masters.

Towards the end of the century another *liber naturalis* became a fruitful source of subjects for scholastic disputation; this was the pseudo-Aristotelian *Problems*, which, although translated earlier, does not seem to have been widely used much before *c.* 1300.[1] About this time, particularly in Paris, there was a tendency in the arts faculty to discuss questions which were less abstract and more down to earth and practical. This was due, not only to the increased circulation of the more practical Aristotelian and pseudo-Aristotelian books, but also to certain other more subtle factors, such as the growing realization that many metaphysical problems could not be satisfactorily solved by purely rational methods, that faith was better in such cases, and, secondly, that the subjects of natural science could best be investigated by reference to natural principles and causes, and through evidence supplied by the senses.[2]

A particularly interesting witness to this state of affairs is the precious codex Bibl. Nat. Lat. 16089, first described by Hauréau in 1896,[3] and more recently, though much more briefly, by Duhem.[4] This manuscript, which once belonged to the Sorbonne, and was written *c.* 1300, contains many questions about natural science (*physica*), some with only the brief determination of the master, others debated at greater length. The names of four of the masters who determined are mentioned; they are, Henri de

---

[1] *c.* 1263 Roger Bacon referred to it as one of those Aristotelian books which is neither commonly known nor completely translated: *Communia nat.*, ed. Steele, *Op. hact. ined.* ii. 12. Also in the *Opus Majus*, completed by 1267, he refers twice to the obscurity of the translation of the *Problems* (ed. J. H. Bridges, ii. 56 and 109), and there is another reference to them in the *Communia math.*, ed. Steele, *Op. hact. ined.* xvi. 5. The quotations in the last three references occur in Bartholomew's translation of the *Problems* made between 1258 and 1266, so there is little doubt that it was to this translation that Bacon was referring and not to the *Vetustissima translatio.* Albertus Magnus does not quote the *Problems* at all in his *Quaest. super De animal.* (1258), and in his later *De animal.* III, 121, *De motib. animal.* I, 2, cap. 5, and *Ethica* VII, 2, cap. 5, he has only indirect references to the subject of Arist. *Prob.* XXX. 1 (953[a]).

[2] Implicit in the teaching of Siger of Brabant, these opinions were stated much more clearly and succinctly by his follower Boethius of Dacia in his *De mundi aeternitate* (before 1277), ed. Geza Sajo. See, in particular, pp. 106 ff. and 68 ff. The discussion of theological questions, 'as concerning the Trinity and incarnation and similar matters', had been forbidden in the faculty of arts since the statute of 1272, *Chart. Univ. Paris,* i, no. 441.

[3] *N.E.* xxxv. 1 (1896), 209–39.   [4] *Système,* vi (1954), 536–42.

Bruxelles, Henri Allemand, Jean Vate, and a certain Ulricus,[1] all of whom taught in the faculty of arts in Paris at the end of the thirteenth or beginning of the fourteenth century.

Out of about 293 questions, not more than ten deal with abstract, Aristotelian physics and metaphysics, and only two deal with the soul or intellect. The questions, as a whole, are almost entirely confined to mundane subjects, such as anthropology and medicine, zoology, botany, mineralogy and alchemy, *experimenta*, meteorology, and geography. There is quite a high percentage of Salernitan questions, but much more emphasis is laid on experiment and alchemy, a subject not discussed at all by the Salernitans. It is, therefore, scarcely surprising that the collection should be influenced by the practical *Quaestiones Nicolai* of Michael Scot, and in fact a fragment of this work is included in the manuscript,[2] and at least one question in the series we are discussing comes from this source.[3]

In another case we find improved observation combined with a practical result in connexion with a Salernitan question which had hitherto been discussed solely from a theoretical point of view. The question was the one which asked why ruminants rise hindquarters first, dating from the time of Adelard, whose opinion about it we have already compared with that of the Salernitans.[4] For the first time it is now pointed out that the animal first kneels before rising, and that, therefore, strictly speaking it neither rises completely hindquarters first nor fore-part first, but chooses a middle way, which, as is this time stressed, it finds easiest and most natural. A practical result of this is that in cattle stalls the front part of the floor is raised to a higher level than the back, 'so that nature, in her workings, may be helped by art'.[5]

The specifically Aristotelian questions are mostly in connexion with

---

[1] Identified by Duhem with Ulrich of Strasbourg, op. cit., p. 538, but this Dominican died at Paris in 1278, P. Glorieux, *Répertoire des maîtres en théologie de Paris au XIIIᵉ siècle*, I, no. 39. He was thus not a contemporary of the other three masters, who were all active after 1289; Duhem, op. cit., pp. 537–8.   [2] f. 135ᵛ.

[3] Namely the question which describes the experiment of growing roses at Christmas time, f. 76. Other questions of an experimental nature are: whether a bladder full of air weighs more than an empty one, f. 62, a question concerning the making of gold *per artem*, f. 62, and another which refers to the testing of must by immersion of an egg, f. 75, a Salernitan question, Q. 84, Pet. f. 14ᵛ, also found in the *Quaestiones Nicolai*.   [4] See above, p. 38.

[5] 'Dico quod perfecte prius surgit retro quam ante, tamen prius ponit se ad genua ante quam surgat retro. causa huius potest esse quia natura in omnibus natura consistentibus facit quod melius est et commodius de possibilibus in natura unuscuiusque, ut apparet 2° de celo et 2° physicorum. nunc autem ita est quod vacca isto modo surgit commodius cuius ratio est quia partes eius posteriores sunt multum ponderose, ut patet ad sensum. habet enim ventrem valde magnum secundum quantitatem sui corporis, et ideo si prius surgeret perfecte ante quam surgeret retro, de difficili posset partes posteriores levare. et si perfecte prius surgeret retro quam aliqualiter surgeret ante, de difficili posset surgere ante. et ideo medio modo in surgendo se habet, ut secundum quod possibile est in sua natura surgat commodius. et ideo videtur quod in stabulis vaccarum loca anteriora fiunt alta, et posteriora bassa, et hoc ut natura sic per artem adiuta possit operari', f. 85ʳ.

the *Problems* and the *De animalibus*, nearly all of the last, or fifth, series of thirty-six anonymous questions quoting references in these works.[1] But the first series of ninety questions[2] disputed by Henri de Bruxelles and Henri Allemand, and the second, anonymous one of seventy-six questions,[3] are both disputations *de quolibet*, as we learn from the explicit and the title respectively,[4] and the third and fourth series of questions by Jean Vate[5] and magister Ulricus[6] seem to be of the same nature. In all these *Quodlibeta* the *Problems* and *De animalibus* continue to inspire some of the questions.

These interests are also found in the medical faculty, although, as one would expect, the questions debated there tended to become much more exclusively medical and anthropological than those discussed in the other faculties. This is the characteristic of perhaps the best example of in-dependent disputations, *de quolibet*, in medicine that has survived from that period—namely the vast *Conciliator* of the Paduan physician, Peter of Abano. Although finished at Padua *c.* 1310, this work is almost certainly partly the fruit of Peter's attendance at the medical faculty in Paris, during his stay in the city from *c.* 1290 to *c.* 1305.[7]

Six questions about the elements are related to Aristotelian physics, but there are no metaphysical, cosmological, or geographical questions, and very few dealing with other branches of *physica*, such as mineralogy, botany, and zoology, apart from their connexion with dietetics and pharmacology. Several of the questions had already been disputed in the *quodlibeta* of famous theologians, others are Salernitan, and like the masters in the arts faculty, Peter freely quotes the pseudo-Aristotelian *Problems* and the *De animalibus*. He was particularly fond of the former work, in connexion with which he had completed both a translation and a commentary by 1310.

The *Conciliator*, then, set the pattern for numerous medical *Quodlibeta* which continued to be disputed and set down throughout the fourteenth century by such physicians as Julian and Albert of Bologna, Dino del Garbo of Florence, and Gentile da Foligno, the self-styled 'fons scientiae medicinae et naturalis philosophiae'.[8]

---

[1] ff. 81v–85v.

[2] ff. 54–61v. Not eleven questions, as stated by Duhem, op. cit., p. 356.

[3] ff. 61v–65.

[4] 'Expliciunt quelibet magistri H. de Brucella et magistri H. Alamanni. Questiones de quolibet: Iª fuit utrum . . . .'   [5] ff. 74–75v, fifty-nine questions.

[6] ff. 75v–76v, thirty-one questions, followed by one question, bringing the total up to 293. Fols. 76v–81 are taken up with *sophismata*, of which one is by Peter of Auvergne, who was a *magister regens* in Paris from 1296 to 1302. He died in 1304.

[7] Ferrari's conjecture that this work was finished in 1310 or even later, and not in 1303 as was formerly thought, is now generally accepted. See Sante Ferrari, 'Per la biografia e per gli scritti di Pietro d'Abano', *M.R.A.L.*, ser. v, vol. xv (1918), 665–73, Sarton, *Introd.* iii. 1, p. 439, and A. C. Crombie, *Grosseteste*, p. 77, n. 4.

[8] For lists of these *quodlibeta* see Thorndike, 'Vatican medieval medical manuscripts', *J.H.M.* viii (1953), 263–83. All the manuscripts he discusses are fourteenth-century or later.

Again, in the arts faculty, the recent attention paid to developments in Aristotelian physics which took place during this century has tended to overshadow the fact that the interest in other branches of natural philosophy, such as the biological sciences, mineralogy, including alchemy, and meteorology, continued unabated. The *Quodlibeta* of Nicole Oresme, for instance, composed *c*. 1370,[1] cover exactly the same ground, and depend on the same sources, as do those in Bibl. Nat. Lat. 16089,[2] and so do those in another series, copied in 1396, and found in a manuscript in company with works by Oresme, Henri de Hesse, Albert of Saxony, and Jean Buridan.[3]

[1] Described by Thorndike, *H.M.E.S.* iii, ch. 27, who used the manuscript in Florence, Bibl. Medicea Laurenziana, Ashburnham 210 (xv cent.). Only the first forty-three problems, listed on ff. 39–40, are disputed in full (ff. 44ᵛ–70ᵛ); the rest, found on ff. 40–44ᵛ, are either simply stated, or have a minimum of discussion.

[2] Medical questions concern the five senses, digestion, nutrition, and generation. A number concern the powers of the soul, dreams, speech, imagination, habit, and other aspects of psychology in which, it appears, Oresme was particularly interested. Others deal with how birds understand each other, the instinct of animals, the causes of tides, magnetism, and the tempering of iron and steel. These subjects represent aspects of Oresme's activity which have not yet been adequately dealt with.

[3] Bibl. Nat. Lat. 2831 (1396), ff. 93–102ᵛ, 'Quedam quolibeta naturalis philosophie', consisting of 126 brief questions and answers, probably the determinations only. Many of the questions are Salernitan. See Duhem, *Système*, vii. 574 ff. For a typical Salernitan question stemming from the *Nicomachean Ethics* and discussed by Buridan and other scholastics, see below, pp. 151 ff.

7

Medieval and Renaissance Translations of Greek Problems, and some Fourteenth- and Fifteenth-Century Collections of Natural Questions

ONE of the most important reasons for the extreme popularity of books of problems in natural philosophy during the three centuries following the thirteenth was the rediscovery of the pseudo-Aristotelian *Problems* *c.* 1300, combined with the desire to imitate the classical tradition, which was such a prominent feature of the later Renaissance.

As E. S. Forster said some thirty years ago, no branch of the Aristotelian corpus has been more neglected than the *Problems*;[1] and it is probably still not generally realized what an impact this work made on the Latin West after the above date, what a large part it played in the scientific and medical thought of the period, and what a vast number of other translations, epitomes, commentaries, and other books of problems of exactly similar nature followed in its wake. Thus although, strictly speaking, the later translations of Greek problems are not in the direct tradition of the Salernitan questions, after *c.* 1300 the two traditions became fused, and collectively played a part in the subsequent history of the sort of questions we have have been discussing. Evidence of this has already been noted in connexion with disputations held in the faculties of arts and medicine at Paris at the end of the thirteenth century.

Peter of Abano had himself translated the pseudo-Aristotelian *Problems* from a Greek text which he had found at Constantinople, as we learn from a passage in the first *differentia* of the *Conciliator*,[2] and from the prologue to his commentary on the *Problems*,[3] which was begun at Paris and

---

[1] E. S. Forster, 'The pseudo-Aristotelian Problems, their Nature and Composition', *C.Q* (1928), pp. 163–5.

[2] 'In quibusdam problematibus Aristoteli attributis per me translatis.'

[3] 'Unde et cum post diu huius expositionis problematum aggregationem, ut discerem grecum in Constantinopolim me transtuli, volumen aliud problematum Aristotelis repperi, quod quidem in linguam iam latinam transduxi. Est autem libri titulus, Liber problematum Aristotelis secundum speciem compilationis incipit' (ed. Venice, 1505, p. 1). This seems to give a better reading than that in the Venice 1482 ed., quoted by Thorndike, 'Peter of Abano and another Commentary on the Problems of Aristotle', *B.H.M.* xxix. 6 (1955), 517. The 1505 printed version of this passage agrees almost exactly with the manuscript version in Bibl. Malatestina, Plut. VI, sin. 2 (XIV cent.), printed in *Aristoteles Latinus*, ii. 893.

finished at Padua by 1310. But no separate text of this translation seems to have survived, and it is not clear to what extent it was used in the commentary. Certainly in most cases the latter is in close agreement with Bartholomew's translation of the *Problems*, and, indeed, it is this which accompanies Peter's commentary in at least seven of the manuscripts,[1] and in all the printed editions, beginning with the *editio princeps* of Mantua 1475.[2] The popularity of this translation, from *c.* 1300 onwards, is also shown by the large number of surviving manuscripts of it, not less than fifty-seven in all, of which forty-two belong to the period *c.* 1300 and the fourteenth century.[3]

In about 1312 Marsilius of Padua[4] came to Paris, bringing with him a copy of Peter's commentary on the *Problems*, which he presented to Jean de Jandun, who was lecturing in the faculty of arts at that time, and who was thus, as he himself tells us, the first in Paris to become acquainted with this work—'Et ego Joannes de Ganduno qui, Deo gratias, credo esse primus inter Parisius regentes in philosophia ad quem praedicta expositio pervenit per dilectissimum meum magistrum Marcilium de Padua'.[5] Jean expounded the commentary in his lectures, and composed a redaction of it, which is extant in several manuscripts,[6] but has never been printed.

---

[1] That, is in Malat. Plut. VI, sin. 2 and 3; Malat. Plut. XXIV, dex. 2; Bibl. Nat. Lat. 6540; Bibl. Nat. Lat. 6541A; and in the three following manuscripts of Jandun's redaction, Vat. lat. 2176; Ghent 72; Erfurt. Ampl., fol. 236. For manuscripts of Peter's commentary see Thorndike, *H.M.E.S.* ii. 921 ff.; the same author's 'Manuscripts of the Writings of Peter of Abano', *B.H.M.* xv (1944), 201–19, and his article quoted above; Sante Ferrari, 'Per la biografia e per gli scritti di Pietro d'Abano', *M.R.A.L.*, ser. 5, xv (Rome, 1918), 678–81. Note, however, that Brit. Mus. Addit. 21978 does not contain Peter's commentary, but only the three translations of the *Problems* by Bartholomew, Giorgio da Trabisonda, and Teodoro Gaza. The remainder of Mazarine 3520, which finishes imperfectly in the middle of the commentary on Part X, prob. 28, is to be found in the Bodleian manuscript, Rawlinson C 116 (13), ff. 51–66, which is not mentioned by Thorndike or Ferrari; this text is the redaction of Peter's commentary made by Jean de Jandun, discussed below.

[2] Other editions were Venice, 1482, ibid. (Locatellus) 1501, ibid. 1505, ibid. 1518, ibid. 1519, Paris, 1520—all in folio.

[3] Fifty-three manuscripts, not including commentaries, abbreviations, and epitomes, are listed in the three volumes of *Aristoteles Latinus*. To these may be added: Ghent, 357 (178ª) (XIV cent.); Bodley 463 (10) (XIV cent.); Brit. Mus. Addit. 21978 (XV cent.); and Michigan Univ. 203 (16) (XIV cent.).

On Bartholomew's translation see: Rose, *Aristoteles pseudepigraphus*, p. 216; M. Grabmann, *Forschungen*, *B.G.P.M.* xvii (1916), 201; G. Sarton, *Introd.* ii. 2, p. 829; S. D. Wingate, *Medieval Latin Versions*, p. 93; *Aristoteles Latinus*, i. 40 and 86. Book I, only, was edited by Dr. R. Seligsohn, *Die Übersetzung der pseudo-Aristotelischen Problemata durch Bartholomaeus von Messina*, Berlin, 1934.

[4] He was Rector of the University from Dec. 1312 to Mar. 1313, *Chart. Univ. Par.* ii, nos. 698–9.

[5] Bibl. Nat. Lat. 6542, f. 1, prologue to Jandun's redaction of Peter of Abano's commentary on the *Problems*.

[6] For the most recent list of these manuscripts, see Stuart MacClintock's *Perversity and Error: Studies on the 'Averroist' John of Jandun*, p. 128, where he lists eleven manuscripts. To these may be added Peterhouse 79 (XIV cent.) and Rawlinson C. 116 (13), which completes Mazarine 3520; see above, n. 1.

Now in the preface to his *Quaestiones super De physico Aristotelis*, Jean complains, like Roger Bacon before him, that the *Problems* is 'commonly found corrupt and incorrect, that it is not much expounded by anyone who is well known or famous, and that, therefore, few study it and fewer understand it sufficiently well, although there are to be found in it numerous most beautiful and marvellously pleasing theoremata, whence', he goes on to say, 'doubtless scholars ought to be extremely grateful to anyone who should both correct this book well and competently expound it.'[1] Did the French master of arts stimulate Peter of Abano to begin his commentary on the *Problems* when the two men were together in Paris, and then arrange for a copy to be sent from Padua as soon as it was finished? Of one thing we can be certain, and that is that, when Jean de Jandun wrote the above-quoted words, he had not yet received Peter's commentary. What is more, the probability is that he did not as yet know that Peter was going to write one. When did Peter start his commentary? In the prologue he states that he collected material for it or, if you prefer, made a redaction of it, a long time ago, 'post diu huius expositionis proble-matum aggregationem', and the explicit tells us he began it at Paris. He must, therefore, have started it some time before *c.* 1305, when he left that city to go to Padua. Quite early in the *Conciliator* he speaks as if he had already completed those parts of the commentary to which he refers.[2] Thus it would appear that Jean started to write his *Quaestiones* on the *Physics* even earlier during the period *c.* 1290–*c.* 1305, that is, before Peter was making much use of the *Problems* in his *Conciliator* and, above all, before he had started his commentary—since, intensely interested as Jean was in the *Problems*, it is inconceivable that he would not know of the activities of a colleague in the same university in connexion with that very book. These facts are borne out by the date 1303 found in the explicit of two manuscripts of the *Quaestiones super De physico*,[3] the validity of which the latest writer on Jandun, Stuart MacClintock, has done his best to annul,[4] in order to confirm another theory of his about the dating of the *Quaestiones super De anima*. It seems to me that, in view of this new

---

[1] 'Et scias quod liber ille de problematibus communiter invenitur corruptus et incorrectus, et non est multum expositus ab aliquo noto aut famoso, et ideo pauci student in eo, et pauciores intelligunt eum sufficienter: quanquam multa et pulcherrima theoremata mirabilis delectationis sunt in eo congregata. unde indubitanter ei qui illum librum bene corrigeret et exponeret competenter multas et magnas gratias deberent reddere studiosi.' Ed. Venice, 1560, sig. † 8b.

[2] Cf. 'Cum etiam considerationem non propius huius operis protendat: de quibus traditum sufficienter in expositionibus problematum, part. 10', *Diff.* 29 (ed. Venice 1548, f. 47ᵛ); 'Harum quoque opinionum destructio aut approbatio non est praesentis inquisitionis, quas siquidem prob. 11 pertractavi', *Diff.* 64 (ed. cit., f. 99ᵛ); 'prohibitione refractionis radiorum motu aquae in ea concidente et proprie velociori, ut declaravi prob. 5', *Diff.* 67 (ed. cit., f. 108ʳ), and there are many other examples.

[3] Vat. Reg. 1342 and Vienna, Dominikanerkloster 402/131.

[4] Op. cit., pp. 110 ff.

evidence, it would be wiser to retain the date 1303 for the completion of the *Quaestiones* on the *Physics*, and, as naturally follows from this, that of 1300 for the *Quaestiones* on the *De anima*, thus, as MacClintock himself suggests, 'pushing Jandun's earliest activity back into the last decade of the thirteenth century'.[1]

The *Quodlibeta* and *Quaestiones* on the *Problems* contained in Bibl. Nat. Lat. 16089, being of uncertain date, are of little help in this case. One can say, however, that they were almost certainly written after Jandun wrote the passage about the *Problems*, quoted above, and that they represented a later state of affairs, being, perhaps, the reflection in the arts faculty of the interest in this book fostered by Peter of Abano in the medical faculty. It is even possible that they were composed a good deal later, when Jandun, having received Peter's commentary *c.* 1312, was himself lecturing on the *Problems*. If this is so, may not some of the questions, particularly the group of thirty-six in the last or fifth series,[2] be *reportationes* of these very lectures of Jandun? I mention this as a possibility, and as a subject for future research.

Another commentary on the *Problems* and an abbreviated compendium of it, in alphabetical order, are ascribed, in two of the manuscripts, to the Oxford scholar, Walter Burley (d. after 1343). Thorndike, who has examined this commentary,[3] without, however, noticing its attribution to Burley, has drawn attention to the fact that the author, 'often rephrases the problem to suit himself, or for the sake of brevity, and sometimes alters the sense as well as the wording of Bartholomew's translation'.[4] The probability is, in fact, that he is using a different translation. At other times he adds questions of his own,[5] which are remarkably like those in the *Quodlibeta* of Bibl. Nat. Lat. 16089. At least one question seems to be taken from Peter of Abano's commentary on the *Problems*. In some cases the author has 'briefly summarized and even enlarged upon and re-ordered the thought of the text in an independent manner . . .', and Thorndike gives an example of this.[6] This aptitude for clear and efficient summarization would suit well the character of the *Doctor planus et perspicuus*, as the fellow of Merton was called.

[1] Ibid., p. 111.
[2] See above, p. 90.
[3] 'Peter of Abano and another commentary on the Problems of Aristotle', *B.H.M.* xxix (1955), 517–23. The best account of Burley and his writings is that by K. Michalski in 'La Physique nouvelle et les différents courants philosophiques au xive siècle', *B.I.A.P.S.L.* (classe de philol., d'hist., et de philos.), Année 1927 Cracow (1928), pp. 93–164. He does not list the commentary on the *Prob.*, or the *Abbreviatio*. In addition to the five manuscripts mentioned by Thorndike, *B.H.M.* xxix (1955), 518, n. 4, there are: Digby 206 (2) (xiv cent.); Oriel 28 (4), (xv cent.); Brit. Mus. Royal 12. E. XVI (xv cent.); the work is ascribed to Burley only in the last manuscript. The *Abbreviatio* of the *Problems* is contained in Peterhouse 220 (xv cent.); Magd. Coll. Oxf. 65 (xv cent.), in which it is ascribed to Burley; Gray's Inn Lib. 2 (xiv cent.).
[4] *B.H.M.* xxix (1955), p. 519.
[5] Some of these questions are listed by Thorndike, ibid., p. 521.
[6] Ibid., p. 523.

Finally, there exist at least two anonymous commentaries, and four epitomes or summaries, all except one of which appear to be of the fourteenth century.[1]

After having done splendid service for nearly 200 years, Bartholomew's translation was at last supplemented, but not entirely superseded, first, by that of the Greek scholar and translator, Giorgio da Trebisonda, (1395–1484), made at Rome towards the close of the first half of the fifteenth century, and then by the better, or at any rate more popular one of his rival, the gifted Teodoro Gaza (1400–76), also made at Rome at the instance of Pope Nicholas V during the period 1451–5, and much corrected later under Sixtus IV.

Giorgio's translation exists only in manuscript,[2] but Gaza's was printed, first at Mantua in [1473], then in three other incunabula,[3] and in at least seventeen editions belonging to the first half of the sixteenth century.[4] Five of these latter editions contain Bartholomew's old translation with Peter of Abano's commentary, as well as the *nova translatio* of Gaza[5]— a striking testimony to the fact that the older, medieval works were not suddenly superseded, but still continued to be studied, side by side with the more modern humanistic material, during a considerable period of the later renaissance.

A word must be said about translations of these *Problems* into languages other than Latin. According to Sarton,[6] Moses ibn Tibbon (*fl.* XIII[2] cent.)

---

[1] For the manuscripts and incipits of these see Note E, p. 208.

[2] Florence, Bibl. Med. Laur., Gaddi, Plut. 89 sup. cod. 84; Bibl. Nat. Lat. 6328; Corpus Christi, Oxf. 105, Brit. Mus. Addit. 21978—all fifteenth century. Incipit 'Quamobrem magni excessus inductivi' (not in Th. and K.).

[3] Rome, 1475; Venice, 1488; ibid. 1495; the two latter editions also contain Valla's translation of the pseudo-Alexandrian *Problems*. See Klebs, 95, nos. 1 and 2, 44, nos. 1 and 2.

[4] Venice (A. Vercellensem), 1501; ibid. (B. Locatellum), 1501; ibid. 1504; ibid. 1505; Lyons [1505] (counterfeit Aldine); Venice, 1513; ibid., 1518; Florence, 1518; Venice, 1519; Paris, 1520; ibid. 1524; Venice, 1524; Paris, 1534; Basel, 1537; Paris, 1539; Basel, 1542 (vol. 2 of the *Opera*); ibid. 1548; Lyons, 1550. In all these editions the pseudo-Aristotelian *Problems* are accompanied with other works, such as the commentary of Peter of Abano, the *Problems* ascribed to Alexander Aphrodisias, and the *De natura animalium*. See next note and below, p. 97, n. 4. In the second half of the century I have noted the following editions: Lyons, 1551; Venice (Junta), 1552; Valencia, 1554; Venice (Tridino), 1560; Lyons, 1561; Venice (Junta), 1562; Basel, 1563; Venice, 1573; Venice (Junta), 1576; Venice (Bindoni), 1576; Lyons, 1579; Lyons, 1580; Venice (Moretti), 1585—where, again, the *Problems* occur in conjunction with other works, usually in one of the volumes comprising a set of the *Opera*. Some manuscripts of the work are: C l m 23718; Dresden Kgl. offentl. Bibl. Db. 80; Donaueschingen, 790; Lucca, 1392; Florence, Bibl. Med. Laur., Gaddi, Plut. 89, sup. cod. 59; Brit. Mus. Harleian 2584 (2); ibid., Addit. 21978—all of which are fifteenth-century.

[5] That is, the four Venetian editions of 1501 (Locatellus), 1505, 1518, 1519, and the Paris one of 1520.

[6] Introd. ii. 2, pp. 849, 860. For a notice of Arabic translations see J. G. Wenrich, *De auctorum graecorum versionibus et commentariis Syriacis, Arabicis, Armeniacis, Persicisque Commentatio*, pp. 150, 153, 154, and Steinschneider, 'Die arabischen Übersetzungen aus dem griechischen', *C.B.*, Beiheft 12 (1893), p. 74. No Latin translations from these Arabic versions seem to have survived; the *Liber Aristotelis continens summam universalium quaestionum*, extant in a Latin translation by Hugo of Santalla, is an astrological work—see Haskins, *Med. Science*, p. 74.

translated them from Arabic into Hebrew in 1264, and in the second half of the fourteenth century they were translated into French by Evrard de Conty (d. 1405), physician to Charles V.[1] It has often been said that Girolamo Manfredi (d. 1492) translated these problems into Italian, with the title, *Il Perche, sive Liber de Homine.* But this book is by no means a translation, although a good deal of the material stems from the *Problems*, so that I have postponed a discussion of it until the end of the chapter.

As regards other Greek problems, in 1302 Peter of Abano seems to have completed a translation of those attributed to Alexander Aphrodiseas;[2] a compilation which, like that ascribed to Aristotle, is now thought to be of much later date, and questions from which formed, as we have seen, the major part of the fragmentary *Vetustissima translatio*, extant since the tenth century. Peter's translation seems to have survived in only two manuscripts,[3] and it has never been printed. Not until the second half of the fifteenth century were any further translations made, and then came three from the pens of well-known Italian humanists; namely, Teodoro Gaza,[4] who, as we saw, had also translated the pseudo-Aristotelian *Problems*, Giorgio Valla[5] (1447–1500), famous humanist and translator from the Greek, who worked chiefly at Venice, and Angelo Poliziano[6] (1545–94), a prominent member of the learned circle who surrounded Lorenzo de Medici, and the intimate friend of Giovanni Pico della Mirandola and Marsilio Ficino.

[1] Sarton, op. cit. iii. 2, p. 1393. Some manuscripts are: Bibl. Nat. français, 210, 211, 563, 564 24281, 24282, N.A. 3371.

[2] See Thorndike, *H.M.E.S.* ii. 878, 918, and F. E. Cranz, 'Alexander Aphrodisiensis', pp. 126 f., in *Catalogus Translationum et Commentariorum: Medieval and Renaissance Latin Translations and Commentaries*, ed. P. O. Kristeller, vol. i. Thorndike seems a little sceptical of the reference to this translation and its ascription to Peter in a fifteenth-century list of his works. However, Peter himself refers to the translation in his *Conciliator, Diff.* v (ed. Venice, 1548, f. 9ᵛ), 'Unde Alexander medicus in problematibus a me translatis'. Incidentally this explains the *dria gnta* quoted by Thorndike, op. cit., p. 878, n. 5, the reading of which should evidently be *differentia quinta* and not *differentiae quinquaginta*, and which refers to the quotation in the *Conciliator* and not to the number of problems in the translation of pseudo-Alexander as Thorndike thought, op. cit., p. 918.

[3] Escorial f-I-11, ff. 31–42 (XIV cent.), Vat. lat. Regin. 747, ff. 62–104 (XVII cent.).

[4] This translation does not appear to have been printed before 1500. The 1504 Aldine ed. seems to be the first, other editions are: Lyons [1505]; Venice, 1513; Paris, 1524; Venice, 1525; Paris, 1534; Basel, 1537 (which has an excellent index); Paris, 1539. In all these it accompanies Gaza's translation of the pseudo-Aristotelian *Problems* and, indeed, the two occur together in most of the editions printed during the second half of the sixteenth century and forming parts of the collected *Opera* of Aristotle. See above, p. 96, n. 4, and Cranz, art. cit., pp. 127 f.

[5] On this most interesting humanist see J. L. Heiberg, *Beiträge zur Gesch. Georg Vallas und seiner Bibliothek. C.B.*, Beiheft xvi. His translation appeared in the two Venice editions of 1488 and 1495, together with Gaza's translation of the pseudo-Aristotelian *Problems*, and after that in the five editions mentioned above, p. 96, n. 5, and in the Venice (Vercellensis) 1501 edition, again together with Gaza's translation of the pseudo-Aristotelian *Problems*. See Cranz, art. cit., pp. 130 ff.

[6] This version first appeared in the editio princeps of the *Opera* of Politian, the Aldine folio of 1498, then in many subsequent editions of the *Opera*. See Cranz, art. cit., pp. 132 ff. From about 1544 onwards it accompanied the *Omnes homines* collection of problems and the *Problemata* of Zimara. See below, p. 130, n. 1.

Finally, in the next century, Johannes Davionus, in his edition of the Greek text of the pseudo-Alexandrian *Problems* accompanied by the Latin translation of Gaza (Paris, 1540–1), translated a few of the problems which had not been dealt with by the latter.[1]

Peter of Abano is also said to have translated yet another set of Greek problems, those ascribed to Cassius the Iatrosophist[2] (*fl. c.* 200), but this translation is now lost, and the work did not become available in Latin until 1541, the date of the first edition of the translation by the prolific Dutch savant, Adrianus Junius (1512–75).[3] The *Quaestiones Salernitanae* and other early collections of questions, show no direct influence by these problems of Cassius, so that one is justified, I think, in assuming that the latter were largely unknown to the medieval Latin West.[4] The same remarks apply to the scientific and medical questions of Plutarch (A.D. *c.* 46–*c.* 120) and to those of the seventh-century Greek historian, Theophylactus Simocatta (d. *c.* A.D. 640), which were also not translated into Latin until the sixteenth century.[5]

We now come to original collections of problems composed during the fourteenth and fifteenth centuries. Two continental collections belonging to this period and containing groups of the earlier, Salernitan prose questions have already been mentioned.[6] An English one, probably composed towards the end of the fourteenth century, is the *De causis naturalibus*

---

[1] See Cranz, art. cit., p. 134. The *Quaestiones naturales et morales*, also attributed to Alexander, though probably also not by him, are not written in the tradition of the *Problems* but in that of the Aristotelian commentaries, therefore I have not dealt with them here. They deal, for the most part, with abstract physics and metaphysics as found in the *Physica* and *De anima*, and with ethical questions based on the *Nicomachean Ethics*.

[2] Sarton, *Introd.* i. 1, p. 324.

[3] *Cassii medici de animalibus medicae Quaestiones et Problemata quae hactenus lucem non videre, interprete Hadriano Junio Hornano medico*. Paris, apud Christ. Wechelum, 1541.

[4] That is, except for the eight questions in the *Vetustissima translatio* which correspond to problems of Cassius, see above, p. 13. Only three of these are found in the Salernitan prose questions, viz. nos. 6, 15, 20; the last was very familiar to the Latin West through Aulus Gellius and Macrobius.

[5] The *Problems* of Plutarch translated by Gianpero da Lucca (d. 1457), of which there exist several incunabula (Klebs 788, nos. 1–4 and 44, nos. 1–2) and sixteenth-century editions, and which often accompanied those of pseudo-Aristotle and pseudo-Alexander, are the entirely classical and antiquarian *Greek and Roman Questions*. The more scientific and medical *Natural Questions* (*De causis naturalibus*) were first translated by Gilbert de Longueil (Gybertus Longolius), appearing in *Ethica seu Moralia opuscula*, Cologne, 1542, Paris, 1544. Adrianus Junius was also the first to give a Latin translation of the *Symposiaca* (Paris, 1547), also largely scientific and medical, a few questions from which had been known in the medieval period through Macrobius, see above, p. 15. The *Physical Problems* of Theophylactus did not appear in Latin until 1598, when the translation by the young Dutch savant, Jacques Kimedoncius, was published at Leyden (reprinted in J. F. Boissonade, *Theophylacti Simocattae Quaestiones physicae et epistolae*). A French version of the problems was given by F. Morel in 1603.

[6] See above, p. 37, n. 1. I have not seen the following: Budapest, Bibl. Mus. Nat., cod. lat. 405 (XIV cent.), ff. 112–19, *Adnotationes physicae et mathematicae*, incip. 'Quare cum homo mortuus gravior sit vivo'; Prague, Bibl. Pub. et Univ. 2056 (XIV–XV cents.), ff. 325ᵛ–331, *Quaestiones de naturalibus* and other medical material; Prague, Bibl. Cap. Met. 1636 (XV cent.), ff. 276–300, *Varia problemata naturalia*.

attributed to the Carmelite, Richard of Lavenham.[1] This contains fifteen meteorological questions and one which discusses the reasons for the central position of the earth in the universe—most of which had been discussed by Adelard and the Salernitans, including the last question. Richard's answers are usually based on later authorities, such as Grosseteste and Albertus Magnus, but occasionally he quotes earlier ones such as Macrobius, in the question about the temperature of well-water in summer and winter, and Urso (*Aphorisms*), in the question about the position of the earth—an interesting witness to the long-continuing influence of this Salernitan master on English scientific thought.[2]

Perhaps another English collection is contained in Brit. Mus. Royal 8. F. vii, ff. 53ᵛ–54, written in England in the fifteenth century, and formerly in the possession of John, Lord Lumley. This consists of twenty-three questions, most of which are ancient Salernitan ones, covering most aspects of *physica*, but with, for the most part, much later answers. Several of these found their way into another series of twenty-seven problems contained in a *Compendium* of Medicine composed *c.* 1507 by the Dutch physician, Reyner Oesterhuysen of Deventer, and also existing only in manuscript, Brit. Mus. Sloane 345, ff. 138–41. But another two collections formed in the fourteenth century, or in the case of the first, perhaps earlier, found their way into print in the fifteenth, and so enjoyed a much wider circulation. The first of these, which became easily the most popular of all the later problem books, is usually attributed to Aristotle, although, as a matter of fact, it has nothing whatever to do with the pseudo-Aristotelian *Problems* translated by Bartholomew and Peter of Abano. Let us call this collection the *Omnes homines*, from the opening words of the incipit.[3] From about 1483 onwards it appeared in no less than twenty Latin editions up to 1500,[4] followed by at least another thirty-six up to 1686.[5] Unlike the problems of Greek origin, it was

---

[1] For the manuscripts and a short description of this treatise see Thorndike, 'Some Medieval and Renaissance Manuscripts on Physics', *P.A.P.S.* civ (2) (1960), 197. A manuscript not listed is Magd. Coll. Oxford 38 (xv cent.), ff. 9–10.

[2] Earlier in the century the Mertonian physician John of Gaddesden quoted Urso in his *Rosa anglica*, written *c.* 1305–17, printed first at Pavia in 1492 and several times subsequently.

[3] 'Omnes homines naturaliter scire desiderant, scribit Aristoteles philosophorum princeps primo metaphysice' (Th. and K. 461). The incipit of the first question is 'Queritur quare inter omnia animalia homo habet faciem versus celum elevatum'. These apply to the printed editions and most of the manuscripts. The earliest manuscript, however, a Bohemian codex preserved at Breslau (Cod. Rehdigerani 458, ff. 44–76ᵛ), written in 1408, omits the preface with the *Omnes homines* incipit, which was probably added at a later date, and has the following incipit: 'Ex paupertate mei ingenioli aliqua probleumata collecturus. Primum sit istud, quare ut dicit Galienus in libro de iumentis quod inter omnia animalia solus homo habet faciem versus celum' (not in Th. and K.). This incipit, with slight modifications, occurs in three other manuscripts: Breslau, Univ. Bibl. IV. Q. 54 (1419); Prague, Bibl. Cap. Met. 1374 (1430); and ibid. 1376 (xv cent.). See below, p. 101, n. 3.

[4] Klebs 95, nos. 3–12, 19–28. The title of 95, 21, is *Probleumata Arestotelis determinantia multas questiones de variis corporum humanorum dispositionibus valde audientibus suaves.*

[5] I have noted the following: Paris, 1501; Cologne, 1506; ibid. [1510]; Antwerp, [1510];

translated into both German and English at an early date. Of the German version there are six incunabula,[1] beginning with the Augsburg 1492 edition, and at least twenty-five editions belonging to the sixteenth and seventeenth centuries, up to 1668.[2] The English version was first printed by the Widow Orwin at London in 1595,[3] and three other editions from the period before 1640 have survived.[4] Later in the seventeenth century, and during the eighteenth and nineteenth centuries, it was many times reprinted,[5] often with different titles and with other spurious Aristotelian material, in chap-book form.[6] The work was also translated into French,

---

Paris, 1514; ibid. 1515; ibid. 1530; Venice, 1532; ibid. 1537; [Francf.?], 1544; Francf. 1548; ibid. 1549; ibid. 1551; Paris, 1552; ibid. 1553; ibid. 1554; ibid. 1558; ibid. 1561; Francf. 1568; Venice, 1568; ibid. 1580; Lyons, 1569; Cologne, 1571; Lyons, 1573; ibid. 1579; London, 1583; Cologne, 1601; Francf. 1609; Venice, 1626; Douai 1631; Leipzig 1633; Amst. 1643; ibid. 1650; Leipzig, 1671; Amst. 1680; ibid. 1686. Doubtless this list is far from complete, and many editions will have disappeared. The titles vary: that of Paris 1558 is *Problemata Aristotelis ac philosophorum medicorumque complurimum ad varias quaestiones cognoscendas . . .*, that of Amst. 1650 is abbreviated to *Aristotelis aliorumque Problemata*. On the Venice 1537 and Francf. 1609 editions, which contain material by Zimara, see below, pp. 129–30.

[1] Klebs 95, nos. 13–18.

[2] To the fifteen mentioned by Graesse, i. 220, the following may be added: Augsb. 1514; ibid. 1531; Strassb. [1540]; ibid. 1543; Francf. 1551; ibid. 1557; ibid. 1566; ibid. 1580; ibid. 1598; Basel, 1668. The title of the Strassb. [1540] ed. reads *Fragstuck Aristotelis, Avicenne, Galeni, unnd Alberti Magni. Darin menschlicher und thierlicher natur eygenschafften durch frag und antwurt, Auch mancherhandt arzneien den menschen zu gut kurz angezeygt werden . . . .* It is edited by (Q. Apollinaris) Walther Hermann Ryff and is remarkable for two full-page woodcuts, one of which is repeated, taken from *Hortus Sanitatis*, Strassb., 1497, and Brunschwig, *Cirurgia*, Strassb., 1497. The two woodcuts in Cammerlander's 1543 edition are quite different, one being based on a cut found in early editions of Ketham's *Fasciculus med.*, and the other being a bloodletting figure used by the same printer (Cammerlander) in his *Ein newe Badenfart*, 1530.

[3] *The Problemes of Aristotle, with other Philosophers and Phisitions. Wherein are contained divers questions, with their answers, touching the estate of mans bodie.* 8° At London Printed by the Widdow Orwin. 1595. *S.T.C.* 762. The Jaggard copy only is listed, but this has since disappeared. However, during the war I was lucky enough to 'pick up' a copy at Folkestone which might have come from the Jaggard library, which was dispersed some years ago. This copy has two title-pages, the imprint of the first being as above, that of the second being 'At Edenborough, Printed by Robert Waldgrave. 1595'. Mr. F. S. Ferguson, to whom I showed the book, has very kindly told me that Joan Orwin of London was the real printer, and that this copy combines both *S.T.C.*, nos. 762 and 763, the intention being that copies could be issued for sale either in England or Scotland, one or other of the titles being suppressed. There are two copies bearing the 'Edenborough' imprint, the Bodleian and that in the Nat. Lib. of Scotland, but the one described above is the only one at present known which carries the London title-page and the true imprint.

[4] *S.T.C.* 764, A. Hatfield, 1597; 765, ibid. 1607. A third was sold at Hodgson's (11/12/47), A.G. for Godfrey Emondson, 1634.

[5] The following are in Wing: nos. A. 3691–4; 1649, 1666, 1670, 1680, 1684, all with a London imprint. An edition of Lond. 1683 is in M. Morton-Smith's Cat. *Rare Books*, no. 2, item 10. Sion Coll. Lib. had an edition Lond. 1689 (*Cat.* ed. W. Reading, Lond. 1724, E B. IX. 45). The *Term* Catalogues (ed. Arber) yield the following London editions: 1679 (i. 364); 1696, the 22nd ed. (ii. 593); 1704, the 23rd ed. (iii. 432). Many editions have therefore disappeared, and those which have survived are often represented by one known copy.

[6] See Sir D'Arcy Power, *The Foundations of Medical History*, ch. 6, for a rather inadequate account of these chap-book editions, *Aristotle's Masterpiece, Experienced Midwife, Book of Problems*, and *Last Legacy*. He lists twenty-five editions of the first, from 1684 to 1930. The *Experienced Midwife* first appeared about 1700 and the *Last Legacy* about 1690. The later

this version appearing first at Lyons in 1554, and several times sub-sequently.[1] As regards Italian versions, Ortensio Lando made great use of it in his *Quattro libri de dubbi* (Venice, 1552), and Bartolomeo Paschetti gave an almost complete translation of it in his imitation of Lando's book, *Dubbi morali et naturali* (Genoa, 1581). As far as I know there is no complete Spanish translation, although Hieronymo Campos used some of the questions in his *Sylva de varias questiones naturales y morales* (Antwerp, 1575).[2]

I have traced twenty-one manuscripts[3] of the work, all fifteenth-century, the earliest having the date 1408, and all except two being of Bohemian, Polish, German, Austrian, Flemish, or Danish provenance. Because of this, because the incunabula printed in Germany far outnumber those printed elsewhere,[4] and because it was translated into German long before any other vernacular translation was made, it seems likely that the collection was compiled in Germany, rather than in France or Italy. In both the printed editions and the manuscripts several 'authorities' are quoted, Aristotle to the greatest extent, followed by Albertus Magnus, Hippocrates, Constantinus, Galen, Avicenna, and Averroes, in order of frequency.[5] Not one of these authorities seems to be later than the second half of the thirteenth century, which makes it very probable that the collection was originally compiled about that period, and that manuscripts

editions contained all four treatises, and also included the *Problems* of Zimara and pseudo-Alexander which usually accompanied the *Omnes homines* problems after *c.* 1544. *Aristotle's New Book of Problems* (3rd ed. Lond. *c.* 1705) is a later, much rarer, imitation.

[1] Some later editions are: Lyons, 1570, 1587; Rouen, 1600; Lyons, 1613, 1618, 1668.

[2] On these three books see further below, pp. 139-40.

[3] Breslau (Wrocław), Cod. Rehdigerani 458, ff. 44-76ᵛ. A Bohemian codex with the explicit 'Consumantur probleumata Aristotelis sub anno domini Milesimo CCCCVIII [1408] post Octavam Nativitatis Beate Marie virginis pro honorabili viro domino preposito de Opatowicz'; Breslau Univ. III. Q. 2, ff. 1-23 (xv cent.); ibid. IV. Q. 54, ff. 186ᵛ-201. 'Scripta per fratrem Jodocum canonicorum regularium de Wratislavia proxima quinta feria ante Agnetis in studio Cracoviensi anno domini MCCCCXIX [1419]'; Cracow, Bibl. Univ. Jagellonicae 1897, ff. 240-97 (1424), written in Leipzig by Johannes de Abenberg; ibid. 2016, ff. 188-208ᵛ (1465-73); ibid. 2110, ff. 337-400 (*c.* 1437); Prague, Bibl. Cap. Metropolitani 1374, ff. 197ᵛ-225 (1430); ibid. 1376, ff. 95-121ᵛ (xv cent.); Erlangen 673, ff. 94-113 (1419), from the Benedictine monastery of St. Aegidius in Nürnberg; C l m 429, ff. 211-24 (1425) 'completa feria tercia . . .' in Brunswick; Erfurt, Ampl. fol. 334, ff. 196-205 (1421); Göttingen Univ. Lüneburg 74, ff. 90-120 (1443); Hanover, Kgl. Offentl. Bibl. 616, ff. 1-66 (xv cent.); Graz Univ. 884, ff. 260-89 (1470); Melk 171, ff. 549-615 (1420-59); Ghent 13, ff. 27-42 (xv cent.), written for Raphael de Marcatelle, abbot of the monastery of St. Bavon; Copenhagen, Thott 580, ff. 351-85 (*c.* 1450), written by a pastor from the diocese of Ripa; ibid., Gl. Kgl. Saml. 1658, ff. 18-24 (xv cent.), the gynaecological questions only, of German provenance; ibid., Ny. Kgl. Saml. 84b, ff. 2ʳ-ᵛ (*c.* 1600), the gynaecological questions only; Mazarine 991, ff. 116-49 (xv cent.); Vat. Lat. 9018, ff. 76 (xv cent.), the gynaecological questions only.

[4] Twenty out of a total of twenty-six.

[5] Other authors quoted once or twice each are: Gilles of Corbeil, *De pulsibus*; pseudo-Boethius, *De disciplina scholarium*; Augustine; Seneca; Theophilus; Porphyrius; Themistius; Isidore; Johannes Sacrobosco (d. 1256); Gilbert de la Porrée (1076-1154), *In sex principiis*; and Eberhard the German (*fl.* before 1280). Also several lines from the Salernitan metrical *Regimen Sanitatis* are quoted.

earlier than 1408 will eventually turn up. The work is ascribed to Albertus Magnus in four of the manuscripts,[1] two of which consist of the gynaecological questions only, with the title *Probleumata Magni Alberti excerpta de secretis mulierum*.[2] These questions, however, have nothing whatever to do with pseudo-Albertus *De secreta mulierum*, a popular gynaecological tract, not in question form, much more astrological and superstitious in character than the *Omnes homines*, and often found printed with two other pseudo-Albertian tracts, the spurious *Liber aggregationis*, and *De mirabilibus mundi*.[3]

Some of the quotations seem to be incorrect; there is no doubt, however, that the compiler used the genuine Albertus Magnus, *De animalibus Lib. 26* (1262–8), and almost certainly the *Quaestiones super De animalibus* (1258). Evidence of use of the former work is particularly clear in two questions about monsters, and it is interesting to see how the compiler has handled this genuine material in order to increase the popularity of the book. In one case we see how a simple statement of Albert's is successively embroidered and rendered more picturesque, from the Erlangen 1419 manuscript up to the printed 1483 Magdeburg edition, when it probably received its final, narrative-like shape.[4] In another case a form of monstrosity ascribed by Albert to a duck is finally attributed to a man, the word 'duck' being suppressed in both manuscripts and printed editions.[5]

---

[1] Erlangen 673; Breslau, Univ. IV. Q.54; Copenhagen, Gl. Kgl. Saml. 1658; Ny. Kgl. Saml. 84b.

[2] That is, the two Copenhagen MSS.

[3] On these three tracts see Thorndike, *H.M.E.S.* ii, ch. 63, and the same author's later 'Further Consideration of the *Experimenta*, *Speculum astronomiae*, and *De secretis mulierum* ascribed to Albertus Magnus', *Speculum*, xxx (1955), 413–43, where note that Thorndike, presumably relying only upon the title, thought that the two Copenhagen fragments belonged to the pseudo-Albertian *De secretis mulierum*; see his article, p. 427.

[4] To obtain a better text of the *Omnes homines*, I have used two manuscripts, Erlangen 673 and Erfurt, Ampl. fol. 334 (the Breslau 1408 codex stops just short of the section on monsters), and the edition of Quentell, Cologne, 1490 (Klebs, 95, no. 21); the later sixteenth- and seventeenth-century editions are apt to be very faulty. Albert. *De animal.* xviii, ch. 6 (ed. Stadler, ii. 1215): 'De monstruosis partibus. Aliquando enim generatus est vitulus caput habens hominis.' Erlangen 673, f. 108ᵛ: 'Item Albertus dicit quod in quadam villa vacca generabat vitulum semihominem, tunc rustici suspicantes pastorem coisse cum vacca, volebant ipsum cremare, si astronomicus, veritatem dicens, non affuisset.' Erfurt, Ampl. fol. 334, f. 206: 'Item Albertus dicit quod in quadam villa vacca peperit vitulum semihominem, et autem rustici suspicantes de pastore huius rei causam nefariam imposuerunt, tandem quod cum vacca volebant ipsum cremare, si astronomicus agnoscens rei veritatem, non affuisset.' Ed. Cologne (1490), sig. e 4: 'Ut contingit temporibus Alberti quod in quadam villa vacca peperit vitulum semihominem: tunc rustici suspicantes de pastore huius [huic] rei causam variam [error for nefariam] imposuerunt, et tandem ipsum cum vacca volebant cremare. sed Albertus astronomie expertus agnoscens rei veritatem, ex constellatione speciali hoc factum esse dixit, et pastorem a manibus eorum redemit.'

[5] Albert., op. cit., ed. Stadler, ii. 1216: 'Nos enim iam vidimus anserem bicorporeum: et in nulla parte erant continua corpora nisi in dorso, et habebat duo capita et quatuor alas et quatuor pedes et ibat ad quamcumque partem convertebatur, et non vixit diu.' Erlangen, f. 108ᵛ: 'Item haec sunt verba Alberti et videtur quod unus [hiatus in MS.] et corpora nulla coniuncta nisi dorso ac habebat 4ᵒʳ aures, duo capita, et 4ᵒʳ pedes et ambulabat ad quamcumque partem.' Erfurt, f. 206: 'Item haec sunt verbi Alberti vidimus bicorporea et tota in nullo erant conjuncta

Other questions seem directly inspired by the *Quaestiones super De animalibus*, such as the questions about long eggs producing male birds and round eggs female, crows not feeding their young before the ninth day, and melancholy animals having long ears, the answers to which all correspond more or less exactly to those given by Albert.[1]

It is strange that among all the Aristotelian works cited, both genuine and spurious, there is no mention of the *Problems*, and a careful examination has convinced me that the compiler made no direct use at all of this work, since, in addition to its not being quoted, in those cases where the questions are the same or similar, the answers are usually different. There is also no evidence that the compiler made any direct use of the pseudo-Alexandrian *Problems*, of which only fragments were available in Latin, in the *Vetustissima translatio*, until it was translated again by Peter of Abano in 1302. These facts are additional evidence that the collection was compiled much earlier than *c.* 1408, perhaps before the end of the thirteenth century, but not before *c.* 1268, because of the use of Albert's *De animalibus*.

As one would expect, considerable use seems to have been made of the Salernitan questions, which were almost certainly the immediate source for many of the Greek problems, particularly for those which belong to the corpus of pseudo-Aristotelian *Problems*, since the answers correspond to those found in the former, rather than to those in the latter work.[2]

The compiler of the *Omnes homines* had confined himself to anthropology, medicine, and zoology, the field covered by the *De animalibus* of Aristotle, choosing in these subjects only the simplest themes, such as the parts and members of the body, and the everyday actions and processes of eating, drinking, sleeping, coitus, conception, birth, menstruation, and abortion.

The second of the two original collections to appear among the incunabula was much more ambitious, and covered a much wider field. This was the *Responsorium curiosorum* of the Dominican, Conrad de Halberstadt,[3] printed at Lübeck in 1476.[4] In the colophon the book is also called

nisi in dorso et habebat duo capita quatuor pedes et quatuor alas et ibat ad quamcumque partem vertebatur.' Ed. Cologne, sig e 4: 'Hec sunt verba Alberti. Vidimus bicorporem, et corpora illius in nullo loco erant conjuncta nisi in dorso, et habebant duo capita, quatuor pedes, quatuor manus, et etiam euntes ad quamcumque partem vertebantur.'

[1] These questions, found on sig. f 1 and e 6ᵛ of the 1490 ed., correspond to *Quaest. De animal.* (ed. Filthaut), vi, qu. 12; viii, qu. 18; i, qu. 37, respectively.

[2] Cf. *Omnes homines*, ed. cit. b 1ᵛ: 'Quare calor solis provocat sternitationem et non calor ignis. Respondetur quod calor solis tantum resolvit et non consumit: ergo vapor resolutus expellitur per sternitationem. sed calor ignis resolvit et consumit, et ergo magis consumit sternitationem quam provocat.' Pet. f. 14: 'Calor solis dissolvere sufficit sed non consumere, unde humoribus dissolutis sed non consumptis fit sternutatio. Calor ignis dissolvere sufficit et consumere, unde nulla sternutatio.' The answer provided by pseudo-Arist. *Prob.* xxxiii. 4 (961ᵇ) is quite different.

[3] It is not certain whether the author was the elder Dominican of this name who *fl.* 1321, or the younger, d. after 1362. See *G.W.* vii, col. 15.

[4] The only manuscript that I know of is that mentioned by Fabricius, *Bibl. lat. med. et inf. aetatis* (1754), i. 413, and said by Schmid to be in the library at Wolfenbüttel.

Mensa philosophica,[1] and undoubtedly this has caused it to be confused, by some scholars, with another book composed not long afterwards which has this name and which will be discussed below. Certainly, for some reason the book has escaped the notice of the principal modern historians of science and medicine,[2] and this in spite of the fact that there are no fewer than seventeen copies, listed by the *Gesamtkatalog*,[3] in English, continental, and American libraries, and although Freytag[4] and M. Denis[5] gave a good description of the book, and pointed out that it was quite different from the *Mensa philosophica* that is usually found in libraries— a warning repeated by Brunet,[6] and, more recently, by T. F. Dunn,[7] in his paper on the *Facetiae* of the latter book.

The *Responsorium* is a rather carelessly printed folio of 134 leaves, and in the prologue the author states that he has composed it, 'because many men willingly enquire about rare and curious things, and gladly hear of and speak about such matters', and 'in order that our brother preachers, who frequently have to be in the company of men of divers states and conditions, may the more agreeably converse with such people, the more readily reply to questions about such things, and know how to discuss them more to the purpose'. He called it *Responsorium curiosorum* because 'I have arranged in it short replies to questions of this sort, such as I have been able to find better and more conveniently in *autoritates autentice*', and divided the book into four parts; 'the first dealing with supercelestial bodies, simple elements, and "mixed" minerals and vegetables, the second, with animals in general, their members and parts, the third, with man *in speciali*, and the fourth, with animals *in speciali*.' Further, he expressly states that he has used the method of short questions and answers, without argument (reasons for and against), because 'I meant this work to be used, not for disputations, but for giving brief replies, and for friendly conversation.'[8]

---

[1] 'Explicit tractatus mense philosophice et responsorii curiosorum.'

[2] The incipit is in Th. and K. (1942), p. 361, but the book receives no mention in *H.M.E.S.* or in Sarton's *Introduction* or in Klebs (1938).

[3] *G.W.* 7423.   [4] *Adparatus Lit.* ii (1753), 816.

[5] *Die Merkwürdigkeiten der k.k. garellischen öffentl. Bibliothek am Theresiano*, Vienna, 1780, pp. 58 ff.   [6] *Manuel*, iii (1862), col. 1636.

[7] The *Facetiae of the Mensa Philosophica*, p. 10.

[8] 'Quia multi homines libenter de raris et curiosis querunt et de talibus delectabiliter audiunt et loquuntur, ideo ut fratres nostri predicatores quos frequenter apud homines diversorum statuum et condicionum esse oportet inter eos gratius conversentur quo ad talia valent aptius respondere et de talibus sciunt etiam convenientius conferre, presens opusculum quod de raris et curiosis questionibus ex diversis breviter compilavi. Responsorium curiosorum nominavi quia breves in eo responsiones ad huiusmodi questiones ordinavi sicut ex autoritatibus autenticis melius et aptius potui invenire. Et istum librum in quattuor libros partiales distinxi. Primus est de corporibus supercelestibus sive elementis simplicibus et aliquibus mixtis scilicet mineralibus et vegetabilibus. Secundus est de animalibus in generali et eorum membris et partibus. Tertius de homine in speciali. Quartus de animalibus in speciali....Ponam autem in singulis questiones breves sine rationibus pro et contra quia non ad disputandum sed ad breviter respondendum et familiariter conferendum illud opusculum ordinavi.' Prologue, f. 15.

Now all these remarks are exceedingly interesting, since they show that educated people, outside the university circles, were already beginning to take an interest in these matters, and that the method of the short *quaestiones et responsiones* was now being used, not only for purely didactic purposes in the class-rooms, but also as the basis for 'polite conversation' among men 'of divers states and conditions'—a form of informal converse which was to be of increasing importance in the sixteenth and seventeenth centuries for the discussion and propagation of scientific ideas, as we shall see. At this period the conversations were confined to the educated classes who could speak Latin, the book was written entirely in this language, and the answers to many of the questions were highly technical, and not simplified and 'watered down' as they were in the vernacular catechisms of the period. At the same time, very few of the questions concerned experiments, the sections on metals and precious stones being mainly astrological, magical, and descriptive, which is what one would expect in a work of this period, chiefly theoretical in tone, and depending on 'authorities', rather than on personal observation and experiment.

This brings us to a discussion of the sources. In the prologue Conrad mentions the pseudo-Aristotelian *Problemata*, Roger Bacon's *Perspectiva*, the *Quaestiones super De animalibus* of Albertus Magnus, Peter of Spain *super Viaticum*, Constantinus, and *diversi doctores alii*.[1]

He freely uses Bartholomew's translation of the *Problems*, on which, it will be remembered, Peter of Abano had composed a commentary which had appeared in print for the first time, together with Bartholomew's translation, the year before the publication of Conrad's book.[2]

The use of Bacon's work on optics and perspective is interesting, and the extracts from it must be among the earliest, if not, indeed, the very first, of that author to appear in print with specific acknowledgement.[3]

As regards Albert's *Quaestiones*, they had probably been used earlier, as we have seen, by the author of the *Omnes homines*, but this work, more elementary than the one we are discussing, was not printed until seven years later; so that we have, in the *Responsorium*, certainly the earliest appearance in print of copious extracts from Albert's important *Quaestiones*, and those in a much more complete form and in a greater number than we have them in the more popular *Omnes homines*.

---

[1] 'Primum autem librum collegi ex probleumatibus arestotelis et de alberto in diversis et Rogerio bactum in perspectivis et diversis aliis. Alios autem tres sequentes ex Aristotile ubisuper et in aliis ex alberto in q(uestiones) Supra de animalibus, ex questionibus Petri hispani super viaticum, Constantinum et diversis doctoribus aliis.' Prol., f. 15.

[2] See above, p. 93.

[3] Jean de Jandun borrows freely from Bacon's *Questions on the Physics* in his *Questions* on that book, 1st ed., Padua, 1475 (*Roger Bacon Essays*, ed. Little, p. 277), but this is without acknowledgement. Later on, Themon Judaei mentioned Bacon's *Perspectiva* as one of his sources in his *Questions on the Meteora*, 1st ed., Pavia, 1480 (Crombie, *Grosseteste*, p. 261). There may be specific quotations from Bacon in other early Aristotelian commentaries, but I know of no such references that appeared in print before 1476.

Besides Peter of Spain's commentary on the *Viaticum* of Constantinus, Conrad used his commentary on Galen's *Tegni*. Neither of these commentaries was included in the Lyons folio (*Opera* Ysaac) of 1515, and both of them still exist only in manuscript.

But in addition to these purely medical works, Conrad used, to an even greater extent, Peter's *Problemata* extracted from his commentary on the *De animalibus*, discussed above[1]—an interesting, early use of this collection, and again the first appearance of any portion of it in print. In at least one case[2] Conrad compares data obtained from Michael Scot's 'old' translation of the *De animalibus* with those obtained from William of Moerbeke's 'new' one, and the views of Albertus Magnus as expressed in his *Quaestiones super De animalibus* with those held in the later *Lib. 26 de animalibus*, thus showing a wide knowledge of the literature connected with this Aristotelian text which was available at the time.

Other works used are: Seneca's *Quaestiones naturales*, the *Saturnalia* of Macrobius, William of Conche's *De philosophia mundi*, the *De plantis* of Nicolaus of Damascus in the translation of Alfred of Sareshel (a work attributed to Aristotle in the Middle Ages), Avicenna's *Canon*, *Alchimista* (*De congelatis*), and commentary on the *De animalibus*, Algazel's *Physica* and *Metaphysica*, and Ptolemy's *Almagest*.

A great many of the questions are Salernitan, but, unlike the author of the *Omnes homines*, Conrad makes no or very little use of the earlier, Salernitan answers, but quotes those furnished by later masters, such as Albertus Magnus and Peter of Spain, who had dealt with the same questions. In a few cases, where he follows older authorities, such as Seneca, Macrobius, and William of Conches, the answers may resemble the Salernitan ones; but, on the whole, Conrad succeeded in producing an extremely useful encyclopedia of the natural sciences, including medicine, in the easily assimilated question-and-answer form, which, for the most part, was based on the most up-to-date and recent authorities in those particular fields. In the catalogue of the Berlin Latin manuscripts, V. Rose describes a *Liber similitudinum naturalium* by the same author (theolog. fol. 315, Rose 502, fourteenth century). This work has six divisions or parts,[3] is written in alphabetical order, and consists of similitudes and adaptations of the various parts of natural philosophy for moralizing purposes. Thus it resembles, exactly, such works as the *Septiformis de moralitatibus rerum naturalium* (1281–91), the *Lumen animae* or *Liber moralitatum rerum naturalium* (edited by M. Farinator in the

---

[1] p. 77.

[2] f. 113, in the question 'utrum mares generentur de ovis oblongis vel rotundis'.

[3] 'Primus est de corporibus simplicibus s. celo et elementis. Secundus de mineralibus s. gemmis et metallis. Tercius de vegetalibus. Quartus de animalibus sive volatilibus sive natatilibus sive gressibilibus sive reptilibus. Quintus de homine et suis partibus et infirmitatibus. Sextus indifferenter de diversis naturalibus, qui pro maiori parte est de probleumaticis.' The incipit, 'Memor ero operum domini', is not in Th. and K. (1937) or *Supplements*.

fifteenth century), and the *Summa de exemplis ac similitudinibus rerum* of
John of San Gimignano (*c.* 1350).[1] This moralizing tendency of the book,
and the fact that it was clearly intended to be used for composing edifying
sermons, rather than in ordinary conversation, differentiates it from the
Responsorium, which is entirely free from ethical and religious motives.
The sources, as mentioned by Rose, are the same as those found in the
latter book, also the sixth part is written in the question-and-answer
form, and consists, apparently, almost entirely of extracts from the
pseudo-Aristotelian *Problems*[2]—another witness of Conrad's love for this
form of exposition, and perhaps the earliest example of its adaptation as a
tool of the sermon makers. The final portion of this sixth part deals with
optics and perspective,[3] and quotes Roger Bacon, John Pecham, Ptolemy,
and Alhazen, and thus reflects the interest in these subjects which Conrad
shows in the *Responsorium*. Yet another rather similar work by this in-
dustrious Dominican, and one which is much more commonly found in
manuscript collections, is the *Tripartitus moralium*,[4] also in alphabetical
order, but this time containing no problems in question-and-answer form,
and not dealing with the parts of natural philosophy.

Nothing like the *Responsorium* in extent, and employing this ancient
Aristotelian form, was to be produced until the sixteenth century and
the full flowering of the Renaissance in Italy. No further editions of this
book seem to have been printed, witness of the fact, perhaps, that its use
was as yet confined to a comparatively narrow field; but not long afterwards[5] there appeared at Cologne a much smaller book with the title
Mensa philosophica, *The Philosophical Banquet*, to which were added, in
later editions, the words, 'prepared in the best manner for studious
youths, the guardian of health, both profitable because of the importance
of its maxims, as well as delightful through the narration of witty tales'

[1] On these encyclopedias see Thorndike, *H.M.E.S.* iii, ch. 32, 'Encyclopedias of the Fourteenth Century', and the same author's *Science and Thought in the Fifteenth Century*, pp. 13–16.
Conrad's works are not included in either of these accounts.

[2] 'In hoc 6 tractu ponam exempla de diversis naturalibus et raris indifferenter qui fere totus
est de probleumatibus Aristotelis ultra 200 probleumata comprehendens.'

[3] 'Habet eciam pauca aliqua de perspectivis et quibusdam aliis que utilia videbantur.'

[4] The three parts deal respectively with: I. De philosophorum et poetarum dictis notabilibus.
II. De antiquorum factis et exemplis memorabilibus. III. De poetarum fabulis ad morum
correctionem utilibus et curiosis. The incipit, 'Sicut dicit Seneca in epistola ad Lucillium',
is in Th. and K. (1937), col. 685, but has reference to what is evidently a different work
(Questions on the mathematical sciences, *Hist. Lit.* 36, 179–80). Some manuscripts are: Lüben
32 (mentioned by Rose in his description of the *Lib. similitud. nat.*); Münster, Regia Bibl.
Paulina, 157 (xv cent.); Göttingen, Theolg. 113 (*c.* 1461); Vienna, Nationalbibl. 1625 (xiv cent.);
Graz, Universitätsbibl. 526 (xv cent.); Prague, Bibl. Pub. et Univ. 130 (xiv–iv cent.); ibid.
556 (xv cent.); Prague, Bibl. Capituli Metropolitani 634 (xiv cent.); ibid. 1079 (xiv cent.).

[5] Klebs gives the first ed. as Cologne, anon. pr. 1480, 676, no. 1. Brunet, *Supplement* (1878),
p. 1010, mentions an edition from the press of Johannes Guldenschaaf in Cologne, *c.* 1475,
which Dunn says is the first, op. cit., p. 9. But Voulliéme, *Der Buchdruck Kölns bis zum Ende
des fünfzehnten Jahrhunderts*, Bonn, 1903, mentions no such edition, and the probability is that
a confusion has arisen with Klebs 676, no. 6, the Guldenschaff ed. of 1485 (Hain, *11075).

(*optime custos valetudinis studiosis juvenibus apparata: non minus senten-tiarum gravitate conducibilis, quam facetiarum enarratione delectabilis*). This time expressly written for students, the pill is well and truly gilded by the addition of a good deal of narrative material. The work is divided into four parts: the first discusses diet and the natures of all kinds of foods and drinks, the second deals with the habits and conditions of those men with whom we associate at table, the third consists of questions by which we are 'philosophically stimulated' when we dine, and the fourth, 'of worthy tales and pastimes to entertain and make us merry at table'.

Short as it is, the book contains a great deal of very interesting material, but the only part to receive much attention from scholars has been the last, which has been well studied and described by historians of *exempla* and *facetiae*.[1] It now seems fairly certain that the work was composed some time in the second half of the fifteenth century, between the *floruit* of Johannes de Durren (d. 1468), who figures in one of the stories, and the date of the first edition, *c.* 1475 or 1480.[2] But no manuscripts of it earlier than the sixteenth century have so far come to light,[3] and the identity of the author is still shrouded in mystery. He was certainly not Michael Scot, whose name appears on the title-pages of seventeenth-century editions. A more likely possibility is that he was the Irish physician, Theobald Anguilbert, who wrote a prefatory epistle, and to whom the work was ascribed in at least three sixteenth-century French editions. It is equally possible, however, that this person may have only been the editor, as other editions indicate. J. T. Welter, who examined the question of authorship in some detail,[4] came to the conclusion that the work was composed by a German Dominican, since it contains a number of stories localized in Germany, a number of German names and references to Germans, and shows a marked preference for stories connected with the Dominican order.

An examination of the scientific and medical sections of the book tends to confirm its German origin. In the first place, I have now discovered that these sections, that is, parts one and three, are literal transcriptions from another, much more voluminous, anonymous work, the *Summa recrea-torum*, of undoubted German provenance, composed before 1412, the date of the earliest manuscript known to me.[5] Like the *Mensa philo-sophica*, this *Summa* contains a good deal of narrative material, and in

---

[1] Besides the study of T. F. Dunn, mentioned above, see G. Frenken, *Die Exempla des Jacob von Vitry*, *Q.U.L.P.M.* v. 1, pp. 73–80, and J. T. Welter, *L'Exemplum dans la littérature religieuse te didactique du moyen âge*, pp. 445 f. There is a translation by A. S. Way, *The Science of Dining*, but the introduction is misleading and of no historical value.

[2] Dunn, op. cit., p. 16.

[3] Only three manuscripts are known: Bibl. Nat. Lat. 8759 (xvi cent.); C l m 9092 (1679); Dublin, Trinity Coll. Lib. 417 (xvii cent.).   [4] In the work cited above.

[5] Prague, Bibl. Pub. et Univ. 207, ff. 51ᵛ–116: 'Completus est liber sub a. d. 1412 V fer. post Viti per Heinricum de Geylnhusen.' Another manuscript is Vienna Nationalbibl. 5371, ff. 185–234, written in a clear fifteenth-century German book hand.

addition several interesting Latin poems, among them three by the *poeta occultus*, Nicolaus de Bibra, who flourished at Erfurt towards the end of the thirteenth century.[1] The prologues in the two books contain similar passages,[2] both quote Macrobius, and there is no doubt that the *Summa*, as a whole, served as a model for the later, much briefer compilation. It contains five parts, the first consisting of 'curious questions', and corresponding exactly to the third part of the *Mensa*, the second discussing 'the natures and qualities of foods and drinks', and corresponding to Part I of the *Mensa*, the third dealing with 'the various properties of things necessary for a feast', of which only a small portion is inserted into Part I of the *Mensa*, the fourth containing 'pleasant stories and poems', none of which seem to be used in the *Mensa*, and the fifth 'worthy examples and laws', material which, again, is not used in the latter treatise. The parts dealing with diet, digestion, and the natures of all kinds of foods and drink consist chiefly of brief quotations from Galen, Hippocrates, Pliny, Dioscorides, Rhazes *In Almansor*, Isaac *De dietis*, Avicenna, Serapion, Constantinus, Averroes, and Arnald de Villanova *De regimine sanitatis*. The questions (Part I in the *Summa*, Part III in the *Mensa*) are in the concise form of the *quaestiones et responsiones*, and are likewise confined to the same gastronomical subjects. But, in addition to most of the authorities mentioned above, the author makes considerable use of the pseudo-Aristotelian *Problems* in the translation of Bartholomew, of the *Quaestiones super De animalibus* of Albertus Magnus, and of the *Problemata de animalibus* of Peter of Spain—exactly that combination which we found in the *Responsorium* of Conrad de Halberstadt, and, in fact, several of the questions and answers correspond exactly to those found in the latter work,[3] yet another

---

[1] On him see G. Bauch, *Die Universität Erfurt im Zeitalter des Frühhumanismus*, pp. 3–11 and *passim*; his poems have been edited by Theobald Fischer in *Geschichtsquellen der Provinz Sachsen*, Bnd. i, 1870.

[2] The prologue in the *Summa* reads 'De summa refectione karissimi refert *Macrobius primo libro Saturnalium* quod studioso animo nichil est iocundius utilius et delectabilius quam honeste colloqui de letis subtilibus ac curiosis questionibus. *Unde omnino videtur expediens* nobilibus dominis et prelatis literatis quod ipsorum convivalis collatio, ymmo gratiosa refectionis dedicatio, aut fit de curiosis questionibus quibus in conviviis subtiliter excitantur aut de naturis rerum esibilium et potabilium quibus in conviviis delectabiliter recreantur, aut de hiis que ad honestum convivium generaliter requiruntur aut de letis historiis et iocundis carminibus quibus studiosi hylariter delectantur, aut de virtuosis exemplis quibus regentes fideliter instituuntur. Idcirco hoc opusculum quod intitulatur summa recreatorum in quinque tractatus est distinguendum', Vienna, Nationalbibl. 5371, f. 185. Compare with this the following passage from the prologue to the *Mensa philosophica*, 'Quia ergo litteratorum mensis et conviviis philosophia conveniens debet interesse, quilibet utique sicut honestius ita utilis et delectabilis esse debet. Quia ut idem dicit *Macrobius libro primo*. Erit in mensa sermo iocundior: ut habeat voluptatis amplius severitatis minus. Oportet enim in convivio versari sermones uti castitate integros ita appetibiles venustate. *Videtur omnino expediens* ut sermo mensalis vel sit de natura rerum quibus vescimur et potamus vel de questionibus mensalibus quibus in mensa exercitamur vel de his et illorum moribus et conditionibus quibus in mensa sociamur, vel de his iocis et solaciis honestis quibus in mensa recreamur et exhilaramur' (ed. Cologne, Winters, [1480]).

[3] e.g. in the section *de vino*, qu. 2 and 3; in the *de carnibus*, qu. 1; *de ovis*, 7 questions out

indication, if any were needed, of the German origin of the *Summa recreatorum*.

But, to return to the *Mensa philosophica*, its skilfully blended mixture of instruction and entertainment proved exceedingly popular, and it was printed many times during the fifteenth and sixteenth centuries.[1] In addition to the nine or ten incunabula of the complete work[2] there are three of Part III printed separately with the title, *Questiones naturales philosophorum*,[3] and this third part, consisting of the questions and answers only, was added to no fewer than eight incunabula which contained the pseudo-Albertian *Liber aggregationis* and *De mirabilibus mundi*,[4] in one case in conjunction with the *Quaestiones naturales* of Adelard of Bath.[5] Thus incunabula containing the questions actually exceed in number those of the whole book—striking evidence of the fact that the third part was the most popular one, and that there was, as yet, no slackening of the all-pervading interest shown in this Aristotelian form of presentation.

Two early English translations of the *Mensa* have survived, but none into any other vernacular language, although it is hard to believe that the work was never translated into French. The first translator was Thomas Twyne (1543–1613), one time master of Canterbury Free School, the protégé of Lord Buckhurst and Sir Francis Walsingham, 'famed not only for medicine, but astrology, and much respected by Dee and Allen'.[6] His version was printed at London in 1576, with the title *The Schoolemaster, or Teacher of Table Phylosophie*, and again in 1583.[7] It is interesting to note that in 1578 Twyne also translated the *Physica christiana* of the Protestant minister and professor, Lambert Daneau, which had been praised by Tycho Brahe, dealt with the whole field of natural philosophy, and was written in the form of the Ciceronian dialogue, embodying questions and answers between master and pupil.[8]

Another translation of the *Mensa philosophica* by W. B. Esq. appeared in 1609, and was reprinted, with additions, in 1614 and 1633, this time with the title, *The Philosophers Banquet. Newly furnished with severall*

of 9 (qu. 3 and 5 being excepted); in the *de piscibus* all 4 questions; *de oleribus* all 6; in the *de fructibus*, qu. 1, 2, 4. A closer examination would no doubt reveal other correspondences.

[1] Dunn gives a list of 29 editions, op. cit., pp. 9–13, which includes two doubtful ones. It seems to me there is also some doubt about no. i, the Cologne *c.* 1475 ed.; see above, p. 107, n. 5. Klebs gives a much better account of the incunabula. The following are not mentioned by Dunn: Paris, F. Regnault, 1509 (Brit. Mus.), Paris, Johannes de Harsy, 1530 (author's collection). The two Brit. Mus. undated editions, Paris, D. Roce, ? 1515, and Paris, I. Frellon, ? 1525, may possibly be the same as the two undated Parisian editions mentioned by Dunn as being in the Bibl. Nat., i.e. nos. 24 and 25 in his list.

[2] Klebs, 676, nos. 1–9.   [3] Ibid. 821, nos. 1–3.

[4] Ibid. 18, nos. 46–53.

[5] Ibid. no. 53. See E. P. Goldschmidt, Cat. 25, item 9; copies are in the Bodleian, and the Hamburg and Memmingen libraries.

[6] Anthony Wood, *Athenae Oxonienses*, London, 1721, col. 387.

[7] *S.T.C.* 24411, 24412.

[8] Ibid. 6231, *The Wonderfull Woorkmanship of the World*. The Latin edition had first appeared at Geneva in 1575.

dishes.[1] The additions found in the second edition are mainly subjoined to the third part, and consist of short observations in natural philosophy, not in question form, 'taken out of Albertus Magnus, Lemnius and others' (pp. 193–206), a *Direction for Studie and Art* (pp. 206–9), *Receyts and Conclusions* (209–12), and a set of questions, mainly from the same sources —all these additions being written in a much-abbreviated, popular style. The fourth part contains only a very few of the stories, and is followed by a page or two of Epigrams, Riddles, and Proverbs.

So far we have only discussed collections of problems which, whether translated from the Greek or composed in Latin, were originally meant for the learned reader or student. It is true that, later on, many of these reached a wider public through vernacular translations. But about 1300, or even earlier, collections of questions began to appear which were composed in the vernacular for a different class of reader. Two of these, which lie entirely outside the Salernitan tradition and resemble oriental rather than Western models, have been ably dealt with by C. V. Langlois in his still invaluable *La Connaissance de la nature et du monde au moyen âge*, and so need not detain us long. The first is the *Livre de Sidrach*, supposedly translated from Arabic into Latin, by order of Frederick II, and subsequently from Latin into French, but which Langlois thought was originally written in the latter language, about the end of the thirteenth century.[2] Written in dialogue form, straightforward, often rather naïve, answers are given to a large number of basic questions, which cover the usual medieval divisions of *physica*, as well as the fields of ethics and theology, which are particularly well represented. The popularity of the work is shown by the large number of surviving manuscripts and printed editions,[3] and by the fact that it was translated into Dutch and English.[4] The second collection, also in dialogue form, is the *Placides et Timeo*, or *Le Livre des secrets aux philosophes*,[5] extant also in several manuscripts, the earliest being dated 1303. A very garbled and much-abbreviated version of this work was printed by Vérard in 1504, and subsequently by other printers, with the title, *Le Cuer de philosophie*.[6] This time resembling rather the pseudo-Aristotelian *Secret of Secrets*, the work contained, in addition to much moralizing, a good deal of physiognomy and astrology. A third collection was composed in Italian verse by the Bolognese astrologer and physician, Cecco d'Ascoli (d. 1327), and incorporated into his

---

[1] No copy has been traced of the first ed., the other two are listed under *S.T.C.* 22062 and 22063.   [2] See Langlois, op. cit., ch. 4.

[3] Paris, Vérard, 1483; ibid. 1496; Valence, 1513; Rouen, 1516; Paris, 1531, &c. Several manuscripts are listed by Langlois.

[4] For the incunabula of the Dutch translation see Klebs 945, nos. 1–3. The English translations are listed under *S.T.C.* 3186–8a. The first was by Hugh of Caumpeden into verse (London, Thomas Godfrey, *c.* 1530), and the second into prose, much abbreviated, by an anonymous translator (Robert Wyer, *c.* 1535).

[5] Langlois, op. cit., ch. 5.

[6] Paris, 1514, ibid. 1520, 1521, 1529, 1534, &c.

curious, didactic poem, *L'acerba*, written in *terza rima*, in imitation of Dante.[1] Although containing much later material dealing with magic and astrology, several of these rhymed questions, unlike the French ones we have been discussing, are Salernitan in origin,[2] and, on the whole, they are much more influenced by Western, Latin sources. Many editions followed the first one, printed at Brescia in 1473.[3]

In the next century, another Bolognese physician, Girolamo Manfredi (*fl. c.* 1460–93), composed his *Liber de Homine*, or *Il Perche* as it was called in later editions, first printed at Bologna in 1474. Written throughout in question-and-answer form, the book was entirely medical in tone, the first part dealing with the preservation of health, under the headings of the six 'non-naturals', diet (food and drink), sleeping and waking, exercise, evacuation (bathing, coitus, urine, faeces, perspiration), air (winds, the seasons, place), and actions of the passions (anger, joy, grief, fear). The second part dealt with the physiognomy of external features, the functions of the lungs, liver, spleen, and gall bladder, and generation. It will be seen that the contents cover roughly the same ground as do those of the pseudo-Aristotelian *Problems*, and indeed many of the questions are nothing more than brief epitomes of these problems. But Manfredi has added much new material, culled from later sources, particularly in the chapters dealing with dietetics, which contain a long didactic poem on this subject. Again, although many of the questions are Salernitan, through having been derived from common Greek sources, the answers do not correspond to the Salernitan ones, being either pseudo-Aristotelian, or derived from the later Arabic–Latin translations. There were two more editions in the fifteenth century, followed by many more in the sixteenth and seventeenth,[4] the later ones being expurgated in those parts which dealt with gynaecology and generation. A Spanish translation appeared *c.* 1570 from the pen of Pedro de Ribas, which was also frequently reprinted;[5] but, as far as I know, the work was never translated into any other language.

These four collections, designed both for the entertainment and instruction of the non-Latin-speaking reader, mark the beginning, in the West, of that taste for popular pseudo-science and medicine which was to become so widespread by the sixteenth and seventeenth centuries.

[1] On Cecco see Thorndike, *H.M.E.S.* ii, ch. 71, where, however, *L'acerba* receives very little attention. The title of the fifth book, in the Venice, 1546 ed., reads 'Qui comincia el quinto Libro che tratta de li problemi naturali circa la sententia mondana'.

[2] See, for instance, my note on Q.130 *lunare iubar*; also one of the Salernitan questions whose answers are analysed at the end of ch. 10 is discussed by Cecco.

[3] See Klebs 259, nos. 1–12, and Brunet i (1860), cols. 1713–14. Tiraboschi says there were nineteen editions up to 1546, *Storia della let. italiana*, v (1795), 194.

[4] Klebs 653, nos. 2 and 3; Brunet iii (1862), col. 1363. It continued to be published until at least as late as 1668.

[5] *El Porque, Libro de problemas, trad. de Toscano en lengua Castellana*, Saragossa. Other editions were: Madrid 1579; ibid. 1581; Alcala 1587; ibid. 1589; Madrid 1598. See Thorndike, *H.M.E.S.* vi. 167, where the derivation from Manfredi is not mentioned.

8

Dietrich Ulsen and the 'Speculator' Broadside

By the end of the fifteenth century, Latin translations of the pseudo-Aristotelian and pseudo-Alexandrian *Problems* had been printed, in some cases in more than one version, and generally in more than one edition. By then, too, had appeared three editions of Adelard's *Quaestiones naturales*, one of Seneca's book with the same title, one of the *Responsorium* of Conrad de Halberstadt, at least twenty of the *Mensa philosophica*, including separate publications of part three, either on its own or in company with other works, and twenty-six of the *Omnes homines*, including those of the German translation. It is curious, in view of their long manuscript tradition and ubiquitous influence, that no one ever thought of printing a selection of the Salernitan *Quaestiones* as such, that is with their correct attribution. The Salernitan *Regimen sanitatis* was printed at least thirty times[1] up to and including the year 1500, with the qualification *Salernitanum* included in the title, the *Quaestiones* not once, as far as we know, by themselves and with this indication of origin. Yet their presence was everywhere felt. As we have seen, many of the questions, either with their original Salernitan answers or later, different ones, had been included in the incunabula of original problem literature.

One of the largest collections of such questions to appear in print was undoubtedly the series of eighty-two comprised in that part of the *Questiones phisicales* which had been incorporated by the humanist physician Dietrich Ulsen into yet another German publication, namely his *Speculator* Broadside, published perhaps *c.* 1501 at Nürnberg. The intimate friend of Conrad Celtis (1459–1508), Ulsen was greatly praised both by the latter and other leading humanists of the time for his skill in poetry, medicine, and astrology. Yet today he is scarcely remembered, even by those most concerned with his period and environment, and a good deal of confusion still exists concerning the facts of his life.[2] It seems fairly clear, however, that he was born at Kampen in Overijssel, which is on the western bank of the Yssel near the Zuyder

[1] See Klebs, 397, No. 7; 815, No. 5; 829, Nos. 1–6; 830, Nos. 1–16; 831, Nos. 1–6.
[2] The account in the *A.D.B.* is both meagre in the extreme and inaccurate. Later accounts, such as those in H. Rupprich's *Briefwechsel des Conrad Celtis*, in A. Hirsch's *Biog. Lex. d. hervor. Aerzte*, v (1934), and even the one in the recent *Verfasserlex. d. deutschen Mittelalters*, iv (1952), are all misleading and far from complete.

Zee,[1] early in the second half of the fifteenth century, probably of lowly stock,[2] and that he received his earliest education at the famous school at Zwolle near by,[3] which was organized by the Brethren of the Common Life; the same school which initiated the studies of Johann Wessel (d. 1489), one of the very earliest and most enlightened of the German humanists.

The course lasted eight years, and here he would learn the subjects of the *trivium*, grammar, dialectic, and rhetoric, taught, not on humanist lines, but according to the old medieval methods of the schools. Here, too, he probably acquired a liking for that mysticism or *devotio moderna*, as it was called, which, stemming from Ruysbroek and Gerard Groote, was fostered at the neighbouring monasteries of Agnietenberg and Windesheim, and of which we find traces in several of his works.

Following R. G. H. Krause (1882), many scholars have stated that Ulsen attended the school at Deventer, which belonged to the same Brethren, and was a pupil there of the famous Alexander Hegius (1433–98).[4] One would like to think that this was so, but the dates do not fit. Krause based his assumption on some poems which Ulsen and Hegius exchanged with each other;[5] but although these indicate that the two men were friends, they certainly give no hint that Ulsen was ever a pupil of Hegius. The explicit of the *Prognosticon* shows that by 1488 Ulsen had obtained his M.A. and completed his medical training. But Hegius did not commence his rectorship of the school of Saint Lebuin in Deventer until 1483;[6] a date which hardly allows time for Ulsen to have attended there under Hegius, matriculate at a university, and obtain, first his M.A., which took anything from three to six years, and then his doctorate in medicine, after a further period in Italy of not less than four years.[7]

---

[1] Therefore he was not technically a Frisian, although always referred to as Theodoricus Ulsenius Phrisius.

[2] If we may literally interpret some lines towards the end of his *De Sancto Judoco Hymnus* (Deventer, *c.* 1507);

> Plaude votivas modulasse laudes
> Fictili plectro phrisium bubulcum
> Re domus parva medicas coactum
> Scandere in artes.

[3] In his *Prognosticon novum* of 1488 (C l m 957) he signs himself Theodorici Ulsenii Campensis Medici, and at the end writes, 'Ex Campis per me Theodoricum Ulsenium Svollensem Artium et Medicinae Doctorem.' See also, J. Ueltzen, 'Das Flugblatt des Arztes Theodoricus Ulsen', *Virchows Archiv*, clxii (1900), 371 ff.

[4] Krause, 'Der Leibarzt Dietrich Ulsenius', *J.V.M.G.* xlvii (1882), 141 ff.; B. Hartmann, *Celtis in Nürnberg*, p. 14; J. Ueltzen, art. cit.; E. P. Goldschmidt, *Hieronymus Münzer*, p. 40; A. Reimann, *Die älteren Pirckheimer*, p. 194 ff.

[5] Contained in C l m 428, f. 237ᵛ.

[6] See P. S. Allen, *Epist. Erasmi*, i. 580 ff.

[7] Some comparable dates are: Hieronymus Münzer, Leipzig 1464–70 (M.A.), then taught for four years at Leipzig, left for Italy in 1474, obtained his doctorate in medicine at Pavia in 1478 (see E. P. Goldschmidt, op. cit., pp. 14 ff.); Hartmann Schedel was at Leipzig from 1456 to 1461, and then at Padua from 1463 to 1466, when he obtained his doctorate. 'In the German

Therefore, until other evidence is forthcoming, it is wisest, I think, to assume that Ulsen only attended the school at Zwolle for his earliest training.

As regards the university to which he must have afterwards gone, Joseph Aschbach stated, as early as 1867, that he studied at Heidelberg; a statement repeated first by Hartmann (1889), and then, more recently, by Rupprich (1934).[1] I have not been able to find the original source for this assertion but, if true, it would fit in with, perhaps, the most probable explanation of where and when Ulsen received instruction in the humanities from Rudolph Agricola (1444–85), whom he names as his master in l. 21 of the *Speculator*.[2] It will be remembered that this great man, the foremost German humanist of his day, went to Heidelberg in the spring of 1484 at the earnest invitation of his friend and patron, Johann von Dalberg, bishop of Worms and Chancellor of the University. There he lectured in an unofficial capacity, and his coming acted as a magnet, attracting scholars from far and wide, who flocked there to sit at the feet of *vir ille plane divinus*, as Erasmus called him. Had Ulsen gone to Heidelberg from Zwolle, he could, just about, still have been there in 1484, and so heard Agricola before going to Italy and getting his doctorate in 1488. Agricola stayed barely a year at Heidelberg, since in the spring of 1485 he accompanied von Dalberg to Rome in the capacity of private secretary. The bishop had been chosen to give an oration to the newly elected pope, Innocent VIII, and when this task had been accomplished the party returned to Germany in July of the same year. On the way Agricola contracted a fever, and although he recovered sufficiently to reach Heidelberg, he died in the arms of Dalberg on 27 October 1485, at the early age of 41. If, therefore, Ulsen had not heard him at Heidelberg in 1484, it is difficult to see when he could have had instruction from him, since from 1468/9 to 1479 Agricola was in Italy, except for one or two brief visits to Germany, and from 1480, after his return to Holland, till 1484, when he accepted Dalberg's invitation, he was chiefly occupied with official business in connexion with the post he held under the Municipal Council of Gröningen, and had little time for lecturing. It is rather significant, too, that two of Ulsen's greatest friends in after life, Conrad Celtis and the Westphalian humanist, Hermann von dem Busche (1468–1534), were

universities the usual period before the Bachelor's degree seems to have been a year and a half, and two years more for the mastership.' H. Rashdall, *Universities*, i. 463 (note 3). As regards the conditions at Bologna for obtaining the degree of doctor in medicine, the same author says, '. . . the candidate was required to be twenty years of age, of five years' standing in the study of medicine and "sufficient in arts". If he had been licensed in arts, four years' study of medicine sufficed.' Ibid. i. 247. The conditions at Padua and Pavia were similar to those at the parent university.

[1] J. Aschbach, *Roswitha u. Conrad Celtes*, p. 36; B. Hartmann, loc. cit.; Rupprich, *Briefw. d. Celtis*, p. 90.

[2] That this refers to Rudolph Agricola and not to the Gregorius Agricola of the riddles will become apparent later on. See below, p. 124.

to be found at Heidelberg in 1484—both having come there in that year, attracted by the fame of Agricola.

Gustav Bauch (1907) says that Ulsen completed his medical training in Italy.[1] Again, I cannot find his original source, but it was certainly the established custom in those days for German students in medicine to go to Italy to complete their training, after having obtained their M.A. at one or other of the German universities. He would probably have gone to Padua or Pavia, the two Italian universities most frequented by the German nation at that time.

At any rate, by 1488 Ulsen had obtained his doctorate and was back in his native land. The *Prognosticon* of that year, almost certainly the first work he wrote,[2] is a short defence of judicial astrology, addressed in the most flattering terms to David of Burgundy, bishop of Utrecht. Without specific originality, it is interesting only for the authorities quoted, which indicate Ulsen's reading at that period, and for the fact that it already shows his leaning towards mysticism and a species of Neoplatonic pantheism which was cultivated at the Florentine Academy in Italy, and which, later on, was to have a profound effect on Celtis and other members of his circle.

Of Ulsen's activities as physician in Kampen we know nothing, but he cannot have remained long at this place, since by 1492 he was practising in Nürnberg.[3] Before this, however, he may have practised in Deventer, where he became friendly with Hegius,[4] and may have met for the first time Bartholomew of Cologne, who was then a master in Hegius's school, and who dedicated two poems to Ulsen in his *Silva Carminum*, published by the Deventer printer, Jacobus de Breda, in 1491. We are rather better informed about Ulsen's Nürnberg period, owing to the seventeen letters which he wrote to Celtis, preserved in the latter's *codex epistolaris* edited

---

[1] G. Bauch, *Aus d. Gesch. d. Mainzer Humanismus*, p. 39; H. Rupprich, op. cit., p. 90.

[2] This we gather from the words, 'Statui ego ingenioli nostri primitias ac lucubratiunculas nonnullas ad reverendissimam dominationem tuam mittere...', in the dedication to the bishop, as well as from the rather immature character of the work itself.

[3] As we learn from Jacob Canter's letter to Celtis, dated 5 Dec. 1492, 'scripsit nuper ad me litteras Theodoricus Ulsenius, qui Noremburgae medicum publice agit, tibi (nisi fallor) haud ignoratus'. Rupprich, op. cit., Letter 49. Ulsen's first letter to Celtis is dated 1492, Letter 55. There seems no basis at all for the supposition that he was state physician in Nürnberg as early as 1486, a fact first stated by A. Blanck, *Die Meklenburgischen Aerzte*, p. 4, who was followed by Lier in *A.D.B.* (1895), by Hirsch in *Biog. Lex. d. hervor. Aerzte*, v. 677 ff., and by the *Verfasserlex. d. deutschen Mittelalters*, iv. 630. Perhaps this date is a misprint for 1496, the date of Ulsen's first publication in Nürnberg. The same doubt attaches to Ellinger's statement that he was state physician in Augsburg in 1486, *Gesch. d. neulat. Lit. Deutschlands*, i. 398, copied by H. Rupprich, op. cit., p. 90. Ellinger's dates for Ulsen's Nürnberg period, 1498–1502, are certainly wrong.

[4] The occasion for the exchange of verses between the two men, mentioned above, p. 114, was Ulsen's departure for Nürnberg. I am sure that J. Ueltzen, art. cit., fixes the date of Ulsen's stay in Deventer much too early, when he says, without quoting his authority, that he practised there, 'in the early eighties, when the plague was prevalent', i.e. *c.* 1484.

by Hans Rupprich in 1934. These letters cover a period of about ten years (*c.* 1492–1501), during which Ulsen was *nominatissimus Archyatrus*, as Danhauser calls him,[1] in the city. Written in a highly conversational, concise, and lively style, they are full of obscure allusions, puns, and a kind of whimsical humour, and reveal an energetic, practical nature—in many ways quite the opposite to that of his more indolent and pleasure-loving friend.

In his capacity as state physician, besides treating private patients, he looked after cases at the public hospital, often, apparently, at his own expense;[2] and from about 1496 onwards was much concerned in finding a cure for syphilis, a disease which had only recently come to Germany. In addition he became a member of two literary societies founded by Celtis, the *Sodalitas Rhenana* (1495) and the *Sodalitas Danubiana* (1497), and must also have found time for teaching and writing. Belonging to his Nürnberg period we have an *Oration* to the Senators (C l m 962), probably written soon after his arrival in the city, an edition of the *Aphorisms* of Hippocrates (Hochfeder 1496), which also contains his *Clinicum pharmacandi modum*, a purely didactic poem on pharmacology and regimen,[3] the Broadside, *Vaticinium in epidemicam scabiem* (H. Maier, 1496),[4] the prose *Cura mali francici* (C l m 963),[5] the *Speculator* Broadside, two poems describing the lives of miracle-working saints,[6] a prose fragment, the *Lumen vitae* (C l m 528), and a number of epigrams and short poems addressed to his fellow humanists, most of which still remain in manuscript.[7] Of all these works the *Vaticinium* is the only one at all remembered today, first because, excluding the Imperial Edict of 7 August 1495, it is the earliest definitely dated work on syphilis to appear in print,[8] and secondly because the fine woodcut in the centre of the Broadside has been

---

[1] In a letter prefixed to his edition of the *Opera* of William of Auvergne, bishop of Paris, Nürnberg, A. Koberger, 1496, reprinted by Freytag, *Adparatus Lit.* iii. 200 ff., and by C. H. Fuchs in his edition of Ulsen's *Vaticinium* Broadside (l. 3), Ulsen had evidently taught Danhauser.

[2] Rupprich, op. cit., Letter 85.

[3] Klebs 520. The only copy extant seems to be that in the Army Medical Library, Washington, see Schullian and Sommer's Catalogue of this library, 241. The *Clinicum* was later edited by Georgius Pictorius in at least three editions of his *Sermones conviviales*, Basel, 1559, 1571, 1596, and two fifteenth-century transcripts of Ulsen's version are found in Nationalbibl. Vienna, Cod. lat. 4772.

[4] Klebs 1004, No. 1, *Einbl.* 1467. Facsimiles, *Virchows Archiv*, 162 (1900), Taf. 12; *I.Z.*, 15 Feb. 1900, No. 2955; Sudhoff, *Erstlinge d. Syphilislit.*, Taf. 5. A second edition appeared at Augsburg, *c.* 1498. Klebs 1004, No. 2; *Einbl.* 1466. Facsimile, Sudhoff, *Erstlinge*, Taf. 6, edited by C. H. Fuchs. A transcript, made in 1501, is contained in Erlangen Univ. Bibl. Cod. lat. 640, ff. 90ᵛ–93ᵛ.

[5] Edited, with German translation, by Sudhoff in *Aus der Frühgesch. der Syphilis*, p. 48 ff.

[6] The *Centimetrum in praeconium Switberti antistis*, C l m 528, 206ᵛ–207, and *Divis martiribus Cosme et Damiano fratribus medicis Sapphicum Carmen*, C l m 14554, ff. 1–2ᵛ.

[7] C l m 428, 486, 528, all transcribed by Hartmann Schedel.

[8] Amongst undated works it was only preceded by Conrad Schellig's *In pustulas malas morbum quem malum de francia vulgus apellat . . . consilium*, printed at Heidelberg at the end of 1495 or beginning of 1496. See Sudhoff–Singer, *The Earliest Printed Literature on Syphilis*.

attributed by many able critics to Dürer.[1] Original in conception and betraying a lively imagination, the poem describes, in narrative form, the astrological origin of the disease, and shows a practical grasp of its nature and symptoms which surpasses that of the majority of his colleagues.[2] The *Cura mali francici* gives us the best summary that we have of Ulsen's general views on medical practice, health, and hygiene. Its fifty aphorisms are much influenced by the Neoplatonic doctrines of Ficino, and contain ideas, particularly in psychological medicine, which are far in advance of those held elsewhere in Germany during the last decades of the fifteenth century, as Sudhoff has pointed out.[3]

On 1 March 1501 Ulsen and other humanists assisted Celtis in a performance of the latter's play, *Ludus Dianae*, acted before Maximilian I at Linz on the Danube, and it was about the same time, as Bauch thinks, that he was crowned Poet Laureate by the emperor.[4] But unfortunately this year also witnessed the downfall of the newly crowned poet-physician. For during it he lost, at one stroke, all his accumulated savings, through the activities of a dishonest merchant in Nürnberg. Thus he was compelled to abandon all his numerous undertakings, sell his books to pay certain debts, and leave the city of his choice, becoming from now on a restless wanderer on the face of the earth.[5] He visited in turn Mainz (1502),[5] Augsburg, where he published an edition of the *De insania Democriti* of Hippocrates (*c.* 1503),[6] Freiburg-im-Breisgau (1504), where he lectured for one year and became friendly with members of the Wimpheling circle, including the Carthusian prior and schoolmaster, Gregorius Reisch,[7] and Cologne,

---

[1] For a discussion of this aspect of the Broadside, see J. Ueltzen, 'Das Flugblatt des Theodoricus Ulsenius mit Dürers Illustration', *Z. Buch.* (1900), i. 151 ff.

[2] It thus anticipates by thirty-four years the more famous poem *De Morbo gallico sive de Syphilide* of Girolamo Fracastoro, Verona, 1530, which also attributes the disease to the malevolent actions of Saturn and Mars (Book I, ll. 413–15), and seems, in other respects, to be influenced by Ulsen's poem; cf. Book I, ll. 45 ff. with *Vaticinium*, ll. 58 ff. where both poets use the simile of spreading fire to illustrate the rapid diffusion of the disease.

[3] In his edition of the work, see above, p. 117, n. 5. Some of these ideas are also found in the writings of Ulsen's one-time master, Dr. Ulrich Pinder of Nürnberg, cf. his *Speculum intellectualis felicitatis humanae*, Nürnberg, 1510. At least two other colleagues of Ulsen, Drs. Hartmann Schedel and Hieronymus Münzer, must have been much influenced by Neoplatonism, to judge by the contents of their libraries. Certainly, in south Germany medieval medicine was undergoing a rapid transformation long before the time of Paracelsus.

[4] See G. Bauch, *Aus d. Gesch. d. Mainzer Humanismus*, pp. 39 ff. Lines 7–8 of the *Speculator* probably refer to this event.

[5] He informs Celtis of this catastrophe in a typical, rather humorous letter, Rupprich, op. cit., Letter 263.

[6] The volume contains a very curious elegy by Ulsen on the death of his friend and fellow countryman, Adolph Occo, the elder, who had died in Augsburg on 24 July 1503. Klebs 522.

[7] See H. Schreiber, *Gesch. d. Albert-Ludwigs-Univ. zu Freiburg* pp. 230 ff. He contributed verses to Wimpheling's *Statuta Synodalia Basiliensis*, *c.* 1507, to the *Bursa Pavonis* of Joannes Eck, Strassb., 1507, and to the second edition of the famous *Margarita philosophica* of Gregorius Reisch, 1504. See R. Ritter von Srbik, 'Die Margarita Philosophica des Greg. Reisch', *A.W.W.D.*, Bd. civ (1941), 90 ff. Srbik thinks that this second edition was printed at Freiburg i.B., and not at Strassburg, as stated on the title.

where he formed one of a band of learned men which the abbot Johannes Trithemius had gathered about him, while attending the Imperial Diet in 1505.[1] Later on in the same year Ulsen arrived in Lübeck in company with the learned and cultured humanist, Nicolaus Marschalk (*c.* 1460–1525), who was on his way to Schwerin to enter the service of the young dukes of Mecklenburg.

Finally, in 1507, Ulsen too was persuaded to enter the ducal service, as far as we know the last appointment he ever held.[2] To this period belongs the *De Sancto Judoco Hymnus* (Deventer, Ric. Paffraet, *c.* 1507), to which Celtis and other friends contributed verses. Some lines towards the end of this poem indicate that Ulsen's declining years were clouded with bitterness and discontent, and seem to hint that he was shortly going to follow in the steps of the hero of his poem and retire from active life.[3] Celtis's poem contributed to this book speaks as if he had already done this[4], and since Celtis died on 4 February 1508, it looks as though his friend must have left the court before this date. The young Duke Erich died of an infectious disease at the end of this year on 22 December, and one would have thought that Ulsen would have stayed on until this event. However, extracts from the account book of the ducal steward, Claus Trutmann, show only two payments to Ulsen, of 10 and 6 gulden respectively, for

[1] Trithemius has left a pleasant description of this little gathering of kindred spirits, *Epist. fam.* 20, *Opera Trithemii*, Frankfurt, 1601, ii. 454.

[2] For the period of Ulsen's stay in Lübeck and Schwerin, see G. C. F. Lisch, 'Ueber des Herzogs Magnus II von Meklenburg Lebensende', *J.V.M.G.* xxxix (1874), 49–58. Ulsen's contract and terms of service are, or were, preserved among the ducal archives, and have been printed in full by A. Blanck, *Die Meklenburgischen Aerzte*, pp. 4 ff. They are interesting and revealing documents.

[3] These lines may be translated as follows: 'I scorn to heap up riches and treasure. Beloved poverty is nowhere corrupted, neither can the murmurs of the crowd truly harm her reputation. My Clio despises the worldly sceptre, the crooked serpent of Geryon, and whatsoever conceals the crimes of impious Kings. From the deceitful shafts of these things will I fly, and thou alone canst show the way, thou who art a tower of strength to the pilgrim who is ready.' Ulsen is here not following the classical description of Geryon in Ovid, Virgil, Hesiod, and others, but that given by Dante, *Inferno*, xvii, ll. 10 ff.

> La faccia sua era faccia d'uom giusto,
> tanto benigna avea di fuor la pelle,
> e d'un serpente tutto l'altro fusto;

Dante makes him the unclean image of fraud,

> E quella sozza imagine di froda,

who carries Dante and Virgil into the abyss of Malebolge, and Ulsen is here using the same image to symbolize fraud and deceit. St. Judocus (d. 699), son of Juthael, King of Brittany, succeeded to the throne, but renounced his kingdom and the world, and retired into a hermitage near Montreuil, which later became a Benedictine Abbey, St. Josse-sur-Mer, and a place of pilgrimage throughout the Middle Ages.

[4]
> Et Maximilianum secutus
> Indicem numine vel Judoci

(He served Maximilian, and even, by the will of God, followed the guidance of St. Judocus). I have followed the reading *indicem* of the later reprint of the poem in P. Suffridus, *De Scriptoribus Frisiae*, Cologne, 1593, p. 53, which makes better sense than the *indice* of the earlier version. Literally, the meaning is pointer or index; in the first and last verses of the *Hymnus* Ulsen refers to St. Judocus as a guiding star.

the year 1508, both for attending Duke Erich, whereas for the previous year he had 107 gulden[1]—which seems to confirm that he left before the end of the year. After that all trace of him vanishes, and it is presumed that he died not long afterwards at 's Hertogenbosch, where he was buried in the choir of the great cathedral of St. John.[2]

The *Speculator* Broadside is, in many ways, the most interesting of Ulsen's works. It has never been critically examined, and only one example is known, which owes its preservation to the physician and chronicler Dr. Hartmann Schedel (1440–1514) of Nürnberg, to whose care and prodigious industry we are indebted for transcriptions of so many writings of the German humanists, including several by Ulsen. Schedel inserted the Broadside, together with others, into his own copy of his famous *Liber Chronicorum* (A. Koburger, 1493)—a copy which is further enriched with copious notes in the hand of the author, and which now forms one of the chief treasures of the Bayerische Staatsbibliothek at Munich.[3] In the centre of the Broadside is an enigmatic woodcut (see Frontispiece), with the strange and elaborate title *Speculator Consiliorum Enigmaticus Microcosmi Protheati Torrens* above it; underneath, two sets of verse riddles, bearing the names of Th(eodoricus) Ulsenius and Gre(gorius) Agricola; and the main poem, in two columns of 82 hexameters each, on either side. The words *Testes Procedant* head the columns, one word on each side, thus heightening the medieval character of the title, and giving the effect of law court procedure, or examination at the bar, which is so familiar a feature in medieval dialogues and debates, and in the later school dramas.

On stylistic evidence alone, from the words, 'Phoebus risen from the Frisian waves' (ll. 5–6), and from the peculiar use of certain rare words, I had attributed the main poem to the pen of Ulsen,[4] and this attribution was recently confirmed by my discovery of an earlier version, or first draft, of the poem in the Westdeutsche Bibliothek at Marburg/Lahn.[5] This has Ulsen's name on the title and a note of recommendation at the end, also bearing his name, which suggests that the whole manuscript may be in the poet's own hand. About the same time I made another

---

[1] See Lisch, art. cit., p. 54.

[2] See Foppens, *Bibl. Belg.* 1739, ii. 1128, and J. Ueltzen, 'Das Flugblatt des Arztes Theodoricus Ulsen', *Virchows Archiv*, clxii (1900), 371 ff.

[3] Described by Dr. A. Ruland, *Serapeum*, xv (1854), 145.

[4] Neither Hain, *Rep. Bib.* *14898, nor Ruland, nor *Einbl.* (1394) attributed the work to Ulsen. The first to do so was J. Ueltzen, 'Das Flugblatt des Theodoricus Ulsenius', *Z. Buch.* (1900), p. 151, on the rather slender grounds of similarity in format to the *Vaticinium* and the presence of Ulsen's name over one set of riddles. Subsequently it was attributed to Ulsen by G. Bauch, *Die Univ. Erfurt*, p. 125, R. Stauber, *Die Schedelsche Bibl.* p. 87, and E. P. Goldschmidt, *H. Münzer*, p. 40. The Broadside is not mentioned at all in the accounts of Ulsen contained in Rupprich, *Briefw. d. Celtis*; Hirsch, *Biog. Lex. d. hervor. Aerzte*, v; and the *Verfasserlex.* iv; neither is it mentioned in Klebs, *Incunabula Scientifica et Medica*.

[5] Berlin, lat. quarto 143 (Rose 152ʳ), ff. 175–6, kept since the war at Marburg/Lahn.

interesting discovery, which was that Ulsen was not the author of the whole of the poem, but of only part of it; that he had, in fact, used about half of the Salernitan *Questiones phisicales*. He gave it a new high-sounding title, added an introduction of thirty lines and a few other lines, omitted the first line from Claudian's *In Rufinum*, and made various other slight alterations. In the earlier draft the title is different, the introduction is more clumsy, and the ending of the poem, also from Ulsen's pen, is obviously in a trial stage.

The note of recommendation at the end runs as follows;

I beg thee, Reverend Father, that these problematical riddles may be discussed among thy companions, and indeed to tell me whether they seem worth publishing. And if there be anyone among you more curious in these matters, let him too, at thy request, determine something about them in any way he likes. If ye should chance to get them published ye would be doing a favour for thy ever grateful Ulsenius, which must be rewarded with a gift.[1]

Who was this prelate whom Ulsen addresses as *paternitatem tuam*? If my conjecture that Phoebe (Diana) in l. 6 of the *Speculator* refers to Bonomus, who certainly acted with Ulsen in the *Ludus Dianae* and is thought to have played the part of Diana, is correct, then this humanist, who became bishop of Trieste in 1501 and was besides one of Ulsen's closest friends, would be the most likely person.[2] But this form of address was also commonly used for an abbot (see Trithemius, *Epist. Familiares, passim*), and in south Germany at that time there seem to have been at least four who were favourable towards the new learning and scientific studies, and with whom Ulsen could have been friendly. First, Johannes Trithemius, abbot of Sponheim in the Palatinate, probably the most learned and famous of them all; a man whom Ulsen would certainly know through the *Sodalitas Rhenana*, of which both men were members, and whom Ulsen visited during his stay in Cologne, in 1505, as we saw. Another possibility is Johann Radenecker, abbot of the Benedictine monastery of St. Aegidius in Nürnberg from 1477 to 1504, a particular friend of both Schedels and an encourager of humanist and scientific studies.[3] Then there was Sebald Bamberger, abbot of the Cistercian monastery of Heilbronn from 1498 to 1581, a friend of Celtis and a scholar who did much to enlarge the library.[4] This monastery was one of those most affected by the spirit of the new learning, culturally it was

---

[1] For text, see below, p. 166.

[2] On him see Rupprich, op. cit., p. 191. C l m 428 contains a letter from Ulsen to Bonomus and verses which were exchanged between the two men. In 1497 Ulsen recommended to his notice a *Centimetrum*, perhaps the one contained in C l m 528. See above, p. 117, n. 6, and Rupprich, op. cit., p. 269.

[3] On him see *Mittelalterliche Bibliothekskat.* iii. 3, p. 426; R. Stauber, op. cit., p. 84; A. Reimann, *Die älteren Pirckheimer*, p. 161; Goldschmidt, op. cit., p. 32.

[4] See Reimann, op. cit., pp. 163 ff., and Rupprich, op. cit., p. 515.

entirely under the influence of Nürnberg, and the monks there were in constant communication with that city and Heidelberg. Hartmann Schedel attended there in his capacity as physician, and doubtless took part in many a learned discussion. In the fourth place one should mention Conrad Mörlin, abbot of the Benedictine monastery of Sts. Ulrich and Affra at Augsburg from 1496 until 1510, under whose rule all kinds of learning, and the arts, greatly flourished.[1] He was a member of the *Sodalitas Literaria Augustana*, another of the literary societies founded by Celtis, of which the Frisian poet-physician Adolph Occo and Blasius Holzel, one of the imperial secretaries, both friends of Ulsen, were also members. The humanist manuscript in my possession which contains a contemporary transcript of the *Speculator* Broadside, also contains Sapphic hymns sung by the writer while attending prayers in this monastery, when Morlin was abbot. The form of address used by Ulsen could also apply to a prior of a Carthusian monastery, who held a similar position to an abbot in other orders, and governed the monks in each separate monastery. George Pirckheimer, prior of the Carthusian monastery in Nürnberg while Ulsen was there, yet another active member of the Celtis circle and encourager of humanism, cannot, therefore, be left out of the picture.[2] Neither can the mysterious *Georgius Truchsess Religiosus Pater et Frater* to whom Ulsen addressed a short letter and epigram (C l m 428), and whom I have been altogether unsuccessful in tracing. It is instructive, too, to remember that about 1490 Hieronymus Münzer, Ulsen's friend and colleague, held a public disputation on magic and witchcraft at the Dominican monastery in Nürnberg. The question debated was whether these pernicious arts and 'abject vanities' could be performed 'according to the principles of natural philosophy',[3] which shows, I think, that the monks there could not have been averse to the new spirit of scientific investigation and inquiry. From this monastery came Johann Kuno (*c.* 1463–1513), the famous Greek scholar and humanist, the friend of Amorbach and Erasmus. A longer search would probably suggest other names, but without further evidence this would not help us much. At the moment all we can be certain about is that the first draft of the *Speculator* was sent for discussion and comment, not to a professor at some university like Celtis, or a colleague like Münzer or Pinder, or a rich patron of the arts and sciences like Willibald Pirckheimer or Sebald Schreyer, but to an influential prelate.

Whether this person was connected with a monastery or not, there is no doubt that a scientific curiosity entirely in keeping with the Italian humanist tradition was very much alive in the monasteries of south Germany towards the end of the fifteenth century. To some extent, perhaps,

---

[1] See Rupprich, op. cit., p. 213.
[2] See Reimann, op. cit., p. 180 ff. One of his protégés was Petrus Danhauser, who had been a pupil of Ulsen.   [3] The question is printed by Goldschmidt, op. cit., pp. 41 ff.

this was a continuation of that scientific curiosity which had been present in north German ecclesiastical circles during the previous century, owing to the lasting influence of Albertus Magnus. But undoubtedly a fresh impulse was received from Italy, which the southern monasteries did a great deal to propagate. The part played by these houses in the spread of humanism and scientific culture has not yet been fully investigated, as Reimann has pointed out.[1]

Let us now glance at the poem itself. Ulsen's introduction, with its pedantic neo-classicisms, unusual medieval words, and strangely forced similes, is characteristic of his work. The references to Etna (ll. 17–19) and to his departure from 'the sulphureous streams' (l. 25) are, perhaps inspired by his Italian visit. The last three lines, also Ulsen's, show traces of that German mysticism which he affected, and echo the oft repeated refrain against moral laxity and degeneration, both typical of pre-Reformation humanism in Germany and symptomatic of the prevailing spiritual unrest and dissatisfaction. Considering the work as a whole, it would be hard to find a more perfect illustration of the continuity of thought between the Middle Ages and the later Renaissance, and of the gradual merging of the one into the other.

In 1492 when Celtis published his inaugural *Oration*, delivered in the University of Ingolstadt, he printed with it an Ode with the title 'The things in which young men should be instructed' (*Quibus instituendi sint adolescentes*).[2] This contained a brief outline of his proposed curriculum of studies at Ingolstadt, which was later to be adopted at the *Collegium* at Vienna, and the poem took the form of a series of exhortations to find out the answers to a number of questions in natural philosophy, including meteorology, astronomy, cosmography, and history. This ode, with its reiterated 'find out why' (*Perge cur*), and insistence on scientific investigation and inquiry, may have supplied a hint to Ulsen in the preparation of his *Speculator*; like the latter, it ends on a moral note—*Perge virtutis generosus artum | callem*—as indeed we should expect. There are traces of this questioning spirit in some other Odes of Celtis, notably in i. 20, ll. 69 ff.; i. 27, ll. 77 ff.; and i. 29, and there is no doubt he did much to encourage and foster what one may call 'the spirit of scientific inquiry' amongst the humanists of his circle. Later on, Ulsen's friend, the poet Hermann von dem Busche, asked in his *Apologia*[3] a series of questions on astronomy, meteorology, and natural philosophy, strikingly similar to those of Celtis, not forgetting the usual moral reflections. Thus, following the lead of the great classic figures of antiquity, Lucretius, Virgil, and Ovid, it was the poets in Germany who now took up the challenge, and helped to stimulate a growing interest in all branches of natural

[1] Op. cit., p. 161.
[2] Printed with translation and commentary in L. W. Forster's *Selections from Conrad Celtis*.
[3] See his *Epigrammatum Liber*, Leipzig, 1504, sig. F₁.

philosophy—a rather significant fact, when one thinks of the tremendous gulf which separates the two cultures today.

A word must be said about the riddles. Several humanists amused themselves by composing these in Latin verse. Like the epigram, it was quite a fashionable employment, especially during the sixteenth century; and in Reusner's *Aenigmatographia* (Frankfurt, 1602) may be found several by such men as Julius Caesar Scaliger, Eobanus Hess, Joachim Camerarius and Adrianus Junius. Those in the *Speculator* Broadside are interesting, if only because they appear to be the earliest printed Latin verse riddles to have survived, and because they add to the comparatively slender stock of late medieval riddles known to have been composed in Europe before 1500.[1] Their form is curious, the answer to each riddle being a word ending in X, and in some cases the first word in a line is the solution to the riddle in the previous line. Most of Ulsen's riddles are exceedingly obscure, like much of his work. One shows the influence of Ficino (no. 8), another, of Apollodorus (no. 3), an exceedingly rare author in the early Renaissance. In complete contrast, those of Gregorius Agricola are all perfectly straightforward and need little comment.

How or when Ulsen came to know this Silesian humanist, I have never been able to find out. His real name was Gregorius Lengesfelt de Vratislavia, and he matriculated at Erfurt during the winter of 1482/3, becoming B.A. in 1485, and M.A. in 1489, a year after the earliest date we have for the commencement of Ulsen's medical practice. Bauch says that he stayed on at Erfurt for some time, studying scholastic philosophy and the *humaniora*, and then returned to Breslau, where he received a professorship, and was greatly in the favour of Bishop Johann IV.[2] In 1504 he became a canon, in 1513 vicar-general, and in 1517 archdeacon, a post he held until his death in 1527. It would thus seem that Lengesfelt was either about the same age as Ulsen, or, as is more probable, younger; and it is difficult to see how Ulsen could have been referring to him as his master in l. 21 of the *Speculator*. It is true we do not know when Lengesfelt returned to Breslau, or whether or not he gave any lectures at Erfurt after 1489. But Ulsen's time, from 1488 to *c.* 1501, the approximate date of the Broadside,[3] seems to have been pretty well filled up, first in his native land, and after 1492 in Nürnberg, where we find him exceedingly busy with his practice, lecturing, and other matters. Thus it is extremely unlikely that he could have attended lectures during this period by Lengesfelt, at either Erfurt or Breslau. His training was finished, and he was then imparting his knowledge to others, not going about in quest of it himself. Apart from anything else, the term *Angelici agricole* suits much better

---

[1] See Archer Taylor's *The Literary Riddle before 1600*. The *Speculator* riddles are not mentioned. These were probably composed before the main poem, since we find them transcribed by Schedel *c.* 1498. See below, p. 157.

[2] Bauch, *Die Univ. Erfurt*, pp. 123 ff.   [3] Concerning this date see Note F, p. 208.

the universally beloved and respected Rudolph than the obscure young humanist from Silesia.

There remains the woodcut, in some ways the most remarkable feature of this interesting Broadside (see Frontispiece). This represents man, the Microcosm, surrounded as far as the waist by the sphere of the Macrocosm, and hanging head downwards from the Empyrean heaven, which is surrounded by the fixed stars and surmounted by the Pelican feeding her young—the emblem of Piety. The man's right hand holds a spade, his left a child's whirligig, whilst both hands grasp a chain connecting him with the radiant image of the Sun. In the centre of the macrocosmic sphere, just over the man's head, is the image of the Moon, which has dominion over the brain. At the bottom of the picture, in the midst of a flowery meadow, there arises the parapet of a well round which is entwined the sinuous body of a serpent bearing a crowned human head. Arising from the waters of the well are two human legs, feet upwards, and from the soles of the feet issue flames. Also emerging from the waters are another flame, a claw-like object, and a creature rather like a lobster which resembles early woodcuts of the watery sign of Cancer. On the left hand of this curious picture we have a series of birds, headed by the Phoenix, and on the right, a column of animals headed by the Salamander.

Now this enigmatical design has, I think, two meanings, an obvious straightforward one, and a more hidden, mystical one. In the first place the picture undoubtedly represents all the subjects embraced by the series of questions in the *Speculator*—the universe, the world, the four elements, man, birds, beasts, and the herbs of the field. It also represents the *vermis sciens* (Satan), the *puteus draconum* (Hell), and the *ethereus radius*, symbolized by the Sun, the three concepts mentioned by Ulsen right at the end of the poem. The spade, emblem of the farmer, is, I think, a punning reference to the two Agricolas of the Broadside; Rudolph, mentioned in l. 21 of the *Speculator*, and Gregorius, the author of the second set of riddles. In both cases punning references exist in the text (*Speculator*, l. 20, and Gregorius' first riddle). If this is so, the whirligig may be a reference to Ulsen, explained by the first line of his set of riddles, in which there may be a pun on the word *turbine*, for *turbo* can mean a whirligig as well as a whirling dance. Apart from this, however, these two emblems could just as well symbolize the two elements, earth and air, or two ages of man, childhood and manhood, play and work, or even indicate that man's best and happiest state was one in which work was combined with recreation. The reader can choose which explanation he likes; perhaps Ulsen intended a combination of several meanings.

As regards the mystical meaning of the picture, below we see man the Microcosm[1] immersed head downwards in a hell upon earth, surrounded

[1] Typified by 'Germanos' in the Broadside, by *rectumque piumque* in the early draft. See my note on l. 163 below, p. 190.

by Satan, the 'cunning worm', and tormented by lesser devils, represented by the claw and image of Cancer and the hell-fires of the evil passions, anger, envy, greed, lust, &c., represented by the flames. Above, we see him as the *microcosmus protheatus* of the title, changed and transformed through piety and confession symbolized by the Pelican,[1] irradiated by the light of reason and truth symbolized by the Moon just over his head, by the chains connecting him with the Sun, and by the *ethereus radius* of the latter, and existing as the central focus of the universe, a being round whom everything revolves, for whom everything exists. In other words, we have here in pictorial form, concepts which we find continually recurring, not only in Ulsen's writings, but in the works of all the pre-Reformation German humanists.

What is remarkable and original, then, is not so much the underlying meaning of the picture, as the method adopted to convey this meaning—the peculiar form of the imagery. One cannot help thinking of the simoniacs and flatterers in Dante's *Inferno*, Canto XIX:

> Io vidi per le coste et per lo fondo
> piena la pietra livida di fori,
> d'un largo tutti e ciascun era tondo.
> Non mi parean men ampi, nè maggiori
> che que' che son nel mio bel San Giovanni,
> fatti per luogo di battezzatori;
>
> .   .   .   .   .
>
> Fuor della bocca a ciascun soperchiava
> d'un peccator li piedi e delle gambe
> infino al grosso, e l'altro dentro stava.
> Le piante erano a tutti accese intrambe.

Here the parallel between Dante's description and the lower part of the woodcut is so striking that we are led to think that the designer of the latter, who may well have been Ulsen himself, must have been influenced by the Inferno. We have already seen traces of this influence in Ulsen's reference to the 'crooked serpent of Geryon' in the *De Sancto Judoco Hymnus*.[2] He could have read the *Divina commedia* in Italy, but at least two of his friends in Nürnberg owned copies; Hartmann Schedel, the edition of Venice, 1497, and Willibald Pirckheimer, probably the Mantua edition of 1472.[3] It is not so easy to find a parallel for the iconography of

---

[1] Cf. A. Neckam, *De nat. rer.* i. 73 and 74, 'De pellicano'. 'Natura in his hominem representat, qui per peccata sua opera bona mortificat; qui postmodum penitentia ductus ornatum respuit vestium, et se ipsum crucians gemitibus dolorem manifestat interiorem. Cor aperit in confessione, et fervore dilectionis opera priora quae facta erant in caritate reviviscunt.'

[2] See above, p. 119, note 3.

[3] See Dr. E. Reicke, *W. Pirckheimers Briefw.*, i. (Munich, 1940), 135, and Stauber, op. cit., pp. 170, 237 ff., &c. The woodcut in the Venice edition shows the sinners in Malebolge upside down in well-like pits, and with flames issuing from the soles of their feet. On the subject of

the upper part, or to tell why the Microcosm should have been depicted hanging head downwards from the Empyrean heaven. Perhaps Ulsen wished to express the Neoplatonic conception of the dual nature of the soul of man—the rational part or mind participating in the nature of God and the angels, and the irrational part participating in the nature of the lower orders of living things—from which it followed that man's desires now lifted him up towards the stars, now debased him towards the earth, but at no time completely alienated him from either; so that he remained, as it were, conjoined to both the highest and the lowest spheres.[1] This train of thought would certainly be represented by Ulsen's inverted image of the Microcosm, partly occupying the celestial regions and partly the centre of the universe, according to that dictum of Pico, 'Medium te mundi posui, ut circumspiceres inde commodius quicquid est in mundo.'[2] But this is not the usual way of depicting the Microcosm in relation to the Macrocosm. In contemporary and later iconography the former is generally placed upright in the centre of the Macrocosmic sphere, and entirely within it.[3]

The whole design, then, is one of great vigour and originality—well calculated to draw attention to the Broadside, to 'catch the eye', and to arouse interest and speculation. We find this same bizarre quality combined with the excessive use of symbols, many of them exceedingly obscure, in the paintings of Hieronymus Bosch (d. 1516). Curiously enough, Ulsen may have spent his last days at 's Hertogenbosch, certainly he was, as we saw, buried in the choir of the Cathedral of St. John there, and one cannot help wondering whether he knew Bosch, who lived and worked in this town. There may have been a point of contact in the Brethren of the Common Life. Bosch was a member of the Brotherhood of Our Lady attached to the Cathedral of St. John, which was affiliated to the Brethren. Ulsen, in his youth, had attended the school at Zwolle, which was also under their direction, and it is quite possible that, without actually being a member of the Brethren, he may have been in close touch with them all his life as his friend Hegius was. Alternatively, he may have joined them after

---

Dante's influence in Germany, see Dr. H. Gravert's article 'Dante in Deutschland', *H.P.B.* cxx (1897), 81–100, 173–89, 321–56, 512–36, 633–52, 789–822. If my surmises are correct, Ulsen is one of the earliest scholars in Germany to be directly influenced by the *Divina commedia*.

[1] 'Illinc cum superioribus, hinc cum inferioribus convenit. Si cum utrisque convenit, appetit utraque. Quapropter naturali quoddam instinctu ascendit ad supera, descendit ad infera. Et dum ascendit, inferiora non deserit, et dum descendit sublimia non relinquit. Nam si alterutrum deserat, ad extremum alterum declinabit, neque vera erit ulterius mundi copula.' Ficino, *Plat. Theol.* iii. 2.

[2] Joannis Pici, *Oratio de Dignitate Hominis.* Cf. also Pico's *Heptaplus,* v. 6. 'Haud aliter principem omnium deum fecisse videmus, qui tota mundi machina constructa postremum omnium hominem in medio illius statuit ad imaginem suam et similitudinem formatum.'

[3] One of the most typical designs, showing this relationship, is to be found in the engraved title to Fludd's *Utriusque Cosmi Maioris scilicet et Minoris Metaphysica Physica Atque Technica Historia,* Tomus i, Tract. i, Oppenheim, 1617.

leaving the service of the dukes of Mecklenburg, and put into actual practice what he seems to indicate in the concluding lines of his *De Sancto
Judoco Hymnus*. This would certainly account for his burial in the choir
of the cathedral. Besides much that was universal amongst all humanists
and free-thinkers of that time, Ulsen and Bosch at least had this in
common—they were both extremely fond of mystification and obscure
enigmas.

9

Sixteenth-Century Books of Problems

IN the fifteenth century the Italian humanists seem to have been too preoccupied with the translation and examination of Greek problems to compose many of their own. In the following one, however, several books of problems, in the direct Peripatetic tradition, were written and published in Italy, as well as elsewhere, and this type of literature reached the height of its popularity.

In the first place, Girgio Valla, who had already translated the pseudo-Alexandrian *Problems*, composed a vast encyclopedia, the *De expetendis et fugiendis rebus*, published by Aldus at Venice in 1501, a year after the humanist's death. Book thirty of this work, called *De physicis quaestionibus*, and published separately with this title at Strassburg in 1529, seems to be modelled on the Greek problems which he had translated, and, to a much less extent, on those attributed to Aristotle and Cassius.[1]

Rather similar, but containing much more Aristotelian material, are the *Problemata* composed by the Averroist and Aristotelian commentator, Marcantonio Zimara (1470–c. 1532) between 1509 and 1514. The earliest editions seem to have completely disappeared; at any rate Zimara's latest biographer Bruno Nardi, writing in 1958, could find none earlier than the Venice edition of 1536.[2] In the following year the work was again published at Venice, this time in conjunction with the *Omnes homines* collection, the *Dicta notabilia Aristotelis* and the *CCC Aristotelis et Averrois propositiones*.[3] In later editions these last two works were omitted and the *Problemata* were always found in conjunction with the *Omnes homines* collection and the pseudo-Alexandrian *Problems*, in the translation of

---

[1] The only originality seems to lie in the fact that, in many cases, his answers differ considerably from those of the Greek compilers. The sections of pseudo-Aristotelian *Problems*, added to the Strassburg [1529] editions of Valla's works, such as the *Problemata Aristotelis de re medica*, added to the *De corporis commodis et incommodis*, and the *Aristotelis Problemata quae ad res bene olidas pertinent*, added to the *De physicis quaestionibus*, are in the translation of Gaza; Valla himself does not seem to have translated these problems.

[2] See Bruno Nardi, *Saggi sull'Aristotelismo Padovano dal secolo XIV al XVI*, pp. 322–55 concerning Marcantonio Zimara, and p. 334 for a notice about the *Problemata*.

[3] There is a copy of this rare book in the Biblioteca Marciana, Venice, fully described in *Manoscritti e Stampe Venete dell'Aristotelismo e Averroismo (secoli X–XVI), Catalogo di Mostra presso la Biblioteca Nazionale Marciana in occasione del XII Congresso Internazionale di Filosofia*, Venice, 1958, No. 214, p. 143.

Poliziano, appearing in this form in all the editions of the French and English translations.[1] The questions mostly deal with human behaviour, ethics, physiology, and medicine, though a very few deal with botany and zoology, and the proportion which had already been dealt with in older collections is, again, very high.

Much more original was the *Novum opus quaestionum* of Ambrogio Leone of Nola (d. *c*. 1524), published in 1523 by Bernadinus and Matthias de Vitali at Venice, in one of the most elegant folio volumes of the period.[2] Leone was a humanist, highly praised by Erasmus, who, after being Professor of Medicine at Naples, was both personal physician and editor in the household of the Venetian printer, Aldus Manutius. Besides writing a history of his native Nola, and *Castigationes adversus Averroem*, he translated from the Greek a chapter of the pseudo-Alexandrian *Quaestiones naturales et morales*, the *De urinis* of Actuarius, and various ethical works of Aristotle.[3]

The *Novum opus*, undoubtedly the most important and interesting of all the books of problems compiled and printed during the sixteenth century, besides covering all the usual fields of *physica* in its most comprehensive, medieval sense, shows the increasing Renaissance interest in technology and the arts by the large number of questions dealing with experiments of all kinds. Specially prominent among these are those dealing with practical metallurgy and the arts of the goldsmith, tinsmith, and armourer.[4] Other questions concern geometry, optics, perspective,[5] the aesthetic appreciation of works of art such as paintings and sculpture,[6]

---

[1] The earliest edition to contain all three collections appears to be that of Frankfurt, 1544. For French and English translations, see above, pp. 100–1. The Frankfurt, 1609, edition of these three collections of *Problemata* received the title of *Trinum magicum*, purported to be edited by Longinus Caesar, and contained in addition the three spurious tracts of Albertus Magnus, i.e. the *De secretis mulierum, Lib. aggregationis*, and *De mirabilibus mundi*. See Thorndike, *H.M.E.S.* vi. 600, who, however, does not distinguish between the problems of Zimara and the *Omnes homines* collection.

[2] The title, in well-proportioned Roman type and in red, is set within a fine Renaissance border, printed in a delicate shade of pale green.

[3] See F. E. Cranz, 'Alexander Aphrodisiensis', *Catalogus translat.*, p. 117 and the literature there cited.

[4] Because of the inaccessibility of the book in this country (it is not in the Brit. Mus., Bodleian, or Camb. Univ. Libs.) I mention a few of the questions; 'Qur erarii fabri qui instannare volunt enea vasa, tunc maxime colophonia resina utuntur. Qur aurifices aurum auro ferruminare exacte volentes chrysocollam adhibent. Qur miscella illa quam aurifices ad ferruminanda duo frusta vel auri vel argenti adiiciunt citius liquefit quam aurum vel argentum. Qur fabri ferrarii volentes ferrum cum ferro solidare, eorum altero cum altero ligato atque aqua madefacto adhibent cretam pulverem redactam.' Some Salernitan physical questions discussed by Leone are those concerning the tempering of iron, the indestructibility of gold in the fire, the formation of sparks by the collision of two objects, the production of fire from quicklime, magnetic attraction, vacuum, and the pouring of oil on the sea to make the latter transparent.

[5] 'Qur in via recta atque longa nobis consistentibus pars viae quo remotior fuerit a nobis, eo videtur arctior adeo ut demum latera veluti lineae concurrentes videantur.'

[6] 'Qur picturam sculpturamve illam admirantur summopere quae simillima est ei rei quam pingendo praesentare conantur, rem vero non adeo admirantur.'

music,[1] anatomy,[2] and medicine. As regards this latter subject, Thorndike has drawn attention to the importance of Leone's question about the use of mercury in the cure of syphilis, in which he gives a very good account of the disease.[3] Finally, the literary side of the Renaissance is well represented by questions about grammar, literature, ethics, mythology, and antiquarianism. In short, the range is truly encyclopedic, and representative of most facets of the later Renaissance movement in Italy.

This work was followed by the *Quaestiones quaedam naturales* of the famous Paduan physician and philosopher, Niccolo Leonico Tomeo (1456–1531), contained in his *Opuscula*, published by the same printers at Venice in 1525.[4] These questions, although not so all-embracing as those of Leone, are yet more original and more typical of the period than those of Valla and Zimara. Out of some 89 problems, 52 deal with animals, birds, insects, reptiles, and fishes, 26 concern anthropology, including physiology and anatomy, and three questions in the latter subject are comparative, the characteristics of man being compared with those of beasts. In all these zoological questions Pliny is still a source, as one would expect, but only about five are recognizable as long-standing, Salernitan questions, the majority stemming from sources such as the new Aristotle, Avicenna, and the later encyclopedists. Five questions are botanical, four deal with what might be termed *experimenta*, e.g. the floating of oil on water (an ancient, Salernitan question), the putrefaction of rain water and fat, and the different effects of heat. Finally, two may be classed under mineralogy, namely those which discuss the indestructibility of the diamond by fire, and the reason why metals were thought to melt easier in very cold weather. Tomeo also composed twenty *Quaestiones amatoriae*, which precede the *Quaestiones naturales* in the 1525 edition, and which deal with the ethics and physiology of love in true Renaissance fashion.

Yet another Paduan humanist-physician, Giulio Paolo Crasso (d. 1574), composed a series of forty-two *Quaestiones naturales et medicae*, which were published posthumously by his son, in a volume containing Latin translations by his father of several writings by Greek physicians, such as Aretaeus, Palladius, Rufus, Theophilus, Galen, and Hippocrates (*Medici antiqui graeci*, Basel, Pet. Perna, 1581). A high proportion of these questions are medical, anatomical, behaviouristic, and ethical; among these

---

[1] 'Qur matutino tempore cantus et instrumenta musica magnopere placent.'

[2] 'Qur quum arcte ligaveris vel brachium vel extremum membrum statim tempore venae intumescunt. Qur in hepate venae duae singulae in oppositis lateribus, in corde item duae atque eodem modo. Qur si una vena sit in toto corpore, ut dictum est, aliae quietae venae in eo, aliae pulsantes inveniuntur, maxime in homine.'

[3] *H.M.E.S.* v. 147. In this work Thorndike gives a brief account of Leone, and lists some of the questions in the *Novum opus*, pp. 143–7. He compares it unfavourably with Adelard's *Quaestiones naturales*, but I think this is being a little too severe; Adelard's questions were not so original as has been thought in the past, and Leone's book was rather more typical of contemporary trends of thought than Adelard's work. See above, Chapter 2.

[4] A manuscript of the questions is contained in Brit. Mus. Sloane 3280 (XVI cent.).

being those dealing with the usefulness of exercise, the effects of the passions, and simple physiology. There is only one botanical question, which discusses variations in the qualities of plants according to situation and climate, one meteorological one about the effects of lightning, and two zoological ones about the defecation of dogs and the audacity of certain beasts. Mineralogy, metallurgy, and physics (*experimenta*) are not represented at all, although superstitious practices are discussed in two questions about the customs of covering the tops of sails with the skins of seals and hyenas to ward off lightning, and of hanging dead chickens to a fig tree to make them more tender. Three questions reflect the Renaissance interest in poetry and the arts; why is poetry more excellent and more philosophical than history; why should poets be either mad or extremely clever; and why do we regard the pictures and images of such terrible things as ferocious beasts and corpses without fear and horror, when the things themselves affect us with these feelings?

In Portugal, Antonio Luiz, a physician of Lisbon, published a folio volume of five books of *Problemata* at that place in 1540.[1] This work was the most ambitious of its kind that had so far been produced, since, besides the comprehensive *physica*, it contained sections on *amatoria*, antique customs, law, magic and demonology, theology and ethics, and the seven liberal arts. The book is altogether more classical and antiquarian in tone than the *Novum opus* of Leone, and Luiz draws freely from the writings of Greek authors such as Aristotle, Plato, Galen, Proclus, Plutarch, and Dionysius. In keeping with this there is a tendency to discuss older questions in abstract, Aristotelian physics, rather than practical problems connected with the later advances in technology and the arts. Thus, optics and perspective receive very little attention, and alchemy and metallurgy are not represented at all; in fact, about the only practical questions are those found in the sections on gardening, agriculture, and medicine. On the whole, then, the work is less representative of the Renaissance movement as a whole, and of the scientific part of it in particular, than Leone's book, in spite of its wide field of inquiry.

The Spanish physician, Leonardus Jacchinus, a native of Catalonia who became Professor of Medicine at Pisa, composed an interesting collection of eighty-four *Quaestiones naturales*, printed for the first time at Lyons in 1540.[2] These consist, mainly, of the usual anthropological and physiological questions about love and generation, sleep and dreams, the effects of the passions, varieties of voice, memory, changes due to climate

---

[1] For a brief account of Luiz, see Thorndike, *H.M.E.S.* v. 550 ff. He also wrote a criticism of Peter of Abano's commentary on the pseudo-Aristotelian *Problems* (Lisbon, 1540), a further witness to his interest in problem literature.

[2] The questions were also contained in later collections of his *Opuscula*, such as those of Basel, 1563, and ibid. 1580. In 1587 a selection of the questions was translated into French and printed at Lyons in a volume containing translations of the *Omnes homines* collection, the problems of pseudo-Alexander, and those of Zimara.

and old age, odours, and tastes. A lesser number deal with meteorology and weather lore, zoology, botany, and ethics. Practical, physical questions are represented by those which discuss the action of burning-glasses, the liquefaction of sulphur, the miscibility of wax, and brick-making. Three problems about the actions of guns illustrate the increasing Renaissance interest in all aspects of military technology, a subject which we have not found discussed in any previous collection of natural questions.

In France the eminent anatomist, Jacques Sylvius (Dubois) (1478–1555), the teacher of Vesalius and Servetus, composed some problems in Latin, modelled on those of pseudo-Alexander, and dealing chiefly with anthropology and medicine. As far as I know these were never published in their original form, but they were translated into French by M. Heret, a friend of Sylvius, and printed at Paris in 1555, together with a French version of the pseudo-Alexandrian *Problems* by the same translator.[1]

Farther north the German physician, Georgius Pictorius of Villingen, the editor of Ulsen's *Clinicum pharmacandi modum*, wrote three centuries of physical questions (*Physicarum quaestionum centuriae tres*), which he published at Basel in 1568 in a composite volume containing other medical works of his.[2]

Pictorius does not pretend to be original, and his questions are preceded by a list of no fewer than seventy 'authorities' which he has laid under contribution, both ancient and modern. His answers are for the most part very brief, and the collection reminds us of the *Omnes homines* problems more than anything else, much of the material in the two works corresponding very closely. This correspondence is particularly evident in the first century of questions, which covers simple anatomy and physiology, the humours, and phlebotomy. The second century deals entirely with food and drink, and is mainly based on the *Canon* of Avicenna and the *De dietis* of Isaac Israeli. The third century is very miscellaneous in character, embracing anthropology, medicine, zoology, botany, and meteorology. There are also several practical questions which discuss various actions of fire and simple experiments with metals, while others deal with the nature of metals and precious stones. It is in this section that Pictorius is most influenced by modern writers such as, among others, Cornelius Agrippa and Marsilio Ficino. But the person to whom he is most indebted is Jerome Cardan; all the practical questions, and all those dealing with metals and gems, as well as many others, both questions and answers, being taken, this time without acknowledgement, from this author's *De subtilitate*, which had been published for the first time eighteen years before (Nürnberg, 1550), and several times in the intervening period.

This book by Cardan was one of those numerous, encyclopedic compendiums of natural philosophy which became so popular in the schools

---

[1] I have not been able to trace a copy of this book in England.
[2] On this book see Thorndike, *H.M.E.S.* vi. 402 ff.

and universities during the sixteenth century. Not all these were scholastic in character; quite often they took the form, either wholly or in part, of the simple question and answer, and thus approximated very closely to the problem books which we have been discussing. They were, in fact, just another manifestation of the tendency to use this Aristotelian question form in works of an increasingly encyclopedic range.

Starting with the *De philosophia mundi* of William of Conches, we have seen this tendency still further developed in the books of Conrad de Halberstadt in Germany, and in those of Valla, Leone, and Luiz south of the Alps. The compendiums were still later stepping stones on the way to the larger encyclopedias of the following century. Another good example in which the non-scholastic question-form was used is the *Quaestiones physicae* (Basel, 1579) of J. T. Freige, which again covered most aspects of the later *physica*, and included geography, agriculture, anthropology, anatomy, and psychology.[1]

But perhaps even nearer to the later encyclopedias was the little-known *Sphinx Philosophica* of Joannes Heidfeld, a professor at Herborn in Nassau, a place which became one of the main strongholds of the whole northern encyclopedic movement during the early years of the seventeenth century. Here, again, the simple question-and-answer technique was used, and although the first edition of 1600 was only a thin octavo of [32]+216 pages, it rapidly expanded, until by 1631 the ninth edition contained no less than 1,382 pages, excluding the preliminary matter and a copious index.[2] This book included, besides the usual branches of *physica*, medicine, theology, ethics, the seven liberal arts, and what Heidfeld called the illiberal arts, such as acrobatics, conjuring, dicing and gaming, the mechanical arts, magic, and alchemy, ending up with various kinds of literary riddles. It became one of the favourite books of James I and was translated into German in 1624 by J. Flitner. The 1612 Latin edition had a long, prefatory poem by Heidfeld's friend and colleague at Herborn University, Johan-Henricus Alsted, whose *Encyclopedia cursus philosophici* (Herborn, 1620) also expanded into the vast *Encyclopedia omnium scientiarum* (Herborn, 1630), one of the best and most influential encyclopedias of the seventeenth century.[3]

---

[1] On this book see Thorndike, *H.M.E.S.* vi. 186 ff. Another edition appeared at Basel in 1585.

[2] Some in-between editions which I have noted are: 1604 (4th ed.); 1605; 1612 (6th ed.); 1616; 1621 (8th ed.). The title of the ninth edition, and possibly of earlier ones as well, was altered to *Sphinx Theologico-Philosophica*.

[3] On the whole encyclopedic movement see Frances A. Yates, *The French Academies of the Sixteenth Century*, chs. 4, 5, 12, and R. F. Young, *Comenius in England*. Comenius had been a pupil of Alsted at Herborn, and so had imbibed his encyclopedic ideas, and probably also those of Heidfeld. Mersenne, in his turn, was interested in the schemes of Comenius and was himself of profound influence on English and continental scientists. Young's date for Alsted's *Encyclopedia cursus philos.*, namely 1608, is surely too early. A precursor of the work was the *Panacea philosophica id est methodus docendi et discendi encyclopaediam*, Herborn, 1610.

We must now say something about the more popular, vernacular question books of the sixteenth century. Curiously enough, it was not Italy that was most prolific in these, but Spain. Moreover, in this country the writers of such books adopted a plan which we have not met with before in connexion with vernacular productions of this kind. Almost without exception the questions were stated in verse, then either answered in verse, or discussed in a prose gloss, or both methods of reply were adopted. This original form of presentation was undoubtedly due to the lasting influence of the *Tenzon* of the Provençal Troubadours, whose poetry and ways of life and thought had been greatly admired and imitated, especially in Castile, in the previous century, during the reign of Don Juan II (1406–54).[1] At first mainly concerned with matters of courtly love, these *preguntas* and *respuestas*, as they were called, gradually came to embrace more serious subjects. Certainly by the sixteenth century they included theology, ethics, and all aspects of natural philosophy, including medicine.

One of the first to use this method for popularizing pseudo-scientific and medical questions was Lopez de Corella, a Professor of Medicine in Tarragona.[2] In 1539 he published a small book with the title, *Secretos de filosophia y medicina puestos a manera d'perque por que mejor se encomienden a la memoria*, which contained several hundred questions. It was written entirely in verse and no answers were given, since, as he rather naïvely says, the learned have no need of them, and as for the unlearned, the mere asking of the questions is sufficient to incite them to study.[3] Perhaps he underestimated the ability and zeal of his readers; at any rate in 1546 he printed 300 of the questions with the answers, both in verse, accompanied by short prose glosses,[4] and, in the following year, a folio volume which, although containing only 250 of the metrical questions, was yet much larger because of the greater length of the prose glosses.[5]

The questions, confined to the medieval field of *physica*, are mostly theoretical in tone, being based on the opinions of a large number of 'authorities' mentioned in the glosses, and of which a list of thirty-seven

But Alsted himself says in the Preface to the Reader in the 1630 edition of his Encyclopedia, 'ab anno 1620 quo primam lucem adspexit Encyclopaedia philosophica'.

[1] The *Tenzon* is the name given to a sort of strife or debate between two poets, who speak in alternate strophes of a poetical composition. See T. F. Crane, *Italian Social Customs of the Sixteenth Century*, pp. 8 ff., and the literature there cited; pp. 16 ff. contain an account of the spread of this form of literature into Spain.

[2] On him see A. H. Morejon, *Hist. Bibliográfica de la Med. Española*, ii. 335; G. Ticknor, *Hist. of Spanish Lit.* ii. 5; A. Hirsch, *Biograph. Lexikon der hervorr. Aerzte*, iii. 837.

[3]   y pondre las dudas sin la responsion
                que para los doctos no es mas menester
                y a los que no saben basta el proponer
                para a preguntarlas les dar aficion.

[4] *Trezientas preguntas de cosas naturales en diferentes materias con las respuestas y alegaciones d'auctores, las quales fueron antes preguntadas, a manera de perque*, Valladolid, 1546.

[5] *Secretos de philosophia y astrologia y medicina y de las quatro mathematicas sciencias, collegidos de muchos y diversos auctores y divididos en cinco quinquagenas de preguntas*, Saragossa, 1547.

is prefixed to the 1546 edition. Used a good deal are the *Problems* of pseudo-Aristotle and pseudo-Alexander, the Aristotelian *libri naturales*, the works of Pliny, Galen, and Hippocrates, and the *Canon* of Avicenna. More recent medicine is represented by the writings of Peter of Abano, Peter of Spain, Gentile da Foligno, Niccolo Falcucci, Jacopo da Forli, Ugo da Siena, Antonio Musa Brasavola, and Michael Savonarola. In questions concerning Aristotelian physics he quotes the commentators Themon Judaei, Albert of Saxony, Marsilius of Inghen, Paulus Venetus, and Ludovicus Coronel. In a question which compares the capacity of a circle with that of a square, which Leone had discussed before him, he quotes the *Tractatus de proportionibus* of Thomas Bradwardine, and in several optical questions makes use of the works of John Pecham and Witelo.

The practical questions are comparatively few; there are no alchemical ones, and about the only ones which deal with metals and the art of the smith are the ancient Salernitan one about the indestructibility of gold, one which asks why hot iron hisses when put into water, and another which discusses why the blacksmith throws water on the forge fire when he is kindling it. Other physical questions discuss: why the flame from *aqua vitae* does not burn (Q. 191, 1547 ed. = Leone, prob. 226), why rain drops are round (Q. 289, 1546 ed., cf. *Speculator*, l. 50), and why the sound of bells is louder near water (Q. 166, 1547 ed., cf. *Quest. phisicales*, l. 33), where he quotes Peter of Abano, *Com. on Arist. Prob.*, part. xi, prob. 8. Thus, although the proportion of old questions is high, Corella as a rule does try to answer them by reference to later authorities.

Much more comprehensive and erudite than Manfredi's *Il Perche*, the books of Corella were the best that had been written in any vernacular language, up to 1547, in the field of natural questions. Certainly the other Spanish problem books did not come up to his standard of scholarship, though perhaps to the unlearned reader some of them may have been more entertaining. Thus the little *Fifty subtle Questions with as many Answers* of Lopez de Yanguas (Medina, *c.* 1540) was entirely in verse and, except for the metrical treatment, dealt in an entirely unoriginal way with ancient, well-tried questions in natural philosophy.[1]

In 1543 there appeared at Zamora a very miscellaneous volume by the famous poet and court physician, Lopez de Villalobos (*c.* 1473–*c.* 1560), which contained forty-one natural and moral problems, two medical dialogues, other satirical material, and the comedy of *Amfitrión*.[2] The

---

[1] *Cincuenta bivas preguntas con otras tantas respuestas.* Other editions were: Medina, *c.* 1543 (Brit. Mus.); Valencia, 1550; and Barcelona, 1618.

[2] *Libro de los problemas que trata de cuerpos naturales y morales, y dos dialogos de medicina, y el tractado de las tres grandes, y una cancion, y la comedia de Anfitrion.* Some later editions were, Saragossa, 1544; ibid. 1550; Seville, 1550; ibid. 1570; ibid. 1574. A modern edition is to be found in the series, edited by B. C. Aribau, *Bibl. de Autores Españoles*, tom. 36, Madrid, 1855, pp. 403–93. See also Ticknor, op. cit. ii. 7 ff.

problems are introduced by a few lines of verse, and are followed by a prose gloss, as in the case of Corella's *Secretos*, but only the first six deal with *physica*, and the field is very limited, being confined to such subjects as the movements of the heavenly bodies, element lore, the saltness of the sea, the nature of light, and the situation of the terrestrial paradise.

Rather more interesting is the *Four Hundred Answers to as Many Questions of the Illustrious Don Fadrique Enriquez, the Admiral of Castile, and other persons*, written by the minorite friar Luys de Escobar, of which there were no less than three editions of Part I in 1545.[1] This first part was written entirely in verse and contained fifty natural questions and answers (Qs. 218–68), the rest dealing with theology (Qs. 1–217) and ethics (Qs. 269–324), or consisting of literary riddles (enigmas, Qs. 325–400). In spite of the strong theological bias of the collection as a whole, these questions give a very good picture of the interests of fashionable society in Spain, during the reign of Charles V.[2] The natural questions, simple and straightforward in character, concern astronomy and astrology, meteorology, anthropology, and medicine, special attention being given to dietetics and the cure of the plague. About the only zoological questions are the ancient ones about the sterility of the mule and the non-micturition of birds, while botany is not represented at all, and physics very badly, one question about the use of mirrors and three about the cooking of eggs only bordering upon this subject. In 1552 Luys published a second book of 400 questions and answers, of which only the first 250 were entirely in verse, the remainder being in prose.[3] These covered, roughly, the same ground as the first 400, but there were far fewer natural questions, and more space was devoted to legal matters, magic, and demonology. One interesting question discussed the possibility of the corruption and transformation of gold, over a number of years, in comparison with those of iron, which take place more rapidly.[4]

The continuing popularity of this sort of literature in Spain, during the first half of the sixteenth century, is shown by two smaller question books. The first is the *Dialogo en verso intitulado Centiloquio de Problemas* of Agustin de Ruescas (1546), in which the 100 questions and answers are in verse, with marginal notes in Latin giving the sources.[5] These latter are similar to those used by Corella, but a greater use is made of Macrobius

---

[1] *Las quatrocientas respuestas a otras tantas preguntas que D. Fadrique Enriquez y otras personas en diversas vezes embiaron a preguntar al auctor*, Valladolid, 1545; Saragossa, 1545 (Diego Hernandez); Saragossa, 1545 (Jorge Coci); Valladolid, 1550; Antwerp, *c.* 1550.

[2] See Ticknor, op. cit. ii. 3 ff.

[3] *La segunda parte de las quatrocientas respuestas a otras preguntas, con las glosas y declaraciones*, Valladolid, 1552.

[4] 'Si se corrompe el oro o alguna parte d'l como una piedra, y se buelve en otro metal o tierra, en esta vida antes del dia del juyzio, si se va naturalmente deshaziendo despues muchos annos que salio de su venero como se deshaze un hierro, aunque el oro no se corrumpa en tan breve tiempo.' Prob. 273.

[5] There was another edition at Alcalá in 1548.

(*Sat.* Book vii), and amongst the moderns we notice such works as Titel-
mann's *Compendium of Natural Philosophy*, the *Colloquia* of Erasmus, and
the *Problemata* of the Portuguese physician, Antonio Luiz, discussed
above. The questions themselves are, almost without exception, ancient
ones that we have met with many times before, covering the fields of
meteorology, anthropology, and medicine, with a very small proportion of
zoology.

The second, and the last of these Spanish problem books that we have
to consider, is the *Summa de philosophia natural* of Alonso de Fuentes,
first published at Seville in 1547, in which the questions only were in
verse, the answers being in prose. This popular compendium of natural
science is exactly in the tradition of the Latin ones already mentioned; but,
although the bulk of the questions are ancient, Fuentes shows, as Thorndike has pointed out, a desire to give a physical explanation of phenomena
wherever possible, in that respect resembling the early Salernitans, and
is not always in agreement with the older authorities.[1] However, in one
Adelardian question about the complexion of plants (*Quaest. nat.*, ch. 2)
his answer is the same as that of the English compiler; and in another from
the same source, about the inability of infants to walk (*Quaest. nat.*, ch.
38), his answer is based on that of William of Conches, which combines
the Salernitan physical answer with Adelard's more philosophical one.[2]
Unfortunately, a corruption of the text has made nonsense of Fuentes's
interpretation of the second half of William's answer.

The *Summa* of Fuentes appears to have been the only one of the Spanish
problem books to have been popular outside Spain, a translation into
Italian by Alfonso di Ulloa appearing at Venice in 1557. In this, the
peculiarly Spanish practice of introducing the questions in verse was
omitted, and both questions and answers were arranged in prose dialogue
form.

About the mid-century two vernacular problem books were composed
in Italy, which seem to have had a much wider influence than the Spanish
ones we have been discussing, and to have set the example for several
later, seventeenth-century books of this kind, in France, England, and
Germany.

The first was the *Problemi naturali e morali* of Hieronimo Garimberto
first printed in a slim octavo at Venice in 1549,[3] and later translated into
French by Jean Louveau (Lyons, 1559). Written in the spirit of the Latin
problemata, the work deals chiefly with human behaviour, physiognomy,
national characteristics, and ethics, with the addition of a few problems
dealing with meteorology, zoology (birds and beasts), and music. But the
problems were intended, as Garimberto says, to please the man in the
street more than the scholar, and are therefore more prolix than their

---

[1] See Thorndike, *H.M.E.S.* vi. 390 ff.   [2] See above, p. 55.
[3] There were at least two later editions of 1550 and 1552, both printed at Venice.

Latin models, 'since principles presumed to be known by the man of letters, cannot be left out when one is writing for the unlearned, neither can certain other pleasant matters, which are introduced to facilitate the reading of obscure passages and give pleasure to the reader, thereby inviting him to read'.[1] The result is certainly an entertaining book, and although many of the questions themselves are ancient, including several Salernitan ones, the treatment of the answers is often lively and original.

In the second place, the eccentric Milanese writer, Ortensio Lando,[2] produced a little book which, although written at first in Latin, was obviously also intended to please a much wider circle of readers than that reached by the more scholarly collections we have been discussing earlier on. This was the *Miscellaneae questiones*, printed by Gabriel Giolito at Venice in 1550, of which a version in Italian, the *Quattro libri de dubbi con le solutioni*, issued from the same press two years later in 1552. Lando used a method exactly opposite to that followed by Garimberto. He epitomized and greatly abbreviated many of the ancient questions and answers, as well as several later ones; his aim being to produce a book, not so much for the enjoyment of reading, as to serve as an aid to memory and so be of use in the fashionable *conversazioni* of the time. The range of subjects was greater than that found in Garimberto's *Problemi*. There were many more natural questions, and the moral and political ones were augmented by those dealing with love and theology, a choice of material which well reflects some of the main interests of the Italian Renaissance. The work proved exceedingly popular, and may be said to mark the beginning in the West of a series of pocket 'helps to discourse'. Several later editions followed,[3] including those of a French translation which first appeared at Lyons in 1558.[4] Two English translations were made from this French version, the first being printed at London in 1566 and 1596,[5] and

---

[1] 'Io volendo giovar al Volgo, sono stato astretto di scrivere volgarmente, e etiandio con prolissità; percioche con gli indotti non si possono lasciar à drieto alcuni principii, i quali si presuppongono per ricevuti ne i litterati; ne si poco pretermettere cert'altre cose dilettevoli e facili, per facilitar i sensi oscuri, e dilettar i lettori; e dilettando invitar lor à leggere.' From the dedicatory epistle.

[2] On him and his writings see Ireneo Sanesi, *Il Cinquecentista Ortensio Lando*, Pistoia, 1893; W. E. A. Axon, 'Ortensio Lando, a humorist of the Renaissance', *T.R.S.L.* xx. 3, pp. 159 ff.; Crane, *Italian Social Customs*, pp. 151-3.

[3] Venice, 1555; ibid. 1556; Piacenza, 1597 (as the work of A. Novelli).

[4] With the title, *Questions diverses et responses d'icelles*. Some other editions with this title were: Lyons, 1570; Paris, 1572; ibid. 1576; Lyons, 1583; ibid. 1596; Rouen, 1610; ibid. 1635. An edition with the title, *Les raisons naturelles et morales de toutes choses qui tombent ordinairement en devis familiers*, appeared at Paris, ?1570, and again at Lyons, 1586 (author's collection).

[5] *S.T.C.* 5059; 5060. *Delectable demaundes and pleasaunt Questions with their severall Aunswers in matters of Love, Natural causes, with Morall and politique devises*, ascribed wrongly to Alain Chartier. This confusion arose because it was thought by Brunet and others to be a translation of the French *Demandes damours avecques les responses*, which has been included among the works of Chartier, see Brunet, *Manuel*, ii (1861), cols. 580-1. Another source of confusion is the *Demaundes joyous*, printed by Wynken de Worde in 1511, *S.T.C.* 6573 (reprinted in 1829

the second in 1640.[1] H. Campos wrote an imitation in Spanish, with the title, *Sylva de varias questiones naturales y morales* (Antwerp, 1575), and another in Italian followed, from the pen of B. Paschetti, the *Dubbi morali e naturali* (Genoa, 1581), in which the section containing natural questions was an almost complete translation of the *Omnes homines* collection.

Both these types of question books, that intended for the enjoyment of reading and that designed to help in conversation, well illustrate the growing interest in scientific, medical, ethical, and social problems of all kinds outside the Latin-speaking circles in Italy, Spain, France, and England during this period.

(London), and in Wright and Halliwell, *Reliquiae Antiquae*, London, 1845, ii. 72–75), which is simply a brief collection of extremely facetious riddles, translated from the French *Les Demandes joyeuses*, Rouen, *c.* 1500, of which there are several later editions; see Brunet, *Manuel*, ii (1861), col. 581.

[1] With the title, *Margariton. A Rich Treasure discovered of Problems and their Resolves*, translated by R. S.; *S.T.C.* 17328, where also it is not attributed to Lando. Both these English editions and the French omit the fourth book of the *Dubbi*, which deals with theological questions.

10

The Treatment of the Questions in the Seventeenth Century

THE tendency to discuss questions of all kinds in the vernacular, which we noticed in the sixteenth century, became much more widespread in the following one. On the other hand, in spite of Francis Bacon's praise of the Aristotelian *Problems* and his recommendation that new ones be composed on similar lines,[1] few such books of problems seem to have been written during this century, in Latin, and for the learned reader. Other literary forms and other ways of expression seem to have been generally preferred for the more serious examination of such problems. In fact there is scarcely a branch of seventeenth-century scientific and medical literature in which they do not occur—both the old ones and the much more numerous new questions dealing with the new or experimental philosophy. To examine in detail all these branches is obviously beyond the scope of this book, but one or two which are specially important because of their fresh approach to the questions should be mentioned.

Thus many of the older questions, including Salernitan ones, were discussed in books of popular errors modelled on Laurent Joubert's *Erreurs populaires et propos vulgaires touchant la médecine et le régime de santé*, first published at Bordeaux in 1578—a genre which had also been recommended by Bacon in his *Advancement of Learning* (1605).[2]

Most of these books discussed errors in popular medicine only,[3] but Sir Thomas Browne's *Pseudodoxia epidemica, or Enquiries into very many received Tenents and commonly presumed Truths* (London, 1646) and F. Bayle's *Problemata physica et medica in quibus varii veterum et recentiorum errores deteguntur* (Toulouse, 1677) embrace the whole field of

---

[1] 'Problems deal with particular doubts; Dogmas with general ones, concerning first principles and the fabric of the universe. Of Problems there is a noble example in the books of Aristotle; a kind of work which certainly deserved not only to be honoured with the praises of posterity, but to be continued by their labours; seeing that new doubts are daily arising.' *The Philosophical Works of Francis Bacon*, ed. J. M. Robertson, p. 467 (*De Augmentis Scientiarum* (1623)). [2] Ed. Robertson, p. 57.

[3] That is, such books as: Scipione Mercurio, *De gli errori popolari*, Venice, 1603; Gaspard Bachot, *Erreurs populaires*, Lyons, 1626; James Primrose, *De vulgi erroribus*, London, 1638 (English translation, by R. Wittie, London, 1651); Henry de Rochas, *La physique réformée*, Paris, 1648.

natural philosophy. The latter book is particularly interesting, since not only is it written in the form of the simple *quaestiones et responsiones*, but the choice of subjects is particularly wide, and we find problems in Cartesian physics as well as those in astronomy, astrology, mineralogy, botany, zoology, anthropology, and medicine, including anatomy.[1] Special features of both these books and, indeed, of the whole class are the tendency to get away from abject reliance on past authorities and the desire to test beliefs by actual experiment.[2]

Other questions of the type we have been discussing were debated in the private academies, which had succeeded those formed in Italy and France during the previous century. Hitherto these institutions had been chiefly concerned with the improvement of the language and moral or religious reform, but they now began to include the study of the sciences, in a completely disinterested and impartial manner.[3] Probably the first academy to discuss such questions, certainly the first to record and publish the results, was that founded by the remarkable protégé of Cardinal Richelieu, the highly original and gifted Théophraste Renaudot (1584–1653). In about 1633 he set up his *Bureau d'Adresse* at the *Grand Coq* in the *Rue de la Calandre* at Paris.[4] There he not only sold his *Gazette*, the first French newspaper, of which he was the originator, but also engaged in numerous activities of a philanthropic nature, such as supplying the poor with free medical treatment and with the addresses of those who might employ them, advancing loans, and arranging sales of houses and unredeemed property. In addition, once a week he held 'conferences' during which questions of the most diverse and encyclopedic nature were discussed with extraordinary enthusiasm by all kinds of people—it being the rule that anyone who was interested in such matters could attend. Renaudot published the results of these conferences held from 1633 to 1641 in four quarto volumes,[5] a fifth, containing the conferences for 1641

---

[1] See Thorndike, *H.M.E.S.* viii. 292 ff. Some Salernitan questions are: the four Greek ones, Prob. 46, why we yawn when we see others do so; Prob. 48, why dead bodies float after a few days (Adelard, *Quaest. nat.*, ch. 47); Prob. 64, why new wine does not inebriate; Prob. 73, on the 'longings' of pregnant women. Another Salernitan one concerns the remora, Prob. 62, whose power is denied by Bayle. He also denies the powers of astrology, no mean act of scepticism for that period.

[2] Bayle, in particular, lays emphasis on experiment, a feature of his book which was not stressed by Thorndike.

[3] On these academies see Crane, *Italian Social Customs*; M. Ornstein (Bronfenbrenner), *The Rôle of Scientific Societies in the Seventeenth Century*; Harcourt Brown, *Scientific Organisations in Seventeenth-Century France*; Frances A. Yates, *The French Academies of the Sixteenth Century*; and L. Thorndike, *H.M.E.S.* viii. ch. 30.

[4] Not mentioned by Ornstein or Thorndike; but see H. Brown, op. cit., ch. 2, and Yates, op. cit., pp. 296 ff.

[5] *Premiere Centurie des Questions traitees ez Conferences du Bureau d'Adresse depuis le 22 jour d'Aoust 1633, jusques au dernier Iuillet 1634*, Paris, 1634, reprinted, 1635, 1636, 1638. *Seconde Centurie . . . 1636; Troisieme Centurie . . . 1639*, rep. 1641; *Quatrieme Centurie . . . 1641*. There was an octavo edition of these centuries printed at Paris, 1655–6, 4 vols. (Bibl. Nat.), and the first four centuries only appeared at Lyons in 1666 in 6 vols., 12mo.

to 1642, being published in octavo in 1655,[1] two years after his death, by his son Eusebius.

In the 'Advice to the Reader' and the Preface to the first century of questions (Paris, 1634) we learn the character and aim of the conferences. Like the humanists of the preceding century, Renaudot maintained that the scholastic disputation of the schools, 'not only obscured all the elegance and pleasure of the discourse, but usually ended in riots and pedantic insults'. Each speaker, therefore, was to state his opinion, clearly and simply, without any syllogistic argument, for or against, and there was to be no summing up or 'determination', the members and the readers of the reports being left entirely free to form their own conclusions. In this way he hoped to avoid all ill feeling, and to ensure the smooth and even running of the meetings. For the same reasons, and so that the judgement of members and readers should be unbiased, the speakers were to remain anonymous. French only was allowed to be spoken, 'in order the more to cultivate the language, in imitation of the ancient Greeks and Romans', and it was the rule to quote authorities as little as possible, both for the sake of brevity, and because 'if a notion is founded on reason, it should stand without the necessity of authority, if not, no authority, save that of the divine law, and the Prince, should have power to sway a mind that is free'. Religion and politics, as being subjects likely to sow discord, were rigorously banned, but, apart from these, the field was unlimited, where 'the young could improve themselves, the old refresh their memory, the learned be admired, others learn, and everyone meet with honest entertainment'.[2] So it was that 'polite entertainments' such as these were the intermediaries between the rather more formal Italian and French academies of the sixteenth century and the *Académie des Sciences* founded by royal charter in 1666, and that the channel through which flowed the tremendous scientific curiosity of the period was diverted from the universities to private establishments.[3] It is, indeed, highly probable that the procedures in Renaudot's *Bureau* influenced those of our own Royal Society founded in 1661. We find the same plea for a simple, unadorned, style of speaking,[4] the avoidance of all disputation and argument,[5] the

---

[1] *Cinquiesme et Dernier Tome du Recueil General des Questions Traittees és Conferences du Bureau d'Addresse, sur toutes sortes de Matieres; Par les plus beaux Esprits de ce temps.* A Paris, chez Cardin Besongne, au Palais, en la Gallerie des Prisonniers, aux Rozes Vermeilles. 1655. 8vo (copy in author's collection).

[2] 'Un divertissement honneste.'

[3] 'It is well known that the universities were the seats of conservatism and virtual neglect of science, rather than the nurseries of the new philosophy (Merton, 'Science in Seventeenth Century England' (*Osiris*, iv, 1938), p. 462); and see also the illuminating article by Phyllis Allen, 'Scientific Studies in the English Universities of the Seventeenth Century', *J.H.I.* x. 2 (1949), 219–53. Things were no better on the Continent during this period.

[4] See Tho. Sprat, *The Hist. of the Royal Society*, London, 1667, part ii, sect. 20, 'Their manner of discourse'.

[5] Sprat, op. cit., part iii, sect. 6.

prejudices against the use of authorities,[1] and the banning of 'all Discourses of Divinity, of State-Affaires, and of News (other than what concerned our business of Philosophy)'[2]—whilst, at the same time, the meetings, like those of the *Bureau*, were held weekly and were open to all interested in such matters, of whatever religion, faction, profession, or nationality.

Renaudot's Conferences were widely advertised in his *Gazette*, and so would quickly come to the knowledge of those Englishmen who were in Paris at the time. But it was not long before some of the actual discourses, or questions, began to be translated into English. The earliest of such translations were those of five of the problems from the fourth century of questions,[3] which were published separately in London in 1640—five years before the original members of the *Invisible College* began their meetings. These questions must have proved popular since they were reissued together, with the title, *Five philosophicall Questions most eloquently and substantially disputed*, in 1650,[4] and again, with the same title, in 1653.[5] In 1664 G. Havers translated the first two centuries of questions,[6] and in the following year, in collaboration with J. Davies of Kidwelly, the third century and parts of the fourth and fifth.[7] Although this method has the disadvantage for us of not indicating which opinion out of several was the favourite one, it does show what different opinions were held at that time about particular questions; and, in the case of the older ones, what progress, if any, had occurred in the attempts to solve them. Many of these latter, of course, were also to be found in the books dealing with the various branches of natural history, and, in particular, in those which specialized in the marvels and rarities of nature and medicine—all written in Latin for the scholarly reader.[8] But the highest percentage of such

[1] Ibid., part ii, sect. 14.

[2] John Wallis, *A Defence of the Royal Society*, London, 1678, p. 7.

[3] 'Whether there be nothing new in the world; Which is most to be esteemed, an inventive wit, judgement or courage; Whether truth beget hatred, and why; Of the Cock, and whether his crying doth affright the Lyon; Why dead bodies bleed in the presence of their Murtherers. Each with a separate title, R. B(adger) for J. Emery, London (1640)', listed together under *S.T.C.* 20884.

[4] Wing, F. 1117.

[5] Not in Wing; the only copy I know of is my own, 'Printed for G:B. in St Dunstans Churchyard in Fleetstreet, 1653.'

[6] *A General Collection of Discourses of the Virtuosi of France upon all sorts of Philosophy and other Natural Knowledge, made in the Assembly of the Beaux-Esprits at Paris*, London, 1664. Wing, R. 1034.

[7] *Another Collection of Philosophical Conferences of the French Virtuosi upon questions of all sorts, for the Improvement of Natural Knowledge*, London, 1665. Wing, R. 1033A.

[8] Such as the *Sylloges Memorabilium medicinae et mirabilium naturae arcanorum* of Joannes Rudolph Camerarius (Cent. I–XII, Strassb., 1624–30); Joh. Jonston's *Thaumatographia naturalis* (Amst., 1632); the *Exercitationes physicae* of A. Senguerdius, Amst., 1658; G. Voigt's *Curiositates physicae* (Gustrow, 1668) and *Deliciae physicae* (Rostock, 1671); and the vast *Elysius Iucundarum Quaestionum Campus* of Gaspar a Reies Franco (Brussels, 1661), a book entirely medieval both in technique and subject-matter.

questions probably occurred in the books of natural problems and in the aids to conversation, both written in the vernacular to meet the ever growing popular demand, among non-Latin-speaking classes, for books dealing with scientific, medical, and ethical questions—rather like the popular wireless programmes of today, which consist of questions and answers.

To the first class of book, which was directly in the tradition of Garimberto's *Problemi naturali e morali* (1549), belonged the *Curiosité naturelle rédigée en questions selon l'ordre alphabétique*, of Scipion Dupleix (1569–1661), Councillor of State and Historiographer of France. Dedicated to Queen Marguerite de Valois, the book first appeared at Paris in 1606, and had an enormous success, being reprinted at least nine times up to and including 1645.[1] A selection of the problems was translated into English, and printed in 1635 with the title *The Resolver or Curiosities of Nature* (London, for N. and J. Okes),[2] whilst a further selection of those questions which had not been translated appeared two years later in a little book of problems compiled by Robert Basset called *Curiosities, or the Cabinet of Nature, containing phylosophical, naturall and morall questions, translated out of Latin, French and Italian authors* (London, N. and J. Okes, 1637).[3] This work also contained translations of some of Lando's *Dubbi*, and so may be said to combine the two classes of books, which, in any case, are very closely associated. Dupleix's book was imitated in 1628 by the French physician, Pierre Bailly, who in that year published at Paris his *Questions naturelles et curieuses*,[4] also in alphabetical order. Finally, in 1647 appeared, again at Paris, the *Mélanges de divers problèmes* of Georges Pellison, elder brother of the famous historian, which was translated into English by H. Some (London, 1662, 1680).[5]

---

[1] Lyons, 1620; Geneva, 1623; Rouen, 1626; Paris, 1631, 1632; Rouen, 1635, 1638, 1640, 1645. Dupleix also wrote popular compendiums of Aristotelian philosophy, viz. of the *Metaphysics*, *Physics*, *Logic*, *Ethics*, and the *Parva naturalia*, all printed a number of times, and written in the vernacular. Like Garimberto he modelled his questions on the Greek problems, but added a good deal of his own: 'Pour le regard des questions contenues en ce traicté, ie m'asseure qu'on en trouvera les résolutions gaillardes et non vulgaires, estant la pluspart extraictes des problèmes d'Aristote, d'Alexandre Aphrodisien, des œuvres des plus excellents Médecins, Naturalistes et autres graves autheurs que i'ay effleurez: y ayant aussi beaucoup contribué du mien, tant à l'invention et disposition, qu'en facilitant les raisons des autres: de sorte que ceux qui auront tant soit peu de iugement pourront soudre une infinité d'autres questions par l'intelligence de celles-cy.' Preface to *La Curiosité naturelle*.

[2] *S.T.C.* 7362.   [3] *S.T.C.* 1557.

[4] *Contenans diverses opinions problématiques, recueillies de la Médecine, touchant le régime de santé. Ou se voient plusieurs Proverbes populaires, fort plaisants et récréatifs qui se proposent iournellement en compagnie.* In spite of this title, and the fact that Joubert's book on popular errors is mentioned in the Epistle to the Reader, the book is much less a condemnation of popular errors than a straightforward book of problems exactly in the manner of Dupleix, who is also mentioned in the Epistle, and it is by no means confined to medicine. As far as I know, it was never translated into English or any other language, although, in some respects, more original in thought than Dupleix's *Curiosité naturelle*.

[5] *A Miscellany of divers problems, containing ingenious solutions of sundry questions, partly moral, partly of other subjects.* Wing, P. 1108, 1109.

In England translations seem to have almost entirely supplanted original works of this kind during this period. I can trace no books of problems, composed as such during the seventeenth century in English, except the extremely facetious and satirical *Philosophical Problems* of R(obert) H(eath) (London, 1659, 1664),[1] an amusing burlesque of the Peripatetic method.[2] On the other hand, we do find smaller collections of such problems added to various books, such as the thirteen added to Henry Cuffe's *Differences of the Ages of Mans Life* (London, 1607, 1633, 1640),[3] and the thirty which form the Appendix to Dr. Gideon Harvey's *Archelogia Philosophica Nova, or New Principles of Philosophy* (London, 1663),[4] both of which contain several ancient questions. Similar questions were also discussed in such works as Francis Bacon's *Sylva Sylvarum* (London 1626) and A. Ross's *Arcana Microcosmi* (London, 1652).[5]

As regards helps to discourse, the genre was well represented in Germany by J. M. Schwimmer's *Diverting and physical Pastime wherein nearly a thousand very delightful, remarkable and useful natural questions are most diligently examined and thoroughly discussed; also very advantageously and agreeably composed, for the singular pleasure of both the learned and the unlearned, and as an elegant, exact and exquisite exercise for their discourse* (Jena u. Leipzig, 1676, 1690, 1702).[6] Another similar book was Gottfried Voigt's *Newly augmented Physical Pastime, wherein three hundred choice and delightful questions from the book of Nature are answered* (Leipzig, 1694; Stettin, 1712).[7] These books, with their limitation to questions and answers, were modelled on Lando's *Dubbi*, rather than on the *Mensa philosophica*.

In England, however, it was this latter book, with its skilful mixture of the serious and the comic, which served as the basic inspiration for the seventeenth-century conversation books. The first to appear was the *Helpe to Discourse or a Miscelany of Merriment, Consisting of wittie Questions and Answers, as also of Epigrams, Epitaphs, Riddles and Jests, with the Countrymans Counsellour*, by W. B. & E. P. (London, 1619, and later editions up

---

[1] Wing, H. 1341, the 1659 ed. only. The full title is *Paradoxical Assertions and Philosophical Problems*. The *Philosophical Problems* has a separate title-page and pagination. In my copy the general title is dated 1664, that of the *Problems*, 1659, and a comparison with the Brit. Mus. 1659 edition shows that the book is a reissue of this, with a new general title. A peculiarity is that in both copies A2 is lacking.

[2] A very similar earlier work in Latin was the *Problematum Miscellaneorum Antaristotelicorum, centuria dimidiata, ad Dominos Studiosos in Academia Leydensi*, of Ludovicus Rouzaeus, 12mo, Leyden, 1616, the character of which is shown by the following words, 'Problemata seria et sublimia sunt, haec vero nostra humilia tantum et nugatoria'.

[3] *S.T.C.* 6103, 6104, 6105.   [4] Wing, H. 1053.   [5] Wing, R. 1947.

[6] *Kurzweiliger und physicalischer Zeitvertreiber, worinnen bei nahe in die Tausend höchstanmuthige, nachdenkliche und recht nützliche Natur-Fragen fleissigst untersuchet, und gründlich erörtert, auch zu Gelehrter und Ungelehrter sonderbarer Ergezzung, netter, reiner und lieblicher Sprach-Übung, höchst-gedeilich und behaglich aufgeführet.*

[7] *Neu-vermehrter physicalischer Zeit-Vertreiber, darinne Drey Hundert auserlesene, anmuthige Fragen aus dem Buch der Natur, beantwortet werden.*

to the seventeenth in 1682).[1] The attribution to William Basse in the *S.T.C.* is doubtful, but whoever W. B. was, he was probably the same person who had made the second translation of the *Mensa* in 1609 (see above, p. 110), since we find considerable portions of the second edition of this translation (1614) incorporated into the *Helpe to Discourse*. This book was followed by the *Helpe to Memorie and Discourse* (2nd ed., London, 1621,[2] another ed., 1630[3]), and W. Winstanley's *New Help to Discourse, or Wit and Mirth intermixt with more serious Matters, consisting of Pleasant Philosophical, Physical, Historical, Moral, and Political Questions and Answers, as also Proverbs, Epitaphs, Epigrams, Riddles, Poesies, Rules for Behaviour etc. with several Wonders, and other Varieties: together with Directions for the true knowledge of several Matters concerning Astronomy, Holydays, and Husbandry, in a plain and easie Method,*[4] of which nine editions appeared between 1669 and 1733.[5] As can be seen from this greatly augmented title, these little books, although consisting essentially of questions and answers, had strayed far beyond the limits of both Lando's *Dubbi* and the *Mensa philosophica* in their self-conscious efforts to please and entertain, but no one will deny that they gave very good value for money.[6]

Finally, towards the end of the century, that eccentric genius John Dunton (1659–1733) had the bright idea of conducting a correspondence through the press, for the purpose of answering any questions that people of all classes and conditions might propose. With this end in view, he published a journal every week, commencing 17 March 1690, called *The Athenian Gazette: or Casuistical Mercury resolving all the most Nice and Curious Questions proposed by the Ingenious of either Sex*. For answering the questions, Dunton is supposed to have had the assistance of several able scholars, such as Richard Sault, Dr. Norris, and Samuel Wesley, who constituted the Athenian Society which used to meet, to discuss the questions sent in, at Mr. Smith's Coffee House in Stocksmarket, London.[7]

One of the aims of the society seems to have been to confute vulgar errors and superstitious beliefs, in the manner of Sir Thomas Browne,[8]

---

[1] *S.T.C.* 1547–54 lists eight editions. Bishop adds four more, John Brand quotes an edition of 1633, *Popular Antiquities*, London, 1849, ii. 56, iii. 202, 403. Wing lists three editions, 1648, 1654, 1663 (E. 23–5), and another, the 17th, London, 1682, was listed in a recent bookseller's catalogue.

[2] *S.T.C.* 13051.

[3] Quoted by Brand, op. cit. iii. 239. Bishop, 13051.2 (Harvard).

[4] The title is copied from the fifth edition, London, 1702 (author's collection).

[5] See Wing, W. 3068–71A, and Case, *Bibliography of English Poetical Miscellanies*, 1935, 141.

[6] In the same tradition is the later chap book, *Aristotle's New Book of Problems*, third ed., London, c. 1705, preface signed S. J. (author's collection).

[7] John Nichols, *Literary Anecdotes of the Eighteenth Century*, v (1812), 68 ff. Pages 59–83 contain a very good account of Dunton and his writings.

[8] 'There are no greater Enemies to Wisdom and Learning than vulgar errors and Super-stition. . . . This learned Society seems to have been very sensible of this, by the great care they have taken, in confuting those erroneous Notions, which are commonly received, as often as

but the answers are often of a most elementary nature, and certainly do not display that acumen and power of reasoning which we find in the earlier books dealing with popular errors, in the more serious vernacular problem books, and in Renaudot's conferences.[1] Like the aids to conversation, the net was set to catch a wider public and it certainly succeeded. The project lasted seven years,[2] and the tradition was carried on in the next century by such publications as the *British Apollo* (1708–11) and the *Weekly Oracle* (1734–7), leading eventually to the modern *Notes and Queries* and other similar journals. For us, perhaps the chief interest of the *Athenian Gazettes* and *Mercuries* is that they show, better than any other publication of the period, the sort of questions with which quite ordinary people of that day occupied themselves, and thus throw considerable light on contemporary customs, beliefs, and ways of life. The popular taste for pseudo-scientific subjects is well represented, and there is a high proportion of older questions, which includes Salernitan ones.

Enough has now been said to show that the Salernitan questions had by no means died out by the seventeenth century. They continued to form an integral part of popular scientific thought, and were discussed, both by the learned and by the unlearned, side by side with those belonging to the sphere of the new experimental and mathematical philosophy. Now the chief characteristic of the older questions was their qualitative nature, that is, they asked why certain things happened, and elicited answers depending solely on physical compositions and properties, usually in relation to the four elements, the humours, and complexions. In physics, which had formed only a very small proportion of the Salernitan questions, this type of question had, by the seventeenth century, been largely superseded by the vastly more interesting and important quantitative questions and answers, embodying *experimenta* which yielded precise numerical data. But the vast majority of the Salernitan questions dealt with

---

they presented themselves in any of the numerous Quaeries that have been sent them: And they have very well observed, that there are a great many omitted by the ingenious Dr Brown, which, are, in my opinion, as necessary to be remov'd, as any he has observed'. *History of the Athenian Society*, London, 1691, p. 15.

[1] It is possible that Renaudot's scheme helped to inspire Dunton with the idea for his *Gazettes*. The Supplements to the first two volumes of the latter (1691) contained much abbreviated translations of several of the questions and answers in Renaudot's conferences. These purported to be contained in a *New Treatise entituled Serious and Gallant Discourses*, translated out of the French, but I have not succeeded in tracing an edition of any such translation, and perhaps it was never separately published.

[2] The *Gazettes* and *Mercuries* from 1690 to 1697, when the scheme ended, ran into twenty folio volumes, each containing thirty single-leaf journals and, in addition, there were supplements to the first five volumes. An index to these five volumes and to their supplements appeared in Dunton's *Young Student's Library*, London, 1692, and a selection of the questions in all the *Gazettes* and *Mercuries* was reprinted in four octavo volumes, London, 1703–10, with the title, *The Athenian Oracle*: finally an abridgement of these appeared in one volume 8vo London, n.d. (*c.* 1740) and 1820.

anthropology, the various branches of medicine, zoology, and, to a less extent, botany, in the sense of plant growth, nourishment, and structure. In these fields, also, the most important progress had taken place in connexion with completely new questions, often brought about by improvements in apparatus and technique, which were entirely beyond the very limited horizon of the Salernitan masters.

Nevertheless the old, qualitative questions persisted, and it is with these that we are more concerned at the moment. It might be asked why they persisted for so long, and why, in certain cases, the answers showed so little change. In the first place, it must be remembered that these questions were originally didactic, and for centuries had served to impress certain doctrines and beliefs on the minds of masters and scholars alike. They had, therefore, a long-standing authoritative value which, in common with that possessed by the great masters, such as Aristotle, Galen, and Hippocrates, was only just beginning to be undermined by the seventeenth century.

Again, a large proportion of the zoological questions concerned fabled attributes of animals, birds, reptiles, and fishes, which had passed into the folk-lore of the people and had been firmly embedded in their minds, through the poetic imagery of the written word and the visual concepts of sculpture and painting. The seventeenth century was an age which delighted in marvels and rarities of all kinds, when, almost daily, there were being brought to the notice of the learned many phenomena in the realms of the biological sciences, which were much more remarkable than those to which they had long been accustomed. It is scarcely surprising, therefore, that the old fables persisted, and the scepticism in these matters of such men as Sir Thomas Browne and Bayle is all the more to be commended.

A smaller number of the zoological questions and the bulk of those in the sphere of anthropology dealt with the common, everyday behaviour of man and beast—actions and processes which undoubtedly took place. These were what one might call the basic questions of perennial interest to all classes of people, whether skilled scientists and physicians or not— and their persistence is understandable for that reason. Not capable of an exact, numerical answer, lying entirely outside the spheres of the technician and the mathematician, these seemingly simple questions were, in fact, during the centuries, found to be among the most difficult that the inquiring mind of man could occupy itself with. In this type of question the answers were not so stable; we have already dealt with some of them in previous chapters and in the seventeenth century we find certain significant changes in the methods of dealing with them. The Salernitans, it will be recalled, had always tried to explain such actions by reference to purely physical characteristics. Later enquirers sought more abstract philosophical, teleological, and ethical causes, until by the seventeenth century there began to appear those based on the psychology of behaviour. Let us illustrate these tendencies by an analysis of the answers to three typical Salernitan questions.

One favourite question discussed why it was that animals swam naturally, but man, who was cleverer than they, had to learn to swim.[1] The Salernitans attributed the greater ease of swimming shown by animals to the eminence of the breast and the hollowness and curvature of the lower parts, which afforded a large surface and so made it easier for them to float. The number of feet also helped the process. Man, on the other hand, is fashioned more or less the same back and front, and is without those lower eminences and hollow protuberances which make it harder for him to float; therefore he cannot swim, except *ex artificio*. Hildegarde of Bingen, writing about 1150, thought that animals swam more easily because they maintained the same natural position both on land and in the water, and were also stronger in their legs, and had more of air in their composition. Man, however, walked upright on land but had to swim in a prone position which was unnatural to him; he was also heavier in proportion and had less air in his composition—and so was by nature less fitted for swimming.[2] When Ambrogio Leone came to discuss the question in 1523, he gave three reasons. The first depended on the solicitude of nature for irrational animals. Since such animals could not teach themselves to swim, they were naturally endowed with this knowledge, to save themselves from drowning should they accidentally fall into the water. Man, on the other hand, being possessed of reason, could teach himself. In the second place, animals and birds move their legs and feet in the same way in both walking and swimming, whereas in man these actions are quite different—he has to learn entirely new actions and motions for swimming. His third reason, depending on the position of the body in swimming and walking, was the same as that given by Hildegarde.[3] Sir Thomas Browne, in his *Pseudodoxia* (1646), mentions, without acknowledgement, the last two reasons of Leone derived from the movements of the limbs and the position of the body.[4] Finally G. Pellison, in the following year, first mentions a psychological reason, namely that man is apt to be preoccupied with the thought that he cannot swim, which makes him either not swim at all or swim badly, 'car infailliblement croire de ne sçavoir pas faire une chose, c'est une disposition à la faire mal, et à n'y réussir point', whereas beasts have no such thoughts. He next mentions the two reasons given by Leone and Browne, based on movements and position, and also one resembling the Salernitan answer which dealt with body structure, saying that oxen and horses have a large

---

[1] Auct. f. 124^v; Pet. f. 34. Q. 97 natare.
[2] *Causae et Curae*, ed. P. Kaiser, Leipzig (Teubner), 1903, p. 110.
[3] *Novum opus questionum*, Prob. 326.
[4] Ed. Sayle, ii (1927), 134.

interior cavity and therefore, like high-walled ships, float more easily. He also says that beasts have longer necks, which makes it easier for them to keep their heads above water. Finally he gives a teleological reason resembling Leone's first one, saying that whereas man can build ships and bridges and use horses for crossing rivers, beasts have no such capabilities and therefore are naturally endowed with the art of swimming.[1]

Another Salernitan question stemming from Aristotle asked why parents loved their children more than the latter loved them.[2] The answer again depended on purely physical characteristics. The child is formed from the sperm of both father and mother, and therefore has its essence from the substance of both. The parents, knowing this, love the child so much the more; but the latter, having nothing of his substance in the parents, for that reason loves them less. Peter of Spain, in his commentary on the *De animalibus*, repeats this reason and also adds another taken from Aristotle, namely that love proceeds forward towards what is better. But being is better than non-being, and the being of the father is the cause of the being of the child, not vice versa; therefore love does not go back from the child to the child's non-being in the father, but forward from the latter to the father's being in the child—which is simply a philosophical interpretation of the physical statement mentioned above.[3]

Aristotle gave four reasons in the *Ethics*; the first resembled the Salernitan answer, the other three were elaborated in the scholastic commentaries on this book,[4] of the thirteenth and fourteenth centuries, before being popularized by Garimberto in the sixteenth.

But first Zimara gave, in effect, the Salernitan answer and a variation of Peter of Spain's second reason—'love does not go backward, but always forward, since it serves for the continuation of the species, so that our natural desire, neglecting things past, looks always forward to future things.'[5] Garimberto repeated this latter reason and then gave the three scholastic ones mentioned above; the first being that the father is certain that he has engendered the child but the latter has no such certainty, since he did not exist at the time of his generation. The second is again philosophical, and depends on the fact that the father has a closer affinity with the child than vice versa. This is proved by the fact that the thing engendered, in comparison with the engenderer, is as the separable part to the whole in which the part is contained; but the whole is not contained in the part. Moreover, that which contains has a closer affinity with that which is contained than vice versa, and from this closer affinity springs a greater love—again, a rather roundabout way of expressing that the father recognizes something

[1] *Mélanges de divers problèmes* (1647), p. 109.
[2] Auct. f. 126ᵛ; *Ethica Nicomachea*, VIII, xii, 2.
[3] Madrid, Bib. Nac. 1877, f. 284ᵛ, also no. 118 of the abstracted *Problemata*.
[4] Notably in those of Albertus Magnus, Thomas Aquinas, Walter Burley, and Jean Buridan.
[5] Prob. 42. Copied by Ortensio Lando in his *Dubbi* (ed. 1556, p. 274).

of himself in the child, but the latter sees nothing of himself in the father. In the third place, Garimberto maintained that affection is increased and confirmed by length of time. The parents begin to love their children as soon as they are born, but the children do not begin to love the parents until they have the use of reason and can distinguish them from other people. The parents, therefore, have a long start over the children as far as the increasing and growth of love is concerned.[1]

Crasso first stressed the active element in loving, saying that the end of loving must always consist in action. But the father is more active than the son, in so far as the latter is an effect of the father's action, and so the father must love more than the son. In the second place, the father is inspired by memory and hope, hoping that he himself will be renewed in his son; factors which do not affect the latter.[2]

Du Pleix (1606) has nothing to add to what has been said before, mentioning the theories which depend on the forward progression of love, the greater time involved, and the presence of the substance of the parents in the child.[3] Pierre Bailly (1628) mentions only two reasons, of which one is the old one, concerning the time factor, but the other completely new, since it stresses the fact that the respect which children naturally owe to their parents diminishes the familiarity and friendship from which love is born, and so does correction and chastisement—certainly the most commonsense reason of all.[4]

The question was debated at some length in Renaudot's *Bureau d'Adresse* on 27 March 1634, when some rather novel opinions, some of them in a lighter vein, were brought forward. Two members denied that the proposition was true, the reason of one being that the love of the child for the parent was pure and disinterested, and therefore better than that of the parent for the child, which was actuated by a desire to be supported by his offspring, and to perpetuate in him his name, coat of arms, and 'something of himself'. The other gave as his reasons: (1) That the whole does not seek the part, but the part, the whole; (2) If the parent loves the child because of a resemblance to himself, this being common to both, the child should love the father just as much, for the same reason; (3) If love is a fire, as the poets say, it should rather mount upwards to the parents, than downwards to the children; and (4) If, in human love, the lover is less perfect than the beloved, the child, who is less perfect than the parent, ought to be the one who loves.

Three other members agreed with the proposition. The first mentioned four commonly held reasons, namely, that the desire of the parent to perpetuate himself in the child made the love of the former greater, not less, and adding the old reason, that we naturally love what proceeds

---

[1] *Problemi* (1549), Prob. 114, following the commentary of Aquinas on the *Ethics*.
[2] *Quaest. nat. et med.* (1581), Prob. 42. [3] *Curiosité nat.*, ed. 1631, p. 11.
[4] *Questions nat.*, p. 28.

from ourselves. He then gives two new reasons, that love is the child of knowledge, but the father has more knowledge, ergo . . ., and God has commanded children to love and honour their parents, as if it were not a natural and usual thing for them to do, whilst no such command has been laid upon the parents to love their children, since this is what they usually do. The second contradicts the first argument against the proposition, saying that it is rather the love of the parent which is free, natural, and disinterested, that of the child being, as it were, the payment of a debt, a recognition of benefits received, and an escape from ingratitude. His second reason was that he who gives loves more than he who receives. Finally, the third member based his reason on the fact that the compassion of parents towards tender and weak children is usually more than that of the children towards parents rendered decrepit by sickness or old age, and love is, above all, fostered by compassion—an answer which resembles that of Cecco d'Ascoli, given in reply to a rather similar question.[1]

The question we are discussing was one of those which W. B. incorporated into his *Helpe to Discourse* (see above, p. 146), and I transcribe it, and the answer, from the 1648 edition.

Q. Why doe the affections of Parents run upward to their Children, and not their Children['s] run downeward to them?

A. Even as the sap in the root of a Tree ascends into the branches thereof, and from the branches returnes not into the root againe, but runs out from thence into seed; so Parents love their children, but children so love not their Parents, but their affections run forward to a further procreation. Whereby it comes to passe, that one Father with more willingnesse brings up ten children, then ten Children in his want sustaine one Father [p. 52].

It is interesting to note that the author adheres to the ancient, Aristotelian answer taught by Peter of Spain, but uses the picturesque and illuminating simile of the sap in the tree—a literary twist that is quite new and entirely in keeping with the popular character of this entertaining little book.

To conclude this brief analysis of problems, let us see how these same French writers deal with another very ancient problem, namely that one which asks why infants cannot walk as soon as they are born, but irrational animals can. We have already discussed this question in Chapters 2 and 4,[2] and shown how both the pseudo-Alexandrian *Problems* and the Salernitan *Quaestiones* had provided physical reasons depending, respectively, on the distribution of innate heat in the body, and on the presence or absence of menstrual blood in the nourishment. We also showed how Adelard of Bath had given a philosophical answer, and said that the

---

[1] 'Why does the father love his youngest son more than himself?', *L'acerba*, v, i (ed. 1546).
[2] See above, pp. 39, 55.

weaker, more tender limbs appertain to the nobler, rational animal, man, while the stronger limbs of beasts are 'out of keeping with the practice of rational virtue'. William of Conches had combined the Salernitan answer with that of Adelard. Hildegarde assigns the cause to the weakness of the infant's legs and feet in comparison with the strength of those of beasts, without going into any more explanations.[1] Peter of Spain, in his commentary on the *De animalibus*, brought in the moist and dry qualities of Galen, saying that man is moister than animals, and that this excess humidity softens the sinews and renders them unfit for walking.[2]

One of the pseudo-Aristotelian problems was 'Why are men more apt than other animals to be lame from birth?',[3] to which one of the answers was, because the legs of beasts are strong, for quadrupeds and birds have bony and sinewy legs, but human legs are fleshy and so, owing to their softness, they more easily become damaged through movements in the uterus. Peter of Abano, in commenting on this problem, said that these were also the reasons why man was slower in learning to walk than animals, and also mentioned the antecedent, Galenic causes of dryness, in the case of beasts, and humidity, in the case of man.[4] The author of the *Quolibeta naturalis philosophiae* in Bibl. Nat. Lat. 2831 determines two causes; the first resembling Adelard's and maintaining that the weaker, more perfect, and nobler composition of man requires nobler organs than beasts do; and the second introducing a new factor, namely the length of life, which is greater in man than in beasts, and therefore 'nature has ordained that the latter should compleat their operations more quickly', implying that man can afford to take a much longer time to learn his functions than beasts can.[5] Cecco d'Ascoli's answer resembles this last one; beasts, he says, are born into the world perfect and have a short life, therefore nature works quickly in them. But man is born imperfect, and depends to a greater extent upon the nursing of his mother.[6]

Conrad de Halberstadt quotes Peter of Spain *super Tegni* (*Galeni*) as the authority for two causes; the first attributing the difficulty of walking to the erect posture of the infant combined with the smallness of the feet, and the second depending on the softness of the body and limbs and corresponding to Peter's above-mentioned explanation in the commentary on the *De animalibus*.[7]

De Pleix, after mentioning the two physical causes of pseudo-Alexander and pseudo-Aristotle, mentions another argument from the fitness of things; if beasts could not walk as soon as they were born, not being endowed with reason, they would quickly perish from the attacks of other beasts and of man himself—an argument which resembles that brought forward by Leone to explain the natural swimming of animals. Finally

---

[1] Op. cit., pp. 109–10.

[2] See Additional Note D (p. 208).

[3] *Prob.* x. 41 (895ᵃ).

[4] Ed. Venice 1505, p. 112.

[5] f. 98.

[6] *L'acerba*, lib. v, ch. 8.

[7] *Responsorium curiosorum* (1476), p. 103.

he mentions an ethical reason, 'it is very expedient that man should be born feeble, so that he may recognize his lowliness and weakness, and so be less proud'.[1] Bailly first mentions the cause referring to dryness and humidity, but says that not all beasts walk as soon as they are born, but only those which are excessively dry, such as certain birds. He then mentions as a cause the fact that beasts have to fend for themselves much sooner than man, who is in the care of his parents for a much longer time, and, finally, the ethical reason of Du Pleix.[2]

This question too, or at least that part of it which confined itself to asking why infants were unable to walk or stand, was discussed in the vernacular helps to conversation. Ortensio Lando in his *Dubbi naturali* briefly replied that the reason for this was the size and weight of the body, to which the French translator added the weakness of the legs.[3] J. M. Schwimmer in his *Physicalischer Zeitvertreiber* (1676) answered at greater length, though with little originality. His first reason was a variation of Conrad de Halberstadt's first solution, and stressed the smallness of the feet in comparison with the size and weight of the body and especially of the head. But he considered this answer inadequate and based his main reason this time on a development of Peter of Spain's other solution which relied on on temperament. The cartilages in the various joints of the body, he said, were weak owing to the predominating moist quality of the child. As the latter gets older his nature becomes drier, and his joints become consequently firmer and more strongly knit together, thus enabling him to stand and walk. This explained too why some children, who were hotter and drier in temperament than others, learnt to walk sooner.[4] Finally, Gottfried Voigt's answer was a much abbreviated version of Schwimmer's.[5]

These three examples, then, show as well as any the sort of treatment that typical Salernitan questions of this kind received at various periods from the twelfth to the seventeenth century. To the original physical reasons there came to be added teleological ones drawn from the fitness of things, those depending on ethics, Aristotelian philosophical reasons, and, finally, psychological ones derived from the rational behaviour of man.

---

[1] Op. cit., ed. 1631, p. 20.   [2] Op. cit., p. 54.
[3] *Dubbi*, ed. 1556, p. 103; *Les raisons naturelles*, 1586, p. 90.
[4] Ed. cit., pp. 168–71.   [5] *Physicalischer Zeitvertreiber* (1694), p. 462.

THE TEXTS

FOR the text of the *Speculator* I have used the Broadside, **H** (Nürnberg, *c.* 1501, Hain 14898, Einbl. 1394), and the five manuscripts, Sloane 1610, **S**; Trinity, Camb. 580 (R. 3. 1), **T**; Berlin, Cod. lat. 4to143 (Rose 152^r), **B**; the author's manuscript, **L**; and, for Ulsen's riddles only, C 1 m 428, **M**.

In five cases the manuscript readings have served to correct obvious errors in the printed Broadside, namely in lines 36, 43, 100, and 145 of the *Speculator*, and in line 9 of Ulsen's set of riddles.

The text of the remainder of the *Questiones phisicales*, not used by Ulsen, is based on **S** and **T**.

Variations in spelling, apart from those which give a different meaning, have not always been noted, and a more modern punctuation has been adopted to facilitate the reading of the texts. Corrupt passages in the manuscript have been thus indicated: ⟨   ⟩.

S. The *Questiones phisicales* occupies ff. 43^v–45^r of a stout folio volume, written throughout on vellum, in a fine thirteenth-century English book hand. The other tracts are all medical works by Ioannitius, Galen, Hippocrates, Theophilus, Philaretus, Aegidius, and Constantinus. The work before the *Questiones* is the prose *De regimine sanitatis* of Galen; that after it, the poem beginning 'Res aloes lignum preciosa sit', variously ascribed to Gilles of Corbeil and Otto of Cremona, and entitled in other manuscripts *Versus de simplicibus aromaticis* (Thorndike and Kibre, *Incipits* (1937), col. 625).

T. This is a folio manuscript, consisting of thirty leaves of vellum, containing part of Neckam's *De laudibus divinae sapientiae*, written early in the fifteenth century. Part only of the *Questiones phisicales* occupies two paper fly-leaves at the end, and is written in a good, clear, sixteenth-century italic hand. Almost certainly an English manuscript given by Thomas Nevile, dean of Canterbury, and Master of Trinity from 1593 to 1615

B. A quarto volume, paper, containing eleven tracts dating from the fifteenth to the eighteenth century, and dealing with a wide variety of subjects, political, theological, medical, and scientific. Ulsen's earlier version of the *Speculator* occupies ff. 175–6, and is the last item in the volume. It is written in a very minute, neat, and scholarly hand, typical of that used by the fifteenth-century German humanists— most probably the autograph of Ulsen himself. The manuscript at one time belonged to the famous classical scholar, Philipp Karl

Buttmann (1764–1829), and a note in his hand states that the two leaves bearing Ulsen's poem were attached to a printed copy of Wimpheling's *Oratio querulosa contra invasores sacerdotum*. The volume is at present lodged in the Westdeutsche Bibl. at Marburg/Lahn.

L. This was formerly item 952 in the *Catalogue of the extraordinary collection of Splendid Manuscripts . . . formed by M. Guglielmo Libri*, Sotheby & Wilkinson, 1859. It is a quarto volume written on paper, and the complete text of the Broadside, the *Speculator*, and the two sets of riddles occupies ff. 2–4ᵛ. It is followed by a prose prophecy, expl. 'finit prophecia Magistri Samuelis Archisynagogi Hierosolimitani, Anno Domini 1492', another prophecy in verse, 'Versus reperti Rome in quodam codice antiquo', and a set of Sapphic Odes describing sixteen pictures of the Passion which then hung in the monastery of Saints Ulrich and Affra at Augsburg. These Odes were sung by the writer while attending prayers in the monastery, when Conrad Mörlin was abbot (1496–1510)—'Ad preces Venerabilis in Christo patris ac domini, domini Conradi abatis Sanctorum Udalrici et Affre Auguste monasterii, has odas cecini in passionem carnigeri dei Jesu Christi contentam in sedecim tabulis, quarum primam tenet Sancta Affra, cum Saphico Carmine, ultimam vero sanctus Udalricus.' The volume is written throughout in a clear German book hand of the early sixteenth century.

M. A volume from Hartmann Schedel's library containing classical, historical, and humanistic works, including poems and letters of Ulsen, Bonomus, Hegius, and Truchsess, transcribed by Schedel *c.* 1498. Ulsen's riddles occur on f. 237.

I

SPECULATOR CONSILIORUM ENIGMATICUS MICROCOSMI PROTHEATI TORRENS

Testes   *Procedant*

Sic ego vesanos senii depello vapores,
Sic notam mihi plasmo viam salientibus astris.
Incepto dubiam radians ubi copia mentem
Obscuros aditus audenti carmine tentet
Xanctus amor patrie. Phrisiis elatus ab undis   5
Pheben Phebus amat docte pia cura Minerve,
Virtutis mihi dulce decus dum grata corolla
Attulit. ignote tranando per avia silve
Discordes videt esse vias cum calle viator
Ambiguus, cernitque brevem sub luce dietam   10
Nunc hos nunc illos aditus et sepe retractat,
Multa notans animo et mestus vestigia torquet:
Sic mihi mutatis placuit sententia ceptis,
Eructat dum fibra novum pro tempore lumen
Pectoris ethereum. ventus pars maxima nostri est   15
Quod sumus et pulvis sub vana cernimur umbra.
Singultat gravis Ethna tonans pumicesque retundit
Ignivomos. sic bella gigas celestia sentit,
Sentit corporei latebrosa pericula templi.
Qualicumque iugo tentem diffundere sulcos   20
Angelici Agricole quo preceptore piatam
Lavimus ecce viam liquide rationis avitam.
Eloquio si digna fides, si candida virtus,
Iam circum gelidos fontes montesque virentes
Sulfureos latices fugiam sub Apollinis umbra,   25
Sedem constituens quercu lauroque labanti
Frondibus intexens solidis, ac viscera vincam
Sambuco et gelida stagnanti felle cicuta.
Psalterio extergam vetulo serpentibus atris
Cornua contexens, clara cantante Camena.   30

Title, Radiosa Microcosmi Veterascentis protheatio Centum Enigmatis The. Ulsenii. Testes Procedant, *omitted,* **B.**   1 Hic, **L**; vesani, **B.**   2 quero, **B.**   4 audens fiducia, **B.** 6 docta, **L**; cura sororis (Minerve *above*), **B.**   7 dum dulce decus, **B**; coralla, **L.**   9 sit esse vias, **B.**   13 Hec mihi, **B.**   14 Eructant dum verba, **B.**   17 Singultit, **H, L**; Sic flammas gravis ethna tonat, **B.**   20 via tentem, **B.**   21 piandam, **H, L.**   26 quercui,

THE ENIGMATIC, IMPETUOUS EXAMINER
OF THE COUNCILS OF THE TRANSFORMED
MICROCOSM

Let the Witnesses Proceed

Thus do I shake off the turbulent vapours of melancholy, and so plot
a course I know athwart the leaping stars.

May a holy love of the Fatherland urge me on, when, full of
doubt yet glowing with eloquence, I assail the dark approaches with
5 daring song. Phoebus, risen from the Frisian waves and in the tender
care of the wise Minerva, loves Phoebe, while the welcome garland has
brought me virtue's highest honour.

10 Like a traveller who, in passing through the wilderness of an unknown
wood, sees that there are different paths, is uncertain which one to
choose, and knowing that the period of daylight is short, explores again
and again now this one, now that, bending his steps hither and thither,
15 full of care and anxiety—so, after various attempts, I am at last resolved
on my course; while, as occasion demands, my inmost bosom emits a new
ethereal lustre. Wind is the greatest part of us, and under the empty
shadows we are beheld but as dust.

Huge and roaring Etna belches forth the fire-spitting pumice, dashing
it down headlong; thus does the giant suffer the effects of his war with the
20 Gods, and feel the perils lurking in his earthly abode.

With a yoke, whate'er it be, let me try to spread abroad the furrows of
the angelic Agricola, for, behold! under his guidance have I washed clean
pure reason's ancient path. If faith and honest virtue are worthy of
25 poetry, now will I forsake the sulphureous streams and make my dwelling
in Apollo's shade, near cool springs and verdant mountains; weaving
together the firm branches of the oak and the tremulous laurel, and when
my bile o'erflows, with elder and cold hemlock will I subdue my bowels.

30 Then, improvising upon an ancient lute, I shall banish the horns from
the poisonous serpents, my Muse clearly singing the while.

H, L.   27 visere, **B.**   28 et fragili prius abdita quoque cicuta, **B.**   29 intendam,
B.   30 Cornua dirumpam cythara plectroque reponens, **B.**

Que primeva foret facies cum cuncta laterent
Informi confunsa globo, coniecta sub una
Mole simul, quam freta sua ratione vetustas
Credidit esse chaos, quam Plato nomine silvam
Designat, quam posterior que temporis huius   35
Est etas appellat ylen, ruditate polita
Incultisque prius cultum sumentibus? unde
Tam stabiles nexus elementis quatuor in se,
Cum teneant causas erecta fronte rebelles?
Que rerum natura latens? quis motus in igne est   40
Nature imperio qui sursum sublevet, aut qui
Mobile subiectum signosum volvat in orbem?
Quis gumfus visum fugiens discordia rerum
Semina concilians concordi pace ligavit?
Quod teneat terram medio, cum pondere vergat   45
Inferius, solusque subest circumfluus aer
Rarior hac, nec cedat ei? quo iure ligatur
Ether ebes, cum cuncta sibi penetrare potestas,
Ut membris solidis humores alteret alter
Inclusos? que sit laticis formalis imago,   50
Spherica vel plana, necnon que tanta poesis
Complexata nitens ut cornua dura cerastes
Accusent lachrymis presens latitare venenum?
Que virtus adamante latens ut mobile ferrum
Efficiat? petulans dum stat sententia vobis,   55
Dicite philosophi que vis magnetica sistit
Hoc ipsum? paleamque trahat quo iure gagates:
Egressum quo iure lapis qua lege cruorem
Stringat emathites? cur nigra peonia partes
Supremas capitis hieronoxa liberet? unde   60
Firmet epar spodium, stomacho que cura galangam
Apropriet, cerebro muscum que causa maritet?
Cur raucescat homo subito quem luce lupina
Perstringit facies? cur federe turtur amico
Marcescens pereat pare depereunte, nec ultro   65

---

31 S *begins, the first line of* S, Sepe mihi dubiam traxhit sententia mentem, *being omitted*;
forent; dum cuncta, S.   32 confusa, S, B ; congesta, S.   35 sed posterior, S ; huius
remota, B.   36 estas, H. L ; ruditate remota, S.   37 que *omitted*, L.   38 elementi,
S.   39 causas habeant, S.   40 est *omitted*, S, B ; *in* S *the order of lines is transposed*,
40, 41, 42 *coming after* 43, 44.   41 aut quid, S.   42 sinuosum, S.   43 quis virtus, B;
nilum, H, B, L.   45 Quid terram medio teneat, S.   47 cedit; ligetur, S.   48 Aer;
tanta sibi, S.   49 alteret altere, S.   51 potestas, S, B.   52 complexata beet, S ; latens, B.
53 tacitum latitare venenum, S.   *In* B *a line is inserted after* 53, Corruptiones primus radius:
et invidie et vitiorum omnes: Cerastes. T *begins here, with the opening line of* S, Sepe mihi
. . . mentem.   54 magnete latens T.   55, 56, 57 *The sentence*, petulans . . . hoc ipsum,
omitted in S, T.   57 paleam moveat, S, T.   58 Egressum sua vasa lapis, S, T.

What was the appearance in the beginning, when all things were confused and lay hid in a formless sphere, thrown together in one mass, which the ancients in their philosophy thought was chaos, Plato called a wood,

35 and this latter age terms hyle—its barbarity having been refined and those who before were unlettered adopting culture? Whence come about such stable bonds in the four elements, when, with bold front, they hold together

40 the opposing causes of things? What is the hidden nature of things? What is that motion in fire, which, by nature's decree, raises it aloft, or which turns around the changing zodiac? What invisible bond, conciliating the discordant seeds of things, has united them in harmony and peace? What

45 bears up the earth in the midst, although it tends to fall by its weight, and when air alone, which is less dense, surrounds it and yet yields not to it? What law governs the sluggish ether, which has the power of penetrating all things, so that air, of one sort or another, can alter the humours enclosed in the solid parts of the body?

50 What is the formal shape of water, spherical or flat? Also, what is that poem which has such charm that, when the cruel horns have been seized, the cerastes let us know by their tears that the potent venom is hidden

55 away?

What virtue is hidden in the diamond, so that it loosens iron? And, whilst your rash mood persists, tell me, o philosophers! what magnetic power holds iron fast? How does jet attract a straw, and the stone haematite staunch the exuded blood? Why does black peony free the top of the

60 head from the falling sickness? How does spodium strengthen the liver, and why is galangal appropriate to the stomach, and musk to the brain?

Why does he who has been dazed by the sight of a wolf suddenly grow

---

59-62 *The sentences,* cur nigra . . . maritet, *omitted in* T, *and the order of lines altered as follows*: 59 & 64, 65, 66, 63, 64 & 87, 88, 67, 68.   60 Yeranoxia, **S**, Hieronaxa, **L**.   61 Tremat epar, **B**; que causa, **S**.   62 Apropiet, **L**.   63 raucescit; subita, **S**, **T**; quem voce, **T**. 64 sadere, **T**.   65 ultra, **S**, **T**.

M

Dignetur carnis nexus renovare iugales?
Cur luces hiemis fugiat detenta sopore
Falso que veris novitate resurgit hyrundo?
Inter aves cur sit fenix avis unica? vel cur
Vipera post partum pereat? cur fetus ab ore   70
Prodit apis? cur concipiat cornicula flatu?
Cur visu solo duris stans incubat ovis
Strutio? cur piscis medios novisse colores
Non possit, luscus medios novisse furores
Non discat? cur nona dies sit nuncia lucis   75
Erepte catulis, contra rugire leonis
Fetum vivificet? cur formam conferat ursus,
Dum lingit lambitque rudem quam mittit ab ore
Materiem simili dum vestit imagine prolem?
Cur talpam tellus, salamandram nutriat ignis?   80
Accusat cur vulnus hians quis criminis auctor,
Dum cruor exudat mortis presente ministro?
Cur lincis radio paries sit pervius? unde
Lux aquile solis radios illesa tuetur?
Cur canis in coitu nexu retinente laboret,   85
Et penam facti cupiens completa iocose
Non impune ferat? cur se castrare fatiget
Castor quando videt iam se cepisse sequentes?
Cur bubo plaudat tenebris odiosa diei
Lumina devitans? cur vespertilio noctem   90
Diligat? unde suas pavo si laude citetur
Pandat opes quas penna tegit, rursusque recondit
Ad laudem si lingua tepet? quo munere mula
Sit sterilis? reddit gravidam cur nepita cattam,
Ventus equam? cur sambuci gravis hernia fumo   95
Infestet commota magis? cur membra bovina
Sublevet ad motum pars ultima cum prior artus
Subportans ostentet onus, cur surgit asellus
Ordine converso? cur bis commutet in anno
Accubitus laterum vervex? nam dum gravis estas   100
Exurit terrena latus convertere dextrum
Ad terram novit, hiemis dum sentit acumen
Hoc subit officium dextro cessante sinistrum.
Cur galli cantus ad motum mobilis ala
Motu preveniat, cur luciferi quasi iura   105

66 sexus, T.   67 lucem, T; detensa, S.   69 fenix solitarius. unde, S, T; avis
omitted in L.   70 per partum, S, T; partus ab ore, T.   71 perdit S; prodat, T,
H, B, L; cunicula, S.   72 vise, B; solis, T.   73 Sturtio, S; pisces; calores, T.
74 possint, T; luscus . . . discat, *omitted in* S, T, B.   76 et cur rugare, S; et cur

65 hoarse? Why does the turtle dove, by mutual contract, pine away and die when her mate perishes, and disdain to renew the carnal bonds of wedlock?

Why does the swallow, held fast by deceitful sleep, vanish in the winter, and appear again at the new-coming of spring? Amongst birds, 70 why is there but one phoenix? Why does the viper die after parturition, and the bee produce her young by means of her mouth? Why does the crow conceive by breath? Why does the ostrich, standing, and by sight alone, hatch her hard eggs? Why is a fish unable to see middle colours, and why is a purblind person never subject to middling attacks of anger? 75 Why does the ninth day bring to puppies the light of which they have, till then, been deprived and, on the other hand, roaring revive the lion cub? Why does the bear, by licking and washing the crude mass which she produces, bestow a shape upon it, and in this way furnish her offspring with 80 a form like her own? Why does earth nourish the mole, and fire the salamander? Why does the gaping wound accuse and show who was the criminal, when blood oozes from it in the presence of the murderer? Why is a wall pervious to the vision of a lynx? How is it that the eagle looks at 85 the sun without hurt? Why, when dogs copulate, are they kept fastened together and, wishing to finish the act, why do they gladly, but not with impunity, suffer the pain of it?

Why does the beaver forthwith torment and castrate himself when he sees that he has been taken by the hunters?

Why does the owl rejoice in the night season, and shun the hateful 90 light of day? Why does the bat love the dark? Why does the peacock disclose the glories hidden in his plumes when he is flattered, and hide them again if the ardour of the flatterer diminishes? By what law is the mule sterile? Why does catmint fertilize the cat, and wind the mare? 95 Why should a severe hernia, disturbed by the smoke of elder wood, cause more pain? Why, in the case of an ox, do the hindquarters lift up the (hind)legs when it gets up, and the forelegs support the weight; and why does an ass arise in the opposite way? Why does the ram change his posi- 100 tion in lying down, twice a year? For when the hot summer scorches the earth, he knows how to turn his right side to the ground; but when he feels the biting cold of winter, the left side takes the place of the right. 105 Why does the cock clap his wings before crowing and, as it were, claim

---

rugire, **T**.   78 lambit linguaque, **S**, **T**.   79 Materiam, **S**, **T**ʼ; dum, *omitted* **L**ʼ; vertit, **T**.
81 Accuset, **S**, **T**.   82 exundat, **S**, **T**.   83 radiis, **S**, **T**.   85 Carnis, **S**ʼ; laborat, **S**, **T**.
86 capiens, **S**ʼ; Et penam . . . ferat, *omitted in* **T**.   87 Castrare laboret, **S**, **T**, **B**.   88 cum
videat, **S**, **T**.   89 tenebras radiosa, **S**ʼ; 89 *and* 90 *combined in* **T**, *as follows*, Cur bubo
tenebras cur vespertilio noctem.   91 cietur, **T**.   92 Pandit; recondat, **S**.   93 laudes,
S, **T**ʼ; de lingua, **S**ʼ; Musa, **T**.   94 Fit, **T**ʼ; reddat, **S**, **T**.   95 Aer equam, **S**, **T**ʼ;
hernio, **S**.   96 Insistet, **S**.   97 dum prior, **S**, **T**.   98 Sustentans subportat honus, **S**ʼ;
Supportans sustentat onus, **T**, **B**ʼ; surgat, **S**, **T**.   100 laterum balans, **S**ʼ; Accubitus
balans, laterum *omitted*, **T**ʼ; gravis est, **H**, **L**ʼ; estus, **B**.   105 Mota prevenit, **T**.

Vendicet usurpans sit gallus preco diei,
Necnon nocturnas distinguat cantibus horas?
Helleboro cur pre cunctis de iure coturnix
Vescatur? cur mortificans sit passeris esca
Iusquiamus cum sit multis mortale venenum?   110
Hec cur fructificet arbor cum nesciat illa
Quid fructus, quid flos herbis semel ipse ministrat
Fructum? dum latis velox fugit annus habenis
Interior cur poma lapis quasi cerasa nullus
Impregnet, totam cur mollia persica pulpam   115
Exterius pandant, nux in conclave recondat?
Cur producta semel semper sua folia servet
Eternum ut viridi ramorum veste superbit,
Dum casus nescit iacturam pinguis oliva?
Perpetuam lauro que confert causa virorem?   120
Cur noctis sub fine diem magis algeat aurum
Accusans properare nitens? que cogat asellum
Lex ut ad urinam moveatur semper aquosis
Si noscat se stare locis, quo iure levato
Mingat crure canis? cur voces psittacus edat   125
Humanas, cur pica loquax latitare volentes
Accuset? cur fata suo iam proxima cantu
Signet holor? cur pestiferi visus basilisci
Sufficit ad mortem? mulier cur leta peracto
Conceptu coitum sitiat, cur bruta recusent   130
Corporis hoc damnum? quedam cur cornua bruto
Vertice promineant, aliis natura negavit
Munus idem? cur Samsonis cum crine resecto
Deperiit virtus, manifeste cur patienti
Maior inest virtus? cur nuncia verba pudoris   135
Singultum reprimant, cur sternutatio simplex
Sit presaga mali, tollat geminata timorem?
Cur leo prostratis parcens instantibus instet
Exacuatque suas cum caude motibus iras?
Cur lepus in vario sexu sit pronus: et usus   140
Nunc maris officio nunc se quasi femina ludat?
Cur mage seva lupo lupa sit cum frigidiore

---

107 distinguit, **T**.   110 Iusquianus, **L**.   111–16 *and* 118 *omitted in* **T**.   112 Quid flos
quid fructus, herbis semel illa ministrat, **S**.   113 Fructus; laxis, **S**.   114 cerasa ullerus, **S**.
118 in viridi semper ramorum, **S**. *lines* 117 *and* 119 *are combined in* **T**, Cur semel eductum
folium conservat oliva.   120 Perpetuum, **S**, **T**. *After* 120 *a line is inserted in* **S**, **T**, *omitted in*
H, **B**, **L**, Cur cogus exurens dampnum non irrogat auro; rogus, **T**.   121 Cur nota; augeat,
S; *This line omitted in* **T**.   122 Admiror nimium totiens quae cogit Asellum, **T**.
123 Fex, **T**.   125 spicatus edit, **S**.   126 loquatur, **S**.   127 proximo, **S**.   129 Sufficet,
T.   130 cum bruta, **S**.   *After* 130 *a line is inserted in* **S**, **T**, *omitted in* **H**, **B**, **L**, Cur

for himself the office of the morning star, usurping the duties of crier by day and marking off the nocturnal hours with his song?

Why does the quail naturally feed on hellebore, in contrast to all other beasts? Why do sparrows feed on the deadly henbane, a mortal poison to many birds? Why does one tree bear fruit and another not, and why do flowers only once provide plants with fruit? While time, swift and untrammelled, hastens onwards, tell me, why does a stone, as it were a worthless object, fill the inside of a cherry, and why do soft peaches display all the fleshy part on the outside, but nuts conceal it tucked away inside?

Why does the juicy olive for ever keep her foliage when it has once appeared, so that she glories continually in her green garment of branches and never knows the loss of a falling leaf? What causes the everlasting verdure of the laurel? Why does the gleaming gold grow colder towards the dawn, telling us that the day is hurrying on its way? What law compels the ass always to urinate, when he finds himself standing in marshy places, and why does the dog perform this function with upraised leg? Why does the parrot utter human words, and the chattering magpie tell us that there are persons wishing to lie concealed?

Why does the swan foretell his approaching death by his song? Why is the mere look of the pestilent basilisk enough to kill? Why does a woman, rejoicing that she has just conceived, then long for coitus, and why do animals reject this abuse of the body? Why in some animals do certain horns vertically project, and why does nature deny this gift to others? Why, when Samson's hair was cut, did his strength vanish, and why was it clearly much greater when he allowed his hair to grow? Why do tidings of disgrace stop the hiccup, and why does a single sneeze presage evil but two banish all fear?

Why does a lion spare those who are lying down, but attack those who are standing, fomenting his wrath with the movements of his tail? Why is the hare liable to adopt different sexes, at one time acting the part of a male, at another, that of a female? Why is the she-wolf fiercer than

---

puer agressum tardus nec bruta molestet; ad gressum, molestat, **T**.   131 Hoc damnum magnum, corporis *omitted*, **T** ; cuidam, **S, T**.   134 manifesto, **S, T**.   137 tollit, **S**. 138 parcat, **S, T** ; parcans, **B** ; sed stantibus instet, **T** ; instat, **B**.   139 cum laudis motibus, **T**. 140 ut usus, **S, T**.   141 nunc sit quasi, **T**.   142 cur frigidiore, **T** ; frigidiori, **S**.

Signetur sexu? cur simia singula simis
Naribus opponat, quasi censor factus odorum?
Cur hidrophobico specialis causa timoris   145
Imprimat unda metum? cur corpora mirrha reservet
Putrida ne sanies adsit? cur muscus odorem
Amissum recipit damnum redimente cloaca?
Solsequio que causa suos expandere flores
Iniungat cum solis adest vapor igneus, et sit   150
Cum noctis caligo venit sub flore sepultum?
Cur serpens renovat depulsa pelle iuventam?
Cur muliebre caput incommoda turpia nescit
Calvicie: cum crebra viros ea damna molestent?
Pregnantes uteris cur strictis legibus usus   155
Innovet affectus, ut quod ratione negetur
Femina deposcat? veneri cur ruta minetur?
Cur philomena sui suspendens organa cantus
Expectet vernale decus? cur pulmo loquatur,
Cor sapiat, chistis fellis cur provocet iras,   160
Splen risum moveat, veneris iecur addat amores?
Germanos cur bilis atrox ratione fugata
Punit ovans, vermisque sciens, puteusque draconum?
Ethereus totum radius lustraverat orbem.

143 singula sucus, S.   144 apponat, S; obiiceat, fractus, T.   145 ydrobico, S; ydroforbitico, H; idroforbicio, B; Hydroforbitico, L.   146 metus; conservet, B.   corpus T.   147
cum sanies assit, T.   148 retinente, T.   150-1 *omitted in* T, 151 *omitted in* S.
152 revocet, S, T.   153 in comota, S; noscat, B.   154 cum dampna viros haec crebra
molestent, S; cur damna viros haec saepe molestant, T.   155 pregnantes stomachos, S, T;
veteris, L.   156 Admovet, T.   157. Affectent, Femina *omitted*, S, T; verni casum cur
ruta, S; veratri (veretri) casum cur ruta, T.   158 Philomela, T.   159 expectat, S, T.
160 iram, T.   161 iecur incitet ignes, S, T.   162 Germanis cur ira ferox, B.
163 vingat ovans. senibus rectumque piumque commordet B.   164 Livor edax vermisque
cadens puteusque draconum, B.   *Lines 162-4 are additions by Ulsen, and not found in* S, T.
In B *only,* 164 *is followed by four other lines, and a note of recommendation by Ulsen:*
    Et reliqui fermenti malini et nequitie hominis viventis ut vides:
      Plebs sathane sathanam sequitur qui degenerando
        A prima causa Lucis ab arce cadit.
Rogo paternitatem tuam ut hec problematica enigmata discutiantur inter tuos contubernales et
quidem an editione digna videantur. Et si quispiam curiosior apud vos est tuo rogatu ultro
aliquid ex eis determinet quocumque stilo. Si educi id nactus fueris rem foveres Ulsenio tuo
gratissimo perpetuo munere dependendam.

her mate, although she is of the colder sex? Why does a monkey put
his snub nose to everything, as if he were a critic of odours? Why
145 do people, and especially those bitten by a mad dog, fear water? Why does
myrrh preserve bodies and keep them from corruption? Why is the lost
odour of musk restored by means of a privy? What causes the heliotrope
150 to display her blossoms in the presence of the sun's fiery rays, and to
slumber underneath them in the darkness of night?

Why does the serpent renew his youth after having cast his skin? Why
is a woman's head unacquainted with the unsightly defects of baldness,
when men suffer ills without number through it? Why should a condi-
155 tion subject to strict laws, in their wombs, so alter pregnant women that
they greedily desire (to eat) that which reason denies?

Why is rue inimical to the act of love? Why does the nightingale,
restraining her vocal organs, await the glory of spring? Why does speech
160 belong to the lungs, and understanding to the heart, and why does the gall
bladder provoke anger, the spleen laughter, and the liver increase the
ardours of love? Why are the Germans maddened by the furious and
exulting bile, a cunning worm, and a pit of dragons?

An ethereal ray once encompassed the whole earth.

NON EST BEATUS QUISPIAM NOCENTIUM

Th. Ulsenii Vox

	Turbine Hamadriadum que vox ciet Ulsenium?	*Grex*
	Edipodem, qui plasmat iter quis turbat eum?	*Spinx*
	Alcidem, qui monstra terat que fata dabunt?	*Linx*
	Quid furit in stomacho quod non nutrit in cerebro?	*Pix*
5	Pix nigra cerbereum virus quid te genuit?	*Fex*
	Fex musis inimica piis quid te peperit?	*Calx*
	Calx lapidum glucten monstrosa palatia quid?	*Merx*
	Inter celestes quod mercurio decus est?	*Fax*
	Urna labando procax quo stat vertigine mens?	*Arx*
10	Sceptra corona bone que tertia signa dee?	*Lanx*
	Monstra regunt orbem monstrosa voce tonabam	

Gre. Agricolae Echo

	Quid iuvat agricolam dentalia dum posuit?	*Grex*
	Gloria prima datur iuveni que Labdacide?	*Spinx*
	Thirsigeri furibunda patris quis plaustra vehit?	*Linx*
	Asphalto que res fit in omnia persimilis?	*Pix*
5	Ima petit liquido demersum gurgite quid?	*Fex*
	Quid calet ut gelidis immersum est fonticulis?	*Calx*
	Ancipites animos quid cogit in omne nefas?	*Merx*
	Parve puer veneris quod nam est insigne tibi?	*Fax*
	Confugium quod, Roma, tibi dum Gallus adest?	*Arx*
10	Perpetue que Sardanapali delitie?	*Lanx*
	Monstroso tonitru reboat monstrosior echo	

XENIUM VALEDICTIONI SACRUM

Title, Echoni sacrum, **M**.   2 dum querit iter, **M**.   9 qua, **H, L** ; labans quo stat petulans vertigine, **M**.   10 dee que tertia signa pie **M**.   11 *This line in* **M** *is the same as the final line in Agricola's Echo.*

NO HARMFUL PERSON IS BLESSED

The Voice of Theodore Ulsen

What voice summons Ulsen from out the giddy dance of the Hamadryads?	*The Multitude*
Who is it that bewilders Oedipus on his travels?	*Sphinx*
What will the Fates bestow on Alcides, for thrashing monsters?	*Lyncaeus*
What rages in the stomach, and nourishes not the brain?	*Pitch*
5 Black pitch, venom of Cerberus, what made thee?	*Dregs*
Dregs, harmful to the sacred Muses, what engendered thee?	*Lime*
What are lime, cement, and huge palaces?	*Possessions*
Among the Gods, what is the attribute of Mercury?	*A Torch*
Where stands the impudent fellow tottering with giddiness like an urn?	*(On the) Citadel*
10 The sceptre and the crown, what is the third emblem of the noble Goddess?	*Scales*
Monsters rule the world, I thundered forth with a monstrous voice.	

The Echo of Gregorius Agricola

What benefits the farmer when he has set aside the plough?	*A Flock (of sheep)*
What was the greatest glory bestowed on the Labdacidean youth?	*Sphinx*
Who draws the madly swaying waggons of the Thyrsus-bearing Sire?	*Lynx(es)*
5 What is exactly like Asphalt?	*Pitch*
What thing, submerged in the watery flood, seeks the bottom?	*Dregs*
What is immersed in icy water in order to become warm?	*Lime*
What compels the waverer to commit every kind of crime?	*Possessions*
Pray, what is thy emblem, o child of Venus?	*A Torch*
When the Gauls are present, what is thy refuge, o Rome?	*The Capitol*
10 What are the constant delights of Sardanapalus?	*Dish(es)*
After the monstrous thunder, resounds an even more monstrous echo	

A GIFT AT PARTING

II

THE REMAINDER OF THE 'QUESTIONES PHISICALES', NOT USED BY ULSEN

based on Sloane 1610 (ll. 131–263), and Trinity, 580 (R. 3. 1).

Cur bonitas subtile magis commendat acetum,
Si terre superinfusum cum perpete motu
Fortiter ebullit? cur lustra ferina peragrans,
Cur visus nescit vestigia, nare sagaci
Non metuens errare canis dependet, et unde   5
Cancer retrogradis gradibus incedere discat?
Cur leo non possit undas transire marinas,
Quin pariat rapidas sompno repente procellas
Insompniis positus? cur sompnia sanguinis hora
Vera facit? cur frigida sit lactuca sapore?   10
Cur faba det vires veneri, complexio cuius
Frigida? cur minuat dans incentiva caloris
Agnus heris? cur quovis mense columba
Pullos multiplicet, aliis hoc iure negato?
Cur viror in flore ius non habet? unde marini   15
Surgant et refluant fluctus? cur circulus imbres
Nuntiet aut ventos qui lune continet orbem?
Cur cornix pennas pluvie presaga fluentis
Irrorat? cur mel fetum pregnantis in alvo
Gustatum signet maculis? nigredo rubori   20
Cur non conveniat varium latura colorem
In brutis? cur arbor aves pro fructibus edat?
Cur capitis turgens soleat signare dolorem
Circulus urine? cur lune plenior orbis
Ossis duriciem replet uberiore medulla?   25
Cur splenis vicium rutilans examine certo
Urine monstrat radius? cur humidus hauster,
Cur boreas siccus, euro que causa calorem
Conferat? algores quo iure favoneus auget?
⟨Cur priorem primo canis aspersa nec illuc⟩   30
Cellula frigescat? maior presumpcio fastus
Cur parvum tumidum faciat, sapiencia magnum

2–5 *omitted* T.   6 gradibus procedat et unde T.   7 Cum leo T.   8 reptante T.
9 Insompnis S, T. possit T.   10 sopori T.   11 dat vires ventri T.   12–13 *the sentence* cur minuat . . . heris, *omitted* T.   13 sale Columba T.   15 vigor T.   17 nunciat S.
21 conveniant S.   22 edit S.   30–31 *omitted* T.

II

TRANSLATION OF THE REMAINDER OF THE 'QUESTIONES PHISICALES', NOT USED BY ULSEN

Why is the quality of fine vinegar better if it vigorously and continuously boils when it is poured on the ground? Why does a dog, traversing the
5 haunts of wild beasts, depend on his clever nose without fear of erring, and why is the spoor not recognized by sight, and how does the crab learn to go backwards? Why is the lion, having just awakened from sleep, unable to pass through the ocean waves without arousing violent storms?
10 Why does the dawn cause true dreams? Why is the lettuce cold in taste? Why do beans, whose nature is cold, increase the venereal powers and the agnus castus, which provokes heat, diminish them? Why does the dove produce her young any month, while this right is denied to other birds?
15 Why has green no right to exist in a flower? What causes the ebbing and flowing of the sea? Why does a circle round the moon foretell rain or winds? Why does a crow who wets his feathers presage rain? Why does eating honey mark the infant in the womb of a pregnant woman with
20 spots? Why does not black combine with red to bring about a variegated colour in animals? Why does a tree produce birds instead of fruit? Why does a circle, swelling out in urine, denote a headache? Why is it
25 that the fuller the moon is, the more is the hard bone replenished with marrow? Why does light shining redly through urine indicate, by infallible trial, a disease of the spleen? Why is the south wind moist, the north dry, and what makes the east wind warm and the west increase the cold?
30 . . . Why should a short man be puffed up with the vaunting presumption of pride, and a tall man be lacking in wisdom? Why is a bell,

Effugiat? cur inter aquas campana sonora
Plus iuvet auditum, tenui circumdata filo
Cur crepet ad pulsum? voces resonabilis ecco   35
Cur iteret? cur in sompnos sit prona senectus
Sicca tamen? cur nocte magis discernere visu
Possit murilegus? que sit compassio porcis,
Ut simul acclament uno paciente? feroces
Cur animos reprimat amplexu virginis atrox   40
Rinoceros? coitus nexus cur bruta statuto
Tempore delectent, et pronum qualibet hora
Sit genus humanum veneri? cur fervidus estus
Estatis putei latices infrigdet, et algens
Algorem castigat hiems? cur vellus ovinum   45
Lanugo crispata tegat, cum predominetur
Humiditas? timidi leporis que causa timorem
Aumentet, vel que sit ei levitatis origo?
Cur oleum latici supernatat? unde redundet
In caseum velox corrupcio si iuvet eius   50
Artificem furtiva venus? cur sistere cogat
Immensam puppim piscis brevis abditus undis
Equoreis? cur has minuat decoctio carnes,
Illas aumentet? que fetu gratia porcam
Multiplicet ditet, aliis cum rarius istud   55
Sit munus? quidam cur potus inebriat, alter
Sobria corda facit? convertibilis cibus unde
Sit lac vel piscis? quid falsos sideris alti
Mentitur casus, dum splendidus evolat ignis
Aere tranquillo? fluidos quid proferat imbres,   60
Quid procreet ventos, quid nubes generet altas,
Fulmina quid iactet, tonitrus que causa sonoros
Producat? cur mane rubor pronunciet imbres
Venturos, si sero venit cras luce sequenti
Subsequitur tranquilla dies? cur signa procelle   65
Previa premonstret commotus in equore piscis?
Cur madidis marmor lachrimis distillet et imbres
Adfore vicinos falso sudore figuret?

---

33 Cur fugiat T.   35 Cur pulsata T; crepat S.   36 somnis sis T.   38 muri-culus T   40 complexu T.   41 nexu T.   42 delectant T.   43–47 *The sentences,* cur fervidus . . . Humiditas, *omitted* T.   47 Et mihi dicatur leporis T.   48 Augmentat T. 49 superenatet T.   50 In casum S; In calido T; iuvat S.   52 puppim, *omitted* S. 54 augmentat T.   54–58 *The sentences,* que fetu gratia . . . lac vel piscis, *omitted* T. 60 fluitos S; procreat T.   61 Quid ventos gignat nubes quid gignat et altas T. 62 Flumina S; iactat S.   63 pronunciat S.   64 sequente T.   66 premonstrat coniunctus T.   67 madidis, *omitted* S; distillat S.   68 Afore S. figurat S; T *ends with this line.*

ringing near water, more pleasant to hear, and being bound with a fine

35 thread why does it crack when it is struck? Why does the resounding echo

repeat words? Why is dry old age still prone to sleep? Why can the cat see

better at night? What is that mutual sympathy of pigs which makes them

cry out together when one of them is in trouble? Why does the savage uni-

40 corn curb his fierce wrath with the virgin's embrace? Why is it that beasts

take pleasure in coitus at definite times, but human beings are ready for

venery at any time? Why does the burning heat of summer cool the waters

of a well and freezing winter restrain their coldness? Why does curly wool

45 cover a sheep's pelt, although moisture predominates there? What in-

creases the fear of the timid hare and what is the cause of its agility? Why

50 does oil float on water? Why does cheese quickly putrefy if its maker

gratifies a secret passion? Why does a little fish, hidden in the ocean waves,

compel a huge ship to stop in its course? Why does cooking shrink one

kind of meat and make another kind swell? By what special favour is the

55 sow enriched and multiplied by breeding, whereas this function happens

less often in other animals? Why does drinking make some merry, others

sad? How is it that milk or fish is changed into nourishment? When

a bright spark flashes out in the serene heavens, what counterfeits the

60 deceptive fall of a star on high? What causes rain, winds, and the lofty

clouds? What hurls the lightning and produces the resounding thunder?

Why does redness in the morning foretell rain, but in the evening the

65 coming of a fine day on the morrow? Why does the commotion of a fish

in the sea foretell a storm? Why does marble shed moist tears and, with

a seeming sweat, tell us that rain is imminent? Why can the stag revive

Cur possit vires cervus revocare per esum
Serpentis? cur non crescant ut cetera nani?   70
Cur non continue leprosus febriat? unde
Conferat ut geminis privetur testibus? unde
Inter aves quas esse facit natura rapaces,
Nequior et maior magis audax femina semper
Mare sit? unde prius floret quam frondeat arbor?   75
Cur timidis ovibus aries sit previus? unde
Artheticis per se nocuum piper esse, iuvare
Dicitur admixtum? cur sol pungente calore
Sternutare facit, nequeat calor igneus? unde
Pre cunctis timeant animalia cuncta cadaver   80
Humanum? cur mors perimat subitanea quosdam?
Cur Iacob varias simul et sine cortice virgas
Ante gregem misit varios ut gingneret agnos?
In mixto lanci musto cur tendit ad imum
Vasis, et in puro missum superenatet ovum?   85
Ungula cur cuidam findatur et integer cuidam
Bruto permaneat? cur quidam frigore magno
Constrictus periit magnum calefactus ad ignem?
Cur generet potius senior paciente puella,
Quam iuvenis vetule commixtus? cur sibi cauda   90
Truncata minui leo toto corpore vires
Sentiat? Unde semel quedam dum volvitur anni
Circulus, et sepe pariant animalia? cur sit
Usque pedes cauda multis protensa, quibusdam
Vix pudibunda tegat? cur non que continet idem   95
Inficiatque virum leprosi sperma sequentem?
Cur doceat brutis natura natare, virisque
Deneget indoctis? cur non ut bruta volucres
Emittant ventum per posteriora sonorum?
Cur cum sit calidum faciat pallere ciminum   100
Utentes? cur pauca vorans [multum egerat], alter
Ordine converso? barba caret unde timetque
Eunuculus, brutis qua menstrua lege negentur?
Cur resupina natet mulier submersa, virumque
Unda ferat pronum? cur ledat lumina lumen   105
Quod nova cera magis quam quod pinguedo ministrat?
Cur careat barba mulier, cur lenior illi,
Grata magis gracilis vox est quam maribus? unde
Fortius effectum solis calor imprimit ymis
Vallibus, et cum sint vicina cacumina soli   110
Continua sint tecta nive, cur bruma sit eius

89 paciente vel pariente S.   101 nutus egeat S.   109 ymnis S.

70 his strength by eating a serpent? Why do dwarfs not grow as other people
do? Why is a sick person not continually feverish? How does it benefit
a man to lose both testicles? Among birds of prey, why is the female
always more vile-tempered, large, and bolder than the male? Why does
75 a tree flower before it has leaves? Why does the ram lead the timid
sheep? Why is pepper, by itself, said to be harmful to arthritics but to
be of use to them when it is mixed with something else? Why does the
piercing heat of the sun cause sneezing, but not the warmth of a fire?
80 Why do all animals fear a human corpse in contrast to their feelings
towards all other corpses? Why does sudden death destroy some people?
Why did Jacob put parti-coloured peeled wands before his flock in order
that parti-coloured lambs might be born? Why does an egg sink to the
bottom when it is put into a dish of must mixed (with water), but swim in
85 pure must? Why is the hoof divided in one animal and in another whole?
Why has a person, constricted with extreme cold, died on being warmed
at a great fire? Why can an old man have children by a young girl much
90 easier than a young man can, who is married to an old woman? Why does
the lion feel the strength of his whole body diminish when his tail is cut off?
Why is it that some animals breed only once during the year and others
do so often? Why is it that in many (animals) the tail stretches to the feet
95 but in others it scarcely covers the hind quarters? Why is it that the sperm
of a leper does not infect the woman who holds that sperm within her, and
yet does infect the next man after him (who lies with the woman)? Why
does nature teach beasts to swim, but not man who is ignorant of this
100 art? Why do not birds blow sounding wind through their posteriors, as
animals do? Why does cumin, although it is hot, make those who use it
grow pale? Why does one person, who eats little, defecate a lot and another
who eats a lot, defecate little? How is it that a eunuch is timid and without
a beard, and by what law are the menses denied to beasts? Why does a
105 drowned woman float face upwards, and a drowned man face downwards?
Why does the light furnished by new wax hurt the eyes more than that
furnished by tallow? Why is a woman beardless, and why has she a gent-
ler, more pleasing, and higher pitched voice than man? Why is the sun's
110 heat stronger in the deepest valleys, and although the mountain peaks are
nearer the sun, why are they continually covered with snow, and why
does winter abound in snow, and hail occur in the hot summer? Why has

Productiva frequens et fervida grandinis estas?
Unde die cretico per fontis reddidit unde
Officium vocis in causone femina potum?
Cur manuum fortis constrictio balbucienti   115
Fecit idem? tibi cur fuerat de vulnere lesus
Musculus amisit sine voce repente loquelam?
Cur de nocte magis morituri lumina claudant
Ultima quam luce? cur vini frigidiores
Inducant morbos longus nec debitus usus?   120
Cur noceant rumpuntque cutem piper atque sinapis
Exterius, nequeant intus suscepta nocere?
Allia cur moveant sine febre commesta calorem,
Pulsibus adiuncta faciant cum caumate febrem?
Cur nocet in girum motus plus quam linearis?   125
Cur non sustineant humana cibaria cruda
Corpora? cur lapsos redimat puericia dentes
Vel fractos, cum nulla viris hec conferat etas?
Cur non exposito lune sed terram subintrans
⟨Quadrupedi lunare iubar nocet ulceret leso?⟩   130
Unde per hos aloe susceptum laxat, et extra
Appositum stringit? cur continue sub acellis
Fetidus est sudor, et copia tanta pilorum?

129 terra **S.**

a woman suffering from an acute fever relinquished her voice by drinking
115 spring water on the critical day? Why has the strong clenching of the hands
had the same affect on a person who stammers? Why, in your case, did a
wounded muscle, with no power of speech, suddenly deprive you of that
function? Why do those who are about to die do so by night, rather than
120 by day? Why does the continual and excessive use of wine induce the
colder diseases? Why is it that pepper and mustard hurt and blister the
skin, applied externally, but are harmless if swallowed? Why does garlic
eaten (whole) provoke heat without fever, but added (to food) by pounding
125 cause both fever and heat? Why does circular motion do more harm than
motion in a straight line? Why are human beings not nourished by raw
foods? Why are fallen or broken teeth compensated for in youth but not
in manhood? Why does moonlight filtering underground ulcerate and
130 hurt a wounded animal, but not do so when the animal is (fully) exposed
to the moon? Why does aloe, taken by the mouth, loosen, and applied externally, constrict? Why is there always a fetid sweat, and such a copious
growth of hair under the armpits?

1. Title. The earlier title might be translated as 'The Radiant Transformation of the Ageing Microcosm, in a hundred Riddles, by The. Ulsen'. *Speculator*—cf. the following line in the *Vaticinium*: 'libera mens clarum *speculator* in ethere.'

2. *plasmo viam*. Cf. a similar use in Ulsen's second riddle—*plasmat iter*.

6. *Pheben Phebus*. Phoebe (Diana) may refer to Ulsen's friend P. Bonomus (see above, p. 121). Phoebus is probably Ulsen, who was always called Phrisius.

7. *grata corolla*: The laurel garland with which it was the custom to crown Poet Laureates. *virtutis* could refer either to poetic merit or to the virtue which was supposed to accompany the study of letters and philosophy, and which was a constantly recurring theme in the works of the German humanists; see above, p. 123.

8. *per avia silve*. The traveller lost in a wood is a motif first employed, in the West, in in the French romances of chivalry *c.* 1150, see E. R. Curtius, *European Lit.*, trans. Trask, London, 1953, p. 362. A famous example is Dante's *Inferno*, I. 5:

> Esta selva selvaggia e aspra e forte.

15–16 *ventus. pulvis. umbra.* Cf. Job vii. 7; Gen. xviii. 27; and Ps. cxliv. 4. Cf. also the words of Trithemius: 'Quid enim sumus miseri mortales, nisi ventus et umbra? . . . Sicut Sophocles in Aiace furentem Ulyssem introducit loquentem:

> Video enim nos nihil existentes aliud quam
> simulachra quotquot vivimus, seu levem umbram.

Trithemius, *Epist. fam.* xliv (ed. 1601, ii. 557).

17–18. *Ethna. gigas.* Cf. Ovid, *Met.* v. 352:

> Degravat Aetna caput, sub qua resupinus harenas
> eiectat flammamque fero vomit ore Typhoeus;

and ibid., v. 319:

> Bella canit superum falsoque in honore gigantas.

Ulsen's train of thought here seems to be: the light of inspiration, or, in the earlier version, inspired words, bursting from his bosom—wind—dust—the mountain Etna, under which the Gods have imprisoned the giant Typhon, who spouts fire from his mouth (an image perhaps conjured up by his Italian visit); see also l. 25 below.

21. *angelice Agricole*. Almost certainly refers to Rudolph Agricola, and not to the Gregorius Agricola of the riddles, see above, p. 124.

28. *sambuco*. Pliny, *Hist. nat.* xxiv. 8 (35): 'caules teneri mitioris sabuci in patinis cocti alvum solvunt.'
cicuta. Ibid. xxv. 25 (95): 'fit ex eo et ad refrigerandum stomachum malagma.'

29–30. *psalterio extergam . . . serpentibus . . . Cornua.* Referring to the charming of the horned serpent, 'cerastes', Pliny, op. cit. viii. 23 (35), a subject to which Ulsen returns later on, see below, note on l. 52.

31. Here Ulsen introduces the *Questiones phisicales*, omitting the opening line of the Sloane MS. taken from Claudian, *In Rufinum*.

34. *chaos*. Cf. Ovid, *Met.* i. 5:

> Ante mare et terras et quod tegit omnia caelum
> unus erat toto naturae vultus in orbe,
> quem dixere chaos: rudis indigestaque moles
> nec quicquam nisi pondus iners congestaque eodem
> non bene iunctarum discordia semina rerum.

Cf. also Celtis, *Ode to Fusilius*, 33:

> Perge confusum chaos intueri;

and ibid. *Germania generalis*, i. 9 ff.:

> O mundi deforme chaos superisque pudendum
> et vos cunctarum discordia semina rerum.

silvam. ilen. Both terms were used throughout the medieval period to denote formless matter. Cf. Isidore, *Etym.* XIII. iii. 1. Macrobius, *Com. in Som. Scip.* i. 12: 'anima ergo cum trahitur ad corpus, in hac prima sui productione silvestrem tumultum, id est hylen, influentem sibi incipit experiri. et hoc est quod Plato notavit in Phaedone . . . .' Another prolific source for the Platonic conception of *silva* was the *Chalcidius–Timaeus*, cf. the *Com.*, ed. Mullach, cccvi ff.

38. *nexus elementis.* Cf. Ovid. *Met.* i. 18–25:

> Frigida pugnabant calidis, umentia siccis, . . .
> dissociata locis concordi pace ligavit.

40. *rerum natura.* Cf. Virgil, *Georgics*, ii. 490:

> Felix qui potuit rerum cognoscere causas.

Neckam, *De laud.*, ed. Wright, p. 492:

> Sed quis naturae vires causasque latentes,
> Arcanas leges enucleare queat?

Celtis, *Ode to Fusilius*, 38:

> Singulis rebus reperire causas.

motus in igne. Cf. Ovid, *Met.* i. 26:

> Ignea convexi vis et sine pondere caeli
> emicuit summaque locum sibi fecit in arce.

Neckam, *De laud.*, p. 422.

42. *mobile subjectum signosum.* Virgil, *Georgics*, i. 238:

> Et via secta per ambas,
> obliquus qua se signorum verteret ordo.

43. *gumfus.* A medieval word also used by Gilles of Corbeil (*De pulsibus*, 304), Cf. above, p. 46.

discordia rerum semina. Ovid, *Met.* i. 9; Celtis, *Germania*, i. 10, both quoted above in note on l. 34. A similar passage is in Celtis, *Ode to Fusilius*, 34 ff.

44. *concordi pace ligavit.* Ovid, *Met.* i. 25, quoted above, in note on l. 38. Cf. also Neckam, *De laud.*, p. 436:

> Sic elementa suae conservant foedera pacis;
> Sic ea concordi foedere jungit amor.

45. *terram medio.* Ovid, *Met.* i. 12:

> Nec circumfuso pendebat in aere tellus
> ponderibus librata suis.

Pliny, *Hist. nat.* ii. 65 (65): 'sed quid hoc refert, alio miraculo exoriente, pendere ipsam, ac non cadere nobiscum.' Cf. also Adelard, *Quaest. nat.*, ch. 48: 'Qua natura terrae globus in medio sustineatur aere?' Urso, *Aphor. Gloss.* 33, and Neckam, *De laud.*, pp. 433 ff.

48. *ether ebes.* Pliny, *Hist. nat.* ii. 5 (4): 'vitalem hunc et per cuncta rerum meabilem totoque consertum.' Lucretius, *De rer. nat.* vi. 1034 ff.:

> Denique res omnes debent in corpore habere
> aera, quandoquidem raro sunt corpore et aer
> omnibus est rebus circumdatus adpositusque.

49. *humores alteret alter.* I think *alter* refers to the kinds of air, which was one of the non-natural causes of diseases, and in fact was said to alter the body more than any of the others. Thus, Maurus in his *Commentary* on the *Isagoge* of Ioannitius says: 'Agens ergo Ioannitius de non-naturalibus, prius agit de aere quia ab aere corpus humanum sepe sepius alteratur quam ab aliqua alia re non-naturali, tanquam a continenti et inspirato' (Bibl. Nat. Lat. 18499, f. 25). He then goes on to describe the five principal kinds of air which produce these alterations: 'ex anni temporibus, ex ortu et occasu stellarum, ex ventis, ex positione terrarum, ex fumositatibus resolutis a paludibus', &c.—a possible source being Constantinus, *Pantegni, Theor.* v. 2–11.

50. *laticis formalis imago.* Pliny, *Hist. nat.* ii. 65 (65): 'sed vulgo maxime haec pugna est, si coactam in verticem aquarum quoque figuram credere cogatur. atqui non aliud in rerum natura adspectu manifestius.' He then draws attention to the roundness of drops of water, and to the curved surface of water contained in a vessel that is full to the brim. Cf. also, Neckam, *De laud.*, p. 398.

52. *cerastes.* Virgil, *Eclogue*, viii. 71:

> Frigidus in pratis cantando rumpitur anguis.

Pliny, *Hist. nat.* viii. 23 (35): 'cerastis corpore eminere cornicula . . . quorum motu, reliquo corpore occultato, sollicitent ad se aves.' Isidore, *Etym.* XII. iv. 18. The birds thought that the moving horns were edible, and so they were caught. But when the serpent was charmed its horns could be seized with impunity. For this use of *accuso* see p. 46, n. 4.

54. *adamante.* There seems to be a contrast here between the power of the diamond, which was thought to cause a magnet to release a piece of iron and let it fall, and the magnetic power, which held the iron fast. Pliny, *Hist. nat.* xxxvii. 4 (15): 'adamas dissidet cum magnete in tantum, ut iuxta positus ferrum non patiatur abstrahi uel, si admotus magnes adprehenderit, rapiat atque auferat.' Isidore, *Etym.* XVI. xiii. 3; Neckam, *De nat. rer.* ii. 94; *De laud.*, p. 471.

56. *vis magnetica.* A favourite question with the poets, cf. Lucretius, *De rer. nat.* vi. 906 ff.; Claudian, *Shorter Poems*, xxix (48); also, Pliny, *Hist. nat.* xxxvi. 16 (25); Isidore, *Etym.* XVI. iv. 1. It was discussed by Urso in *Aphor. Gloss.* 26, in Auct. f. 122, and by Neckam, *De nat. rer.* ii. 93.

57. *gagates*, Solinus, *Polyhist.*, ch. 25; 'attritu calfactus applicita detinet aeque ut succinum.' This property is not mentioned by Pliny and Isidore. Neckam, *De laud.*, p. 468.

59. *emathites.* Pliny, *Hist. nat.* xxxvi. 20 (37): 'sistit profluvia mulierum potus.' Platearius, *Circa inst.*, ed. P. Dorveaux, Paris, 1913, p. 88; Neckam, *De laud.*, p. 470.
peonia. Theodorus Priscianus, *Physica*, ed. Rose, p. 253: 'paeoniae radix magnum praesidium praestat, si collo alligatam frequentius odoretur.' Constantinus, *De gradibus* (1536), p. 358; Neckam, *De laud.*, p. 470.

61. *epar spodium.* Constantinus, *De grad.* (1536), p. 370: 'calorem epatis refrigerat.'
stomacho galangam. Constantinus, *De grad.*, p. 372: 'stomachum phlegmaticum corroborat, vim digestivam adiuvat, ventositatem dissolvit.' Platearius, *Circa inst.* (1913), p. 90.

62. *cerebro muscum.* Constantinus, *De grad.*, p. 354: 'dolorem capitis de frigido et humido curat.' *Pantegni, Theor.* v. 31: 'Sternutationes de musco et croco . . . cerebrum confortant.' Platearius, *Circa inst.* (1913), p. 130. Cf. ll. 2621–2 of the *Schola Salern.* (ed. de Renzi, v. 77):

> Pulmo liquiritia, mace cor, stomachusque galanga,
> gaudet hepar spodio, splen cappare, cerebrum moscho.

63. *luce lupina.* Virgil, *Ecl.* ix. 53:

Vox quoque Moerim

iam fugit ipsa; lupi Moerim videre priores.

Pliny, *Hist. nat.* viii. 22 (34); Isidore, *Etym.* xii. ii. 24; Auct. f. 149; Neckam, *De laud.*, p. 488; Browne, *Pseudodoxia*, iii. 8.

64. *turtur.* Aelian, *De nat. animal.* iii. 44; St. Basil, *Hom.* viii. 6; *Physiologus Theobaldi*, ed. Rendell, p. 94; Auct. f. 149ᵛ; Neckam, *De nat. rer.* i. 59; *De laud.*, p. 392.

68. *hyrundo.* Pliny, *Hist. nat.* x. 24 (34): 'Abeunt et hirundines hibernis mensibus.'

69. *fenix.* Pliny, *Hist. nat.* x. 2 (2): 'Arabiae phoenicem haud scio an fabulose, unum in toto orbe.' Isidore, *Etym.* xii. vii. 22. Bibl. Nat. Lat. 18081, f. 212. (*Physiologus*, (*Dicta Chrysost.* 27) and Ovid (*Met.* xv. 392 ff.) do not mention the uniqueness of the bird, neither does Neckam (*De nat. rer.* i. 34–35, *De laud.* p. 377)). Browne, *Pseudodoxia*, iii. 12.

70. *vipera.* Pliny, *Hist. nat.* x. 62 (82): 'itaque ceteri tarditatis impatientes perrumpunt latera occisa parente.' St. Basil, *Hom.* ix. 5; Isidore, *Etym.* xii. iv. 10; *Physiolog. Dicta Chrysost.* 11; Neckam, *De nat. rer.* ii. 105; Browne, *Pseudodoxia*, iii. 16.

71. *apis.* Cf. Urso, *Aphor. Gloss.* 2: 'Praeterea si forma matricis fuerit talis quod unum solum habeat orificium ysofago adiunctum, quia in eo viget desiderium et deportatio, et semen per os suscipitur ad conceptionem et in matrice, conceptus eius naturaliter solutis habenis per os in partu emittitur, quod per apes patet, quae ore concipiunt et ore pariunt.' See also Pet. f. 17ᵛ. The source for this extraordinary belief is, perhaps, the *De sensibus* of Belenus-Apollonius, quoted by Arnold of Saxony in his *De finibus rerum naturalium* (*c.* 1225).

In one such quotation we read: 'In eodem Belletus, carnem vacce vel tauri comminuas et misceas cum lazech ut putrescat, generantur ex ea apes multe sine pedibus, et cum in se generantur, apes tunc ore suo concipiunt semen suum et ore pariunt' (Bodl. lat. misc. e. 34 (xiii cent.), f. 15ᵛ). A more corrupt rendering of this passage is given in Emil Stange's *Arnoldus Saxo, der älteste encyklopädist des dreizehnten jahrhunderts*, p. 60. On Arnold, see E. Stange, *Die Encyklopädie des Arnoldus Saxo*, Erfurt, 1905–6; A. Birkenmajer, *Le Rôle*, pp. 11–13; Paul Lehmann, *Mitteilungen aus Handschriften*, iv. 61–63 (*S.B.A.W.* 1933, Hft. 9); M. Grabmann, *Methoden und Hilfsmittel des Aristotelesstudiums im Mittelalter*, pp. 109 ff. (*S.B.A.W.* 1939, Hft. 5); Sarton, *Introd.* ii. 592. Lehmann, in his enumeration of manuscripts of the work, does not mention the Bodleian MS., from which I quote, and which seems more correct than those used by Stange. On Belenus-Apollonius see my note on p. 73 above. As far as I know, the Arabic original of the *De sensibus* has not yet been discovered. The use of ideas from it by Urso and the Salernitan masters would seem to indicate that it was known in south Italy well before the time of Arnold of Saxony. For another possible use of the *De sensibus* in the *Questiones phisicales* see below, note to line 95.

71. *cornicula.* Probably a confusion has arisen with the raven (corvus), with which the superstition was traditionally associated. In the Salernitan prose questions it is discussed in the same question as that which concerns the oral parturition of the bee —'Quedam animalia ore concipiunt et ore pariunt ut apes, quedam ore concipiunt et per inferiora pariunt ut corvi, quedam e converso ut mustelle, quedam per inferiora et concipiunt et pariunt ut mulieres et quedam alia animalia' (Pet. f. 17ʳ⁻ᵛ). The source in the west could be Pliny, *Hist. nat.* x. 12 (15): 'ore eos parere aut coire vulgus arbitratur ideoque gravidas, si ederint corvinum ovum, per os partum reddere', who, however, differs in saying that the eggs are also produced from the mouth. A much more likely source is the Arab author Jorach or Jorath, to whom the belief is attributed by the encyclopedists, Arnold of Saxony, *De finibus*, ii. 3: 'In libro de animalibus Jorach, per

os concipit corvus, et per inferiora eius egrediuntur ova' (Bodl. lat. misc. e. 34, f. 27; E. Stange, *Arnoldus Saxo*, p. 48), and Vincent of Beauvais, *Speculum nat.* xvi. 61: 'Jorath ubi supra, corvus per os concipit.' *Jorach de animalibus* is also quoted, although not in connexion with the raven, by Bartholomew of England, in his *De proprietatibus rerum* (*c.* 1230), and Albertus Magnus, in his *Lib. de animalibus,* but nothing is known of this author, and neither the Arabic original of his book nor the Latin translation has so far come to light. As in the case of the *De sensibus* of Belenus-Apollonius, it seems likely that this book of Jorach was known to the Salernitan masters before it reached the northern encyclopedists, which is, of course, exactly what one would expect with a work of Arab origin. Albertus Magnus mentions this belief about the raven, but attributes it to Anaxagoras, and takes pains to refute it, *De animal.* xvii, tract 1, ch. 5. Neckam, *De laud.,* p. 385, quotes no authority. Even after the complete refutation by Albertus Magnus, the Dutch physician Levinus Lemnius could say in 1559: 'Also there are some Crows in the Low Countries that conceive by their mouth, which they call Rock Jackdaws', *Occulta naturae miracula,* English translation, London, 1658, p. 287. The *cunicula* of **S** is evidently a scribe's error, corrected in later manuscripts.

For another possible use of Jorach, see below, note to l. 109.

73. *strutio.* The source for this tradition is probably some early bestiary or version of *Physiologus.* It is found in the French *Li Livres des natures des bestes* contained in Arsenal 283 (XIII cent.), prepared by the clerk Pieres at the command of Philippe de Dreux, bishop of Beauvais (1175–1217), and itself derived from an older Latin or Greek version, see Cahier et Martin, *Mélanges d'archéologie*, Paris, ii (1851), 85 ff.; iii (1853), 203 ff.; iv (1856), 55 ff. The passage is as follows: 'et par nature que Dex li a doné en son regart, amaine en ses oes pochins tot altresi comme se la beste les covast', Cahier et Martin, iii. 258. Bibl. Nat. Lat. 18081, f. 225. Neckam, *De nat. rer.* i. 50 has: 'Visu solo ita fovet ova sua in arena recondita, ut ex illis egrediantur pulli in lucem', which very words are copied by Vincent, *Spec. nat.* xvi. 239, who, attributes them, however, to *Phisiologus.* Since the tradition is in an early version of this compilation, it is more reasonable to suppose that both Neckam and Vincent were quoting from some lost Latin *Physiologus,* rather than that the latter author was using the former without acknowledgement. Lauchert notes that the tradition is found in the more corrupt Greek versions of *Physiologus,* such as the B text in Pitra, *Spicilegium Solesmense,* Paris, iii (1855). F. Lauchert, *Gesch. d. Physiologus,* p. 38. Albertus Magnus refutes the belief: 'Aliquando autem custodit ea et respicit ad locum in quo iacent: et ideo rumor falsus exivit quod visu ea foveat', *De animal.* xxiii. 139.

73. *piscis.* Urso, *Aphor. Gloss.* 38: 'Unde visus perfectior efficitur in tantum ut extremos colores et medios sine confusione perpendant. Animalia vero palpebris carentia oculorum continua apertione ad continuam operante spirituum disgregationem imperfecte vident in tantum ut solos extremos et non medios colores inconfuse percipiant, utpote pisces et hiis similia animalia' (Trinity 1154, f. 171). Neckam repeats this belief, and also adds an interesting practical result of it, namely that fishermen wear clothes of a middle colour, in order not to scare the fish: 'Extremos item secernunt colores, et non medios. Rubeum autem colorem inter extremos annumerabis. Hinc est quod piscatores in arte sua instructi, rubeis non utuntur colobiis, nec albis nec nigris, sed pannis medio colore coloratis, ne scilicet territi pisces fugam ineant', *De nat. rer.* ii. 22. *De laud.,* p. 404.

74. *luscus.* There are two sources of confusion in this sentence, which, curiously enough, is not in **S**, **T**, or **B**. In the first place, *luscus* strictly means one-eyed, but *lusciosus* or *luscitiosus,* purblind, seems called for, whatever meaning one gives to the rest of the sentence. In the second place, although the Broadside gives

furores, and I have used this word in my translation, it is possible that this is an error for *colores*, which is retained, with *furores*, in **L**, but with cancellation marks *çọḷọṛẹṣ*), probably to show which word was used in the Broadside. The explanation of *furores* lies in the fact that the purblind, i.e. those who saw badly by day, especially in the half light of evening, but well at night (cf. Isidore, *Etym.* x. 163: 'Luscus, quod lucem ex parte sciat, sicut luscitiosus, qui vesperi nihil videt'), were supposed to have grey or pale-coloured eyes ('Oculus vero glaucus e contrario de die debilis est, de nocte vero fortis', Bartholomew, *De prop. rer.* v. 6). But these eyes denoted excessive timidity, 'Glauci et albidi timidum et fugacem vehementer hominem nuntiant', *Physiognomonia* of Apuleius, Eudoxus, and Aristotle, ed. Rose, *Anecdota*, i (1864), 120. Thus it would be quite in order to say that the purblind are not subject even to moderate passions or attacks of anger. But this involves a rare use of *medios*, quite different from its application in the previous sentence, and also a loss of continuity in ideas. On the other hand, if we retain *colores*, we also retain the previous more usual interpretation of *medios*, and the sentence carries on and elaborates the ideas expressed in the one before it. Just as in fish the continually open eyes cause a dispersion of the visible spirits, and so imperfect sight, in the purblind both these effects are brought about by the pallor of their eyes. This is explained by Urso earlier on in the same Gloss which we quoted in the last note: 'Quedam animalia pro albedine oculorum et subtilitate visibilis spiritus in nocte vident et non in die. In die namque, pro aeris claritate oculos tenebrante, cooperante oculorum albedine ad disgregationem, visibilis spiritus utpote subtilis et clarus, facile disgregatus, deperditur, sicque visus spirituum obtenebratur perditione. In nocte vero, aeris obscuritate congregatus confortatur et confortatus aerem inter rem videntem et rem videndam sui claritate illustrat, sic ad rem oppositam cernendam reparatur', Urso, *Aphor. Gloss.* 38 (Trinity 1154, f. 170ᵛ). It is true that this is applied to owls, but it could equally well serve as an explanation of the poor sight of purblind people by day. Neckam copies this, word for word, *De nat. rer.* ii. 153. (See also Albertus Magnus, *De animal.* xix. 12.) In retaining *colores*, therefore, we also have the association of ideas found together in what is probably the original source for these questions, viz. Urso's *Gloss.*, whereas I have not succeeded in tracing the '*luscus* [*lusciosus*]—*oculi glauci et albidi*—*medios furores*' combination in any other Salernitan collection. These must be among the earliest references to colour blindness in fish (and, with less certainty, in man) available in the Latin West.

Ulsen did not use this sentence in his first draft of the poem. Why did he insert it in his final redaction? Perhaps he had come across a more complete text of the *Questiones phisicales*, which contained this sentence; perhaps, also, this text used *colores*. In that case it is possible that Ulsen, not liking the repetition, changed this word to *furores*. The rather unusual use of *medios* would be quite to his taste, and by the end of the fifteenth century the physiognomical characteristics of eyes would be well known.

76. *catulis*. Pliny, *Hist. nat.* viii. 40 (62): 'gignunt caecos . . . quidam tradunt, si unus gignatur, nono die cernere.' Urso, *Com. Elem.* (Trinity 1154, f. 111): 'Videmus namque catulum canis clausis oculis nasci, unde natura IX dierum spacio ad eorum operationem laborat.' Auct. f. 154ᵛ; Neckam, *De nat. rer.* ii. 157; *De laud.*, p. 490.

leonis fetum. Isidore, *Etym.* xII. ii. 5: 'Cum genuerint catulum, tribus diebus et tribus noctibus catulus dormire fertur; tunc deinde patris fremitu vel rugitu veluti treme-factus cubilis locus suscitare dicitur catulum dormientem.' *Physiologus Theobaldi*, ed. Rendell (1928), p. 64; Urso, *Com. Elem.* (Trinity 1154, f. 111); Auct. f. 122ᵛ; Neckam, *De nat. rer.* ii. 148; *De laud.*, p. 486.

77. *ursus*. A belief mentioned by Ovid, *Met.* xv. 379 ff. Also by Pliny, *Hist. nat.* viii. 36 (54); Isidore, *Etym.* xII. ii. 22; Neckam, *De nat. rer.* ii. 130; *De laud.*, p. 488; Browne, *Pseudodoxia*, iii. 6.

80. *talpam. salamandram.* These ideas are found in the old French *Li Livres des natures des bestes*, quoted above, in the note on l. 73. *talpam*, 'qu'èle vit de pure terre', Cahier et Martin, *Mélanges*, iii (1853), 274; *salamandram*, 'Phisiologes nos dit qu'èle est de tel nature qu'èle vit de pur fu, et si s'en paist', ibid., p. 271. Urso, *Com. elem.*: 'profunda terre inhabitat et terra fovetur, ut talpa . . . in igne vivit et nutritur ut salamandra' (Trinity, 1154, f. 137ᵛ). Neckam says nothing about the nourishment of the mole but about the salamander says:

> Frigida flammigero salamandra fovetur ab igne,

De laud., p. 374. Pliny does not mention the nourishment of either beast; Isidore, *Etym.* XII. iii. 5, says only that the mole feeds on roots.

81. *vulnus.* An extraordinarily widespread belief, which persisted until the seventeenth century. There is a reference to the belief in the *Nibelungenlied* (XII cent.), xvii. 1043 ff., see the article 'Bier Right' by W. G. Aitchison Robertson, *Vᵐᵉ Congrès Int. d'Hist. de la Méd.*, Geneva, 1926, pp. 192 ff. The first to discuss it seriously in the Latin West however, would appear to be the Salernitan masters, see Urso, *Aphor. Gloss.* 26, whose very words were used by Neckam in *De nat. rer.* ii. 98, and Auct. f. 148. Subsequently the question is found in nearly all medieval and Renaissance collections. For this use of *accuso*, see p. 46, n. 4.

83. *lincis radio.* A tradition well known to the classical poets, cf. Horace, *Epist.* i. 1, and Cicero, *Epist. fam.* ix. 2, and to Pliny, *Hist. nat.* ii. 17 (15). Urso discusses the reason for this penetrating vision of the lynx, *Aphor. Gloss.* 38 (Trinity 1154, f. 171): 'In lynce vero tanta visibilis spiritus claritas est et subtilitas, ut irradiatione sui obscurum aerem in angustos poros parietis contentum illustrando, ad videndam rem ultra parietem positam moveatur', whose words are, again, copied by Neckam, *De nat. rer.* ii. 153, see also his *De laud.*, p. 489.

84. *lux aquile.* Pliny, *Hist. nat.* x. 3 (3): 'pullos suos percutiens subinde cogit adversos intueri solis radios.' Isidore, *Etym.* XII. vii. 2. Discussed by Urso, *Aphor. Gloss.* 38, immediately after his explanation of the lynx's vision. He is followed by Neckam, *De nat. rer.* ii. 153, *De laud.*, p. 377.

85. *canis.* Pliny, *Hist. nat.* x. 63 (83): 'avertuntur et canes, phocae, lupi, in medioque coitu, invitique etiam cohaerent.' Lucretius, *De rer. nat.* iv. 1203 ff. Cf. also pseudo-Alexander, *Prob.* (trans. Gaza), i. 73: 'Quam ob causam canes soli ex omnium animantium numero colligari post coitum venereum soleant?'

88. *castor.* Pliny, *Hist. nat.* xxxii. 3 (13): 'amputari hos ab ipsis, cum capiantur negat Sextius.' Isidore, *Etym.* XII. ii. 21; *Physiologus Dicta Chrysost.* 16; Neckam, *De nat. rer.* ii. 140; *De laud.*, p. 488; Browne, *Pseudodoxia*, iii. 4.

89. *bubo.* Isidore, *Etym.* XII. vii. 40: 'Noctua dicitur pro eo quod nocte circumvolat et per diem non possit videre.' Urso discusses the vision of owls in *Aphor. Gloss.* 38 and 107, and is copied by Neckam, *De nat. rer.* ii. 153—see above, note on l. 74.

90. *vespertilio.* Isidore, *Etym.* XII. vii. 36; Auct. f. 121.

91. *pavo.* It was commonly held that the peacock displayed his tail when he was praised, Pliny, x. 20 (22): 'gemmantes laudatus expandit colores', but not nearly so widely known was the belief that he hid his tail again, 'if the ardour of the flatterer diminished', mentioned by Ovid, *Ars Amat.* i. 627:

> Laudatas ostendit avis Iunonia pinnas:
> Si tacitus spectes, illa recondit opes,

quoted by Neckam, *De nat. rer.* i. 39. See also Bibl. Nat. Lat. 18081, f. 216ᵛ. Ulsen used these lines in the *Speculator* again, in a poem which he contributed to Joannes Eck's *Bursa Pavonis* (Strassburg, 1507):

> In primis querere corde vacet
> regius unde suas Pavo si laude citetur
>   pandat opes speculis quas sacra penna tegit,
>   rursus et abscondat quoties pia lingua tacebit.

93. *mula.* A Greek question, pseudo-Alexander, *Prob.* i. 132: 'Cur mulae parere nequeant?' Pliny, *Hist. nat.* viii. 44 (69); Auct. f. 128; Neckam, *De nat. rer.* ii. 159; *De laud.*, p. 490.

94. *nepita cattam.* A question which probably originated in Salerno. Urso discusses it, together with the next question about the impregnation of mares by wind, in *Aphor. Gloss.* 23: 'Hinc solvitur quaestio, quare cata ad confricationem sui in nepitam, equa ex positione sui ad ventum, et aves veris humido tempore ad coitum moveantur et conceptionem vel nidificationem. Quod ea ratione fieri credimus, quia ad coitum tria necessaria existunt, calor scilicet dissolvens, ut artifex, humor dissolvendus, ut materia, spiritus dissoluta ad locum generationis seminis vel fetus impellens, ut instrumentum. Occulta igitur quadam discretione nature, cum in cata tantum calor desit, incitatus ex aere, confricatione calamenti calefacto, per exsolutionem, aliis duobus presentibus, ad iam dictam actionem facile incitatur. In equa vero cum spiritus assit, quando defectus, borea flante se vento exponit, ut ex ingresso aere spiritu augmentato et conforto duobus aliis presentibus, ad coitum et conceptionem moveatur' (Trinity 1154, f. 162ᵛ), The emphasis here seems to be on the action of coitus, but in the Salernitan prose questions we have, after a discussion on the impregnation of mares, the following: 'Idem potest dici de cata que dum tempore caloris nepite se fricat, vigor nepite in eam subintrans, in tantum eius spiritum corroborat ut concipiat fetus et pariat' (Pet. f. 4ᵛ).

It is likely that from this Salernitan source, the belief passed to Cornelius Agrippa, who says: 'Sic feles sive catus gaudet nepeta herba, ad cuius affricationem concipere traditur, et defectum masculi supplere: et equae in Cappadocia se flatui venti exponunt atque ex eius afflatu et attractu concipiunt', *De occult. philos.* i. 17. Wecker, in his *De secretis* (1559) and Sinibaldus in his *Geneanthropeiae* (1642) both quote Agrippa for the belief.

95. *ventus equam.* See previous note. This belief was much more widespread than the one about the cat, being often referred to in classical times. Cf. Virgil, *Georgics*, iii. 273 ff.:

>   Illae
> ore omnes versae in Zephyrum stant rupibus altis
> exceptantque levis auras, et saepe sine ullis
> coniugiis vento gravidae (mirabile dictu)
> saxa per et scopulos et depressas convallis
> diffugiunt . . . .

Pliny, *Hist. nat.* viii. 42 (67); Auct. f. 145; Neckam, *De nat. rer.* ii. 158. See the article by C. Zirkle, 'Animals Impregnated by the Wind', *Isis*, xxv (1936), 95–130.

sambuci. Another question of which the probable source is the Arabic–Latin *De sensibus* of Belenus-Apollonius; see note on l. 71 above. The relevant passage is quoted by Arnold of Saxony in his *De finibus*, as follows: 'In eodem (*lib. de sensibus*) Belletus, si accendatur ignis coram ernioso ex viridibus lignis ficulneorum, trepidant eius testiculi' (Bodl. lat. misc. e. 34, f. 17; E. Stange, 1885, p. 60, 1905/6, p. 84). Here the hernia is said to be affected by the burning of fresh fig-tree wood, not of elder wood; in Wecker, *De secretis*, however, we find both kinds of wood mentioned: 'Ut hernioso crepitent testiculi. Ubi eum igni accedere conspicies, et calefacere, sambuci vel ficus igni viridia immittito ligna, ut comburantur, sic enim crepitum dabunt, ut secedere illinc cogatur. An id evenit, quam eructat aura, illi vento simili qui quoque eis officere solet' (1642 ed., p. 659). It seems likely that *crepitent* is a corruption of *trepident*, the verb used in Arnold's quotation; certainly this latter verb is the more suitable of the two, as applied to *testiculi*, and would agree more with the *commota* of the Salernitan questions. As regards Wecker's explanation, the south wind was supposed to make hernias swell, cf. Campenella, *De sensu rerum*: 'Nam hernia aliove morbo affecti, bene austrum norunt, quo tumescunt' (1637 ed., p. 19). Wecker's authority for the above malicious experiment is Baptista Porta, but I cannot find it in his *Magiae naturalis libri*.

96. *membra bovina*. An Adelardian question (*Quaest. nat.*, ch. 9), which I have discussed above, on two occasions, pp. 38, 89. It also occurs in the Salernitan prose collection, Pet. f. 11ᵛ, and amongst the *quodlibeta* disputed in the faculty of arts at Paris, *c.* 1300 (Bib. Nat. Lat. 16089, f. 85).

100. *vervex*. A legend for which Aelian is, perhaps, responsible: 'Aries sex hibernos menses, ut audio, in laevum latus jacens somno fruitur; contraque ab aequinoctio verno in dextrum incumbens somnum capit. Ad utrumque igitur aequinoctium ipsam aries mutat cubandi rationem' (*De nat. animal.* x. 18). This work of Aelian was not translated into Latin until the sixteenth century (by Pierre Gilles in 1533, revised and completed by Conrad Gesner in 1556); it is probable, therefore, that the story first gained a footing in the Latin West through the Salernitan masters (it also occurs in the prose questions, Auct. f. 126), from whom it passed to Neckam (*De laud.*, p. 491). It was well known to the encyclopedists of the thirteenth century. It was not known to Pliny, Solinus, St. Basil, or Isidore, and does not occur in any version of *Physiologus* that I have seen.

104. *galli cantus*. Pliny, *Hist. nat.* x. 21 (24): 'norunt sidera, et ternas distinguunt horas interdiu cantu ... diemque venientem nuntiant cantu, ipsum vero cantum plausu laterum'. The *praeco dei* is an echo from one of the most beautiful hymns of St. Ambrose:

> Aeterne rerum conditor,
> noctem diemque qui regis,
> et temporum das tempora,
> ut alleves fastidium;
>
> praeco diei iam sonat,
> noctis profundae pervigil,
> nocturna lux viantibus,
> a nocte noctem segregans.

A. S. Walpole, *Early Latin Hymns*, Cambridge, 1922, p. 30. Bibl. Nat. Lat. 18081, f. 224. Cf. Neckam, *De nat. rer.* i. 75; *De laud.*, pp. 391 and 489. He also uses the term *praeco diei*.

108. *coturnix*. Pliny does not specify the seed: 'coturnicibus veneni semen gratissimus cibus', *Hist. nat.* x. 23 (33). St. Basil specifically mentions Hellebore, *Hom.* v. 4. Neckam copies Pliny and Solinus, *De nat. rer.* i. 70.

109. *passeris*. This characteristic of the sparrow is not mentioned by any of the pre-thirteenth-century encyclopedists, but is mentioned by Arnold of Saxony, who quotes the *De animalibus* of the Arab author Jorach: 'In lib. Jorach. nulli avium accidit magis caducus [morbus] quam passeri et coturnici et his, qui comedunt iusquiamum.' Bodl. lat. misc. e. 34, f. 28 (Stange, 1885, p. 50). This may well be, therefore, another early use of Jorach by the Salernitan masters. See my note on l. 71 above.

112. *fructus. flos*. Cf. Pliny, *Hist. nat.* xvi. 25–26 (40–46); Urso, *Com. Elem.* (Trinity 1154, f. 87 ff.), where the flowering and fruiting of trees is discussed. A somewhat similar question occurs in the Salernitan prose questions: 'Unde proveniat quod quedam arbores et flores et fructus producunt, quedam nec flores nec fructus, quedam

flores et non fructus, quedam fructus et non flores.' (Auct. ff. 123, 154ᵛ). Cf. Neckam *De nat. rer.* ii. 75.

114–16. *cerasa. persica. nux.* Pliny, *Hist. nat.* xv. 28 (34): 'alia bacis quarum intus lignum et extra caro, ut olivis, cerasis . . . aliorum intus corpus et foris lignum ut nucum. aliis foris corpus, intus lignum, ut persicis et prunis.' This is a Greek question cf. pseudo-Alexander *Prob.* (trans. Gaza), ii. 14: 'Cur ex fructibus alii partem inutilem intus contineant, ut palmulae, pruna, persica: alii extrinsecus ea ipsa contineant, ut nuces et mala punica?' In the Latin West, the question was first discussed in Isaac, *Lib. Diet. Univ.* trans. Constantinus (*Opera Isaaci*, Lyons, 1515, f. lviiᵛ), from which source it doubtless passed to the Salernitan masters. Cf. Urso, *Aphor. Gloss.* 106; *Com. Elem.*, Trinity 1154, ff. 131 ff., and the Salernitan prose questions, Auct. f. 123 (several times repeated).

119–20. *oliva. lauro.* Pliny, *Hist. nat.* xvi. 19–20 (32–33): 'Praeterea arborum aliis decidunt folia, aliae sempiterna coma virent. . . . harum generis non decidunt oleae, lauro, palmae.' Another question discussed by Isaac, *Lib. Diet. Univ.*, ed cit., f. lviiᵛ. William of Conches has a rather similar question, *Dragmaticon*, ed. 1567, p. 231; cf. also Auct. f. 156ᵛ, and Neckam *De laud.*, p. 485:

> Perpetuo laurus stat nobilitata virore.

121. *aurum.* One of the few cases in which I have been unable to find any other reference earlier than Neckam. He, however, says that gold gets moist towards the dawn, not that it gets colder, *De nat. rer.* ii. 53: 'Sicut autem aurum madefit appropinquante aurora', and *De laud.*, p. 464;

> Sese conformat naturae sanguinis aurum,
> Et quociens instat sanguinis hora, madet.
> Forsitan externis haec efficit aeris humor,
> Forsitan interior vis operator idem.

Thomas of Cantimpré, *De nat. rer.* (1228–44), has: 'Aurum contra diem frigescit, ut dicitur, et sic cognoscunt homines habentes aurum in digitis quando diescit' (Arundel 323, f. 89ᵛ). Vincent, *Spec. nat.* vii. 7, copies this. It seems likely that there was some source known to the Salernitans and Thomas which Neckam interpreted wrongly. The fact that gold is unharmed in the fire, mentioned in the line inserted in S and T, is more widely known: cf. Pliny, *Hist. nat.* xxxiii. 3 (19): 'tuto etiam in incendiis rogisque.' Cf. Auct. 138ᵛ. For this use of the verb *accuso*, see p. 46, n. 4.

122. *asellum.* Auct. f. 138ᵛ has: 'Quare asinus cum venerit ad locum ubi alii mixerint, statim mingat?', which is not quite the same question. Bartholomew, *De prop. rer.* xviii. 7, has: 'quando cogitur aquam vel rivum evadere, in ipso mingit', which must refer to the same characteristic. Pliny, *Hist. nat.* viii. 43 (68), says that asses are exceedingly afraid of water, so much so that they take care not to get their feet wet: 'per ignes ad fetus tendunt: eaedem, si rivus minimus intersit, horrent etiam pedes omnino tinguere.' Neckam does not mention this habit of the ass, and I am unable to say through what source it reached the Salernitan masters.

125. *canis.* Pliny, *Hist. nat.* viii. 16 (18): 'urinam mares crure sublato reddere ut canes.'

psittacus. Pliny, *Hist. nat.* x. 42 (58): 'super omnia humanas voces reddunt.' Isidore, *Etym.* XII. vii. 24; Neckam, *De nat. rer.* i. 36; *De laud.*, p. 378.

126. *pica loquax.* A story mentioned by Neckam, *De nat. rer.* i. 69: 'Commendabilis tamen est pica in hoc, quod curiae vel cortis in qua nidificat, prospicit indemnitati, et insidias latitantium multo prodit clamore, adeo ut a proposito infelici territi nonnunquam revocentur', also *De laud.*, p. 388. Vincent repeats the tale, and attributes it to *Physiologus* (*Spec. nat.* xvi. 131), and the probability is that it originated in some version of this compilation, which served as a source for the Salernitans, Neckam and Vincent. I cannot find it in any extant version. For this use of *accuso*, see p. 46, n. 4.

128. *holor*. A belief as common as the previous one is rare. Pliny, *Hist. nat.* x. 23 (32): 'olorum morte narratur flebilis cantus, falso, ut arbitror, aliquot experimentis.' Neckam, *De nat. rer.* i. 100; *De laud.*, p. 381.

visus basilisci. Another very common and early belief. Pliny, *Hist. nat.* xxix. 4 (19): 'Basilisci . . . qui hominem, vel si adspiciat tantum, dicitur interemere.' Isidore, *Etym.* XII. iv. 6; Auct. f. 127. Neckam, *De nat. rer.* ii. 153: 'Basiliscus solo visu hominem necare perhibetur.'

129. *mulier*. This belongs to the group of Salernitan gynaecological questions used by William of Conches, and discussed above, p. 53 (Auct. f. 1201; William, *De philos.* iv. 14). A possible source is Pliny, *Hist. nat.* vii. 11 (9): 'Praeter mulierem, pauca animalia coitum novere gravida.' The question is common in later collections of natural questions.

cur puer ad gressum. This question, inserted in S and T, belongs to the same Salernitan group, Auct. f. 119; William, *De philos.* iv. 9. Cf. Macrobius, *Sat.* vii. 7: 'cum calor semper generationis causa fit, feminae ideo celerius quam pueri fiunt idoneae ad generandum, quia calent amplius.'

131. *cornua*. An Adelardian question (*Quaest. nat.*, ch. 15), see above, p. 39; also discussed by Urso, *Aphor. Gloss.* 2, and found in the prose collection, Auct. f. 130ᵛ. Cf. Pliny, *Hist. nat.* xi. 37 (45).

133. *Samsonis*. A biblical question, also found in the prose Salernitan collection, Pet. f. 33.

136. *singultum*. A Greek question, cf. pseudo-Alexander, *Prob.* (trans. Gaza), i. 46: 'Quam ob causam qui ex pane singultiunt, solvantur singultu cum triste aliquid audierint?' Cf. Constantinus, *Viaticum*, iv. 8: 'Extinguitur omne genus singultuum si infirmo timenda vel anxia nuncientur, natura enim ex cogitatione singultum impedit' Auct. f. 146.

sternutatio. Although there are many references in classical literature to omens of sneezing to the left or to the right, and at certain times, also to the custom of salutation at sneezing, references to prognostication from the number of sneezes are rare. The earliest I can find seems to be that in John of Salisbury's *Polycraticus* (1159), ii. 1: 'Quid enim refert ad consequentiam rerum, si quis semel aut amplius sternutavit?' The question is dealt with in the prose Salernitan questions, Auct. f. 144. There is a chapter on prognosticating from the number of sneezes in the popular *Physionomia* or *De secretis naturae* of Michael Scot (ch. 57 in the Frankfurt 1624 ed., printed with the spurious Albertus Magnus, *De secretis mulierum*). The grammarian William Horman (d. 1535), vice-provost of Eton, knew of the superstition and mentioned it in his *Vulgaria* (Pynson, 1519): 'Bina aut terna sternutatio salutaris, solitaria vero gravis. Two or iii nesys be holsom: one is a shrewd token.' The belief may well have a medical origin, sneezing twice being regarded by physicians as a sign that a person would recover from a severe illness. See Forestus, *De cerebri morbis*, Scholia on Observat. 127: 'Sic observatum, si aegrotans vir semel dumtaxat sternuat, quod is morbi ferocia succumbet. Si vero geminet, bisque sternuat, profligato morbo revalescet.' It is possible, therefore, that this is a superstition which, in the West, originated in and spread from Salerno during the twelfth century.

138. *leo*. Pliny, *Hist. nat.* viii. 16 (19): 'Leoni tantum ex feris clementia in supplices. prostratis parcit . . . . leonum animi index cauda, sicut et equorum aures.' Isidore, *Etym.* XII. ii. 4, 6. The reference to the motions of the tail occurs in pseudo-Alexander, *Prob.* (trans. Gaza), i. 144. The first question is dealt with by Neckam, *De nat. rer.* ii. 148; *De laud.*, p. 486.

140. *lepus*. Pliny, *Hist. nat.* viii. 55 (81): 'idem utramque vim singulis inesse ac sine mare aeque gignere.' Pet. f. 36ᵛ. Neckam, *De nat. rer.* ii. 134; Browne, *Pseudodoxia*, iii. 17.

142. *lupa*. Aristotle ascribed this characteristic only to the females of the leopard and the bear, *Hist. animal.* 608^{a-b}. Pliny follows him, *Hist. nat.* xi. 49 (110): 'Mares in omni genere fortiores sunt praeterquam pantheris et ursis.' Vincent, *Spec. nat.* xxii. 24, follows Aristotle and Pliny. The only other reference which I can find where the wolf takes the place of the bear is in Michael Scot's translation of the *Abbreviatio Avicenne de animalibus* (*c.* 1232): 'mulieres secundum plurimum sunt obedientes et maioris domationis et timoris et debilitatis praeter leopardas et lupas, extimatur quod femine quedam earum sunt audaciores et discretiores', *Opera Avicenne*, Venice, 1508, ii. f. 38. In this case we have to accept, either that this question is a later interpolation, or that the contents of at least part of this Arab text were known in Salerno well before Michael Scot made his translation.

143. *simia*. I have not traced a reference to this particular characteristic of the monkey in any earlier literary source. Neckam, in speaking of the *murena*, says, *De laudibus*, p. 407:

> Miror discernens quas naribus admovet escas,
> Isto se reficit simia laeta cibo,

which is the nearest that he gets to the subject of this question.

145. *hidrophobico*. The symptoms of hydrophobia were well known throughout the Middle Ages, cf. Pliny, *Hist. nat.* viii. 40 (63); Constantinus, *Viaticum*, vii. 13; Auct. f. 159; Neckam, *De nat. rer.* ii. 157.

146. *mirrha*. Platearius, *Circa instans* (1913), p. 135: 'Dom li prodom ancienement soloient afeitier les cors des homenz morz qu'ils ne porrissent.' This property of myrrh is also mentioned in the *De plantis* of the Arab author Jorach, quoted by Arnold of Saxony, *De finibus rerum nat.* Bodl. lat. misc. e. 34, f. 5^v (E. Stange, 1885, p. 44): 'omnia corpora salva a corruptione conservat et a contactu reptilium, et venena ipsorum repellit.'

147. *muscus*. Matthaeus Platearius, *Circa instans*: 'Se il a perdu sa force par ce que il a esté descovert ou par autre chouse, metez le ou vaissel meismes tot descovert el pertuis d'une privee, et illuec recoverra tote sa force' (ed. cit., p. 130). Jorach mentions this method for recovering the powers of Opobalsamum: 'Et si ex aliqua causa virtus eius destruitur, aere foetido rectificatur' (Bodl. lat. misc. e. 34, f. 5; E. Stange, 1885, p. 43). The question is discussed in the prose Salernitan collection, Auct. f. 157, but has been omitted by Neckam. The explanation probably lies in the fact that musk is restored by the fumes of ammonia, *Pharmaceutical Formulas*, 5th ed., 1902, p. 153: 'Ammonia has a wonderful influence in developing the odour of musk, and restores it when lost.' This gas would be present in the fumes given off by a stale privy owing to the decomposition of urine. The use of natural musk for perfumery has almost completely died out in Europe, the artificial variety being preferred for a number of reasons. It is, therefore, hardly surprising that a number of wholesale perfumers whom I questioned had never heard of this method of reviving musk, well known, apparently, sixty years ago and a heritage from the twelfth century. It would be interesting to know whether the method is still practised in the East. Cf. Campenella *De sensu rerum* (1637) 147.

149. *solsequio*. This is the same as the heliotropium. Pliny, *Hist. nat.* ii. 41 (41): 'herbam unam, quae vocatur heliotropium, abeuntem solem intueri semper omnibusque horis cum eo verti, vel nubilo obumbrante.' Isidore, *Etym.* XVII. ix. 37. Among the riddles of Aldhelm (VI^2 cent.) is one: 'De Heliotropia sive Solissequa', in which he says: 'Occiduo claudor, sic orto sole patesco' (Thomas Wright, *The Anglo-Latin Satirical Poets and Epigrammatists*, London, 1872, ii. 539). Cf. Urso, *Aphor. Gloss.* 32, and Neckam, *De nat. rer.* ii. 58.

152. *serpens.* Ovid, *Met. ix.* 266:

> Utque novus serpens posita cum pelle senecta,
> luxuriare solet, squamaque nitere recenti.

Isidore, *Etym.* XII. iv. 46; *Physiologus Theob.*, ed. Rendell, p. 70.

153. *muliebre caput.* Pliny, *Hist. nat.* xi. 37 (47): 'defluvium eorum in muliere rarum, in spadonibus non visum, nec in ullo ante veneris usum.' This was one of the questions mentioned by Baudry of Bourgueil in his poetical description of theoretical medicine, made about 1100, see above, p. 13. It is a very common one in medieval and Renaissance natural questions and *problemata*.

155. *pregnantes uteris.* This refers to the well-known 'longings' of pregnant women or their unnatural desires to eat strange things. The question is Greek, and had been available in the West since at least the ninth century in the so-called *Vetustissima translatio* of ancient Greek problems (see above, pp. 12 ff., ed. V. Rose, *Aristoteles pseudepigraphus*, 1863, p. 673, and cf. also pseudo-Alexander, *Prob.* trans. Gaza, ii. 69), and in the early Latin translations of the *Gynaecia* of Soranus (see Caelius Aurelianus, *Gynaecia*, ed. M. F. Drabkin and I. E. Drabkin, Baltimore, 1951, pp. 22 ff.). See also Constantinus, *Viaticum*, iv. 4. The question occurs in Auct. f. 149ᵛ, and in several later collections, and was discussed by Urso, *Aphor. Gloss.* 22.

157. *ruta.* Pliny, *Hist. nat.* xx. 13 (51): 'itemque generationem impediri hoc cibo.' Constantinus, *De grad.* (1536), p. 386; Urso, *Aphor. Gloss.* 21; Neckam, *De laud.*, p. 474.

158. *philomena.* Pliny, *Hist. nat.* x. 29 (43): 'mox aestu aucto in totum alia vox fit, nec modulata aut varia; mutatur et color. postremo hieme ipsa non cernitur.' Neckam, *De laud.*, p. 390:

> Cui clemens verni temporis aura placet.

159–61. *pulmo. cor. chistis fellis. splen. iecur.* The source for this series of questions is almost certainly Isidore, *Etym.* XI. i. 124–7: 'unde et pulmones vocati sunt. ... Nam splene ridemus, felle irascimur, corde sapimus, iecore amamus.' The questions occur in Auct. f. 137.

162. *Germanos.* The bad temper of the Germans was proverbial, Seneca, *De ira*, ii. 15: 'Ut scias, inquit, iram habere in se generosi aliquid, liberas videbis gentes quae iracundissimae sunt, ut Germanos et Scythas.' Le Roux de Lincy, *Le Livre de proverbes français*, Paris, 1842, i. 187: 'Li plus ireur sont en Alemaingne.'

163. *vermisque sciens puteusque draconum.* The first term undoubtedly refers to Satan, and the second, I think, to hell or the whole tribe of lesser devils which inhabit it. Both concepts are represented in the remarkable woodcut of the Broadside, see above pp. 125 ff. In this final redaction both terms are linked with anger (*bilis atrox*), and refer to things which especially torment the Germans. In the earlier version, however, anger (*ira ferox*) alone has reference to the Germans, the other two terms, of which the first is now *vermis cadens*, being linked with 'all-consuming spite' (*livor edax*), and referring to things which torment 'the noble and the good' (*rectumque piumque*); a train of thought which is carried on in the four following, irregular lines, which are not present in the Broadside.

163. *ethereus radius.* This final line is not in the earlier version. It is, perhaps, represented in the woodcut by the image of the Sun, and Ulsen is probably referring to the metaphysical light of truth. His works, as well as those of his contemporaries, are full of references to this metaphysical light. Since the verb is in the Pluperfect (*lustraverat*), Ulsen may have wished to indicate the spiritually better state of the world before the fall of Adam, or before Satan and his tribe were cast into hell.

NOTES ON THE VERSE RIDDLES

1. There does not seem, today, much point in the first riddle; it probably had a meaning for contemporaries, which is now lost.

3. The Latin of this sentence, which, like the previous one, consists of a name, a clause, and a question, is corrupt. *Alcidem* should probably be emended to the Dative, *Alcidae*. It should also be noted that although the object of the question is plural (*quae*), the answer *linx* is singular. Similarly, in Ulsen's last riddle, the singular answer *lanx* corresponds to the plural *que tertia signa* of the question, although *lances*, a pair of scales, not a single pan of a balance, would obviously be more appropriate; while in Agricola's third riddle, the answer should be *linces*, not a single lynx, and in his last one, *lances* would be more appropriate than *lanx*, a single dish. The idea was, evidently, to keep to the 'x' ending in the answer, even if it was not grammatically correct or was otherwise not suitable; as long as it conveyed the general idea, that was all that mattered. As it happens, in the riddle under discussion the singular answer is more appropriate, since it must refer to Lyncaeus, the son of Hercules (Alcides) and Tiphyse, a relationship mentioned only by Apollodorus, *The Library*, II. vii. 8, and not, as far as I am aware, contained in the extant works of any medieval or Renaissance author. It is rather surprising, therefore, that Ulsen should have got hold of this information. Early manuscripts of Apollodorus are rare, see the Introduction by Frazer to the Loeb edition, and the work was not printed until 1555; thus he is an author hardly ever quoted by late medieval and Renaissance scholars. On the other hand, there seems to be no other connexion between Hercules and Lynx in the whole of classical literature.

4, 5. The answer *fex*, dregs, or sediment, is most probably explained by the method of making pitch, described by Pliny and others, in which pieces of pine wood are distilled by primitive methods and the liquor drawn forth by pipes. The first liquor that flows is clear, but the last darker, and this can again be boiled with vinegar in bronze cauldrons, and so further thickened and darkened (Pliny, *Hist. nat.* xvi. 11 (21–22)). The resultant residue was called *pix navalis*, ship pitch or tar, and Brasavolus says that its blackness is due to the action of the fire: 'pix navalis notissima est, ex pinu, et picea fit, pinguissimis harum arborum assulis acceptis resina plenis in struem congeruntur, et igne apposito in fictitium canalem fluit resina accensa, quae extincta pix vocatur, et nigredinem ab igne acquisivit: a nobis pix navalis, ab antiquis liquida nuncupatur', Ant. Mus. Brasavoli, *Examen omnium simplicium*, Lyons, 1546, p. 659. Further, on the authority of Vincent, this ship pitch was sometimes called *fex navalis*: 'dicunt tamen quidam quod liquida sit fex navalis quae dum excoquitur pix liquida quasi fex residet' (*Spec. nat.* xiii. 101). I can find no authority at all for the poisonous properties of this pitch as described by Ulsen. The most that can be said is that, in pharmacy, this variety seems to have been used only in the making of plasters, and, perhaps, if taken by mouth it would have toxic effects, especially on the stomach. On the other hand the clear resin would appear to have been taken internally as an antidote against poison: 'sed illa melior est que est lucida, levis et munda, bibita venenis occurrit' (Vincent, *Spec. nat.* xiii. 102). There seems no explanation for the terms *non nutrit in cerebro* of line 4 and *cerbereum virus* of line 5, unless Ulsen used these words for purely literary purposes and because of their similarity in sound.

6. It looks, at first sight, as though Ulsen was continuing the chain of ideas, and was still referring to the *pix nigra*, or *fex navalis*, in this riddle; since, because of its harmful effects, one could, I suppose, designate it as 'inimical to the sacred Muses'. On the other hand, there is no record of lime (*calx*) being used in its preparation, and it is unlikely that he would formulate two consecutive riddles, both concerning the preparation of the same substance. *Fex* could also refer to the lees or dregs of wine, and, as

it happens, there are references to the practice of adding lime and gypsum to wine, and particularly to must, or new wine. Pliny, *Hist. nat.* xiv. 19 (24): 'Africa gypso mitigat asperitatem nec non aliquibus partibus sui calce', and xxxvi. 22 (48): 'ad vina calce uti, quoniam sic musta condiunt.' Such wine was, according to Vincent, employed as a remedy against poison, but was otherwise of little or no use, and even bad for the nerves and liable to cause a headache: 'Vinum gipsatum venenis omnibus est contrarium. Est autem calidum, nervisque contrarium acceptum. Caput etiam gravat et totum corpus similiter vesice quoque inutile' (*Spec. nat.* xiv. 234). Must by itself was also exceedingly harmful, see Vincent, ibid. xiv. 126 'De musto'. The ancients confused *gypsum* with *calx* (Pliny, *Hist. nat.* xxxvi. 24 (59): 'cognata calci res gypsum est. plura eius genera', Isidore, *Etym.* XVI. iii. 9, and Vincent, *Spec. nat.* viii. 11) and it was used for similar purposes. On the whole then it seems likely that Ulsen was referring to new wine to which lime had been added, and used the word *fex* to maintain the continuity—the first word in riddles 5, 6, and 7 being the solution to the previous riddle. Why he did not compose all the riddles in this way, it is impossible to say; perhaps he found that the task would be too difficult.

8. The only association of a torch with Mercury that I can find is in Ficino, *De trip. vit.*, ch. 18, and in Agrippa, *De occult. philos.* ii. 43, who both describe a magical, astrological image of Mercury which holds in its left hand either a cock or a torch. We have already discussed the influence of Ficino on Ulsen and his contemporaries in Nürnberg (see above, p. 118), and it would have been quite easy for the Dutch physician to have obtained this information, either in the latter place or when he was in Italy.

9. The key to this riddle is to be found in the couplet written by Ulsen at the end of his first draught of the poem,

Plebs sathane sathanam sequitur qui degenerando
A prima causa lucis ab arce cadit.

By *procax mens* he means Satan, and by *arx*, the citadel of heaven.

10. This riddle refers to the emblem of Justice.

11. Tyrannical rulers were often referred to by freedom-loving humanists as monsters. Ulsen was rather fond of referring to monsters, perhaps not always meaning rulers. Compare his obscure letter to Celtis dated 4 March 1496 (No. 104 in Rupprich, *Briefw. des Celtis*), which contains a passage beginning 'Quidni monstrosa numina monstrosos supplices efficient?', and a reference to an earlier, *iocosum epistolium*, now lost, which may have contained the key to both this letter and the references in the riddles of Ulsen and Agricola.

GRE. AGRICOLA'S (LENGESFELT'S) RIDDLES

In contrast to Ulsen's, these riddles are all perfectly straightforward, and need very little comment.

1. This contains a pun on the word *agricola*.

2. Labdacus was the father of Laius, who was the father of Oedipus.

3. *Thirsigeri patris*. Bacchus, whose chariot was often depicted drawn by lynxes and tigers.

6. Symphosius (v cent.) has a similar riddle about quicklime (Riddle 75):

Frigesco lymphis, calidis incendor ab undis.

8. Boccaccio gives the reason for the attribution of a torch to Cupid: 'Fax autem illi superaddita ostendit animorum incendia, exustione continua captivos infestantia', *De Gen. Deorum*, Basel, 1532, p. 222.

9. Referring to the legend of Manlius Capitolinus, who held the Capitol against the Gauls, in 390 B.C. Virgil, *Aeneid*, viii. 652 ff.

THE TWO SAYINGS IN LARGER TYPE

The first of these, printed over the two sets of riddles, *Non est beatus quispiam nocentium*, resembles line 38 of the *Vaticinium in Epidemicam Scabiem*, 'scelus est laudare nocentes'. The second, *Xenium Valedictioni Sacrum*, placed under the riddles, resembles the title of Ulsen's short poem, the *Valedictioni Sacrum*, which accompanies his *Cura Mali Francici*, edited by Sudhoff in 1912; see above, p. 118. The latter poem was a farewell to Apollo, whom he asks to forgive him for forsaking poetry and turning towards medicine. In this case perhaps the most likely explanation is that the words refer to Ulsen's impending departure from Nürnberg after the disastrous loss of his savings in 1501.

NOTES ON THE 'QUESTIONES PHISICALES'

1. *acetum.* An ancient method of testing vinegar, mentioned by Platearius, *Circa instans*: 'Et se vos volés savoir s'il est bons, vos l'esproveroiz einsi: metez desus le fer froit ou en la terre, et s'il est bons, il boudra', ed. P. Dorveaux, pp. 17 ff. The question is discussed at length in the *Compendium medicinae* of Gilbertus Anglicus, Lyons, 1510, ff. 48 ff.

5. *canis.* Cf. the description of Claudian, 'hae nare sagaces', *De Consul. Stilich.* iii. 299. Auct. f. 156ᵛ: 'quare canis percipit cervum remoto odore, et non aliud animal vicinum?' Neckam, *De nat. rer.* ii. 157: 'Narium sagacitate legunt ferarum vestigia et certis indiciis produnt ipsarum latebras.'

6. *cancer.* Pliny, *Hist. nat.* ix. 31 (51): 'cancri in pavore et retrorsi pari velocitate redeunt.'

7. *leo.* This undoubtedly refers to the story of the lion and the knight, as told by Neckam, *De nat. rer.* ii. 148: 'Excitatus postea a somno leo, et fide et virtute praestantissimus, sinus carbasi tumentes cernens, nunc gemitum edit nunc rugitu implet littora. Quid fidus non cogat amor? Fluctus marinos et procellarum indignationes inundantium contemnit, mari se committit animal generosum. Invidit audaciae ipsius Neptunus, et procellosis inundationum impetibus pro dolor! submersit.' The lion was thus only the indirect cause of the storm, which was actually stirred up by the envious Neptune.

Insompniis positus (*Insompnis* in the manuscripts). An example of synizesis, see V. Ussani, *Insomnia. Saggio di critica semantica*, Rome 1955, p. 84. Cf. *sompno positus*, Virgil, *Aeneid*, iv. 527.

The story perhaps came from some version of *Physiologus*, at present unknown.

9. *sompnia sanguinis hora.* We have already come across the use of the term *sanguinis hora* to denote the dawn, when quoting Neckam in the note on l. 121 of the *Speculator*. It arose because the sanguine humour was thought to predominate at that time, 'In aurora autem humor sanguinis principaliter dominatur', Bartholomew, *De prop. rerum*, ix. 21. The truth of morning dreams is mentioned by Horace, *Sat.* i. 10:

Post mediam noctem visus, cum somnia vera,

and Ovid, *Her.* xix. 195. Avicenna, in his *De anima*, iv. 2, gave reasons for this belief: 'Praeter hoc etiam non sunt vera somnia pleraque nisi que videntur in mane. Omnes enim cognitationes hac hora quiescunt, et motus humorum sunt finiti.' This work became known in the West after 1150, through the translation of Gundissalinus and his collaborators, and it is this source which is quoted by Peter of Abano, when discussing the same question in his *Conciliator, Diff.* 157. This fact about dreams was known, however, in the Latin West much earlier, as it is mentioned by Adelard in his *De eodem* (1105–10): 'Hinc illud aliud, quod in somnis anima, quia quodammodo tunc liberior est a vexatione sensuum, aciem stringit et de futuris etiam aut verum aut verisimile quandoque deprehendit et sub aurora minus fallitur, utpote iam digestis cibis expeditior', ed. Willner, 1903, p. 13. The belief that the tranquil and calm soul, and one free from the perturbations caused by the actions of the senses and the processes of digestion, can experience true dreams and predict the future perhaps stems from Posidonius, and is found in both Cicero, *De divinatione*, i. 60 and 121, and Chalcidius, *Com. in Timaeus*, ed. Mullach, ccxlix and ccli (see C. Blum, *Studies in the Dream Book of Artemidorus*, Uppsala, 1936, pp. 58–61). But the only early Latin source for the special association of this period of tranquillity with the morning would seem to be the Latin translation of the *Solutiones* of Priscianus Lydus (see above, pp. 1–2)—'Quaestio tertia, de somniis. Circa enim ver et autumnum turbida et falsa, veluti ab ipsa continuo aesca, matutina vero, cessante iam perturbatione, pura' (ed. Bywater, p. 62; ed. Dübner, p. 565). I would suggest that, through these five traditional sources, Cicero, Horace, Ovid, Chalcidius, and Priscianus Lydus, this particular portion of dream lore became known both to Adelard and the Salernitans, long before the diffusion of Arabic–Latin translations.

10. *lactuca.* Pliny, *Hist. nat.* xix. 8 (38): 'est quidem natura omnibus refrigeratrix.' Isaac, *De diet. part.* (trans. Const., ed. 1515, f. 125).

11. *faba.* According to Constantinus, three things are necessary for the production of semen—nourishment, ventosity, and warmth. Beans supply the first two, the third is supplied by hot spices, such as pepper and ginger. A mixture of these latter substances and beans was, therefore, thought to be aphrodisiac: 'fabe nutriunt et ventositatem generant, tamen quia nutrimenta earum frigiditati collimitant, uno carent et duo possident: piper vero longum, zingiber, piper nigrum, et his similia tantum calida, nullumque eorum attingentia que sunt genus seminis. Si tamen horum aliquid fabe commiscueris, efficitur nutrimentum quod generat semen, quia hec tria possidet.' Constantinus, *De coitu* (*Opera*, Basel, 1536, p. 305).

12. *agnus heris.* This must refer to the *agnus castus*, or chaste tree (vitex, a species of verbena). Pliny, *Hist. nat.* xxiv. 9 (38): 'ad venerem impetus inhibent.' Constantinus, *De Grad.* (1536), p. 378; Neckam, *De laud.*, p. 474.

13. *columba.* Pliny, *Hist. nat.* x. 53 (74): 'columbae deciens anno pariunt, quaedam et undeciens.'

15. *viror in flore.* Urso discusses the colours of flowers in several places, particularly *De com. elem.* (Trinity 1154, f. 138^v–139). A similar question is found in the Salernitan prose collection, 'Quare flores herbe unius coloris sunt, folia alterius?' (Auct. f. 144^v), where, again, the causes of the various colours in flowers are discussed. Cf. Neckam, *De laud.*, p. 485:

Quare
Flos nullus viridis, sit tamen herba virens,

and *De nat. rer.* ii. 56.

16. *marini fluctus.* A very common question in the traditional Latin sources. Cf. Virgil, *Georg.* ii. 479–80; Pliny, *Hist. nat.* ii. 97 (99); Macrobius, *In som. Scip.* ii. 9; Pet. f. 35^v; Neckam, *De nat. rer.* ii. 17.

17. *circulus imbres.* Pliny, xviii. 35 (79): 'si quartam orbis rutilus cingit et ventos et imbres praemonebit.'

18. *cornix.* Pliny, xviii. 35 (87): 'et cum terrestres volucres contra aquam clangores dabunt perfundentesque sese, sed maxime cornix.' Neckam, *De nat. rer.* i. 62; *De laud.* p. 386.

19. *mel fetum.* I have no doubt that this is a typically Salernitan question, although I have not succeeded in tracing its exact origin. Constantinus, in speaking of honey, says, 'Colerici et iuvenes caveant, quia coleram generat rubeam, calidos morbos et acutos, in aestate maxime. In his enim corporibus prius in coleram rubeam quam in sanguine mutatur', *Pantegni, Theor.* v. 27. Doubtless it was this excess of red bile in the mother which was supposed to mark the foetus with spots of the same colour. Thomas Fienus explains how this happens, in his *De viribus imaginationis* (1608): 'Possunt etiam maculae in foetum induci, sanguine vel bile, vel melancholia in aliquam partem externam motu illo decumbentibus, qui in partis alimentum transeuntes, cutem simili colore inficiant: vel pravis aliquibus e corpore matris humoribus ad foetum transmissis qui partem, quam alunt, pravo colore tingant' (ed. Leyden, 1635, p. 262). The question is not in the extant prose Salternitan collections. Neckam mentions the

belief twice, *De nat. rer.* ii. 155: 'Sumptum a pregnante . . mel certa sui in corpore tenero relinquit indicia', and *De laud.*, p. 492:

> Praebet item puero maculam, si vescitur illo
> Mater, dum ventris cellula claudit eum.

21. *varium . . . colorem.* The ultimate source for the uniformity of coloration in animals is Arist. *De gen. animal.* v. 6. Based on this is pseudo-Alexander *Prob.* (tr. Valla), iii. 4: 'Cur silvestres bestiae unicolores sunt?', which corresponds to Bussemaker's *Prob. inedita*, 129 (Arist. *Opera*, Paris, iv, 1857, p. 316). This problem is not included in the extant fragment of the *Vetustissima translatio* (see above, p. 13), so that the earliest available Latin source at the moment is Michael Scot's translation of the *De animalibus*. See above, p. 25, for a note on some similar Greek questions used by Adelard for which there are no earlier, extant, intermediate Latin sources.

22. *arbor aves.* The late Dr. J. Seide thought that this legend of birds growing on trees was of oriental origin, and that it first reached the West in some version of *Physiologus*. He says that from the twelfth century onwards the belief quite frequently formed the subject of questions concerning the Jewish dietary laws, dealt with by the rabbinical authorities in England, France, and Germany; the first to mention the legend being rabbi Jacob Tam (1100–71), of Rameru near Troyes. See the article, 'The Barnacle Goose Myth in the Hebrew Literature of the Middle Ages', *Centaurus*, vii. 2 (1961), 206–11. The legend is found in the French, *Li Livres des natures des bestes* (ed. C. Cahier, *Mélanges d'archéologie*, ii (1851), 216), based on an earlier twelfth-century *Physiologus*, and it is also mentioned by Giraldus Cambrensis, *Topog. Hib.* (*c. 1185*) (ed. J. F. Dimock, 1867, p. 47). Urso discussed it in his *De effectib. qualitat.* (ed. C. Matthaes, 1918, p. 29) and *Aphor. Gloss.* 28, and it is found in the Salernitan prose questions (Auct. f. 131). See also Neckam, *De nat. rer.* i. 48. A Greek or Oriental origin of the belief certainly fits in with its being found at an early date in Salerno, from which place it could easily have spread, with the other Salernitan material, over the rest of Western Europe.

24. *Circulus urine.* Aegidius Corboliensis, *De urinis*:

> Spissus in urina si circulus est et aquosus,
> Cellula posterior phlegmate pressa dolet,

ed. L. Choulant, *Carmina medica*, p. 13.

25. *medulla.* Pliny, *Hist. nat.* ii. 99 (102): 'hoc esse quod terras saturet accedensque corpora impleat, abscedens inaniat.' He then mentions the effect of the moon on shellfish and human blood, but not on bone marrow. This latter effect is, however, mentioned by Urso, *Aphor. Gloss.* 32: 'Hinc est quod omnia medullosa in plenilunio medullis implentur, in semilunio pauperantur.' The question is found in the prose Salernitan collection, Bibl. Nat. Lat. 18081, f. 212.

27. *urine radius.* Urso, *De urinis*: 'Urina rufa vel subrufa in substantia si sit limpidissima vicium splenis vel epatis significat', ed. Giacosa, *Mag. Sal.*, p. 286.

27–29. *hauster. boreas. euro. favoneus.* Favourite meteorological questions. Cf. Pliny, *Hist. nat.* ii. 47 (48); Seneca, *Quaest. nat.* v; Neckam, *De laud.*, p. 423.

31. *cellula frigescat.* The text of l. 30 is corrupt and since the question is not found among the extant prose Salernitan collections, and the exact source is not known, it is impossible to say, with any certainty, what the author's meaning is. *Canis* may have reference to the dog days, a period of great heat, and the *aspersa . . . cellula frigescat*, to the practice of sprinkling a small room with water, in order to cool it; a process exactly described by the Salernitan Johannes Afflacius in his *De febribus et urinis*, ed. De Renzi, *Col. Salernit.* ii. 741.

32. *parvum tumidum.* A Greek question, which usually referred to the greater wisdom of the short man. as compared with that of the tall man. Cf. pseudo-Alexander,

Prob. (tr. Gaza), i. 25: 'Cur homines qui brevi sunt corpore, prudentiores magna ex parte sunt, quam qui longo?' The idea had been available in the Latin West, since at least the twelfth century, in the translation of an anonymous Greek *Physiognomonia* compiled from the writings of Loxus, Aristotle, and Polemon: 'Cum vero magno corpori caro mollis est vel color est frigidus, inefficaces sunt. . . . Rursum cum corpus parvum molli carne circumdatum est et colorem ex frigidioribus sortitum est, facile perficit coepta et est efficax', ed. V. Rose, *Anecdota*, i. 156; ed. R. Foerster, *Scrip. Physiog.* ii. 117. Cf. Aristotle, *Physiognomonica*, ed. Bussemaker, *Opera Arist.* iv. 14. The question was discussed by Urso, *Aphor. Gloss.* 6 and 40, and is in the Salernitan prose collection, Pet. f. 10: 'Cur vix invenitur longus sapiens, parvus humilis?' (Auct. f. 149). The former refers to a proverb beginning: 'Si videris longum sapientem et fortem, et parvum humilem etc.', and the idea is conveyed in the English proverb:

> Fair and sluttish, black and proud,
> Long and lazy, little and loud.

J. Ray, *A Collection of English Proverbs*, 2nd ed., Cambridge, 1678, p. 61. The question was an exceedingly popular one, forming the subject of a long quodlibetical disputation by Richard of Middleton in 1286 (*Quod.* ii, qu. 18), occurring in several Renaissance collections of *problemata* and, finally, being debated at the 42nd Conference of Théophraste Renaudot, held at his *Bureau d'Adresse* in Paris on 7 June 1634. See above, pp. 142 ff., for an account of his Conferences.

33. *campana.* A question similar to the one about the bell sounding better near water occurs in the prose Salernitan collection: 'Quare propter foramina superius clarius sonat tintinnabulum' (Auct. f. 154). Neckam has: 'Clarior item censetur sonus campanae suspensae juxta aquarum fluenta' (*De nat. rer.* i. 22). The second question about the bell breaking if it is struck when bound with a thread is discussed by Urso, *Aphor. Gloss.* 7, and also occurs in Auct. f. 129 (repeated twice), and in Neckam, loc. cit. The experiment survived until the sixteenth century and is found among the *Experimenta* of the Renaissance schoolmaster, Joachim Fortius Ringelberg, *Opera*, Lyons, 1531, p. 612.

35. *ecco.* Another Greek question, pseudo-Alexander, *Prob.* (trans. Gaza), i. 130: 'Cur vaste synceraeque speluncae et loca excelsa puraque soleant resonare?'; Lucretius *De rer. nat.* iv. 570; Pliny, *Hist. nat.* ii. 44 (44) and xxxvi. 15 (23); Bibl. Nat. Lat. 18081, f. 216; Neckam, *De nat. rer.* i. 20: 'Multi etiam quadam sciendi curiositate solliciti sunt ad inquirendum quid sit echo.'

36. *in sompnos.* This seems to be opposite to the tenets of classical medicine. Old age was usually associated with dryness, and consequent insomnia. Cf. Macrobius, *Sat.* vii. 10: 'inde senecta sicca est inopia naturalis humoris. . . . Hinc est, quod et vigiliis aetas gravior afficitur'; pseudo-Alexander, *Prob.* (tr. Gaza), i. 2: 'Cur excrementis abundare, ac vigiles esse senes consueverunt?' An emendation to *insōmnīīs* could be made to suit the scansion of the line, by synizesis of *īīs*. It is, therefore, uncertain whether an error has crept into this question, or whether it is based on an opinion opposite to the usual one, as in a later question, Q. 104, *mulier submersa.*

38. *murilegus.* The night vision of animals was a very common subject for discussion: pseudo-Alexander, *Prob.* i. 66; Isidore, *Etym.* XII. ii. 38; Adelard, *Quaest. nat.* 12; Urso, *Aphor. Gloss.* 38; Auct. f. 149ᵛ; Neckam, *De laud.*, p. 490. See notes on S. 74 and 89.

compassio porcis. It is possible that this belief arose from the misunderstanding of a corrupt passage in Pliny. The passage is as follows: 'compertum agnitam vocem suarii furto abactis, mersoque navigio inclinatione lateris unius remeasse', *Hist. nat.* viii. 51 (77). Bartholomew gave a summary of Pliny's chapter on the pig, and when he came to the above passage, he interpreted it as follows: 'mutuo se diligunt, et mutuam vocem noscunt. unde uno clamante omnes occurrunt et ipsum pro viribus iuvare satagunt et contendunt, *De prop. rerum*, xviii. 85. A fuller version of Pliny's story is given by Aelian, *De nat. animal*. viii. 19, and in this he tells how the swineherd waited until the pirates had got some distance from the land, and then hailed his pigs. The latter, knowing their owner's voice, immediately rushed to one side of the ship so that the vessel overturned, and all the pirates were drowned; but the wise pigs swam safely to shore. Bartholomew distorts the story, making it appear that the pigs know their own voices, not that of the swineherd, and that they rush to help when one of them cries out, not in answer to the voice of their master. Such a misunderstanding could easily have occurred through a corrupt rendering of Pliny's passage; and it is interesting to note that it was this corrupt version that was probably kuown to the Salernitan masters, and that, therefore, many years before Bartholomew wrote his encyclopedia, it was this incorrect version of Pliny's story that was in circulation. After-wards it was further promulgated in Vincent's *Speculum Naturale*, xviii. 78, and in the sixteenth century by Gesner (Topsell's trans. *Hist. of Four-footed Beasts*, London, 1607, p. 675).

41. *rinoceros*. Isidore, *Etym*. XII. ii. 13: 'virgo puella praeponitur, quae venienti sinum aperit, in quo ille omni ferocitate deposita caput ponit, sicque soporatus velut inermis capitur.' The story passed into the older versions of *Physiologus* (cf. *Dicta Chrysostomi*, ch. 3), and became a favourite subject for medieval iconography. Auct. f. 133; Neckam, *De nat. rer*. ii. 104; *De laud*., p. 490.

coitus nexus. An Aristotelian question, *Prob*. x. 47 (896ᵃ), known in the West through Pliny, *Hist. nat*. x. 63 (83): 'ceteris animalibus stati per tempora anni concubitus; homini, ut dictum est, omnibus horis dierum noctiumque.'

44. *putei latices*. Another Greek question, pseudo-Alexander *Prob*. (tr. Gaza), i. 54, known in traditional Latin sources through Lucretius, *De rer. nat*. vi. 840; Seneca, *Quaest. nat*. iv. 2; and Macrobius, *Sat*. vii. 8. The question was an exceedingly popular one, occurring in Auct. f. 128, William of Conches, *De philos*. iii. 19; Neckam, *De nat. rer*. ii. 12; and in many subsequent collections.

45. *vellus ovium*. The curliness of the hair was thought by Aristotle to be due to warmth and dryness, *Hist. Animal*. iii. 10 (917ᵇ), *Prob*. xiv. 4 (909ᵃ), an idea trans-mitted by Macrobius, *Sat*. vii. 10, and Constantinus, *Pantegni, Theor*., ed. 1539, p. 10, to mention only two of many possible Latin sources. But moisture was thought to pre-dominate in sheep; Hildegarde, *Physica*, vii. 15: 'Ovis, sive aries, sive agna sit, frigida est, sed tamen bove calidior, et etiam humida et simplex est' (*Pat. lat*. 197, col. 1324). Neckam, *De laud*., p. 490,

Humiditas disponit ovem sociata calori.

The question no doubt arose from the association of these two conflicting ideas; I have not found it anywhere else.

47. *leporis*. Isidore, *Etym*. XII. i. 23: 'Lepus . . . velox est enim animal et satis timidum' (Pet. f. 31). Neckam, *De nat. rer*. ii. 134; *De laud*., p. 489.

49. *oleum*. Lucretius, *De rer. nat*. vi. 1073; Pliny, *Hist. nat*. xv. 7 (7): 'coquitur id in aqua, innatansque oleum tollitur.'

50. *caseum*. A typically Salernitan question, found in the collection contained in Brit. Mus. Royal, 12. G. IV, f. 128: 'Quare mulieres coeuntes corruptos faciunt caseos, et homines mustum turbulentum ita quod vix clarificatur?' The corruption was thought to be caused by excess heat escaping from the hands: 'Solutio, in coitu calescit totum corpus unde superfluitas fumosa ad manus veniens corrumpit caseos, ad pedes corrumpit racemos et mustum.'

52. *piscis brevis*. A reference to the well-known story of the remora or echeneis. Lucan, *Pharsalia*, vi. 674:

> Non puppim retinens, euro tendente rudentis,
> In mediis echeneis aquis.

Pliny, *Hist. nat.* ix. 25 (41); Isidore, *Etym.* XII. vi. 34; Neckam, *De laud.*, p. 405. A very common question in subsequent collections, and one much discussed in the seventeenth century in connection with occult properties; see Thorndike, 'Medieval Magic in the Seventeenth Century', *Speculum*, xxviii (1953), 695 ff. Sir Thomas Browne was one of the first to doubt the belief, *Pseudodoxia*, iii. 28.

53. *decoctio carnis*. The question, as it stands here, is rather obscure. A clearer version of it is given in Bibl. Nat. Lat. 18081, f. 225: 'Quare caro decrepiti animalis dum coquitur minuatur, iuvenculi autem crescat?' The properties of the flesh of old and young beasts are discussed at length in Isaac, *De Dietis univ. et partic.*, but I can find no other reference to the effects of cooking discussed in this Salernitan question.

54. *porcam*. An Aristotelian question which refers to the extreme fecundity of the pig, as compared with other animals. *Prob.* x, 14 (892^a); pseudo-Alexander, *Prob.* (tr. Gaza) ii. 64; Pliny, *Hist. nat.* viii. 51 (77); x. 63 (83), 65 (84): 'ex omnibus, quae perfectos fetus, sues tantum et numerosos edunt, nam plures contra naturam solidipedum aut bisulcorum.'

56. *potus*. pseudo-Arist. *Prob.* xxx. 1 (953^b) discusses the different effects of wine. Compare also, Pliny, *Hist. nat.* xiv. 22 (28); Seneca, *Epist. ad Lucilium*, 83.

57. *convertibilis cibus*. Dietetic tracts formed an essential part of pre-Constantinian practical medicine in the West. Two main theories of nutrition were available in the twelfth century, the one depending on the four elementary qualities, advocated by Adelard, and the other based on Galenic principles of digestion, promulgated by the Constantinian translations and taught by the Salernitan masters. See above, p. 23.

58–59. *sideris casus*. A question discussed by Adelard, *Quaest. nat.* 73, and William of Conches, *De philos.* iii. 12, see above, p. 51. Cf. Ovid, *Met.* ii. 321:

> Ut interdum de caelo stella sereno
> etsi non cecidit, potuit cecidisse videri.

Pliny, *Hist. nat.* ii. 25 (23); Seneca, *Quaest. nat.* i. i; Neckam, *De laud.*, p. 364:

> In medio sistunt libratam flamina nubem,
> Quae solis radiis splendida facta micat.
> Mentitur stellam, sed cur crinita videtur?

60–62. *imbres. ventos. nubes. fulmina. tonitrus*. Typical meteorological questions, which formed part of almost every collection of natural questions, from those of Seneca onwards. In the Latin West they were originally inspired by the classical poets; cf. Virgil, *Geor.* ii. 475; Ovid, *Met.* xv. 69; Horace, *Epist.* i. 12; Pliny, *Hist. nat.* ii; Isidore, *Etym.* XIII; Urso, *Aphor. Gloss.* 6; Neckam, *De laud.*, pp. 397 ff., 423.

63. *mane rubor*. Pliny, *Hist. nat.* xviii. 35 (78): 'si circa occidentem rubescent nubes, serenitatem et futuri diei spondent.' Urso, *Aphor. Gloss.* 32; Bibl. Nat. Lat. 18081, f. 216^v; Neckam, *De laud.*, p. 424.

66. *commotus piscis*. Pliny, *Hist. nat.* xviii. 35 (87): 'delphini tranquillo mari lascivientes flatum, ex qua veniant parte.' Neckam, *De laud.*, p. 404.

67. *marmor lacrimis*. Cf. Virgil, *Geor.* i. 480:

> Et maestum inlacrimat templis ebur aeraque sudant.

Auct. f. 154: 'Quare marmora sudant?'; Gay's *Trivia* (1716), i:

> Church monuments foretell the changing air;
> Then Niobe dissolves into a tear,
> And sweats with secret grief.

69. *cervus*. Pliny only says that deer fight with serpents, and that their breath draws them from the holes in which they lurk, not that they renew their strength by the eating of serpents. *Hist. nat.* viii. 32 (50): 'et his cum serpente pugna: vestigant cavernas nariumque spiritu extrahunt renitentes', and Aelian has the same story, *De nat. animal.* ii. 9. The earliest in the Latin West to mention the curative effect of the serpents would appear to be Isidore, *Etym.* XII. i. 18: 'Hi serpentium inimici cum se gravatos infirmitate persenserint, spiritu narium eos extrahunt de cavernis, et superata pernicie veneni eorum pabulo reparantur.' Cf. *Physiologus Theob.*, ed. Rendell, p. 81; Auct. f. 124ᵛ; Neckam, *De laud.*, p. 489:

Serpentis virtute soles reparare juventam.

70. *nani*. Isidore, *Etym.* XI. iii. 7: 'alia parvitate totius corporis, ut nani, vel quos Graeci Pygmaeos vocant.' The question is an Aristotelian one, *Prob.* x. 12 (892ᵃ).

71. *leprosus febriat*. *leprosus* here means, 'a sick person', not a leper, and the question refers to the intermittent fevers, tertian, quartan, &c. Fever was not a characteristic symptom of leprosy. Pre-Constantinian classical medical texts, and the Constantinian translations, contained good descriptions of these various kinds of fevers.

72. *testibus*. Amongst the somewhat dubious advantages enjoyed by eunuchs are the facts that they do not suffer from varicocele, and do not become bald. See pseudo-Arist., *Prob.* x. 37 (894ᵇ), x. 57 (897ᵇ), and Pliny, *Hist. nat.* xi. 37 (47).

73. *aves rapaces*. There seems to be no earlier authority for this belief, than the Salernitan prose questions, cf. Auct. f. 148. Neckam quotes the question, *De nat. rer.* i. 79: 'Solet dubitari a quibusdam qua de causa inter aves rapaces foeminae sint maiores et audaciores masculis, et diutius durent.'

75. *arbor*. Pliny, *Hist. nat.* xvi. 25 (39): 'concipiunt [sata] variis diebus et pro sua quaeque natura alia protinus, ut animalia, tardius aliqua et diutius gravida partus gerunt, quod germinatio ideo vocatur. pariunt vero, cum florent. Ibid. 25 (41): 'quae-dam statim in germinatione florent properantque in eo.' Cf. Auct. f. 123: 'Quare quedam arbores citius frondes emittant, quedam tardius?'

76. *aries*. The practice of training one of the rams for bellwether, who takes the lead of the flock, is mentioned by Aristotle, *Hist. animal.* vi. 19 (573ᵇ); but this capability of the ram, is not, as far as I know, mentioned in any of the traditional Latin sources. The question occurs in the prose Salernitan questions, Pet. f. 14ᵛ, but is not repre-sented in any of Neckam's works.

77. *artheticis piper*. Pepper was an ingredient of pills used for the cure of gout and other arthritic diseases, Constantinus, *Viaticum*, vi. 19; but I can find no other authority for the belief that the spice, by itself, was harmful in such cases.

79. *sternutare*. Undoubtedly a Greek question, cf. pseudo-Arist. *Prob.* xxxiii. 4 (961ᵇ). Constantinus mentions *splendor solis* among the causes of sneezing, *Viaticum*, i. 21, and the question was discussed in the prose Salernitan collection, Auct. f. 138ᵛ, and in many subsequent collections of *problemata*, being among those answered by Francis Bacon, *Nat. hist.* (1626), Cent. vii, Exp. 687, by John Dunton's '*Athenian Society* in 1691 (*Athenian Mercury*, vol. ii. no. 8, qu. 6), and by that person, or society, who published the *Weekly Oracle or Universal Library*, in imitation of Dunton's pro-ject, London, 1737, p. 98.

80. *cadaver*. Adelard has a similar question: 'Quare defunctorum corpora vivi pertimescamus?', *Quaest. nat.* 46. Urso discusses another similar question in *Aphor. Gloss.* 24: 'Unde mortuos tanto plus timemus, quanto plus vivos amavimus?', which is also found in Auct. f. 148ᵛ. Only the Peterhouse MS. has exactly the same question: 'Quare homo mortuus pre ceteris animalibus timetur?' (f. 37ᵛ).

81. *mors subitanea*. Pliny, *Hist. nat.* vii. 53 (54): 'In primis autem miraculo sunt, summaque frequentia mortes repentinae, hoc est summa vitae felicitas, quas esse naturales docebimus.' Discussed in Constantinus, *Pantegni, Theor.* iv. 7.

82. *Iacob. varias virgas*. This story from *Genesis* xxx. 37 ff. is an old favourite with medieval and Renaissance authors, particularly with those who treat of natural magic and the influence of the imagination. Augustine was the first to popularize this aspect of the story in Western Europe, quoting it, as evidence of the power of the imagination, at least four times, *De civ. dei*, xii. 25 and xviii. 5; *De trin.* iii. 12; *Contra Jul.* ix. Isidore mentions the belief, *Etym.* xii. i. 58, Urso discusses it, *Aphor. Gloss.* 24, and it is found in the Salernitan prose collection, Pet. f. 10ᵛ.

85. *ovum*. The Salernitan masters seem to have been the first to describe this experiment, which is also found in Pet. f. 14ᵛ. After them, it is described by Neckam, *De laud.*, p. 430, and by Michael Scot, in his *Questiones Nicolai Peripatetici*, qu. 49 (Bibl. Nat. Lat. 7156, f. 47), see above, p. 76. In the sixteenth century the experiment was perpetuated in the books of writers on natural magic, such as Wecker, *De secretis* (1559), lib. v (Basel, 1662, p. 181), and Porta, *Magia nat.* (1558), xviii. 6, in which an apple or pear takes the place of the egg.

86. *ungula*. Pliny, *Hist. nat.* xi. 45–46 (105–6); Auct. f. 124ᵛ.

87. *frigore magno*. The Greek problems discuss why it is that those who are chilled feel pain if they are taken straight to the fire, whereas they do not do so if they are warmed gradually (Arist. *Prob.* viii. 18 (888ᵇ), and pseudo-Alexander, *Prob.* (tr. Gaza) i, 42), but the patient's death is not mentioned. Constantinus, *Pantegni, Theor.* iii. 7, discusses death by exposure to extreme cold, but does not mention the part played by the too sudden contrast of excessive heat. The only identical reference is in Auct. f. 125: 'Queritur, quidam transiens per nivosa loca arreptus est algore et congelata sunt omnia eius membra, deinde adductus est ad maximum ignem et calefactus est, subito acceptus a nausea exspiravit.' Probably this very accident had happened to travellers crossing over the Alps into Italy, in which case this would be one of the rare medical questions based not so much on literary authority as on contemporary experience.

89. *senior paciente puella*. Pliny, *Hist. nat.* vii. 14 (12): 'Mulier post quinquagensimum annum non gignit . . . nam in viris Masinissam regem, post lxxxvi annum generasse filium . . . clarum est.' Macrobius, *Sat.* vii .7: 'Sed si vis intellegere in generatione veram rationem caloris, considera viros longe diutius perseverare in generando quam mulieres in pariendo.'

91. *leo*. The belief that the lion loses all his strength if his tail is cut off is found nowhere else, except in the prose Salernitan collection, Auct. f. 124: 'Queritur cur leo tantam fortitudinem habeat in cauda pre ceteris animalibus, quod ea truncata in toto corpore debilitatur.' Perhaps this is another example of a survival from an unknown version of *Physiologus*, or from some such work as Jorach, *De animalibus*, See above, notes on l. 7, and on *Speculator*, ll. 71, 109, 126.

92–93. *semel quedam . . . et sepe pariant animalia*. Pliny, *Hist. nat.* x. 63 (83), discusses the frequency of parturition in animals.

94. *cauda*. Pliny, *Hist. nat.* xi. 50 (111) discusses long and short tails. Auct. f. 124: 'Quedam animalia quare complemento caude careant?'

96. *leprosi sperma*. Another question belonging to that early group of gynaecological questions discussed by William of Conches and the Salernitans and probably of Greek origin (see above, pp. 53 ff.). Two other questions from this group are in the *Speculator*, S. 129, *mulier* and *cur puer ad gressum*. This question about the transference of leprosy was also discussed by Adelard, *Quaest. nat.*, ch. 41 (see above, p. 38 and Note A, p. 205).

The wording of the question in Auct. f. 119^v is as follows: 'Quaeritur si leprosus accedit ad mulierem mulier non leditur, qui vero post illum prius ad eam accedit, quare leprosus efficitur.' See also, Neckam, *De laud.*, p. 478, and Gilbert Anglicus, *Comp. med.*, Lyons, 1510, f. 337.

97. *natare*. I have discussed this question, and its treatment from the twelfth to the seventeenth century, above, pp. 150 ff. It occurs in Auct. f. 124^v (repeated twice), and is discussed by Hildegarde, *Causae et Curae* (ed. Kaiser, p. 110); Ambrogio Leone, *Novum opus* (1523), Prob. 326; Browne, *Pseudodoxia*, iv. 6; and G. Pellison, *Mélanges de divers problèmes* (1647), p. 109.

98. *volucres*. This is a Greek question, allied to the one about the non-micturition of birds, which I have discussed above, p. 74. Cf. pseudo-Arist., *Prob.* x. 144 (895^b): 'Why is it that beasts of burden and cattle, horned animals and birds, do not eruct?' In the answer occurs the sentence: 'Birds and horned animals neither eruct nor break wind.' The question is found in Pet. f. 14^v, Bibl. Nat. Lat. 18081, f. 222 and Brit. Mus. Royal 12. G. IV, f. 129^v.

100. *ciminum*. Pliny, *Hist. nat.* xx. 14 (57): 'verumtamen omne pallorem gignit bibentibus.' Constantinus, *De grad.* (1536), p. 375; Urso, *Aphor. Gloss.* 21; Auct. f. 149.

101. *pauca vorans*. This question also occurs in Bibl. Nat. Lat. 18081, f. 222^v, where Constantinus is quoted by name in the answer and, in fact, the question is based on Constantinus, *Pantegni, Theor.* vi. 33: 'De accidentibus in egestione apparentibus.' In this case, therefore, we have good grounds for emending the corruption of the text.

103. *eunuculus*. The Greek problems discuss the failure of eunuchs to grow beards, pseudo-Arist. *Prob.* x. 42 (895^a); pseudo-Alexander, *Prob.* (tr. Gaza) ii. 97; *Vetust. trans.*, Prob. 4. Cf. Macrobius, *Sat.* vii. 7: 'Calor est enim qui pilos creat, unde et eunuchis desunt.' As regards their timidity, this must be accounted as part of their effeminacy, pseudo-Arist. *Prob.* x. 36 (894^b); pseudo-Alexander, *Prob.* i. 6. The former characteristic only is discussed in the Salernitan prose collection, Pet. f. 11^v.

menstrua. Pliny, *Hist. nat.* vii. 15 (13): 'Solum autem animal menstruale mulier est.' Auct. f. 149^v; Neckam, *De nat. rer.* ii. 156.

104. *mulier submersa*. Pliny states exactly the opposite, giving a moral rather than a physical reason for the woman's body's floating face down: 'virorum cadavera supina fluitare, feminarum prona, velut pudori defunctarum parcente natura', *Hist. nat.* vii. 17 (18). A host of later sixteenth- and seventeenth-century writers have all followed Pliny, and advanced more or less elaborate physical reasons for the different ways of floating of male and female bodies. It is clear that the version in the *Questiones phisicales* is not an error, since it agrees with that in the prose collection, Auct. f. 127 (repeated on f. 147^v) and Pet. f. 8, where the reasons adduced are opposite to those brought forward by the later writers. This is one rare case, therefore, where 'authority' has not played the decisive part in a decision, and where there has occurred a complete reversal of opinion in the continuous transmission of an idea. We have to wait until 1646 until Pliny's belief is again doubted by Sir Thomas Browne and some of the reasons alleged by later writers refuted, *Pseudodoxia*, iv. 6.

105. *lumina*. A Salernitan question discussed in Pet. f. 20 and Bibl. Nat. Lat. 18081, f. 222^v, but, as far as I know, nowhere else.

107-8. *barba mulier. vox*. Both Greek questions. Compare, for the former, pseudo-Alexander, *Prob.* (tr. Gaza), i. 5; Macrobius, *Sat.* vii. 7; Pet. f. 11^v; and for the latter, pseudo-Arist. *Prob.* xi. 16 (900^b); pseudo-Alexander, *Prob.* i. 95; Macrobius, *Sat.* vii. 10; Pet. f. 11. These two questions, like the one about women and baldness (S. 153), are among the basic elementary questions mentioned by Baudry of Bourgueil *c.* 1100; see above, p. 13.

109. *solis calor*. Another popular question, stemming from Seneca, *Quaest. nat.* iv. 10. 11, discussed by Maurus, *super Isagoge Ioannitii* (Bibl. Nat. Lat. 18499, f. 26ᵛ); Urso, *Aphor. Gloss.* 6, and, at an earlier period, by William of Conches, *De philos.* iv. 5; Neckam, *De laud.*, p. 425.

111–12. (*nivis*) *bruma. grandinis. estas.* Pliny, *Hist. nat.* ii. 60 (61): 'per hiemem nives cadere, non grandines.' Seneca, *Quaest. nat.* iv. 4. 1: 'Quaeritur autem quare hieme ningat, non grandinet, vere iam frigore infracto grando cadat.' William of Conches, *De philos.* iii. 9: 'Quare nives nunquam contingant in aestate, cum in eo contingat grando?' Urso, *Aphor. Gloss.* 59; Auct. f. 156: 'Quare grandines fiunt in estate magis quam in hieme?' Neckam, *De laud.*, p. 397:

> Cernit bruma nivem, sed spicula grandinis aestas.

114. *officium vocis*. Auct. f. 125ᵛ: 'Queritur, quedam femina passa est acutem febrem, que dum crisis fieret ⟨multum⟩ recentis aque potavit et statim vocem amisit, quare.' The second *unde* may represent *undae*. This, like the next three medical questions, may well be founded on contemporary clinical experience at Salerno.

115. *balbucienti*. Auct. f. 125: 'Queritur de quodam balbutiente qui cum stringeretur per manum amittebat loquelam.'

116. *de vulnere lesus*. Auct. f. 126: 'Quidam vulneratus in brachiis vel in colo, quare amisit loquelam?' The use of *tibi*, if not a corruption, is curious, being the only personal reference in the whole poem. Perhaps this very accident had happened to the person to whom the poem was dedicated or sent.

118. *nocte magis morituri*. Pet. f. 37; Royal 12. G. IV, f. 127ᵛ; Bibl. Nat. Lat. 18081, f. 222ᵛ. Discussed by Peter of Abano, *Conciliator, Diff.* 103. I can find no anterior literary sources for these four medical questions.

119. *vini frigidiores*. Macrobius, *Sat.* vii. 6: 'Multis autem et morbus ille, quem παράλυσιν Graeci vocant, sic nimio vino ut multo algore contingit.' The Greek origin of the question is also betrayed by pseudo-Arist. *Prob.* iii. 1 (871ᵃ), and *Vetust. trans.* prob. 17; Pet. f. 8ᵛ.

121. *piper atque sinapis*. Another Greek question, transmitted by Macrobius. pseudo-Alexander, *Prob.* (tr. Gaza) i. 28; Macrobius, *Sat.* vii. 9; Pet. f. 1.

123. *allia*. It seems likely that this question refers to the different actions of garlic eaten whole and after it has been crushed—in the latter case the heating effect being much stronger. A very similar question occurs in pseudo-Alexander, *Prob.* (tr. Gaza), i. 65: 'Cur piper et sinapi si solida devorentur, calfacere nequeant, si contusa nimirum queant?' The effects of crushing onions, pepper, mustard, and garlic are discussed by Urso, *Aphor. Gloss.* 21, and we learn from Maurus that foods seasoned with pepper and garlic were thought to be a possible cause of fever, *super Isagoge Ioanitii*, Bibl. Nat. Lat. 18499, f. 31.

125. *in gyrum motus*. pseudo-Alexander, *Prob.* (tr. Valla) (ed. 1505, p. 275); tr. Poliziano, *Prob.* 131; not in Gaza's translation. Macrobius, *Sat.* vii. 9; Pet. f. 9ᵛ.

126. *cibaria cruda*. Macrobius popularized this question in his discussion, in chapters 4 and 5 of the *Saturnalia*, book vii, concerning the benefits of a simple or uniform diet, in comparison with those of a mixed or varied one. Also, the harmfulness of raw uncooked food was stressed in such pre-Constantinian dietetic treatises as the *Epistola Anthimi ad Theodoricum regem* (ed. Rose, *Anecdota*, ii). Auct. f. 124.

127. *dentes*. Pliny, *Hist. nat.* vii. 16 (15): 'Ceterum editis primores septimo mense gigni dentes priusque in supera fere parte, haud dubium est, septimo eosdem decidere anno aliosque suffici.' Auct. f. 124 (repeated twice).

130. *lunare iubar.* The source for the idea that concentrated moonbeams were harmful to wounds is, perhaps, the following passage in Urso, *Aphor. Gloss.* 32: 'Praeterea secundum sui circuli quadraturam, ut Constantinus inquit, in egrotantibus ad expellenda aquea, ut humores, virtutem expulsivam coadiuvat. Et dum mediantibus suis radiis per angusta foramina missis, vulneribus multa humiditas infunditur, utpote putribiliora incurabilia fiunt' (Trinity, 1154, f. 168ᵛ ff.). Pet. f. 30, has: 'Quare equus redoratus [*sic*], si totus exponitur radiis lune non moritur, si autem radius lune tangat per fenestram sive per aliud foramen, ulcera eius moritur ?' In Brit. Mus. Royal, 12. G. iv, f. 127, the question is: 'Quare equus redorsatus et vulneratus in dorso, si totus nudus soli exponatur, non leditur, si vero per foramen lune radii penetrant ad vulnus, moritur aut multum leditur ?' The effect on the wounds of human beings, mentioned by Urso (I cannot find it in any of the extant works of Constantinus) is, for some inexplicable reason, transferred to those of horses (quadrupeds in the *Questiones phisicales*), and the story has been connected with horses ever since. Neckam describes it at length, *De nat. rer.* ii. 153, it is mentioned by Vincent, *Spec. nat.* xv. 8, and has even been put into Italian verse by Cecco d'Ascoli, *L'acerba,* v. 2 (ed. 1546):

> Perche sel razo suo entra per buco
> Et far cavallo col piegato dorso
> Che cio non ven sin campo lo conduco.

On this work, see above, p. 112.

131. *aloe.* Pliny, *Hist. nat.* xxvii. 4 (5): 'natura eius spissare, densare, et leniter calfacere: usus multi, sed principalis alvum solvere . . . vulnerum quoque sanguinem et undecumque fluentem sistit per se vel ex aceto.' Constantinus, *De grad.* (1536), p. 354; Pet. f. 23.

132. *subacellis.* A Greek question, pseudo-Arist., *Prob.* xiii. 8 (908ᵇ); pseudo-Alexander, *Prob.* i. 9; Isidore, *Etym.* xi. i. 65.

ADDITIONAL NOTES

A (p. 38, n. 5)

Adelard, *Quaest.*, ch. 41: 'Est igitur virilis quidem natura secundum esse calidior, muliebris vero frigidior [Macrobius, *Sat.* vii. 7]. Et virilis quidem ad siccitatem pertinet, muliebris vero ad humiditatem. Unde si quando elephantiosi semen suscipiat, frigida et humida proprietas a tali eam affectione defendit. In qua tamen cum pars seminis inefficax remaneat, cum ad eandem vir accedit, cum siccitate tum calore ingruente ex similitudine qualitatum affectionem sibi accidit ut inducat. Sicut enim frigiditas et humiditas expellunt, ita caliditas et siccitas suapte natura attrahunt'. Auct. F. 3. 10. f. 121 and 156ᵛ: 'Mulier naturaliter frigidam et compactam substanciam (habet) quod potest cognosci per pilos quia non est pilosa. Cum ergo leprosus cum ea concumbit licet sperma eiciat, tamen propter compactam substanciam penetrare non potest matricis substanciam et ad alias partes corporis transmitti ut eas inficiat, unde leprosa non efficitur . . . sed cum contingit virum proxime coire, ex ipso motu virge et ex ipso spiritu inde procedente, dum sperma leprosi dissolvitur, poros virge apertos subintrat et potissime meatum virge, quod in modum veneni serpendo, paulatim inficit totum corpus ita ut leprosus permanet. Unde dicimus quod in illis sic factis leprosis primo apparent ulcera in virga et postea alibi.' It is easy to see how later Renaissance physicians, such as Niccolo Leoniceno, mistook the disease for syphilis. Adelard refers to the Greek *elephantiasis*, a word which, as Leoniceno pointed out in his *Libellus de epidemia quam vulgo morbum Gallicum vocant*, Venice, 1497, was used by the Greeks to describe a disease exactly resembling the leprosy of the Arabian physicians. It is probable, therefore, that Adelard's question was inspired by some hitherto untraced Greek source. It is not in the pseudo-Aristotelian collection, or in the *Problemata inedita* of Bussemaker, or in those ascribed to Alexander and Cassius, neither is it among those discussed by Plutarch. Oribasius says that coitus is very harmful in leprosy, and that women and eunuchs are seldom infected (*Collect. med.* xlv. ch. 29; *Œuvres*, tom. iv (1862), 82), but gives no reasons. Paulus Aegineta (iv. 1), and Aetius (*Serm.* 13, ch. 120), have chapters on the disease, but do not mention its connexion with coitus. Neither is this relation mentioned by Constantinus (*lepra* is described in *Pantegni, Theor.* viii. 15; *Viaticum*, vii. 17; and in the tract *De elephantia, Opera Albucasis* (Basel, 1541), pp. 322–8, where, in spite of the title, the disease is referred to as *lepra*: 'Ex his enim humoribus corruptis nascitur infirmitas quae lepra solet nuncupari'). We shall find the question again in the writings of the Chartrian, William of Conches, see pp. 55–56, and it was discussed by the Salernitans (see my note on Q. 96), and by Gilbert Anglicus in his *Comp. Med.* (ed. Lyons, 1510, f. 337). The following question, *Quaest. nat.* 42, also about coitus, is definitely Greek, being prob. 26 in the *Vetust. trans.* ed. by Rose.

B (p. 51, n. 3).

Cl. Picard-Parra has pointed out that William made great use of Seneca's *Quaestiones naturales* in the later *Dragmaticon*, and implied that he did not use it so much, if at all, in the *De philosophia*. 'Une utilisation des Quaestiones naturales de Sénèque au milieu du XIIᵉ siècle', *R.M.A.L.* v (2) (1949), 115–26, cf. p. 119, n. 10, and p. 126, where it is suggested that William found in the *Quaestiones* confirmation of what he knew already about the subject of winds, and that this work was, at the time of writing the *Dragmaticon*, a comparatively recent rediscovery at the school of Chartres. This is confirmed by a comparison of the answers given by Adelard and William (in the *De Philosophia*) with the relative material in Seneca's text, when it will be found that

William is much closer to Adelard than to the stoic philosopher; cf. the following examples.

1. Adelard, ch. 55: '*Flumina vero*, si nescis, quae cursum perpetuum habent, *circularem* naturaliter nacta sunt motum. In se ipsa igitur redeunt et quod eundo fluxerunt, redeundo restituunt.' Ibid., ch. 54: '*Licent enim a mari salsa prodissent*, tamen, dum per viscera terrae ea quodam modo cribrantis multipliciter transeunt, in eadem salsuginem deponunt.' *De philos*. iii, chs. 16 and 17: '*Cum ex principio hoc salso, omnes aquae nascantur*, et ad idem revertantur . . . (Neque enim credendum est aquas annihilari, sed *circulariter* reverti) unde est quod quaedam aquae sunt dulces, quaedam salsae? Cuius haec solutio: cum terra cavernosa sit, aqua ex labilitate sua subintrat, quae per cataractas transiens, colatur et attenuatur, salsumque amittit saporem, quae ad terrae superficiem erumpens, fontes et diversos rivulos dulcis saporis inde gignit.' Seneca, *Quaest. nat*. iii. 5: 'Quidam iudicant terram quicquid aquarum emisit rursus accipere, et ob hoc maria non crescere quia quod influxit non in suum vertunt sed protinus reddunt. Occulto enim itinere subit terras, et palam venit, secreto revertitur. Colaturque in transitu mare, quod per multiplices terrarum anfractus verberatum amaritudinem ponit et pravitatem: in tanta soli varietate saporem exuit et in sinceram aquam transit' (ed. Oltramare, i. 121).

2. Adelard, ch. 56: 'Cum enim in visceribus terrae multiformem flumina cursum dividant, fieri potest, ut tale quandoque incurrant territorium, quod undique lapideis obstrusum molibus, ea *sursum* quidem, si ita patet exitus, *cogat effluere*.' *De philos*. iii. 18: 'Ubi enim fons finita est cataracta. Inde aqua propter spissitudinem terrae, non valens ultra defluere, *cogitur sursum ebullire*.' Seneca, *Quaest. nat*. iii. 26: 'Omnis autem natura umor ad inferius et ad inane defertur. Illo itaque recepta flumina cursus egere secreto, sed, cum primum aliquid solidi quod obstaret occurrit, perrupta parte quae minus ad exitum repugnavit, repetiere cursum suum' (ed. Oltramare, i. 145).

This correspondence is also found in those meteorological questions and answers which do not stem from Seneca, and is especially evident in the following examples.

1. Adelard, ch. 69; '*Quod si proprium haberet ignem*, nocivum haberet ardorem; nam et fructus exureret et fontes siccaret et tellurem a vicino flagrans in pulverem redigeret.' *De philos*. ii. 31: '*Si enim proprium haberet calorem*, cum vicina sit terrae, per singulos menses, aestus caloris, frigus hiemis in terram ageret, tanquam continuis inaequalitatibus, nihil vivere possit'; where William, however, adds the contrary effects of cold.

2. Adelard, ch. 71: 'Considera igitur, quid ex hac tua prava commoditate secuturum sit. Si enim recta linea et zodiacus et stellae suae per aetherem diducta forent, is semper esset rerum status, quicunque esse potest *sole in aequinoxiali degente linea*. *Ver itaque haberemus perpetuum*, sicque numquam aestatem vel hiemem. Ablata vero hieme auferretur et seminum plurima putrefactio, ea absente periret eorum vivificatio. Nullum enim semen ad vitam nascitur, nisi prius corrumpatur. At vero aestate abrasa, superfluae humiditatis rerum periret desiccatio, ea sublata nulla eorundem sequeretur maturatio.' *De philos*. ii. 27: 'Sed dicet aliquis: Si ita se moveret, ver esset in ariete, *quod aequaliter distaret, quod aequaliter nobis semper temperiem faceret veris*, nec aliquid mali inde proveniret. Nos dicimus contra, pessimum inde provenire malum. Nunquam enim terra intus conciperet, quod agit in hieme, neque fructus si aliqui nascerentur, ad maturitatem tenderent, sine quibus nullus animantium vivere posset.'

3. Adelard, ch. 72: 'Si itaque extimae sphaerae subditarumque stellarum *idem esset cursus*, dum totus aer subiectus moveretur, nos etiam secum aut impediret aut implicaret *impetus*.' *De philos*. ii. 25: 'Cum firmamentum ab ortu in occasum volvatur, si planetae *similiter moverentur*, esset tantus *impetus*, quod in terra nihil stare vel vivere posset.'

I have not succeeded in tracing any traditional Latin common source for these questions which might have furnished material for both Adelard and William.

C (p. 58, n. 6)

'Sed quid est in causa, quod quedam arbores ut sunt buxus et laurus, quadam pre-rogativa estate et hyeme virent et nunquam frondes amittunt? Ad quod dicitur quod natura lauri est inobediens effectui solis. . . . Cum igitur natura lauri, que est arbor viscosa, frigida, et humida, hyemali frigori resistat, nequaquam causa sicut ceteras arbores in quibus humor siccatur, hyems exurit: frigiditas namque viscositati coniuncta in lauro semper humiditatem conservat. Quod etiam sola frigiditas humiditatem conservet, in editis montium contingit videre, ubi quia aer est frigidus, pre nimia frigiditate nix et glacies, que nichil aliud sunt nisi aqua congelata, conservantur, et solis consumptivo calori frigore obviante et adiuvante resistunt.' *De naturis*, p. 32, where, though the passage is still corrupt, even after Birkenmajer's emendations from the Berlin codex, it is quite clear that, according to Daniel, the main factor in preserving the humidity of the leaves is the coldness of the plant, which, joined to its viscosity, enables it to resist the drying action of the sun's heat during the summer months. The Salernitan answer depends on the thickness of the leaf stalk: 'Que exilia sunt, arbori debiliter herentia, hieme occidunt, que vero grossa firmiter sunt herentia, minime cadunt' (Auct. f. 156ᵛ). According to Isaac, the cause of the lack of moisture in the leaves is not so much the drying action of the sun during the summer months, as the attraction from them of moisture by the roots, to temper the heat which has been driven down-wards by the cold of winter. In evergreens the roots are numerous and large, therefore they can draw enough moisture from the earth without taking it from the leaves, and in addition, the humours in the latter are thick and earthy, so that they resist the attraction of the roots, which only absorb the more subtle parts. Thus enough moisture remains in the branches and leaves to nourish them through the winter (*De diet. univ.*, *Isaaci Opera*, Lyons, 1515, f. lviiᵛ).

D (p. 78, n. 5)

(1) Madrid, Bibl. Nac. 1877, f. 258b: 'Quare animal volatile caret urina cum bibant aves, item quare omne animal mingens est egerens et non revertitur, propter quid aves rapaces minime potant?' (cf. Adelard ch. 10, discussed p. 74). 'Dicendum quod egestio est principaliter superfluitas cibi, et urina potus. Cibus requiritur ut deperditum restauretur, potus ut cibum deferat per membra, ergo per hanc viam ordinatur ad cibum, et non revertitur, et ideo omne animal quod recipit potum recipit cibum. Sed in animalibus communiter est magis necessarius cibus quam potus, et ex opposito superfluitates et egestiones magis debent expelli cibi quam potus, et ita si eicitur superfluitas potus, eicitur etiam cum urina alia superfluitas que est egestio, et ideo si mingit, egerit, et non revertitur. Preterea potus ordinatur ad alterandum calorem naturalem in corpore, sed cibus ad restaurandum deperditum, et ita cibus est magis necessarius quam potus, et ita si expellit superfluitatem potus, expellit superfluitatem cibi. Ad aliud dicendum quod volatilia, loquendo in parabola generali, valde sunt calida et sicca; et quia simile appetit suum simile, et cibus sit siccior quam potus, quantum-cumque sit humidius, ideo magis appetunt cibum quam potum. Sed tamen plus et minus, nam quedam sunt habentia suum nutrimentum cum quo est humidum, sicut carnes crude in viventibus de rapina est patens, et ista minime potant. Quedam comedunt gramina et radices et herbas, in quibus minor est humiditas, et ideo magis potant. Quia tamen parum potant, sicut dictum est, ideo natura non accipit nisi quod sibi fuit necessarium ad refrenandum et alterandum calorem innatum. Ideo non fuit ibi super-fluitas que urina vocatur. Ex iam dictis paret solutio ad questionem que postea fiebat de animalibus rapacibus, quare minime potant.' Question 32 of the 128 *Questiones* corresponds to this, and it will be sufficient to show the methods of the compiler, if I give only the first part of the answer (using MSS. Bibl. Nat. Lat. 7798, Ashmole 1471, and Marciana lat. f.a. 534). 'et quia egestio est superfluitas cibi, urina potus, et cibus est

ad restaurandum deperditum, potus ad deferendum cibum per corpus, et sic potus ordinatur ad cibum, et non convertitur, ideo omne animal quod potum recipit, recipit cibum. Sed in animalibus communiter magis necessarius est cibus quam potus, et ideo eius superfluitas magis debet expelli quam potus, et ideo si eicitur superfluitas potus, eiciuntur et alia, etiam si mingat, egerat, sed non convertitur.' The sentence *Preterea . . . ciba* is omitted by the compiler.

(2) 'Propter quid homo tardius incedit ceteris animalibus incessu pedum?' f. 258ᵛa (cf. Adelard, ch. 38, discussed on pp. 153 ff.). 'Dicit philosophus in fine cap. VII, mulieres graviter ambulant ex eo quod sunt valde frigide et humide. Ut dicit Galen, virtutes remollit, remollitio autem in nervis est causa gravis ambulationis. Dicit enim Galen quod nervi quanto sunt sicciores, tanto sunt meliores, nisi ad tantam siccitatem ducantur quod rumpantur. Dicit etiam Galen quod cecati sumus in ultimo limositatis et humiditatis. Quia igitur humiditas sit quod potens est, remollit nervos; que quidem remollitio est causa gravis ambulationis. Ideo homo gravius ambulat quam aliquod aliud animal.' This question is not included in the 128 *Questiones*.

E (p. 96, n. 1)

1. *Propter quid magne superhabundancie egritudines graves causant? Ratio illius est, nam causant.* Anonymous commentary found in C l m 4710 (15th cent.); C l m 12021 (15th cent.); Göttingen, Theolog. 124 (1364); Cracow, Univ. Jagellonica 654 (1366). Not in Th. & K.

2. *Propter quid urina.* Portion of a commentary by an anonymous 'Bononiensem', found in Venice, Marciana lat., f.a. 263 (V. xii. 85) (14th cent.) Th. & K. (1937) 497. (*Post problemata naturalia circa odorem.*)

(3) In libro de probleumatibus aristotelis sunt 4 partes.' Anonymous epitome in Vat. Lat. 901 (14th cent.), Th. & K. (1937) 326.

4. *Particula prima de hiis que circa medicinalia evenire solent.* Anonymous epitome found in Prague, Bibl. Pub. et Univ. 117 (14th cent.) and ibid. 1426 (14th–15th cent.) Not in Th. & K.

5. *In isto problemate querit philosophus quare magne superhabundancie et magni defectus causant egritudines. Explicit summa problematum aristotelis sub brevibus verbis.* Anonymous epitome in Bruges, Bibl. Pub. 481 (14th cent.) Not in Th. & K. Each problem is introduced by the words of Bartholomew's translation.

6. *Propter quid est quod magne superhabundancie. . . . Respondetur quod.* Anonymous epitome in Bibl. Nat. Lat. 14728 (15th cent.). Not in Th. & K.

F (p. 124, n. 3)

In Einblattdrucke (1914), No. 1394, the *Speculator* Broadside is ascribed to Caspar Hochfeder, with the date *c.* 1497, probably because this printer left Nürnberg at that time. But since other printers in Nürnberg, notably Georg Stuchs, used Hochfeder's types after this date, the evidence of the types is not alone conclusive. In my view the evidence of the text points to a date *c.* 1501. There is first the reference to Ulsen's crowning as Poet Laureate (*Speculator*, 7–8). Supporting Bauch's view that this took place in 1501 is the fact that the earliest reference to him as Poet Laureate is that found in the notice of his admission to the medical faculty of Mainz on March 27, 1502 (quoted by Bauch, loc. cit. above, p. 118, n. 4), and it is only after this date that he calls himself Poet Laureate in the titles of several poems which he contributed to works by other humanists. Secondly, there is the strong probability that the Phoebe of l. 6 refers to Bonomus with his role of Diana in the *Ludus Dianae* of 1501. Finally, the most likely explanation for the inscription *Xenium Valedictioni Sacrum* is that this refers to his impending departure from Nürnberg after the disaster of 1501 (see above, p. 118).

Bibliographies

ABBREVIATIONS

I. *Bibliographical References*

Bishop. W. W. Bishop, *A Checklist of American copies of 'Short-Title Catalogue' Books*. Ann Arbor, 1944.

Brunet. J. C. Brunet, *Manuel du Libraire et de l'Amateur de Livres*, 6 vols. Paris 1860–65, Supplement, 2 vols. Paris, 1878–80.

Einbl. *Einblattdrucke des XV. Jahrhunderts hrsg. von der Kommission für den Gesamtkat. der Wiegendrucke*. Halle, 1914.

Graesse. J. G. T. Graesse, *Trésor des livres rares et précieux*. 7 vols. Dresden 1859–69.

G.W. *Gesamtkatalog der Wiegendrucke*. 7 vols. Leipzig, 1925–38.

Hain. L. Hain. *Repertorium Bibliographicum, saec. XV*. 4 vols. Stuttgart–Paris, 1826–38. Supplement by W. A. Copinger. 3 vols. London, 1895–1902.

Klebs. A. C. Klebs, *Incunabula Scientifica et Medica. Osiris*, iv, Bruges 1938, part i.

S.T.C. A. W. Pollard and G. R. Redgrave, *A Short-Title Catalogue of Books printed in England, Scotland, and Ireland, and of English Books printed abroad 1475–1640*. London, 1926.

Wing. D. Wing. *Short-Title Catalogue of Books printed in England, Scotland, Ireland, Wales and British America and of English Books printed in other Countries, 1641–1700*, 3 vols. New York, 1945–51.

II. *Journals and Collections*

A.B.A.W. *Abhandlungen der bayerischen Akad. der Wissenschaften* (Philos., philol. u. hist. Klasse). Munich.

A.D.B. *Allgemeine deutsche Biographie*. 56 vols. Leipzig, 1855–1912.

A.G.M.N. *Abhandlungen zur Geschichte der Medizin und der Naturwissenschaften.* Berlin.

A.G.M.N.T. *Archiv für Gesch. der Mathematik, Naturwissenschaften u. der Technik.* Leipzig (continuation of *A.G.N.T.*).

A.G.N.T. *Archiv für die Gesch. der Naturwissenschaften u. der Technik. Leipzig.*

A.G.W.G. *Abhandlungen der Gesellschaft für Wissenschaften zu Göttingen* (Philol.-hist. Klasse). Berlin.

A.H.D.L. *Archives d'histoire doctrinale et littéraire du Moyen Âge.* Paris.

A.H.G. *Archiv für hessische Gesch.* Darmstadt.

A.L.L.G. *Archiv für lateinische Lexikographie u. Grammatik.* Leipzig.

A.P.A.W. *Abhandlungen der preussischen Akad. der Wissenschaften* (Philos.-hist. Klasse). Berlin.

A.W.W.D. *Akad. der Wissenschaften in Wien Denkschriften* (Mathemat.-naturwissenschaftl. Klasse). Vienna.

B.G.P.M. *Beiträge zur Gesch. der Philosophie des Mittelalters.* Münster.

B.H.M. *Bulletin of the History of Medicine.* Baltimore.

B.I.A.P.S.L. *Bulletin international de l'acad. polonaise des sciences et des lettres* (Classe d'hist. et de philos.). Cracow.

B.I.H.M. *Bulletin of the Institute of the Hist. of Medicine.* Baltimore (continuation of *B.H.M.* for 1933–9).

C.B. *Centralblatt für Bibliothekswesen.* Leipzig.

C.H.J. Cambridge Historical Journal. Cambridge.
C.M.L. Corpus medicorum latinorum. Leipzig–Berlin.
C.P. Classical Philology. Chicago.
C.Q. Classical Quarterly. London.
C.T. Cahiers de Tunisie. Tunis.
D.L. Deutsche Literaturzeitung. Berlin.
E.H.R. English Historical Review. London.
H.P.B. Historisch-politische Blätter. Munich.
H.Z. Historische Zeitschrift. Munich.
I.Z. Illustrierte Zeitung. Leipzig.
J.A. Journal asiatique. Paris.
J.H.I. Journal of the Hist. of Ideas. New York.
J.H.M. Journal of the Hist. of Medicine. New Haven, Conn.
J.V.M.G. Jahrbücher des Vereins für meklenburgische Gesch. Schwerin.
J.W.I. Journal of the Warburg Institute. London.
L.C.C. Library of Christian Classics. (S.C.M. Press) London.
M.P. Modern Philology. Chicago.
M.R.A.L. Memorie della R. Acad. dei Lincei (Classe di scienze morali, storiche e filol.) Rome.
M.R.S. Mediaeval and Renaissance Studies. (Warburg Inst.) London.
M.S. Medieval Studies. Toronto.
N.E. Notices et extraits des manuscrits de la Bibl. Nat. et des autres bibliothèques. Paris.
O.H.S. Oxford Historical Soc. Publications. Oxford.
P.A.P.S. Proceedings of the American Philosophical Society. Philadelphia.
P.B.A. Proceedings of the British Academy. London.
P.J. Philosophisches Jahrbuch der Görres-Gesellschaft. Bonn.
P.L. Patrologia Latina, ed. J. P. Migne. Paris.
Q.S.G.N.M. Quellen u. Studien zur Gesch. der Naturwissenschaften u. der Medizin. Berlin (a continuation of *A.G.M.N.T.*).
Q.U.L.P.M. Quellen u. Untersuchungen zur lat. Philologie des Mittelalters. Munich.
R.M.A.L. Revue du Moyen Âge latin. Strassburg.
R.N.P. Revue néoscolastique de philosophie. Louvain.
R.O.C. Revue de l'orient chrétien. Paris.
R.S.I. Rivista storia italiana. Turin.
S.A.W.W. Sitzungsberichte der Akad. der Wissenschaften in Wien (Philos.-hist. Klasse). Vienna.
S.B.A.W. Sitzungsberichte der bayerischen Akad. der Wissenschaften. (Philos., philol. u. hist. Klasse). Munich.
S.G.M. Studien zur Gesch. der Medizin. Leipzig, 1907–34.
S.H.A.W. Sitzungsberichte der heidelberger Akad. der Wissenschaften (Philos.-hist. Klasse). Heidelberg.
S.P.L.S.A. Studi periodici di letteratura e storia dell'antiquità. Pavia.
S.R. Studies in the Renaissance. Austin (Univ. of Texas).
S.R.G. Scriptores Rerum Germanicarum (*in usum scholarum ex Monumentis Germaniae Historicis recusi*). Hanover.
S.T.G.M. Studien u. Texte zur Geistesgesch. d. Mittelalters. Leiden–Cologne.
Sudhoffs Archiv. Sudhoffs Archiv für Gesch. der Medizin u. der Naturwissenschaften. Berlin–Wiesbaden.
T.R.H.S. Transactions of the Royal Historical Society. London.
T.R.S.L. Transactions of the Royal Society of Letters. London.
Virchows Archiv. Virchows Archiv für pathologische Anatomie u. Physiologie. Berlin.
Z. Büch. Zeitschrift für Bücherfreunde. Bielefeld–Leipzig.
Z.D.M.G. Zeitschrift der deutschen morgenländischen Gesellschaft. Leipzig.

BIBLIOGRAPHY

THIS does not include works mentioned only once or twice in the notes on the *Speculator* and *Questiones*, neither does it mention all the editions of books of problems, but only those used for the purpose of this study. A fuller account of these editions, and of the translations, will be found in chapters seven, nine, and ten.

(a) *Primary sources*

ABANO, PETER OF. *Expositio problematum Aristotelis.* See under pseudo-Aristotle, *Problemata*, Venice, 1505.

ABANO, PETER OF. *Conciliator controversiarum quae inter philosophos et medicos versantur.* Venice, apud Iuntas, 1548.

ADELARD OF BATH. *De eodem et diverso*, hrsg. H. Willner. *B.G.P.M.* iv. 1, 1903.

ADELARD OF BATH. *Quaestiones naturales*, hrsg. M. Müller. *B.G.P.M.* xxxi. 2, 1934.

ADELARD OF BATH. *Dodi Ve-Nechdi . . . to which is added the first English trans. of Adelard of Bath's Quaestiones*, by H. Gollancz. Oxford, 1920.

AELIAN. *De natura animalium, varia Historia, Epistolae et Fragmenta*, recog. R. Hercher. Paris, 1858.

AETIUS AMIDENUS. *Contractae ex veteribus medicinae Tetrabiblos*, trans. J. Cornarius. Lyons, 1549.

ALAIN DE LILLE. *Anticlaudianus*, ed. R. Bossuat. Paris, 1955.

ALBERTUS MAGNUS. *Opera Omnia*, ed. A. Borgnet, 38 vols. Paris, 1890–9.

ALBERTUS MAGNUS. *De animalibus Libri XXVI*, hrsg. H. Stadler. *B.G.P.M.* xv, xvi, 1916, 1921.

ALBERTUS MAGNUS. *Liber de Natura et Origine Animae. Liber de Principiis Motus Processivi. Quaestiones super de Animalibus*, ed. Ephrem Filthaut O.P. Münster, 1955 (*Opera Omnia, tom. xii*).

PSEUDO-ALBERTUS MAGNUS. *De secretis mulierum . . . eiusdem De virtutibus herbarum, lapidum et animalium . . . item De mirabilibus mundi . . . Adjecimus Michaelis Scoti philosophi De secretis naturae opusculum.* Strassburg, L. Zetner, 1625.

ALBUCASIS. *Methodus medendi cum instrumentis ad omnes fere morbos depictis.* Basel, 1541.

PSEUDO-ALEXANDER APHRODISEAS. *Problemata*, trans. G. Valla. See under pseudo-Aristotle, *Problemata*, Venice, 1505.

PSEUDO-ALEXANDER APHRODISEAS. *Problemata*, trans. Th. Gaza. See under pseudo-Aristotle, *Problemata*. Basel, 1537.

PSEUDO-ALEXANDER APHRODISEAS. *Les Problèmes*, trad. par M. Heret. Paris, 1555.

PSEUDO-ALEXANDER APHRODISEAS. *Problemata*, trans. A. Poliziano. See under pseudo-Aristotle, *Problemata*. Amsterdam, 1650.

ALFARABI. *De ortu scientiarum*, hrsg. C. Baeumker. *B.G.P.M.* xix. 3, 1916.

ALFRED OF SARESHEL. *De motu cordis*, hrsg. C. Baeumker. *B.G.P.M.* xxiii. 1–2, 1923.

Altercatio Hadriani Augusti et Epicteti Philosophi, by L. W. Daly and W. Suchier. The Univ. of Illinois Press, Urbana, 1939.

ARISTOTLE. *Opera Omnia*, Gr. et Lat., ed. Dübner, Bussemaker, Heitz, 5 vols. Paris (Firmin–Didot), 1848–74.

ARISTOTLE. *Works*, translated under the editorship of J. A. Smith and Sir David Ross, 12 vols. Oxford, 1908–52.

ARISTOTLE. *Fragmenta*, ed. V. Rose. Leipzig, 1886.

PSEUDO-ARISTOTLE. *Aristoteles pseudepigraphus*, ed. V. Rose. Leipzig, 1863.

PSEUDO-ARISTOTLE. *Problemata Aristotelis cum duplici translatione antiqua* [by Bartholomew of Messina] *videlicet et nova sive Theodori Gaze, cum expositione Petri Aponi. Tabula secundum magistrum Petrum de tussignano per alphabetum. Problemata Alexandri aphrodisei. Problemata Plutarchi.* Venice, 1505. (The Alexandri *Prob.* are translated by G. Valla; those of Plutarch, by Peter of Lucca.)

PSEUDO-ARISTOTLE. *Problematum Aristotelis sectiones duaedequadraginta. Problematum Alexandri Aphrodisiei Libri duo. Theodoro Gaza interprete.* Basel, 1537.

PSEUDO-ARISTOTLE. *Les Problèmes,* trad. par J. Barthélemy-Saint Hilaire, 2 vols. Paris, 1891.

PSEUDO-ARISTOTLE. *Problems,* Gr., ed. Ruelle, Knoellinger, Klek. Leipzig, 1922.

PSEUDO-ARISTOTLE. *Die Übersetzung der pseudo-aristotelischen Problemata durch Bartholomaeus von Messina,* hrsg. R. Seligsohn. Berlin, 1934.

PSEUDO-ARISTOTLE. *Probleumata Arestotelis determinantia multas questiones de variis corporum humanorum dispositionibus valde audientibus suaves Cum eiusdem Arestotelis vita et morte metrice descripta Subiunctis metrorum cum interlineali glosa sententialibus expositionibus.* Cologne, Quentell, *c.* 1490—Klebs, 95, no. 21.

PSEUDO-ARISTOTLE. *Aristotelis aliorumque Problemata cui de novo accessere Jul. Caesaris Scaligeri Problemata Gelliana.* Amsterdam, 1650. (*Marci Antonii Zimarae Problemata his addit . . . item Alexandri Aphrodisaei super Quaestionibus nonnullis Physicis Solutionum liber, Angelo Politiano interprete.*)

ARNOLD OF SAXONY. *Die Encyklopädie des Arnoldus Saxo,* hrsg. Emil Stange. Erfurt, 1905–6.

AURELIUS. *De acutis passionibus,* ed. Daremberg, *Janus* (Breslau) ii. (1847), 472–7.

AVICENNA. *Opera—Logyca, Sufficientia, De celo et mundo, De anima, De animalibus, De intelligentiis, Alpharabius de intelligentiis, Philosophia prima* (Metaphysica). Venice, 1508.

BACHOT, GASPARD, *Erreurs populaires touchant la médecine et régime de santé.* Lyons, 1626.

BACON, FRANCIS. *Philosophical Works,* ed. J. M. Robertson. London, 1905.

BACON, FRANCIS. *Sylva Sylvarum, or a Natural History.* London, 1626.

BACON, ROGER. *Opus majus,* ed. J. H. Bridges, 3 vols. London, 1897–1900.

BACON, ROGER. *Opera hactenus inedita,* ed. R. Steel, F. Delorme, A. G. Little, E. Withington, 16 fasciculi. Oxford, 1909–40.

BAILLY, PIERRE. *Questions naturelles et curieuses.* Paris, 1628.

BARTHOLOMEW OF COLOGNE. *Silva carminum.* Deventer, 1491.

BARTHOLOMEW OF ENGLAND. *De proprietatibus rerum.* Strassburg, 1485.

S. BASIL OF CAESAREA. *Homélies sur l'Hexaéméron,* texte et trad. de Stanislas Giet. Paris, 1949 (*Sources chrétiennes,* 26).

BASSETT, ROBERT. *Curiosities, or the Cabinet of Nature, containing phylosophical, naturall, and morall questions,* translated out of Latin, French, and Italian authors. London, 1637.

BAUDRI DE BOURGUEIL. *Les Œuvres poétiques,* ed. Phyllis Abrahams. Paris, 1926.

BAYLE, F. *Problemata physica et medica, in quibus varii veterum et recentiorum errores deteguntur.* Toulouse, 1677.

PSEUDO-BOETHIUS. *De disciplina scholarium.* Cologne, Quentell, 1493. *P.L.* 64, cols. 1223–38.

BOETHIUS DE DACIE. *Quaestio de Aeternitate Mundi,* ed. Geza Sajo. Budapest, 1954.

The British Apollo or Curious Amusements for the Ingenious. London, 1708–11.

BROWNE, SIR THOMAS. *Works,* ed. by Charles Sayle, 3 vols. Edinburgh, 1927.

BUSCH, HERMANN VON DEM. *Epigrammatum Liber.* Leipzig, 1504.

CAELIUS AURELIANUS. *De morbis acutis et chronicis,* rec. J. C. Amman. Amsterdam, 1722.

CAELIUS AURELIANUS. *Gynaecia*, ed. M. F. and I. E. Drabkin. Baltimore, 1951.

CAMERARIUS, JOACHIM. *Decuriae XXI συμμικτων προβληματων seu variarum et diversarum quaestionum de natura, moribus, sermone. In quibus allegoriae et etymologiae multae insunt. . . . Appendix problematum, varias et diversas quaestiones morales, naturales mathematicas, poeticas et mythologicas complectens.* Geneva, 1594–6. (Greek and Latin, entirely classical in tone.)

CAMERARIUS, JOANNIS RUDOLPH. *Sylloges Memorabilium medicinae et mirabilium naturae arcanorum. Cent. I–XII.* Strassburg, 1624–30.

CAMPOS, H. *Sylva de varias questiones naturales y morales.* Antwerp, 1575.

CARDAN, JEROME. *De Subtilitate Libri XXI*, Lyons, 1559.

CASSIODORUS. *Institutiones*, ed. R. A. B. Mynors. Oxford, 1937.

CASSIUS MEDICUS. *De animalibus medicae quaestiones et problemata*, interp. Hadriano Junio. Paris, 1541.

CECCO D'ASCOLI. *L'acerba.* Venice, 1546. Interp. A. Crespi, Ascoli Piceno, 1927.

CELSUS, A. CORNELIUS. *Opera quae supersunt*, rec. F. Marx. Leipzig, 1915 (*C.M.L.* i).

CELTIS, CONRAD. *Briefwechsel*, ed. H. Rupprich. Munich, 1934.

CELTIS, CONRAD. *Selections*, ed. with translation and commentary, by Leonard Forster. Cambridge, 1948.

CHALCIDIUS. *Timaeus ex Platonis Dialogo translatus et in eundem Commentarius*, ed. Mullach, *Fragmenta Philosophorum Graecorum*, ii (Paris, 1882), 147–258.

CICERO, *De Oratore*, with Introd. and notes by A. S. Wilkins, 2 vols. Oxford, 1888.

CLARENBALD OF ARRAS. *Der Kommentar des Clarenbaldus von Arras zu Boethius De Trinitate*, hrsg. von W. Jansen. Breslau, 1926.

CLAUDIAN. *Works*, trans. M. Platnauer, 2 vols. London, 1922 (Loeb Lib.).

CONRAD DE HALBERSTADT. *Responsorium Curiosorum.* Lübeck, 1476.

CONSTANTINUS AFRICANUS. See under Isaac Israeli, *Opera*, 1515.

CONSTANTINUS AFRICANUS. *Opera*, 2 vols. Basel, 1536, 1539.

CRASSO, GIULIO PAOLO. *Medici Antiqui Graeci.* Basel, ex officina Petri Pernae, 1581. (Contains his *Quaestiones naturales et medicae*, ii. 94–108.)

Cueur de Philosophie. Paris, 1504.

CUFFE, HENRY. *The Differences of the Ages of Mans Life.* London, 1607.

DANIEL OF MORLEY. *Lib. de naturis inferiorum et superiorum*, hrsg. K. Sudhoff. *A.G.N.T.* VIII. i (Leipzig, 1917), 1–40, corrected by Birkenmajer ibid. IX. i (1920), 45–51.

DANTE ALIGHIERI. *La Divina Commedia, testo critico rifatto da Giuseppe Vandelli.* Milan, 1949.

DUNTON, JOHN. *Athenian Gazettes and Mercuries*, 20 vols. London, 1690–7 (with Supplements to vols. 1–5).

DUNTON, JOHN. *History of the Athenian Society* (written by Mr. Gildon). London, 1691.

DUNTON, JOHN. *Young Student's Library.* London, 1691 (with indexes to vols. 1–5 of the *Gazettes*, and of the Supplements to them, as well as to the *History of the Athenian Soc.*, and to the *Young Student's Lib.*).

DUPLEIX, SCIPIO, *La Curiosité naturelle rédigée en questions selon l'ordre alphabétique.* Paris, 1631.

ESCOBAR, LUYS DE. *Las quatrocientas respuestas a otras tantas preguntas que D. Fadrique Enriquez y otras personas en diversas vezes embiaron a preguntar al auctor . . . .* Valladolid, 1545.

ESCOBAR, LUYS DE. *La segunda parte de las quatrocientas respuestas a otras preguntas, con las glosas y declaraciones.* Valladolid, 1552.

Experimentarius medicinae. Strassburg, apud J. Schottum, 1544.

FICINO, MARSILIO. *Platonica Theologia de immortalitate animorum*, 2nd ed. Venice, 1524–5.

FICINO, MARSILIO. *De vita libri tres.* Lyons, 1566.

FRACASTORO, GIROLAMO. *Syphilis or the French disease.* Text and trans. by Heneage Wynne-Finch. London, 1935.

FREIGE, J. T. *Quaestiones physicae.* Basel, 1579.

FUENTES, ALONSO DE. *Summa de philosophia natural en la qual assi mismo se tracta de Astrulugia y Astronomia y otras sciencias.* Seville, 1547.

GALEN. *Opera ex septima Iuntarum editione* (13 parts, including Synopsis and Index). Venice (Junta), 1579.

GARIMBERTO, HIERONYMO. *Problemi naturali e morali.* Venice, 1549.

GELLIUS, AULUS. *Noctes Atticae,* trans. J. C. Rolfe, 3 vols. London, 1927–8 (Loeb Lib.).

GILBERT ANGLICUS. *Compendium medicinae.* Lyons, 1510.

GILLES OF CORBEIL. *Carmina medica,* ed. L. Choulant. Leipzig, 1826.

GILLES OF CORBEIL. *Viaticus,* ed. V. Rose. Leipzig, 1907.

GODFREY OF SAINT-VICTOR. *Fons philosophiae,* ed. P. Michaud-Quantin. Louvain, 1956.

GODFREY OF SAINT-VICTOR. *Microcosmus,* ed. Ph. Delhaye. Lille, 1951.

GUNDISSALINUS, DOMINICUS. *De Divisione Philosophiae,* hrsg. L. Baur. *B.G.P.M.* iv. 2–3, 1903.

HARVEY, GIDEON. *Archelogia Philosophica Nova, or New Principles of Philosophy.* London, 1663.

H(EATH), R(OBERT). *Philosophical Problems,* 2nd ed. London, 1664.

HEIDFELD, JOHANN. *Sphinx philosophica.* Herborn, 1600 (1st ed.); *Sphinx Theologico-philosophica,* Herborn, 1631 (9th ed.)

Helpe to Discourse (by W. B. & E. P.), 13th ed. London, 1648.

Helpe to memorie and discourse, 2nd ed. London, 1621.

HERMANN OF CARINTHIA. *De Essentiis,* ed. P. Manuel Alonso. Univ. Pontificia, Comillas (Santander), 1946.

S. HILDEGARD OF BINGEN. *Causae et Curae,* ed. P. Kaiser. Leipzig, 1903.

HORACE. *Satires, Epistles, Ars Poetica,* trans. H. R. Fairclough, London, 1926 (Loeb Lib.).

HUGH OF SAINT-VICTOR. *Opera,* ed. Migne. *P.L.* 175–7, Paris, 1879–80.

HUGH OF SAINT VICTOR. *Didascalicon,* ed. C. H. Buttimer. Washington, D.C., 1939.

ISIDORE OF SEVILLE. *Etymologiarum,* rec. W. M. Lindsay, 2 vols. Oxford, 1911.

ISAAC ISRAELI. *Opera: Lib. de definitionibus; de elementis; dietarum universalium, cum com. Petri Hispani; dietarum particularium, cum com. eiusdem; de urinis, cum com. eiusdem; de febribus; Pantechni decem libri theorices et decem practices; cum tractatu de gradibus medicinarum Constantini; Viaticum Ysaac quod Constantinus sibi attribuit; de oculis Constantini; de stomacho Constantini; virtutum de simplici medicina Constantini; Compendium megatechni Galeni Constantino compositum.* Lyons, 1515.

JACCHINUS, LEONARDUS. *Quaestionum naturalium libellus.* Lyons, 1540.

JEAN DE JANDUN. *Quaestiones super de physico Aristotelis.* Venice, 1560.

JOHN OF GADDESDEN. *Rosa Anglica.* Pavia, 1492.

JOHN OF SALISBURY. *Opera,* ed. Migne. *P.L.* 199, Paris, 1855.

JONSTON, JOHN. *Thaumatographia naturalis.* Amsterdam, 1632.

JOUBERT, LAURENT. *Erreurs populaires et propos vulgaires touchant la médecine et le régime de santé.* Bordeaux, 1578.

LANDO, ORTENSIO. *Miscellaneae Quaestiones.* Venice, 1550.

LANDO, ORTENSIO. *Quattro libri de dubbi.* Venice, 1552.

LEONE, AMBROGIO. *Novum opus quaestionum seu problematum ut pulcherrimorum ita utilissimorum tum aliis plerisque in rebus cognoscendis tum maxime in philosophia et medicina scientia.* Venice (Bern. et Matthias de Vitali), 1523.

LOPEZ DE CORELLA, ALONSO. *Secretos de filosophia y medicina . . . puestos a manera d'perque por que mejor se incomienden a la memoria.* 1539.

LOPEZ DE CORELLA, ALONSO. *Trezientas preguntas de cosas naturales en diferentes materias con las respuestas y alegaciones d'auctores, las quales fueron antes preguntadas a manera de perque.* Valladolid, 1546.

LOPEZ DE CORELLA, ALONSO. *Secretos de philosophia y astrologia y medicina y de las quatro mathematicas sciencias, collegidos de muchos y diversos auctores y divididos en cinco quinquagenas de preguntas.* Saragossa, 1547.

LOPEZ DE VILLALOBOS, FRANCISCO. *Libro de los problemas que trata de cuerpos naturales y morales, y dos dialogos de medicina, y el tractado de las tres grandes, y una cancion, y la comedia de Anfitrion,* Bibl. de Autores Españoles, tom. 36 (Madrid, 1855), pp. 403–93.

LOPEZ DE YANGUAS, HERNANDO. *Cincuenta bivas preguntas con otras tantas respuestas.* Medina, *c.* 1540.

LUCRETIUS. *De rerum natura,* trans. W. H. D. Rouse. London, 1947 (Loeb Lib.).

LUIZ, ANTONIO. *Problematum, libri quinque.* Lisbon, 1539–40.

MACROBIUS. *In Somnium Scipionis,* ed. F. Eyssenhardt. Leipzig, 1893.

MACROBIUS. *Commentary on the Dream of Scipio,* trans. W. H. Stahl. New York (Col. Univ. Press), 1952.

MACROBIUS. *Saturnalia,* texte et trad. par H. Bornecque et F. Richard, 2 vols. Paris, 1937.

MANFREDI, GIROLAMO. *Il perchè, sive liber de homine.* Bologna, 1474.

MARCELLUS. *Medicamentis,* ed. G. Helmreich. Leipzig, 1889.

MARTIANUS CAPELLA. *De nuptiis philologiae et mercurii,* ed. F. Eyssenhardt. Leipzig, 1866.

Mensa philosophica. Cologne, Conrad Winters, [1480] (Klebs, 676, no. 2).

MERCURIO, SCIPIONE. *Degli errori popolari.* Venice, 1603.

NECKAM, ALEXANDER. *De naturis rerum libri duo. De laudibus divinae sapientiae,* ed. Thomas Wright (Rolls ser.). London, 1863.

NEMESIUS OF EMESA. *Premnon physicon (in the Latin trans. of Alfanus),* ed. K. Burkhard. Leipzig, 1917.

NEMESIUS OF EMESA. *On the Nature of Man,* ed. W. Telfer. London, 1955 (L.C.C iv).

NICOLAUS OF DAMASCUS. *De plantis (in the trans. of Alfred of Sareshel),* ed. E. H. F Meyer. Leipzig, 1841.

ORIBASIUS. *Œuvres,* ed. C. Daremberg, V. C. Bussemaker, A. Molinier, 6 vols. Paris, 1851–76.

ORIBASIUS LATINUS, hrsg. H. Mørland, i. Oslo, 1940.

OVID. *Metamorphoses,* trans. F. J. Miller, 2 vols. London, 1946 (Loeb Lib.).

PASCHETTI, B. *Dubbi morali e naturali.* Genoa, 1581.

Passionarius Galeni (Gariopontus). Lyons, 1526.

PAULUS AEGINETA. *Opera,* trans. Günther of Andernach. Paris, 1532.

PELLISON, GEORGE. *Mélanges de divers problèmes.* Paris, 1647.

PETER OF EBOLI. *Petro Ansolini de Ebulo, De Rebus Siculis,* a cura di Ettore Rota. Castello, 1904 (Muratori, *Rer. Italic. Script.* 31).

PETER OF SPAIN. See Isaac Israeli, *Opera.* Lyons, 1515.

PETER OF SPAIN. *Scientia libri de anima,* ed. M. Alonso. Madrid, 1941 (*Obras Filosóficas* I).

PETER OF SPAIN. *Com. al 'De anima' de Aristóteles,* ed. M. Alonso. Madrid, 1944 (*Obras filosóficas* II).

Physiologus. Dicta Chrysostomi, hrsg. Gustav Heider. Vienna, 1851.

Physiologus. Li Livres des natures des bestes, ed. C. Cahier, *Mélanges d'archéologie,* Paris: ii (1851), 85–100, 106–232; iii (1853), 203–88; iv (1856), 55–87.

Physiologus. A Metrical Bestiary . . . by Bishop Theobald, text and trans. by A. W. Rendell. London, 1928.

Physiologus. The Bestiary of Guillaume le Clerk, trans. G. C. Druce. Ashford, Kent, 1936.

Physiologus latinus, versio b, ed. F. J. Carmody. Paris, 1939.

Physiologus latinus, versio y, ed. F. J. Carmody. Univ. of California, 1941 (*C.P.* xii. 7).

Physiologus. Der Millstätter Physiologus und seine Verwandten von Hermann Menhardt. Klagenfurt, 1956. (This contains an excellent summary of the literature up to date.)

PICO DELLA MIRANDOLA, GIOVANNI. *Opera omnia*. Reggio, 1506.

PICTORIUS, GEORGIUS. *Sermones conviviales*. Basel, 1559.

PICTORIUS, GEORGIUS. *Physicarum quaestionum centuriae tres*. Basel, 1568.

PINDER, ULRICH. *Speculum intellectuale*. Nürnberg (F. Peypus), 1510.

PLATEARIUS. *Circa instans, Le Livre des simples médecines*, trad. par P. Dorveaux. Paris, 1913.

PLINY THE ELDER. *Historia Naturalis*, ed. K. Mayhoff, 6 vols. Leipzig, 1906–9.

PLUTARCH. *Problemata*. See pseudo-Aristotle, *Probl.* 1505.

PLUTARCH. *De causis naturalibus*, trans. Gilbert de Longueil. Cologne, 1542.

PLUTARCH. *Symposiaca*, trans. Adrianus Junius. Paris, 1547.

POLIZIANO, ANGELO. *Opera*. Venice, 1498.

PRIMROSE, JAMES. *De vulgi erroribus in medicina*. London, 1638.

PRISCIANUS LYDUS. *Solutiones*, ed. F. Dübner, in *Plotini Enneades, Porphyrii et Procli Institutiones* (Paris, 1855), pp. 545–79.

PRISCIANUS LYDUS. *Solutiones*, ed. I. Bywater, *Supplementum Aristotelicum*, i. part 2. Berlin, 1886.

PRISCIANUS, THEODORUS. *Euporiston*, ed. V. Rose. Leipzig, 1894.

PTOLOMEY OF LUCCA. *Historia Ecclesiastica*. Milan, 1727 (Muratori, *Rer. italic. scrip.* xi).

REIES FRANCO, GASPAR A. *Elysius Iucundarum Quaestionum Campus*. Brussels, 1661.

RENAUDOT, THÉOPHRASTE. *Premiere centurie des questions traitees ez Conferences du Bureau d'Adresse*. Paris, 1634. *Seconde cent.* 1636. *Troisiesme cent.* 1639. *Quatriesme cent.* 1641. *Cinquiesme cent.* 1655.

REUSNER, NICOLAUS. *Aenigmatographia*. Frankfurt, 1602.

RICHER. *Historiarum libri* III, rec. G. Waitz. Hanover, 1877 (*S.R.G. in usum scholarum*).

ROCHAS, HENRI DE. *La physique reformée, contenant la refutation des erreurs populaires et le triomphe des veritez philosophiques*. Paris, 1648.

ROSS, ALEXANDER. Arcana Microcosmi, or The hid Secrets of Man's Body discovered. With a Refutation of Doctor Brown's Vulgar Errors, the Lord Bacon's Natural History, and Dr. Harvy's Book De Generatione, Comenius, and Others. London, 1652.

ROUZAEUS, LUDOVICUS. *Miscellaneorum Anaristotelicorum centuria dimidiata*. Leyden, 1616.

RUESCAS, ALONSO DE. *Dialogo en verso intitulado Centiloquio de Problemas*. 1546.

SCHWIMMER, J. M. *Kurzweiliger und physicalischer Zeitvertreiber*. Leipzig, 1676.

SENECA, L. ANNAEUS. *Naturales Quaestiones*, ed. A. Gercke. Leipzig (Teubner), 1907.

SENECA, L. ANNAEUS. *Physical Science in the time of Nero, being a translation of the Quaestiones Naturales of Seneca*, J. Clarke and A. Geikie. London, 1910.

SENECA, L. ANNAEUS. *Sénèque, Questions naturelles*, texte établi et trad. P. Oltramare, 2 vols. Paris, 1929.

SENECA, L. ANNAEUS. 'Seneca's *naturales Quaestiones*. The Text Emended and Explained', W. H. Alexander, *Univ. of California Publications in Classical Philology* xiii, no. 8 (1948), 241–332.

SENGUERDIUS, A. *Exercitationes physicae*. Amsterdam, 1658.

SIDRACH. *Le Livre de Sidrach*. Paris (Vérard), 1486.

SPRAT, Thomas. *The History of the Royal Society*. London, 1667.

TADDEO DI ALDEROTTO (Thaddeus Florentinus). *Expositiones in arduum aphorismorum Ipocrati.* . . . Venice, 1527.

THEOPHYLACTUS SIMOCATTA. *Quaestiones physices et epistolas, gr. et lat.*, ed. J. F. Boissonade. Paris, 1835.

TOMEO, NICCOLO LEONICO. *Opuscula*. Venice, 1525.

TORINUS, ALBANUS. *De re medica*. Basel, 1528.

TRITHEMIUS, JOHANNES. *Opera*, ed. M. Freher, 2 vols. Frankfurt, 1601.

ULSEN, DIETRICH. *Hippocrates Aphorismi sive Sententiae*. Nürnberg, Caspar Hochfeder, after 5 April 1496.

ULSEN, DIETRICH. *Vaticinium in epidemicam scabiem*. Nürnberg (Hans Maier), 1 Aug. 1496; Augsburg (Johann Froschauer), *c.* 1498. Ed. C. H. Fuchs, Göttingen, 1850.

ULSEN, DIETRICH. *Speculator consiliorum enigmaticus*. Nürnberg, *c.* 1501.

ULSEN, DIETRICH. *De Insania Democriti*. Augsburg (Johann Froschauer), *c.* 1503.

ULSEN, DIETRICH. *De Sancto Judoco Hymnus*. Deventer (Richardus Paffraet), *c.* 1507.

URSO OF CALABRIA. *De urinis*, ed. Giacosa, *Magistri Salernitani* (Turin, 1901), pp. 283–90.

URSO OF CALABRIA. *De effectibus qualitatum. De effectibus medicinarum*, ed. C. Matthaes in his dissertation, *Der salernitaner Arzt Urso . . . und sein beiden Schriften.* . . . Borna–Leipzig, 1918.

URSO OF CALABRIA. *De gradibus*, ed. K. Sudhoff, in *Sudhoffs Archiv*, XII (1920), 135–8.

URSO OF CALABRIA. 'Die medizinisch-naturphilosophischen Aphorismen und Kommentare des Magister Urso Salernitanus', hrsg. R. Creutz. *Q.S.G.N.M.* V. 1 (Berlin, 1936), 1–192.

VALLA, GIORGIO. *De expetendis et fugiendis rebus*. Venice (Aldus), 1501.

VALLA, GIORGIO. *De physicis quaestionibus*. Strassburg, 1529.

VINCENT OF BEAUVAIS. *Speculum naturale*. Venice, 1494.

VIRGIL. *Georgics*, trans. H. R. Fairclough. London, 1922 (Loeb Lib.).

VOIGT, GOTTFRIED. *Curiositates physicae*. Güstrow, 1668.

VOIGT, GOTTFRIED. *Deliciae physicae*. Rostock, 1671.

VOIGT, GOTTFRIED. *Neu-vermehrter physicalischer Zeit-Vertreiber*. Leipzig, 1694.

WALLIS, JOHN. *A Defence of the Royal Society*. London, 1678.

WALSINGHAM, THOMAS. *Gesta Abbatum Monast. S. Albani*, ed. H. T. Riley, vol. i. (1867). Rolls ser., 28. iv. 1.

WECKER, J. *De Secretis*, lib. xvii. Basel, 1662.

The Weekly Oracle or Universal Library, published by a Society of Gentlemen, London, 1734–7 (reprinted London, 1737).

WILLIAM OF CONCHES. *Dialogus de substantiis physicis ante annos ducentos confectus a Vuilhelmo Aneponymo Philosopho*. Strassburg, 1567. (This is the *Dragmaticon*.)

WILLIAM OF CONCHES. *De philosophia mundi*, ed. Migne. *P.L.* 90, cols. 1127–78 (under pseudo-Bede); ed. Migne, *P.L.* 172, cols. 39–102 (under Honorius of Autun).

WINSTANLEY, WILLIAM. *The New Help to Discourse*, 5th ed. London, 1702.

ZIMARA, MARCANTONIO. *Problemata*. See under pseudo-Aristotle, *Problemata*, 1650.

4218 *Bibliographies*

(b) Secondary, historical sources

ALLEN, PHYLLIS. 'Scientific studies in the English universities of the seventeenth century', *J.H.I.* x. 2 (1949), 219–53.

ALLEN, P. S. *Epistolae Erasmi*, i. Oxford, 1906.

D'ALVERNY, M.-TH. 'Notes sur les traductions médiévales des œuvres philosophiques d'Avicenne', *A.H.D.L.* xix (1953), 337–58.

ALONSO, P. MANUEL ALONSO, S. I. *Temas filosóficos medievales*. Comillas (Santander), 1959.

AMARI, M. 'Questions philosophiques adressées aux savants musulmans par l'empereur Frédéric II', *J.A.* vth ser., i (1853), 240–74 (continued by A. F. Mehren, *J.A.* viith ser., xiv (1879), 341–454).

ANTONIO, NICOLAS. *Bibliotheca Hispana vetus*. Madrid, 1780.

ARISTOTLE. *An excerpt from the general catalogue of printed books in the British Museum*. London, 1933.

Aristoteles Latinus. Codices descripsit G. Lacombe, in societatem operis adsumptis A. Birkenmajer, M. Dulong, A. Franceschini, L. Minio-Paluello. Pars prior, Rome, 1939; Pars post., Cambridge, 1954. Supplementa altera, Bruges–Paris, 1961.

ARISTOTLE. *Manoscritti e stampe Venete dell'Aristotelismo e Averroismo (secoli X–XVI) (Catalogo di mostra presso la Biblioteca Nazionale Marciana, in occasione del XII Congresso Internazionale di Filosofia)*. Venice, 1958.

ARISTOTLE. See Riley, L. W., *Aristotle Texts and Commentaries to 1700*. Philadelphia, 1961.

ASCHBACH, J. *Roswitha und Conrad Celtis*. Vienna, 1867 (2nd ed., 1868).

ASTRUC, J. *Mémoires pour servir à l'histoire de la Faculté de médecine de Montpellier*. Paris, 1767.

AXON, W. E. A. 'Ortensio Lando, a humorist of the Renaissance', *T.R.S.L.* xx. 3 (1899), 159 ff.

BAUCH, GUSTAV. *Die Universität Erfurt im Zeitalter des Frühhumanismus*. Breslau, 1904.

BAUCH, GUSTAV. 'Aus der Gesch. des Mainzer Humanismus', *A.H.G.* N.F. v (Darmstadt, 1907), 3–86.

BAUMGARTNER, M. *Die Philosophie des Alanus de Insulis*. *B.G.P.M.* ii. 4, 1896.

BECCARIA, A. 'Il ritorno delle scienza classica', *R.S.I.* II. i (1937), 24 ff.

BECCARIA, A. *I codici di medicina del periodo presalernitano*. Rome, 1956.

BÉDORET, H. 'Les Premières Traductions tolédanes de philosophie. Œuvres d'Alfarabi', *R.N.P.* (1938), pp. 80–97.

BÉDORET, H. 'Les Premières Traductions tolédanes de philosophie. Œuvres d'Avicenne', *R.N.P.* (1938), pp. 374–400.

BIRKENMAJER, A. *Le Rôle joué par les médecins et les naturalistes dans la reception d'Aristote aux XIIe et XIIIe siècles (La Pologne au VIe congrès international des sciences historiques, Oslo, 1928)*, Warsaw, 1930.

BIRKENMAJER, A. 'Découverte de fragments manuscrits de David de Dinant', *R.N.P.* (1933), pp. 220–9.

BIRKENMAJER, A. *Classement des ouvrages attribués à Aristote par le Moyen Âge latin*, Cracow, 1932.

BLANCK, A. *Die Meklenburgischen Aerzte*. Schwerin, 1874.

BLIEMETZRIEDER, F. 'Literarische Vorlagen des *Liber de Naturis* des Daniel von Morley', *A.G.M.N.T.* X (1927), 338–44.

BLIEMETZRIEDER, F. *Adelhard von Bath*. Munich, 1935 (rev. by F. Pelster, in *D.L.* (1936), cols. 1472–4).

BONCAMPAGNI, B. *Gherardo Cremonese*. Rome, 1851.

BROOK, Z. N. and C. N. L. 'Hereford Cathedral dignitaries in the twelfth century. Supplement', *C.H.J.* viii. 3 (1946), 179–85.

BROWN, HARCOURT. *Scientific Organisations in the Seventeenth Century*. Baltimore, 1934.

CALLUS, D. A. 'Introduction of Aristotelian Learning to Oxford', *P.B.A.* xix (1943), 229–84.

CALLUS, D. A. 'The treatise of John Blund on the Soul', *Autour d'Aristote — Recueil d'études de philosophie ancienne et médiévale offert à Monseigneur A. Mansion* (Louvain, 1955), pp. 471–95.

CAPES, W. W. *Charters and Records of Hereford Cathedral*, 1908.

CAPPARONI, P. *Magistri Salernitani nondum cogniti*. London, 1923 (Wellcome Hist. Med. Mus., Research Studies No. 2).

CAPPARONI, P. 'Il trattato de quattuor humoribus di Alfano', *Casinensia (Miscellanea di studi Cassinesi)* (Montecassino, 1929), i. 151–6.

CLERVAL, A. *Les Écoles de Chartres au Moyen Âge*. Paris, 1895.

CORNER, G. W. *Anatomical Texts of the Earlier Middle Ages*. Washington, 1927.

COURCELLE, P. *Les Lettres grecques en Occident, de Macrobe à Cassiodore*, new ed., Paris, 1948.

CRANE, T. F. *Italian Social Customs of the Sixteenth Century*. New Haven Conn., 1920.

CRANZ, F. E. 'Alexander Aphrodisiensis', *Catalogus translationum et commentariorum*, ed. P. O. Kristeller, vol. i (Washington, D.C., 1960), 77–135.

CREUTZ, R. 'Urso der Letzte des hochsalerno Arzt, Philosoph, Theologe', *A.G.M.N.* Heft 5. Berlin, 1934.

CROMBIE, A. C. *Robert Grosseteste and the Origins of Experimental Science, 1100–1700*. Oxford, 1953 (reprinted 1963).

DENIFLE, H., and CHATELAINE, A. *Chartularium Universitatis Parisiensis*, 4 vols. Paris, 1889–97.

DENIS, M. *Die Merkwürdigkeiten der k. k. garellischen öffentl. Bibliothek am Theresiano*. Vienna, 1780.

DIAZ Y DIAZ, M. C. *Index Scriptorum Latinorum Medii Aevi Hispanorum*. Madrid, 1959.

DIELS, H. *Die Handschriften der antiken Aerzte. A.P.A.W.* (Philos.-hist. Klasse). Berlin, 2 vols., 1905–6 (1907 Erster Nachtrag).

DUBREUIL-CHAMBARDEL, L. *Les Médecins dans l'ouest de la France aux XIe et XIIe siècles*. Paris, 1914.

DUHEM, PIERRE. *Le Système du monde*, tomes i–x. Paris, 1913–59.

DUNN, T. F. *The Facetiae of the Mensa Philosophica*. Washington Univ., 1934 (*Studies in Lang. and Lit.* N.S., No. 5).

EASTON, S. C. *Roger Bacon and his Search for a Universal Science*. Oxford, 1952.

ELLINGER, G. *Gesch. der neulateinischen Lit. Deutschlands*, vol. i. Berlin, 1929.

EMDEN, A. B. *A Biographical Register of the University of Oxford to A.D. 1500*, 3 vols. Oxford, 1958.

ESPOSITO, M. 'On some unpublished poems attributed to Alexander Neckam', *E.H.R.* xxx (1915), 450–71.

FABRICIUS, J. A. *Bibliotheca latina mediae et infimae aetatis*, 6 vols. Patavia, 1754.

FERRARI, SANTE. *I tempi, la vita, le dottrine di Pietro d'Abano*. Genoa, 1900.

FERRARI, SANTE. 'Per la biografia e per gli scritti di Pietro d'Abano', *M.R.A.L.*, ser. 5, vol. xv (Rome, 1918), 629–727.

FESTUGIÈRE, R. P. *La Révélation d'Hermès Trismégiste*. Vol. I, *L'Astrologie et les sciences occultes*. Paris, 1950 (2nd ed.).

FOPPENS, J. F. *Bibliotheca Belgica*, 2 vols. Brussels, 1739.

FORSTER, E. S. 'The pseudo-Aristotelian Problems, their nature and composition', *C.Q.* (1928), pp. 163–5.

FRANCESCHINI, E. 'Sulle versioni latine medievali del περὶ χρωμάτων', *Autour d'Aristote* (Louvain, 1955), pp. 451–69.

FRENKEN, G. *Die Exempla des Jacob von Vitry. Q.U.L.P.M.*, vol. 1. Munich, 1914.

FREYTAG, F. G. *Adparatus Litterarius*, 3 vols. Leipzig, 1752–5.

GARUFI, C. A. *Necrologio del Liber Confratrum di S. Matteo di Salerno.* Rome, 1922.

GIACOSA, P. *Magistri Salernitani nondum editi* (text and portfolio of plates). Turin, 1901.

GLORIEUX, L'ABBÉ P. *La Littérature quodlibétique de 1260–1320*, 2 vols. La Saulchoir, Kain, 1925; Paris, 1935.

GLORIEUX, L'ABBÉ P. *Répertoire des Maîtres en Théologie de Paris au XIIIe siècle*, 2 vols. Paris, 1933–4.

GOLDSCHMIDT, E. P. *Hieronymus Münzer und seine Bibliothek.* London, Warburg Inst., 1938.

GOLDSCHMIDT, E. P. *Medieval Texts and Their First Appearance in Print.* Oxford, 1943 (Supplement to the *Bibliographical Soc. Trans.*, no. 16).

GRABMANN, M. *Die Geschichte der scholastischen Methode.* 2 vols. Freiburg i. B. 1909–11 (reprinted Graz, 1956). (*G.S.M.*)

GRABMANN, M. *Forschungen über die lateinischen Aristotelesübersetzungen des XIII. Jahrhunderts. B.G.P.M.* xvii. 5–6, 1916.

GRABMANN, M. *Mittelalterliches Geistesleben*, 3 vols. Munich, 1926. 36. 56. (*M.G.*)

GRABMANN, M. *Mittelalterliche lat. Aristotelesübersetzungen und Aristoteleskommentare in Handschriften spanischer Bibliotheken. S.B.A.W.* (1928), Heft 5.

GRABMANN, M. *Handschriftliche Forschungen und Mitteilungen zum Schrifttum des Wilhelm von Conches. S.B.A.W.* (1935), Heft 10.

GRABMANN, M. *Handschriftliche Forschungen und Funde zu den philosophischen Schriften des Petrus Hispanus. S.B.A.W.* (1936), Heft 9.

GRAVERT, H. 'Dante in Deutschland', *H.P.B.* CXX (Munich, 1897), pp. 81–100, 173–89, 321–56, 512–36, 633–52, 789–822.

GREGORY, TULLIO. *Anima Mundi. La filosofia di Guglielmo di Conches e la scuola di Chartres.* Florence, 1955.

HANDERSON, H. E. *Gilbertus Anglicus.* Cleveland, Ohio, 1918.

HARTMANN, B. *Konrad Celtis in Nürnberg.* Berlin, 1889.

HARTMANN, F. *Die Literatur von Früh- und Hochsalerno.* Borna–Leipzig, 1919.

HASKINS, C. H. *Studies in the History of Mediaeval Science*, Cambridge (Mass.), 1924, 2nd ed., 1927.

HASKINS, C. H. *Studies in Mediaeval Culture.* Cambridge (Mass.), 1929.

HAURÉAU, B. *Hist. de la philosophie scolastique*, 2 vols. Paris, 1872–80.

HAURÉAU, B. 'Notice sur le numéro 16089 des manuscrits latins de la Bibliothèque Nationale', *N.E.* xxxv. 1 (1896), 209–39.

HEIBERG, J. L. *Beiträge zur Gesch. Georg Valla's und seiner Bibliothek (C.B.* Beiheft 16). Leipzig, 1896.

HERRMANN, M. *Rezeption des Humanismus in Nürnberg.* Berlin, 1898.

HIRSCH, A. *Biographisches Lexikon der hervorragenden Ärzte*, 6 vols. Berlin, 1929–35.

HIRZEL, R. *Der Dialog*, 2 vols. Leipzig, 1895.

HUNT, R. W. 'English learning in the late twelfth century', *T.R.H.S.*, 4th ser., xix (1936), 19–35.

JAMES, M. R. *The Ancient Libraries of Canterbury and Dover.* Cambridge, 1903.

JAMES, M. R. *Lists of Manuscripts formerly owned by Dr. John Dee.* Oxford, 1921 (Supplement to the *Bibliographical Soc. Trans.*, no. 1).

KLIBANSKY, R. *The Continuity of the Platonic Tradition during the Middle Ages.* London (Warburg Inst.), 1939 (reissue 1950).

KRAUSE, K. E. H. 'Der Liebarzt Dietrich Ulsenius', *J.V.M.G.* xlvii, (Schwerin, 1882, 141–5.

KRISTELLER, P. O. 'The School of Salerno', *B.H.M.* xvii. 2 (Baltimore, 1945), 138–94 (reprinted in *Studies* (1956), pp. 495–551).

KRISTELLER, P. O. *Studies in Renaissance Thought and Letters*, Rome, 1956.

KRISTELLER, P. O. 'Nuove fonti per la medicina Salernitana del secolo XII' (*Rassegna Storica Salernitana*, Anno xviii, nos. 1–4). Salerno, 1958.

KRISTELLER, P. O. 'Beiträge der Schule von Salerno zur Entwicklung der scholastischen Wissenschaft im 12. Jahrhundert', *Artes Liberales*, hrsg. J. Koch, *S.T.G.M.*, Bd. v (Leiden–Cologne, 1959), pp. 84–90.

KRISTELLER, P. O. (editor). *Catalogus Translationum et Commentariorum: Medieval and Renaissance Latin Translations and Commentaries*, vol. i, Washington, D. C., 1960.

KURDZIAŁEK, M. 'Anatomische und embryologische Ausserungen Davids von Dinant', *Sudhoffs Archiv*, XLV 1 (1961), 1–22.

LANGLOIS, C. V. *La Connaissance de la nature et du monde au Moyen Âge.* Paris, 1911.

LAUCHERT, F. *Gesch. der Physiologus.* Strassburg, 1889.

LEHMANN, P. *Mitteilungen aus Handschriften.* i–ix. *S.B.A.W.* 1929–51.

LEHMANN, P. *Pseudo-Antike Literature des Mittelalters.* Leipzig, 1927 (*Stud. der Bibl. Warburg*).

LELAND, J. *Commentarii de Scriptoribus Britannicis*, ed. A. Hall. 2 vols. Oxford, 1709.

LISCH, G. C. F. 'Ueber des Herzogs Magnus II von Meklenburg Lebensende', *J.V.M.G.* XXXIX (Schwerin, 1874), 49–58.

LITTLE, A. G. *Roger Bacon Essays*, ed. Little. Oxford, 1914.

LITTLE, A. G., and PELSTER, F. *Oxford Theology and Theologians, c. A.D. 1282–1302.* Oxford, 1934 (*O.H.S.*, vol. xcvi).

LOEW (LOWE), E. A. *The Beneventan Script.* Oxford, 1914.

MACCLINTOCK, STUART. *Perversity and Error. Studies on the Averroist John of Jandun.* Indiana Univ. Press, 1956.

MACKINNEY, L. C. *Early Medieval Medicine.* Baltimore, 1937.

MERTON, R. K. 'Science, Technology and Society in Seventeenth-Century England', *Osiris*, iv (1938), 360–632.

MICHALSKI, K. 'La Physique nouvelle et les différents courants philosophiques au XIVᵉ siècle', *B.I.A.P.S.L.*, année 1927 (Cracow, 1928), 93–164.

MINIO-PALUELLO, L. 'Jacobus Veneticus Grecus', *Traditio* viii (1952), 265–304.

MINIO-PALUELLO, L. 'The *Ars Disserendi* of Adam of Balsham "Parvipontanus"', *M.R.S.* iii (1954), 116–69.

Mittelalterliche Bibliothekskat. Deutschlands u. der Schweiz, III, Bistum Bamberg, bearb. P. Ruf. Munich, 1939.

MOREJON, ANTONIO HERNANDEZ. *Historia Bibliografica de la Medicina Española*, vols. 1 and 2. Madrid, 1842–3.

MÜLLER, M. 'Die Stellung des Daniel von Morley in der Wissenschaft des Mittelalters', *P.J.* XLI. 3 (1928), 301–37.

NARDI, BRUNO. *Saggi sull'Aristotelismo Padovano dal secolo XIV al XVI.* Florence, 1958.

NAU, F. 'Une Ancienne Traduction latine du Bélinous arabe', *R.O.C.* XII (1907), 99–106.

NEUBURGER, MAX. 'Die Medizin im Macrobius und Theodoretus', *Janus*, XXVIII (1924), pp. 155–72.

NORMANN, H. *Disputatio Platonis et Aristotelis*: ein apokrypher Dialog aus dem früher Mittelalter', *Sudhoffs Archiv*, XXIII (1930), 68–86.

ORNSTEIN, M. (Bronfenbrenner). *The Rôle of Scientific Societies in the Seventeenth Century.* New York, 1938.

PARÉ, G., BRUNET, A., and TREMBLAY, P. *La Renaissance du XIIᵉ siècle. Les écoles et l'enseignement.* Paris–Ottawa, 1933.

PARENT, J. M. *La Doctrine de la création dans l'École de Chartres.* Paris–Ottawa, 1938.

PICARD-PARRA, C. 'Une utilisation des *Quaestiones Naturales* de Sénèque au milieu du XIIᵉ siècle', *R.M.A.L.* V, no. 2 (1949), 115–26.

PITRA, J. B. *Spicilegium solesmense*, iii. Paris, 1855.

PORCHER, J. 'Le *De disciplina scholarium*, traité du XIIIᵉ siècle faussement attribué à Boèce', *Position des thèses de l'École nationale des Chartes*. Paris, 1921.

POWER, SIR D'ARCY. *The Foundations of Medical History*. Baltimore, 1931.

PRANTL, C. 'Über die Probleme des Aristoteles', *A.B.A.W.* VI (1851), 339–77.

RABY, F. J. E. *A History of Secular Latin Poetry in the Middle Ages*, 2 vols. Oxford, 1934 (2nd ed., 1958).

RABY, F. J. E. *A History of Christian Latin Poetry from the beginnings to the close of the Middle Ages*, 2nd ed. Oxford, 1953.

RASHDALL, H. *The Universities of Europe in the Middle Ages*, ed. F. M. Powicke and A. B. Emden, 3 vols., reprinted Oxford, 1951.

REIMANN, A. *Die älteren Pirckheimer*, hrsg. H. Rupprich. Leipzig, 1944.

RENZI, S. de. *Collectio Salernitana*, 5 vols. Naples, 1852–9.

RICHTER, E. *De Aristotelis Problematis*, Bonn, 1885.

RILEY, L. W., *Aristotle Texts and Commentaries to 1700 in the University of Pennsylvania Library*. Philadelphia, 1961.

ROBINSON, J. A., and JAMES, M. R. *The Manuscripts of Westminster Abbey*, Cambridge, 1909.

ROSE, V. *Anecdota Graeca et Graecolatina*, 2 vols. Berlin, 1864–70.

ROSE, V. 'Ptolomeus und die Schule von Toledo', *Hermes*, VIII (1874), 327–49.

RULAND, A. 'Das Exemplar von Hartmanni Schedelii *Chronicon* lat. Norimbergae 1493 welches der Verfasser Hartmann Schedel selbst besass', *Serapeum*, XV (1854), 145 ff.

RUSKA, J. *Tabula Smaragdina, ein Beitrag zur Gesch. der hermetischen Lit.* Heidelberg, 1926.

RUSSELL, J. C. 'Hereford and Arabic Science in England about 1175–1200', *Isis*, xviii (1932), 14–25.

RUSSELL, J. C. *Dictionary of Writers of Thirteenth-century England*. London, 1936.

SACY, S. DE. 'Le Livre du secret de la créature par le sage Bélinous', *N.E.* iv (1799), pp. 108–58.

SARTON, G. *Introduction to the History of Science*, 3 vols. Baltimore, 1927–47.

SBORDONE, F. 'La tradizione manoscritta del *Physiologus* latino', *S.P.L.S.A.*, N.S. 27 Pavia (1949), pp. 246–80.

SCHEDLER, P. M. *Die Philosophie des Macrobius und ihr Einfluss auf die Wissenschaft des christlichen Mittelalters*. *B.G.P.M.* xiii. 1, 1916.

SCHIPA, M. 'Una triade illustre di Montecassino', *Casinensia*, i (1929), 157–60.

SCHIPPERGES, H. 'Die frühen Übersetzer der arabischen Medizin in chronologischer Sicht', *Sudhoffs Archiv*, XXXIX. 1 (1955), 53–93.

SCHREIBER, H. *Gesch. der Albert-Ludwigs-Univ. zu Freiburg im Bresgau*. 2 vols. Freiburg i. B., 1857.

SCHWARZ, I. *Die medizinischen Handschriften der kgl. Universitätsbibliothek in Würzburg*. Würzburg, 1907.

SIGERIST, H. E. 'The Latin Medical Literature of the Early Middle Ages', *J.H.M.* xiii. 2 (1958), 127–46.

SILVERSTEIN, T. 'The fabulous cosmogony of Bernard Silvestris', *M.P.* xlvi. 2 (1948), 92–116.

SILVERSTEIN, T. 'Daniel of Morley, English Cosmogonist and Student of Arabic Science', *M.S.* x (1948), 179–96.

SILVERSTEIN, T. 'Adelard, Aristotle and the *De natura deorum*', *C.P.* xlvii (1952), 82–86.

SILVERSTEIN, T. 'Hermann of Carinthia and Greek: A problem in the New Science of the twelfth century', *Medioevo e Rinascimento. Studi in onore di Bruno Nardi* (Florence, 1955), ii. 681–99.

SILVERSTEIN, T. 'Liber Hermetis Mercurii Triplicis de VI rerum principiis', *A.H.D.L.* xxii (1956), 217–302.

SRBIK, RITTER VON. 'Die *Margarita Philosophica* des Gregor Reisch (1525), ein Beitrag zur Gesch. d. Naturwissenschaften in Deutschland', *A.W.W.D.* civ (Vienna, 1941), 83–205.

STADLER, H. 'Neue Bruchstücke der *Quaestiones medicinales* des pseudo-Soranus', *A.L.L.G.* xiv (1906), 361–8.

STANGE, E. *Arnoldus Saxo, der älteste Encyklopädist des dreizehnten Jahrhunderts.* Inaugural dissertation. Halle, 1885.

STAPPER, R. *Papst Johannes xxi (Petrus Hispanus)*, Münster, 1898.

STAUBER, R. *Die Schedelsche Bibliothek.* Freiburg i. B., 1908.

STEINER, A. 'The Authorship of the *De disciplina scholarium*', *Speculum*, xii (1937), 81–84.

STEINSCHNEIDER, M. 'Die arabischen Übersetzungen aus dem Griechischen', *C.B.* v (1889), xii (1893), and *Z.D.M.G.*, l (1896), 161 ff. (A.U.). Reprinted, Graz, 1960.

STEINSCHNEIDER, M. *Die griechischen Aerzte in arabischen Uebersetzungen. Virchows Archiv*, Bd. 124, Folge XII, iv (1891) (reprint in *Die ärabischen übersetzungen aus dem Griechischen.* Graz, 1960).

STEINSCHNEIDER, M. 'Apollonius von Thyana (oder Balinus) bei den Arabern', *Z.D.M.G.* XLV (1891), 439–46.

STEINSCHNEIDER, M. *Die europäischen Übersetzungen aus dem Arabischen bis Mitte des 17. Jahrhunderts. S.A.W.W.* CXLIX. 4 (1905), CLI. 1 (1906) (reprinted Graz 1956). (*E.U.*).

STUBBS, W. *Seventeen Lectures on the Study of Medieval and Modern History and Kindred Subjects.* Oxford, 1886.

SUDHOFF, K. *Aus der Frühgesch. der Syphilislit.* Leipzig, 1912. *S.G.M.* 9.

SUDHOFF, K. *Erstlinge der Syphilislit.* Munich, 1912.

SUDHOFF, K. 'Die Salernitaner Handschrift in Breslau', *Sudhoffs Archiv*, XII (1920), 101–48.

SUDHOFF, K., and MEYER-STEINEG, T. *Gesch. der Medizin im Überblick.* Jena, 1921.

SUDHOFF, K., and SINGER, C. *The Earliest Printed Literature on Syphilis.* Florence, 1925.

SUDHOFF, K. 'Die vierte salernitaner Anatomie', *Sudhoffs Archiv*, XX (1928), 33–50.

SUDHOFF, K. 'Salerno, Montpellier und Paris, *c.* 1200', *Sudhoffs Archiv*, XX (1928), 51–62.

SUDHOFF, K. 'Constantin, der erste Vermittler muslimischer Wissenschaft ins Abendland und die beiden salernitaner Frühscholastiker Maurus und Urso als Exponenten dieser Vermittlung', *Archeion*, XIV (1932), 359–69.

SUFFRIDUS, P. *De Scriptoribus Frisiae.* Cologne, 1593.

TAYLOR, A. *The Literary Riddle before 1600.* Univ. of California Press, 1948.

TEMKIN, O. 'Alexandrian studies on Galen's *De sectis*', *B.I.H.M.* iii (1935), 405–30.

THOMPSON, J. W. 'The introduction of Arabic science into Lorraine in the tenth century', *Isis*, xii (1929), 184 ff.

THORNDIKE, L. *A History of Magic and Experimental Science*, 8 vols. N.Y., 1923–58 (*H.M.E.S.*).

THORNDIKE, L. *Science and Thought in the Fifteenth Century.* N.Y., 1929.

THORNDIKE, L. 'Vatican Latin manuscripts in the history of science and medicine', *Isis*, xiii (1929–30), 53–102.

THORNDIKE, L. 'Manuscripts of the writings of Peter of Abano', *B.H.M.* xv (1944), 201–19.

THORNDIKE, L. 'More manuscripts of the *Dragmaticon* and *Philosophia* of William of Conches', *Speculum*, xx (1945), 84–87.

THORNDIKE, L. 'Mediaeval magic and science in the seventeenth century', *Speculum*, xxviii. 4 (1953), 692–704.

THORNDIKE, L. 'Vatican mediaeval medical manuscripts', *J.H.M.* viii. 3 (1953), 263–83.

THORNDIKE, L. 'Peter of Abano and another Commentary on the Problems of Aristotle' *B.H.M.* xxix (1955), 517–23.

THORNDIKE, L. 'Further consideration of the *Experimenta, Speculum astronomiae,* and *De Secretis mulierum* ascribed to Albertus Magnus', *Speculum,* xxx (1955), 413–43.

THORNDIKE, L. 'Unde versus', *Traditio,* xi (1955), 163–93.

THORNDIKE, L. 'Notes on medical texts in manuscripts at London and Oxford', *Janus,* XLVIII (1959), 141–202.

THORNDIKE, L. 'Questiones Alani', *Isis,* li (1960), pp. 181–5.

THORNDIKE, L. 'Some Medieval and Renaissance manuscripts on physics', *P.A.P.S.* civ, no. 2 (1960), 188–201.

THORNDIKE, L. and KIBRE, P. *A Catalogue of Incipits of Medieval Scientific Writings in Latin.* Cambridge, Mass., 1937. (Th. and K. 1937). 'Additional Incipits . . .', *Speculum,* xiv. 1 (1939), 93–105; 'More Incipits . . .', *Speculum,* xvii. 3 (1942), 342–66; 'Further Incipits . . .', *Speculum,* xxvi. 4 (1951), 673–95.

TICKNOR, G. *History of Spanish Literature,* 3 vols. Boston, 1888.

TIRABOSCHI, G. Storia della letteratura italiana. Tom. i–ix, Venice, 1795–6.

UELTZEN, J. 'Das Flugblatt des Theodoricus Ulsenius mit Dürers Illustration', *Z. Büch.* I (1900), 151–2.

UELTZEN, J. 'Das Bild des Pestkranken, wahrscheinlich eine Jugendarbeit Albrecht Dürers', *I.Z.* (1900), no. 2955, p. 242.

UELTZEN, J. 'Das Flugblatt des Arztes Theodoricus Ulsenius vom Jahre 1496 über den deutschen Ursprung der Syphilis und seine Illustration', *Virchows Archiv,* CLXII (1900), 371 ff.

VAN STEENBERGHEN, F. *Aristotle in the West.* Louvain, 1955.

Verfasserlexikon des deutschen Mittelalters, Hrsg. W. Stammler und K. Langosch, 5 vols. Berlin–Leipzig, 1933–55.

VIEILLARD, C. *Gilles de Corbeil.* Paris, 1909.

WALTHER, H. *Initia carminum ac versuum medii aevi,* i. Göttingen, 1959.

WELLCOME HISTORICAL MEDICAL LIBRARY. *A Catalogue of Printed Books.* Vol. I, *Books printed before 1641.* London, 1962.

WELTER, J. T. *L'Exemplum dans la littérature religieuse et didactique du Moyen Âge.* Paris, 1927.

WENRICH, J. G. *De Auctorum Graecorum versionibus et commentariis Syriacis, Arabicis, Armeniacis, Persicisque Commentatio.* Leipzig, 1842.

WHITTAKER, T. *Macrobius, or Philosophy, Science and Letters in the Year 400.* Cambridge, 1923.

WICKERSHEIMER, E. *Commentaires de la Faculté de Médecine.* Paris, 1915.

WICKERSHEIMER, E. *Dict. biographique des médecins en France au Moyen Âge,* 2 vols. Paris, 1936.

WINGATE, S. D. *The Medieval Latin Versions of the Aristotelian Scientific Corpus.* London, 1931.

WLASCHKY, M. 'Sapientia artis medicinae', *Kyklos,* i (1928), 103–13.

YAHIA, BOUBAKER BEN. 'Constantin l'Africain et l'école de Salerne', *C.T.* iii (1955), 49–59.

YATES, FRANCIS, A. *The French Academies of the Sixteenth Century.* London (Warburg Inst.), 1947.

YOUNG, P. *Catalogus Librorum Manuscriptorum Bibl. Wigorniensis (1622–23),* ed. I. Atkins and N. R. Ker. Cambridge, 1944.

YOUNG, R. F. *Comenius in England.* Oxford, 1932.

INDEX OF MANUSCRIPTS

SUBJECT INDEX
FOR THE *QUESTIONES PHISICALES*

The numbers refer to lines, S in the *Speculator*, Q in the remainder of the *Questiones*.

GENERAL INDEX